Lecture Notes in Computer Science 15997

The series Lecture Notes in Computer Science (LNCS), including its subseries Lecture Notes in Artificial Intelligence (LNAI) and Lecture Notes in Bioinformatics (LNBI), has established itself as a medium for the publication of new developments in computer science and information technology research, teaching, and education.

LNCS enjoys close cooperation with the computer science R & D community, the series counts many renowned academics among its volume editors and paper authors, and collaborates with prestigious societies. Its mission is to serve this international community by providing an invaluable service, mainly focused on the publication of conference and workshop proceedings and postproceedings. LNCS commenced publication in 1973.

Bart Coppens · Bruno Volckaert ·
Vincent Naessens · Bjorn De Sutter
Editors

Availability, Reliability and Security

ARES 2025 International Workshops
Ghent, Belgium, August 11–14, 2025
Proceedings, Part IV

Springer

Editors
Bart Coppens
Ghent University
Ghent, Belgium

Bruno Volckaert
Ghent University
Ghent, Belgium

Vincent Naessens
KU Leuven
Ghent, Belgium

Bjorn De Sutter
Ghent University
Ghent, Belgium

ISSN 0302-9743 ISSN 1611-3349 (electronic)
Lecture Notes in Computer Science
ISBN 978-3-032-00638-7 ISBN 978-3-032-00639-4 (eBook)
https://doi.org/10.1007/978-3-032-00639-4

This Springer imprint is published by the registered company Springer Nature Switzerland AG
The registered company address is: Gewerbestrasse 11, 6330 Cham, Switzerland

ARES Workshops 2025 Foreword

Alongside the main track of the 20th International Conference on Availability, Reliability and Security (ARES), the organizers received 17 regular workshop proposals, of which eventually 15 were accepted as workshops. A total of 173 papers were submitted over these workshops, of which 79 were accepted for publication and presentation at ARES 2025. All papers that were not desk rejected received a minimum of 3 double-blind reviews by TPC members, and in the case of conflicts of interest with the workshop organizers, the workshop chairs assigned reviewers and decided on the paper review ranking. As organizers, we believe the resulting workshops will allow for insightful discussions and interesting exchanges of ideas on advances made within the security field.

As workshop chairs we would like to use this space to thank all organizers for their hard work on promoting and managing their workshops. We'd also like to give a special thank you to the TPC members who provided—under strict time constraints—constructive reviews for both accepted and rejected papers. We sincerely believe the workshop programs contribute a lot to maintaining a vibrant ARES community. Therefore, from us to you, a massive thank you.

August 2025

Bart Coppens
Bruno Volckaert
Vincent Naessens
Bjorn De Sutter

ARES Workshops 2025 Organization

General Chair

Bjorn De Sutter	Ghent University, Belgium

General Workshop Chairs

Bart Coppens	Ghent University, Belgium
Bruno Volckaert	Ghent University, Belgium

Proceedings Chairs

Vincent Naessens	KU Leuven, Belgium
Michiel Willocx	KU Leuven, Belgium

Workshop Chairs

Aleksandra Mileva	Goce Delcev University, North Macedonia
Alessandro Aldini	University of Urbino, Italy
Amir Sharif	Fondazione Bruno Kessler, Italy
Amna Shifa	University of Galway, Ireland
Anastasija Collen	University of Geneva, Switzerland
Andrea Saracino	Scuola Superiore Universitaria Sant'Anna di Pisa, Italy
Andrew Marrington	Zayed University, UAE
Angelo Consoli	Scuola Universitaria Professionale della Svizzera Italiana (SUPSI), Switzerland
Artur Janicki	Warsaw University of Technology, Poland
Christoph Schmittner	Austrian Institute of Technology, Austria
Costas Lambrinoudakis	University of Piraeus, Greece
Daniela Pöhn	Universität der Bundeswehr München, Germany
Daniele Canavese	IRIT-CNRS, France
Gregorio Martinez Pérez	University of Murcia, Spain
Günther Pernul	University of Regensburg, Germany
Habtamu Abie	Norwegian Computing Center, Norway

Halvor Holtskog	Norwegian University of Science and Technology, Norway
Hamida Seba	University Lyon 1, France
Helge Janicke	Edith Cowan University, Australia
Javier Lopez	University of Malaga, Spain
Joerg Keller	FernUniversität in Hagen, Germany
Jorge Maestre Vidal	Indra, Spain
Kacper Gradoń	Warsaw University of Technology, Poland
Katarzyna Kamińska	Warsaw University of Technology, Poland
Kim-Kwang Raymond Choo	University of Texas at San Antonio, USA
Leandros Maglaras	De Montfort University, UK
Leonardo Regano	University of Cagliari, Italy
Luca Caviglione	CNR – IMATI, Italy
Mamoona Asghar	University of Galway, Ireland
Mansoor Ahmed	Maynooth University, Ireland
Marco Antonio Sotelo Monge	Indra, Spain
Marco Rasori	National Research Council, Italy
Markus Helfert	Maynooth University, Ireland
Marta Irene García Cid	Indra, Spain
Martin Husák	Masaryk University, Czech Republic
Martin Steinebach	Fraunhofer Institute SIT|ATHENE, Germany
Mauro Conti	University of Padua, Italy
Meriem Benyahya	University of Geneva, Switzerland
Mohamed Ali Kandi	IRIT-University of Toulouse, France
Mohamed-Lamine Messai	University Lyon 2, France
Muhammad Irfan Khalid	University of Agder, Norway
Nadia Kanwal	Keele University, UK
Nils Gruschka	University of Oslo, Norway
Pedro R. M. Inácio	Universidade da Beira Interior, Portugal
Peter Kieseberg	FH St. Pölten, Austria
Philipp Amann	Europol EC3, The Netherlands
Richard Overill	King's College London, UK
Richard Smith	De Montfort University, UK
Salvador Llopis Sanchez	Universitat Politècnica de Valencia, Spain
Sandeep Pirbhulal	Norwegian Computing Center, Oslo, Norway
Simone Fischer-Hübner	Karlstad University, Chalmers University of Technology & Gothenburg University, Sweden
Sokratis Katsikas	Norwegian University of Science and Technology, Norway
Stephen Fisher Davies	Airbus, UK
Steven Furnell	University of Nottingham, UK
Thomas Brandstetter	Limes Security/FHSTP, Austria

Virginia N. L. Franqueira	University of Kent, UK
Wojciech Mazurczyk	Warsaw University of Technology, Poland

CPRA 2025 Preface

This volume presents the proceedings of the workshop on Cybersecurity and Privacy Risk Assessments (CPRA), held in conjunction with the 20th International Conference on Availability, Reliability and Security (ARES), which took place in Ghent, Belgium, August 11–14, 2025.

The CPRA brought together computer scientists, researchers, practitioners, and industry experts to explore emerging methodologies for assessing evolving cybersecurity and privacy risks. Discussions addressed the limitations of traditional risk assessment methodologies, particularly their reliance on extensive manual processes and lack of clear guidance and reproducibility, issues that are increasingly problematic in the context of evolving Cyber Physical System (CPS) technologies. On that note, CPRA emphasized the importance of enhancing risk assessment methodologies at different levels, including the risk scoring, risk treatment decision and vulnerabilities' prioritization. The workshop focused on refining standardized approaches, such as ISO/SAE 21434 and ISO 42010, while addressing their limitations through innovative methods, such as dynamic decision support systems, viewpoint based-models, and data-driven approaches, built on top of traditional Threat Analysis and Risk Assessment (TARA), Data Protection Impact Assessments (DPIAs), and risk prioritization techniques.

Furthermore, the workshop explored the interplay between regulatory compliance and the role of human factors in risk management, particularly in balancing legal, technical, and societal requirements. Special attention was given to the challenges posed by the subjective interpretation of risks among diverse stakeholders, and how these perceptions can be integrated into more objective and structured assessment frameworks.

The papers of the workshops were grouped into the following topical sections: (i) Security risk assessment enhancements; (ii) Data privacy assessments; and (iii) Risk prioritization.

The workshop papers included in this volume were selected through a rigorous review process, with an acceptance rate of $\geq$50%. Out of eight submissions, four papers were accepted for presentation at the workshop. Manuscripts were double-blind reviewed by at least three experts, assigned based on relevant expertise of program committee members. Evaluation criteria included relevance to the workshop theme, originality of the research, clarity of the methods and results, approach and correctness of the validation, interest to the general, scientific and practitioner public as well as overall quality of the manuscript. All conflicts of interest were declared and verified by the workshop chairs, who ensured that no program committee member served as a co-author on any reviewed paper.

August 2025

Meriem Benyahya
Anastasija Collen
Christoph Schmittner

CPRA 2025 Organization

Workshop Chairs

Meriem Benyahya	University of Geneva, Switzerland
Anastasija Collen	University of Geneva, Switzerland
Christoph Schmittner	Austrian Institute of Technology, Austria

Program Committee

Tariq Bontekoe	University of Groningen, Netherlands
Simon Bouget	Division Digitala System, Sweden
Luigi Briguglio	CyberEthics Lab., Italy
Vittoria Cozza	University of Verona, Italy
Piroska Haller	University of Medicine, Pharmacy, Sciences and Technology of Targu Mures, Romania
Nicolas Harrand	Stockholm University, Sweden
Sokratis Katsikas	Norwegian University of Science and Technology, Norway
Teri Lenard	University of Medicine, Pharmacy, Science and Technology of Targu Mures, Romania
McKenna McCall	Carnegie Mellon University, Pittsburgh, USA
Mohamed Amine Merzouk	Polytechnique Montréal, Canada
Niels Alexander Nijdam	University of Geneva, Switzerland
Federica Paci	University of Verona, Italy
Laurens Sion	KU Leuven, Belgium

Sponsors

AI4CSM	DOI: 10.3030/101007326	https://ai4csm.eu/
AIMS50	DOI: 10.3030/101112089	https://www.aims50.eu/
AutoTRUST	DOI: 10.3030/101148123	https://autotrust-he.eu/
OPEVA	DOI: 10.3030/101097267	https://opeva.eu/
ShapeFuture	DOI: 10.3030/101139996	https://shapefuture.eu/
ULTIMO	DOI: 10.3030/101077587	https://ultimo-he.eu/

EDId 2025 Preface

The identity environment has evolved into a complex and dynamic ecosystem that demands seamless interoperability, stronger security measures, and user-centric experiences in an increasingly interconnected digital world. As digital transformation accelerates across sectors, the challenges surrounding digital identity systems have grown in scope and complexity. The rise of decentralized architectures, cross-border data flows, and mounting concerns over surveillance, data misuse, and exclusion have made identity management a focal point for innovation and critical inquiry.

One significant development in this space is the introduction of the European Digital Identity (EUDI) Wallet, which aims to provide EU citizens and residents with a trusted, secure, and interoperable solution for managing their digital identity across borders. The EUDI Wallet exemplifies the shift toward user-controlled identity models. It also raises critical questions around standardization, governance, and inclusion—issues beyond the European context. Addressing these questions requires a collaborative effort that bridges disciplinary boundaries.

The 2nd International Workshop on Emerging Digital Identities (EDId) aimed to foster dialogue, share emerging research, and catalyze innovative solutions. EDId explores the evolving digital identity landscape by engaging with various topics—from implementing secure authentication protocols and interoperability standards to the legal and regulatory dimensions of data protection, privacy, and digital rights.

This workshop accepted 6 manuscripts out of a total of 13 submissions. At least three reviewers followed a double-blind approach to peer review the manuscripts. The reviewers, who were part of the Program Committee, were composed of 19 experts in digital identities. Based on their valuable reviews, 6 papers were accepted to be published in the LNCS volume by Springer and presented at the workshop.

We thank all the participants, including the authors, the reviewers, the invited keynote speaker, and the attendees, for their valuable work and significant efforts, which contributed to the workshop's success. We hope that this workshop will advance the development of emerging digital identities.

August 2025

Nils Gruschka
Daniela Pöhn
Amir Sharif

EDId 2025 Organization

Workshop Chairs

Nils Gruschka	University of Oslo, Norway
Daniela Pöhn	Universität der Bundeswehr München, Germany
Amir Sharif	Fondazione Bruno Kessler, Italy

Program Committee

Hamed Arshad	Cegal, Norway
Diana G. Berbecaru	Politecnico di Torino, Italy
Tamas Bisztray	University of Oslo, Norway
Julien Bringer	Kallistech, France
Francesco Buccafurri	Università degli Studi Mediterranea di Reggio Calabria, Italy
Andre Büttner	University of Oslo, Norway
Roberto Carbone	Fondazione Bruno Kessler, Italy
Lothar Fritsch	OsloMet, Norway
Michael Grabatin	Universität der Bundeswehr München, Germany
Wolfgang Hommel	Universität der Bundeswehr München, Germany
Meiko Jensen	Karlstad University, Sweden
Sandra Kostic	FU Berlin & Fraunhofer AISEC, Germany
Sara Lazzaro	Università degli Studi Mediterranea di Reggio Calabria, Italy
Stefan More	Graz University of Technology, Austria
Cecilia Pasquini	Fondazione Bruno Kessler, Italy
Marco Pernpruner	Fondazione Bruno Kessler, Italy
Silvio Ranise	Fondazione Bruno Kessler & University of Trento, Italy
Guido Schmitz	Lancaster University Leipzig, UK
Giada Sciarretta	Fondazione Bruno Kessler, Italy

Additional Reviewer

Tahir Ahmad

SPETViD 2025 Preface

Multimodal data combines information from various modalities, such as text, images, audio, video, and 3D models, captured by diverse devices and sensors. As this type of data becomes increasingly integrated into security and AI-driven applications, ensuring privacy, integrity, and robustness is more critical than ever. In this context, Privacy-Enhancing Technologies (PETs) play a crucial role in mitigating privacy risks. PETs enable responsible innovation and secure data usage in domains such as healthcare, finance, and artificial intelligence, while also supporting the adoption of data-driven technologies in smart ecosystems.

The 2nd International Workshop on Security and Privacy Enhancing Technologies for Multimodal Data (SPETViD 2025) was held in conjunction with the 20th International Conference on Availability, Reliability, and Security (ARES 2025), which took place in Ghent, Belgium, August 11–14, 2025. SPETViD provides a focused forum for researchers, practitioners, and policymakers to address the growing concerns about privacy and security. The workshop promotes the exploration of technical, legal, and ethical perspectives for safeguarding multimodal data, particularly in areas related to smart environments, surveillance, and collaborative AI systems.

For SPETViD 2025, we received 6 full-length submissions, one of which was desk-rejected. All full-length papers underwent a rigorous double-blind peer review process, with each submission reviewed by at least three independent reviewers from a diverse program committee of international experts in privacy, security, AI, and data ethics. Based on these reviews and discussions among the chairs, three full papers were accepted for oral presentation and are included in this LNCS volume. All submissions were handled independently and fairly, including those co-authored by members of the organizing or program committees. In such cases, the review process was managed without the involvement of conflicted individuals to maintain the integrity of the double-blind review standards.

We thank all authors who submitted their work to SPETViD 2025 and extend our gratitude to the reviewers for their valuable and timely feedback. We are also grateful to the ARES 2025 organisers and our workshop participants for contributing to an engaging and impactful event. We hope that the contributions presented in this volume will inspire continued research and collaboration in designing and deploying secure, privacy-preserving, and ethically aligned technologies for multimodal data systems.

August 2025

Amna Shifa
Mamoona Asgher
Nadia Kanwal

SPETViD 2025 Organization

Workshop Chairs

Amna Shifa	University of Galway, Ireland
Mamoona Asghar	University of Galway, Ireland
Nadia Kanwal	Keele University, UK

Program Committee

Asra Aslam	Sheffield University, UK
Farzana Zahid	University of Waikato, New Zealand
Gazi Erkan Bostanci	Ankara University, Turkey
Ifeoluwapo Aribilola	Insight SFI Research Centre for Data Analytics, Ireland
Ihsan Ullah	University of Galway, Ireland
Malika Bendechache	University of Galway, Ireland
Mary Pidgeon	Technological University of the Shannon: Midlands Mid-West, Ireland
Mehwish Tahir	Technological University of the Shannon, Ireland
Muhammad Babar Imtiaz	Technological University of the Shannon, Ireland
Muhammad Jehanzaib Yousuf	Technological University of the Shannon, Ireland
Muhammad Samar Ansari	University of Chester, UK
Rónán Kennedy	University of Galway, Ireland
Seamus Dowling	Atlantic Technological University, Ireland
Shoaib Ehsan	University of Southampton, UK

GRASEC 2025 Preface

This book constitutes the refereed proceedings of the 6th International Workshop on Graph-based Approaches for CyberSecurity (GRASEC 2025), held in conjunction with the 20th International Conference on Availability, Reliability and Security (ARES 2025), which took place in Ghent, Belgium, on August 11–14, 2025. The GRASEC Workshop aims to highlight the latest research and experience in graph-based approaches in cybersecurity.

The three full papers included in this volume were carefully reviewed and selected from seven submissions. Each paper underwent a rigorous double-blind review process, with a minimum of three independent reviews. The acceptance rate for this edition of the workshop is 42%. The program committee was composed of 10 experts in the field of the workshop, representing diverse institutions and countries, which contributed to a rich and balanced evaluation process.

As the scale and complexity of modern digital systems continue to grow, ensuring their security becomes increasingly challenging. Traditional methods often fall short in addressing the dynamic, high-volume, and heterogeneous nature of cybersecurity data. Graph-based approaches offer a powerful alternative by capturing relationships, dependencies, and structures that are otherwise difficult to model. Graph theory, graph mining, and knowledge graphs enable the representation and analysis of complex systems, adversarial behaviors, and system interactions. These models support enhanced detection of threats such as botnet activity, network intrusions, and malware propagation. Furthermore, graph visualizations provide a human-understandable view of cyber events, supporting faster and more accurate decision-making. The GRASEC workshop brings together a multidisciplinary community of researchers, practitioners, and industry experts working at the intersection of cybersecurity and graph analytics. This event fosters knowledge exchange across theoretical foundations, practical implementations, and real-world case studies. Key topics include attack graph modeling, threat prediction, anomaly detection using graph data, graph embeddings, and knowledge graph applications in security.

We believe that the work presented in these proceedings will contribute significantly to advancing the field and inspire future research. We would like to thank all the authors for their high-quality submissions, the program committee for their thorough and constructive reviews, and the participants for their valuable engagement. We also express our gratitude to the ARES organizers for their support in hosting this workshop.

August 2025

Martin Husák
Mohamed-Lamine Messai
Hamida Seba

GRASEC 2025 Organization

Workshop Chairs

Martin Husák	Masaryk University, Czech Republic
Mohamed-Lamine Messai	University Lyon 2, France
Hamida Seba	University Lyon 1, France

Program Committee

Ajay Venkat Nagrale	Meta, USA
Belal Alsinglawi	Zayed University, UAE
Francesco Mercaldo	University of Molise, Italy
Imre Lendák	ELT University, Hungary
Milan Čermák	Masaryk University, Czech Republic
Mohamed Haddad	University Lyon 1, France
Mohammed Nafi	University of Rennes, France
Mudita Khurana	Meta, USA
Pierre Parrend	University of Strasbourg, France
Walid Megherbi	University Lyon 1, France

BASS 2025 Preface

The BASS (Behavioral Authentication for System Security) workshop was organized to bring together researchers and practitioners from industry and academia who are working on behavioral analysis techniques for enhancing IT security. Over recent years, behavioral features have attracted growing interest as they enable continuous and unobtrusive user authentication, anomaly and intrusion detection, and risk mitigation across diverse systems and contexts. BASS welcomed contributions on theoretical foundations, practical implementations, and privacy-preserving methods related to behavior-based profiling, authentication, and anomaly detection. In particular, topics ranged from software behavior analysis, user-behavior modeling and classification, and ontologies for behavior representation, to privacy-preserving behavioral analysis, explainability, and forensic applications. The workshop built on previous editions co-located with SECRYPT 2018 and ARES (2019, 2021, and 2024), continuing the tradition of fostering discussion on novel behavioral techniques for system security.

All submitted workshop papers underwent a double-blind review process, with each manuscript receiving four independent reviews to ensure a rigorous evaluation. Out of six workshop papers submitted, three were accepted for presentation and inclusion in these proceedings. Conflicts of interest were managed in accordance with the conference's ethical guidelines to ensure objective review.

We thank all authors for their high-quality submissions and the Program Committee and external reviewers for their thorough and constructive feedback. We are also grateful to the organizers of ARES and to Springer for their support in bringing these proceedings to fruition.

August 2025

Alessandro Aldini
Marco Rasori
Andrea Saracino

BASS 2025 Organization

Workshop Chairs

Alessandro Aldini	University of Urbino, Italy
Marco Rasori	National Research Council, Italy
Andrea Saracino	Scuola Superiore Universitaria Sant'Anna di Pisa, Italy

Program Committee

Wesam Alabbasi	Scuola Superiore Universitaria Sant'Anna di Pisa, Italy
Luca Ardito	Politecnico di Torino, Italy
Vasileios Gkioulos	Norwegian University of Science and Technology, Norway
Erisa Karafili	University of Southampton, UK
Weizhi Meng	Lancaster University, UK
Pericle Perazzo	University of Pisa, Italy
Giulio Rossolini	Scuola Superiore Universitaria Sant'Anna di Pisa, Italy
Marco Tiloca	Research Institutes of Sweden, Sweden
Shucheng Yu	Stevens Institute of Technology, USA
Nicola Zannone	Eindhoven University of Technology, Netherland

Additional Reviewer

Jiarui Li

Contents – Part IV

Proceedings of the Fifth International Workshop on Behavioral Authentication for System Security (BASS 2025)

Proceedings of the First International Workshop on Cybersecurity and Privacy Risk Assessments (CPRA 2025)

CPRA 2025 Preface

This volume presents the proceedings of the workshop on Cybersecurity and Privacy Risk Assessments (CPRA), held in conjunction with the 20th International Conference on Availability, Reliability and Security (ARES), which took place in Ghent, Belgium, August 11–14, 2025.

The CPRA brought together computer scientists, researchers, practitioners, and industry experts to explore emerging methodologies for assessing evolving cybersecurity and privacy risks. Discussions addressed the limitations of traditional risk assessment methodologies, particularly their reliance on extensive manual processes and lack of clear guidance and reproducibility, issues that are increasingly problematic in the context of evolving Cyber Physical System (CPS) technologies. On that note, CPRA emphasized the importance of enhancing risk assessment methodologies at different levels, including the risk scoring, risk treatment decision and vulnerabilities' prioritization. The workshop focused on refining standardized approaches, such as ISO/SAE 21434 and ISO 42010, while addressing their limitations through innovative methods, such as dynamic decision support systems, viewpoint based-models, and data-driven approaches, built on top of traditional Threat Analysis and Risk Assessment (TARA), Data Protection Impact Assessments (DPIAs), and risk prioritization techniques.

Furthermore, the workshop explored the interplay between regulatory compliance and the role of human factors in risk management, particularly in balancing legal, technical, and societal requirements. Special attention was given to the challenges posed by the subjective interpretation of risks among diverse stakeholders, and how these perceptions can be integrated into more objective and structured assessment frameworks.

The papers of the workshops were grouped into the following topical sections: (i) Security risk assessment enhancements; (ii) Data privacy assessments; and (iii) Risk prioritization.

The workshop papers included in this volume were selected through a rigorous review process, with an acceptance rate of $\geq$50%. Out of eight submissions, four papers were accepted for presentation at the workshop. Manuscripts were double-blind reviewed by at least three experts, assigned based on relevant expertise of program committee members. Evaluation criteria included relevance to the workshop theme, originality of the research, clarity of the methods and results, approach and correctness of the validation, interest to the general, scientific and practitioner public as well as overall quality of the manuscript. All conflicts of interest were declared and verified by the workshop chairs, who ensured that no program committee member served as a co-author on any reviewed paper.

August 2025

Meriem Benyahya
Anastasija Collen
Christoph Schmittner

CPRA 2025 Organization

Workshop Chairs

Meriem Benyahya	University of Geneva, Switzerland
Anastasija Collen	University of Geneva, Switzerland
Christoph Schmittner	Austrian Institute of Technology, Austria

Program Committee

Tariq Bontekoe	University of Groningen, Netherlands
Simon Bouget	Division Digitala System, Sweden
Luigi Briguglio	CyberEthics Lab., Italy
Vittoria Cozza	University of Verona, Italy
Piroska Haller	University of Medicine, Pharmacy, Sciences and Technology of Targu Mures, Romania
Nicolas Harrand	Stockholm University, Sweden
Sokratis Katsikas	Norwegian University of Science and Technology, Norway
Teri Lenard	University of Medicine, Pharmacy, Science and Technology of Targu Mures, Romania
McKenna McCall	Carnegie Mellon University, Pittsburgh, USA
Mohamed Amine Merzouk	Polytechnique Montréal, Canada
Niels Alexander Nijdam	University of Geneva, Switzerland
Federica Paci	University of Verona, Italy
Laurens Sion	KU Leuven, Belgium

Sponsors

AI4CSM	DOI: 10.3030/101007326	https://ai4csm.eu/
AIMS50	DOI: 10.3030/101112089	https://www.aims50.eu/
AutoTRUST	DOI: 10.3030/101148123	https://autotrust-he.eu/
OPEVA	DOI: 10.3030/101097267	https://opeva.eu/
ShapeFuture	DOI: 10.3030/101139996	https://shapefuture.eu/
ULTIMO	DOI: 10.3030/101077587	https://ultimo-he.eu/

Securing the Road Ahead: Supporting Decision Making in Automotive Cybersecurity Risk Treatment

Manfred Vielberth[1(✉)], Robin Siepmann[2], Magdalena Glas[2], and Günther Pernul[2]

[1] Faculty of Computer Science, Deggendorf Institute of Technology, Deggendorf, Germany
manfred.vielberth@th-deg.de

[2] Chair of Information Systems, University of Regensburg, Regensburg, Germany
{robin.siepmann,magdalena.glas,guenther.pernul}@ur.de

Abstract. In the automotive industry, as in most other sectors, risk management is essential for maintaining a balanced security posture while ensuring reasonable cybersecurity spending. ISO 21434 clearly defines the process for automotive Threat Analysis and Risk Assessment (TARA) for identifying cybersecurity risks. However, it lacks detailed guidance on subsequent risk treatment decision-making, leading to a lack of reproducibility and transparency in automotive projects. To address this issue, we propose a framework that defines a structured decision-making process and provides guidance for experts on suitable cybersecurity control sets. Our framework evaluates all potential control options based on their cost-effectiveness, aiming to mitigate high risks to an acceptable level. Through a case study and interviews with six industry experts, we assessed its feasibility and iteratively refined the framework based on the experts' feedback.

Keywords: Threat Analysis and Risk Assessment · Automotive Security · Risk Treatment Decision · Risk Management · Decision Support

1 Introduction

The vision for future cities encompasses an interconnected environment with high traffic efficiency, ideally leading to reduced energy waste, pollution, and accidents. A key component of this vision is the trend of V2X (vehicle-to-everything) technology, where vehicles connect with their surroundings, including other vehicles and infrastructure. However, enabling such a transformative change requires robust security for these connections and systems. While achieving 100% security is unattainable, effective risk management is essential. Risk management not only supports a security-by-design approach by identifying risks early in the development process but also allows security architects to select appropriate

B. Coppens et al. (Eds.): ARES 2025 Workshops, LNCS 15997, pp. 5–22, 2025.
https://doi.org/10.1007/978-3-032-00639-4_1

countermeasures in a pragmatic and resource-aware manner. In the automotive industry, this risk management approach is defined in ISO 21434 [1] as Threat Analysis and Risk Assessment (TARA). It details how cybersecurity risks are identified, from identifying damage scenarios to rating the feasibility of potential attacks. The result is a list of risks rated from very low to very high. However, ISO 21434 [1] lacks detail on the subsequent steps, specifically on connecting those risk values with an appropriate risk treatment decision. Additionally, economic considerations are rarely incorporated into the decision-making process, further limiting transparency and traceability in control selection. It is essential to evaluate whether a high-risk classification demands intervention, or if acceptance is a reasonable alternative when mitigation costs outweigh potential benefits.

Motivating Example. The following example illustrates this problem. Assume an Electronic Control Unit (ECU) of a vehicle, that is controlling the exterior lights. To keep this example simple, it consists of a microcontroller, a flash storage unit, and several interfaces, such as Controller Area Networks (CAN) or Local Interconnect Networks (LIN) to other components. Given the critical nature of lighting systems in terms of passenger and road user safety, the security of this component is paramount. A measure to protect the communication with other ECUs would be to implement SecOC (Secure Onboard Communication) for the CAN interface, which ensures the authenticity of messages. However, the implementation of this control can incur significant expenses, particularly when considering the synchronization requirements between multiple ECUs. It falls on an expert to decide about the implementation of this control. However, due to the absence of guidance, the only possibility is to take ad hoc decisions with limited transparency and reproducibility. Therefore, we raise the following research question:

> **RQ:** How can risk treatment decisions in automotive security be made in a reproducible and transparent manner?

To address this research question, we propose a framework designed to guide experts in selecting cybersecurity controls. Developed and refined in collaboration with industry experts, the framework integrates feedback from practical applications to enhance its relevance and usability. To demonstrate its feasibility, we conduct an illustrative case study along a real use case. The final framework provides a structured, data-driven approach for systematically evaluating control options, enabling reproducible and justifiable risk treatment decisions. It also incorporates cost-benefit as a key criterion for recommending viable security controls.

2 Background and Related Work

2.1 Threat Analysis and Risk Assessment (TARA)

The TARA process is a systematic approach to identifying cybersecurity-relevant threats and risks. Research has taken up the topic of TARA [5,14,22]. Nevertheless, the following description focuses on the description outlined by Benyahya et al. [6] and ISO 21434 [1] (illustrated in Fig. 1), due to its broad recognition within the industry.

The TARA process builds upon the input of an item definition, which outlines the components and interfaces under analysis and specifies its boundaries. Based on the item definition, the first key step is **asset identification**, where cybersecurity-relevant assets and their properties are identified.

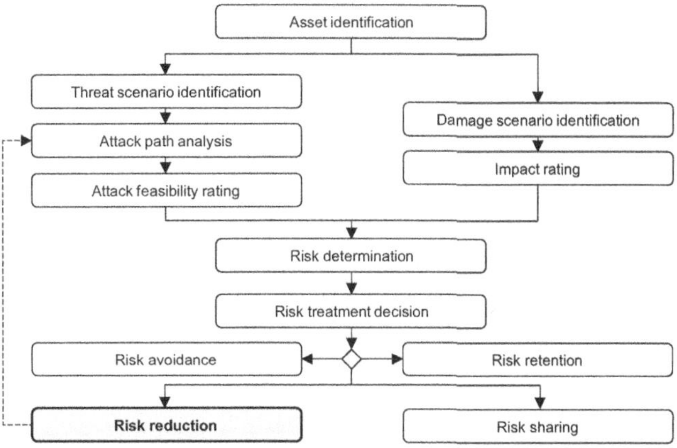

Fig. 1. Schematic representation of the TARA process based on ISO 21434 [1,14]. The focus of this paper lies on the step *Risk reduction*.

The next step in the process is the **identification of threat scenarios**. A threat scenario outlines how an asset could be compromised through a cybersecurity attack, For the exterior lighting ECU example from the introduction, a potential threat scenario could involve an attacker injecting malicious CAN messages to manipulate the headlights.

To assess the likelihood of a threat scenario occurring, the first step is to map out the possible attack paths. This **attack path analysis** involves examining each step an attacker has to take to exploit the system to realize a threat scenario. To perform an attack path analysis, ISO 21434 outlines several methodologies, with one of the most widely adopted being the use of attack trees, which visually represent the sequential steps an attacker could follow [1,12].

To determine the likelihood of an attack, the **attack feasibility rating** evaluates the effort an attacker would need to successfully execute a given attack. This rating considers key factors such as the technical complexity of the attack, the required tools, and the needed level of expertise. For instance, if the CAN communication between the ECU and other components lacks authentication, the attack feasibility would be rated high (or very high), as injecting unauthorized messages would require only basic skills and little effort.

Any adverse event, such as the failure of the exterior lights, could lead to potential **damage scenarios**, including serious injuries or fatalities due to reduced visibility for the driver and other road users. Based on that, the **impact rating** aims to measure the adverse consequences and outcomes for road users and other stakeholders for each damage scenario, with ratings across four main dimensions: safety, financial, operational, and privacy.

The next step in the TARA process is **risk determination**, where the overall risk level of each identified threat scenario is calculated by combining the Impact Rating and the Attack Feasibility Rating, typically using risk matrices or mathematical formulas. Risk values are generally categorized on a scale from 1 to 5, where 1 indicates minimal risk, and 5 represents the most critical threats.

The final step in the TARA process is the **risk treatment decision**, where appropriate strategies must be selected to address each identified risk, based on the previously determined risk values. In the broader field of cybersecurity and risk management, there is a general consensus on four primary risk treatment strategies: **Risk avoidance** eliminates the source of risk (e.g., not implementing vulnerable features). **Risk reduction** applies cybersecurity controls to manage and reduce risks to an acceptable level. **Risk sharing** shifts risk to a third party, often via contracts or insurance. And finally, **risk acceptance** allows for irreducible risks and especially low risks to be accepted.

2.2 Related Work

Up to this point, the TARA process has been well-defined and extensively explored in the literature. However, beyond this stage the ISO 21434 and research provide limited guidance on choosing appropriate risk treatment options. This lack of guidance in ISO 21434 is not limited to the automotive industry or this specific standard; rather, it represents a broader challenge in cybersecurity risk management. Comparable standards, such as the NIST Special Publication 800-82 [21], which focuses on Operational Technology (OT) Security, also do not provide comprehensive solutions or clear guidelines for decision-making. Similarly, Gordon et al. [11] point out that, while the NIST Cybersecurity Framework acknowledges the importance of integrating cost-benefit considerations into cybersecurity risk management, it lacks concrete guidance on how such analyses should be conducted.

This is despite the fact that monetary-based security controls assessments and the optimization of cybersecurity investments have been a subject of research for decades, particularly in the field of information security [10]. However, most of these works emphasize overarching investment strategies and focus on high-level economic models rather than offering systematic guidance for the selection and prioritization of security controls in practical applications. For instance, Nowey et al. [18] analyze different security investment evaluation methods, comparing their practicality and efficiency, while Weishäupl et al. [23] examine decision-making frameworks and assessment systems in cybersecurity investment strategies. A common challenge across these studies is the accurate quantification of control effectiveness, which remains complex due to inherent uncertainties in risk estimations and a lack of empirical evaluation data.

Prior research has explored Multi-Criteria Decision-Making (MCDM) approaches, which assess multiple factors to determine the most suitable alternatives [19], thereby offering a structured method to integrate non-monetary factors into control selection. Mohamed et al. [17] demonstrate this by integrating MCDM techniques with the MITRE ATT&CK framework for optimizing security measures. To operationalize such approaches, decision support systems (DSS) have emerged as essential tools in cybersecurity and risk management for a variety of use cases. Akbar et al. [3], for example, present a comprehensive literature review on the advancement of decision support tools for risk management. They highlight that while risk identification has been extensively addressed, research on decision support applications for risk mitigation remains largely underexplored. Nevertheless, a few approaches have been proposed that offer direct guidance on selecting appropriate security controls for specific use cases. For example, Almeida et al. [4] introduce a decision-support framework based on the ISO/IEC 27000 series, designed to assist security managers in prioritizing security controls to mitigate risks. Their framework incorporates an optimization model that aims to determine the optimal selection of security measures by balancing two key objectives: minimizing investment costs for security implementation and reducing residual risks. Alternative approaches have been proposed to optimize security control portfolios under constraints by identifying the most suitable combination of controls. For instance, Léveillé and Jaskolka [16] apply game-theoretic principles to the control selection problem to generate valid control sets for selection. Another noteworthy approach is Kiesling et al. [13], who utilize attack simulations on system components to determine the most effective control combinations. Similarly, Yevseyeva et al. [24] present an approach to security controls subset selection by formulating it as a portfolio optimization problem.

However, while these studies provide valuable insights, most research in this domain focuses on IT security controls, which differ significantly from product security controls. Unlike flexible IT security measures that can be implemented or adjusted post-deployment, product security controls must be embedded early in the design and development process due to hardware and embedded system constraints. In automotive cybersecurity, late-stage modifications are often impractical or highly resource-intensive, making technical design controls the primary means of ensuring security in line with the "Security-by-Design" principle. Consequently, IT security strategies are not fully transferable to the static, pre-integrated nature of security for products, such as a ECU.

3 Methodology

Due to the practice-driven nature of cybersecurity decision-making in automotive TARA, we apply Action Design Research (ADR) [20], an approach that aims to bridge theory and practice by iteratively creating a research artifact in collaboration with experts of the respective domain. As such, we collaborated with TARA experts through iterative discussions and semi-structured interviews.

Thereby, we adapted the ADR approach leading to five iterative steps, which are outlined in the following and depicted in Fig. 2.

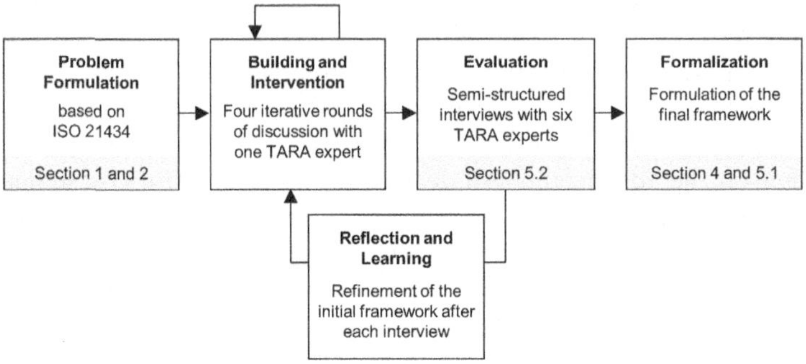

Fig. 2. Overview of how the Action Design Research (ADR) method was applied

1) Problem Formulation. Our study addresses the lack of structured decision-making support for selecting cybersecurity controls in the automotive industry. A detailed problem formulation is provided in Sect. 1.

2) Building and Intervention. The initial process was developed based on insights gained from observing TARA applications in practice, along with the structured outputs of a TARA process as defined in ISO 21434. The framework was then iteratively refined through four structured sessions with an industry TARA expert. A key design principle was ensuring alignment with the TARA process so that the proposed framework begins precisely where ISO 21434 guidance ends. The inputs for the decision-support process were directly mapped to the outputs of TARA, ensuring seamless integration. The initial version was evaluated using fictional yet practically relevant scenarios, in which predefined TARA-based risk values and estimated control implementation costs were used to assess the feasibility of the framework.

3) Evaluation. To assess the framework's relevance and applicability it was then evaluated with six industry experts. The detailed evaluation process is outlined in Sect. 5.

4) Reflection and Learning. Following each expert interview, we systematically analyzed the findings and discussed key insights. This reflective process allowed for continuous learning and adaptation, enhancing the framework's practicality and alignment with real-world decision-making.

5) Formalization of Learning. The results of the previous steps were consolidated into a formalized decision-support framework as demonstrated in this paper.

4 Framework

The framework presented in this section provides an approach for evaluating available control options to support control selection. By leveraging the outputs of a TARA, this approach supplements industry standards, in particular the ISO 21434. To further address the research question, the presented process equips cybersecurity experts with the necessary information to make transparent and justified decisions.

Due to the varied definitions of "decision support" in the literature, it is important to clarify that this process does not constitute a traditional decision support system (DSS) but rather provides the foundation for developing one. While not the focus of this paper, an automated implementation of the process could readily classify as a DSS [8,9]. The proposed decision-support process is not designed to identify a single optimal solution, replacing the control selection process entirely. Instead, it serves as a decision aid, offering well-founded recommendations to support stakeholders in making informed choices.

4.1 Decision Support Process

The proposed decision support process, illustrated in Fig. 3, begins with the **generation of control sets**. This step requires identifying all *available controls* that are applicable according to the TARA. Additionally, project-specific *constraints* must be considered to determine whether a control set is feasible. For example, some controls may be mandatory and must always be included in any valid set, while others may only be effective when combined with specific complementary controls. The next step, **residual risk determination**, focuses on assessing the residual risks that remain after applying a given control set. Specifically, when a control set is applied, it reduces certain risks identified in the TARA. These adjusted, lower risk values are referred to as the *residual risk values*. To calculate these, all controls included in the respective set are integrated into the underlying TARA model, and the overall risk profile is recalculated accordingly. This procedure is repeated for each generated control set, allowing a systematic evaluation of how much each set reduces the overall risk compared to the initial, uncontrolled state. The **evaluation of risk reduction capability** aims to quantify how effectively each control set mitigates risk by comparing the *residual risk values* to the *initial risk values*. As a next step, **cost-benefit evaluation** step requires *cost estimations* for all control sets, which need to be provided by the responsible engineers or developers. In a well-managed project, these estimations are typically available from the outset, meaning no additional effort is needed to obtain them for this process. Based on this information, it becomes possible to assess the trade-off between the risk reduction capability and the associated implementation costs. Finally, the process concludes with **pre-selecting control sets**, where the most promising alternatives are identified using predefined selection and filtering criteria. This step involves applying risk thresholds and prioritization parameters to ensure that only the most suitable sets for a given use case that align with an organization's security goals are retained for further consideration. This provides stakeholders with a quick overview of the most suitable control combinations, along with the necessary information to examine these alternatives in greater detail.

By performing these steps, the proposed decision support process aims to achieve three key objectives. First, it reduces arbitrary control selection by employing a structured, systematic, and reproducible approach. Additionally, it facilitates well-founded decision-making by providing relevant information about available alternatives. Finally, the traceable nature of the process provides a robust basis for validation, communication and justification of final decisions.

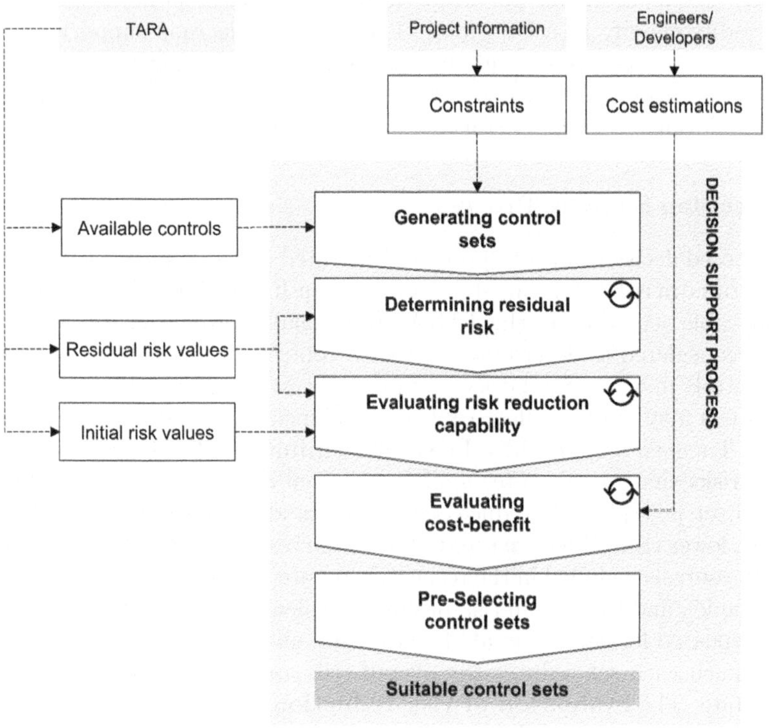

Fig. 3. Conceptual framework of the decision support process. Circular arrows indicate that a step is repeated for every control set.

4.2 Process Instantiation (Step-by-Step Algorithm)

To further demonstrate the functionality and applicability of the proposed framework, this section presents a step-by-step algorithm outlining how the decision-support process could be instantiated.

For the algorithm, the risks output by the TARA process are conceptualized as vectors, with each entry representing a single estimated risk value on a scale from 1 to 5:

$$R = [5, 4, 3, \ldots, 2]$$

Step 1: Generating Control Sets. The control sets are generated by computing the power set (all possible combinations) of the available controls S that were input into the process. Given that the empty set (i.e., no control implemented) does not affect the initial risk values, it can be ignored, as the initial risk values are already accounted for as an additional input to the framework.
The total number of possible control combinations is determined by:

$$2^n - 1,$$

where n represents the number of available controls. Each combination represents a control set S_y that could potentially be implemented:

$$S_y \subseteq S, \quad S_y \neq \emptyset,$$

where $S = \{C_1, C_2, \ldots, C_n\}$ is the set of all available controls.
Each generated control set S_y is then assessed against a predefined set of mandatory controls M, which represents controls that are required for implementation:

$$M \subseteq S.$$

A control set S_y is only retained if it contains all mandatory controls; otherwise, it is discarded:

$$S_y \text{ is valid if } M \subseteq S_y.$$

This filtering mechanism ensures that only practically feasible and applicable control sets proceed to the subsequent analysis.

Step 2: Determining Residual Risk Values. For each control set S_y, every individual control within the set is incorporated into the TARA model, and the resulting risk values (residual risks) R_y are calculated for this set (function f). Consequently, each control set yields exactly one residual risk vector:

$$R_y = f(S_y)$$

As the general methodology for determining risk values has already been described in previous sections, this step will not be further elaborated. However, it should be noted that the calculation of residual risk values heavily depends on the specific TARA modeling methodology employed. By determining the residual risks for each control set, this step ensures that even complex interactions between controls, which may be challenging to anticipate in advance, are accounted for accurately.

Step 3: Evaluating Risk Reduction Capability. The total initial risk R_{total} is computed by summing all entries in the risk vector R:

$$R_{\text{total}} = \sum_{i=1}^{n} R_i$$

This value serves as a baseline for evaluating the risk reduction capabilities of the different control sets.

For each control set, the total residual risk $R_{\text{total},y}$ as the sum of all elements in the risk vector R_y

$$R_{\text{total},y} = \sum_{i=1}^{m} R_{i,y}$$

The absolute risk reduction ΔR_y achieved by each control set is determined as the difference between the total initial risk and the total residual risk:

$$\Delta R_y = R_{\text{total}} - R_{\text{total},y}$$

Step 4: Evaluating Cost-Benefit. For each generated control set S_y, the total implementation cost K_{S_y} is calculated as the sum of the costs of the individual controls included in the set:

$$K_{S_y} = \sum_{C \in S_y} K_C,$$

where K_C represents the estimated implementation cost of each control C within a set S. This step provides a quantitative measure of the resources required for each control set, forming the basis for cost-effectiveness comparisons.

The cost-effectiveness E of each control set is calculated by dividing its achieved risk reduction ΔR_y by its total implementation cost K_{S_y}:

$$\text{E} = \frac{\Delta R_y}{K_{S_y}} \text{ with } K_{S_y} > 0$$

This metric provides a normalized measure of how efficiently each control set reduces risk relative to its cost, enabling a structured prioritization of control sets.

Step 5: Pre-Selecting Control Sets. Each residual risk vector R_y is evaluated to identify the number of individual residual risk values exceeding the defined threshold t. Only the control sets that minimize the count of risk values exceeding the threshold are retained for further analysis:

$$S_y^* = \arg\min_{S_y} |\{R_i \in R_y \mid R_i > t\}|$$

This step ensures that the focus remains on identifying the sets achieving the greatest risk reduction among high risks before considering costs as a secondary selection criterion. Skipping this filtering step could result in selecting sets that may offer higher total risk reduction or greater cost-effectiveness but contain an excessive number of unacceptable residual risks. Therefore, the threshold t reflects the organization's risk tolerance.

Table 1. Overview of Control Set Alternatives

ID	S	R_{total}	Δ R	K	E
Initial TARA (Empty Set)	{ }	30	–	–	–
Set 1	C1	22	8	600	0.013
Set 2	C2	24	6	1400	0.004
Set 3	C3	22	8	1600	0.005
Set 4	C1, C2	22	8	2000	0.004
Set 5	C1, C3	15	15	2200	0.007
Set 6	C2, C3	17	13	3000	0.004
Set 7	C1, C2, C3	14	16	3600	0.005

Note: S: Control set, C: Control, R: Risk, E: Cost Effectiveness, K: Cost, C1: Secure Boot, C2: Secure Software Update, C3: Secure Onboard Communication

5 Evaluation

In the following, we present an illustrative control selection scenario based on the motivating example from Sect. 1, which also served as a demonstration in the expert interviews. We then describe how the expert interviews were conducted and summarize their findings and how it helped us to improve the framework.

5.1 Exemplary Control Selection Scenario

This section presents an exemplary control selection case study based on the realistic yet simplified scenario introduced in Sect. 1 (motivating example). The numbers used in this case study (e.g., risk values, cost estimations) are therefore purely demonstrative, but developed in collaboration with the industry expert that was directly involved in the development of the framework. The purpose of this example is to illustrate how the proposed decision-support process could be applied in a real-world setting by following the step-by-step algorithm outlined in the previous section.

For the system under consideration, the TARA process has already been conducted to estimate the initial risks. The system comprises eight identified threat scenarios, encompassing various cybersecurity challenges, such as firmware tampering and exploitation of communication channels.

Since the impact rating typically covers four distinct impact categories, safety, financial, operational, and privacy, each threat scenario also generated four separate risk values corresponding to these categories. Ideally, these risk values should be considered separately. However, to simplify the calculation process, these four risk values per threat scenario were treated as a single combined vector value. Consequently, in the given example, this approach resulted in risk value vectors with a length of eight. To address the identified risks, three controls were considered for implementation:

- **Secure Boot (C1)**: Ensures that only authorized software is executed during system startup, mitigating risks associated with unauthorized firmware or software modifications.
- **Secure Software Update (C2)**: Provides mechanisms for authenticated and integrity-verified updates, addressing vulnerabilities related to tampered updates.
- **Secure Onboard Communication (C3)**: Implements authentication protocols to protect data transmissions via CAN from interception or manipulation.

Additionally, an expert familiar with the project estimated the implementation cost of each control using a standardized methodology defined by the organization.

The resulting control sets were generated as presented in Table 1. Subsequently, the residual risk values for each set were determined by incorporating the corresponding controls into the TARA model, using the previously described Attack Potential-Based approach to recalculate the resulting risk values. To further quantify the risk reduction capabilities of each set and to incorporate the cost dimension into the decision-making process, the absolute risk reduction, total implementation cost, and cost-effectiveness were also determined, as described in the previous section.

The results were compiled in a structured table (see Table 1) providing an overview of the prepared information, allowing for easy comparison between control sets. This structured presentation not only enables decision-makers to quickly evaluate different options but also contributes to a well-documented and transparent control selection process.

Before the final recommendations, however, the control sets were pre-selected based on a predefined risk threshold of $t = 2$, which was collaboratively determined by the cybersecurity expert and the client. For this reason, each residual risk vector was evaluated to count the number of individual residual risk values exceeding this threshold.

The threshold was set to 2, and the minimum number of counted values exceeding this threshold per control set was identified to be 1, as depicted in Table 2. Consequently, only the three control sets that met this criterion (Set 5, Set 6, Set 7) were retained for the final recommendation, ensuring that all remaining control sets have the lowest possible number of high-priority residual risks among the given options.

A key observation from the recommendations is that the highest-ranked control set, Set 5 (Secure Boot + Secure Onboard Communication), was identified as the most suitable and cost-effective solution based on the applied parameters and selection criteria. However, the second-highest ranked set, Set 7, which includes all three controls, achieved an even slightly higher total risk reduction, albeit at a higher cost. The responsible cybersecurity expert can immediately recognize this distinction and conduct a more detailed comparison of these two sets. In doing so, it becomes apparent that the differences in risk reduction between the sets are not purely additive but can be traced back to partial functional overlaps

Table 2. Pre-selection of Control Set Alternatives

ID	R	$\|R_i > t\|$	Suggested
Initial TARA	[**3**, **4**, **3**, **4**, **5**, **4**, **3**, **4**]	8	
Set 1	[2, 2, 1, **4**, **5**, **4**, **3**, 1]	4	
Set 2	[2, 2, 2, **4**, **5**, **4**, **3**, 2]	4	
Set 3	[**3**, **4**, **3**, 2, **3**, 2, 2, **3**]	5	
Set 4	[2, 2, 1, **4**, **5**, **4**, **3**, 1]	4	
Set 5	[2, 2, 1, 2, **3**, 2, 2, 1]	1	✓
Set 6	[2, 2, 2, 2, **3**, 2, 2, 2]	1	✓
Set 7	[2, 1, 1, 2, **3**, 2, 2, 1]	1	✓

Note: S: Risk set, R: Risk vector, RV: Risk value, t: risk threshold (t=2 in this example)

between Secure Boot and Secure Software Update. Such insights provide the expert with an even deeper understanding to assess whether the additional benefits of Secure Software Update justify the increased cost or if the much cheaper Set 5 already provides sufficient security for the specific project requirements.

This exemplifies why the goal of the decision-support process should not be to identify a single "best" solution but rather to systematically prepare information and narrow down the viable options based on predefined criteria, ultimately presenting the most suitable alternatives for a given use case. By structuring the output in a clear and comparative format, the process allows decision-makers to efficiently evaluate and compare the most suitable options based on quantifiable indicators and systematically prepared information, thereby fostering a more data-driven and less arbitrary decision-making process.

5.2 Expert Interviews

Method and Procedure. The initial framework, developed through several rounds of discussion with one TARA expert, was subsequently evaluated and refined through expert interviews. We recruited six experts from the automotive sector who are either directly involved in the TARA process (e.g., cybersecurity analysts and architects) or indirectly engaged (e.g., decision-makers). To this end, we employed purposive sampling, selectively recruiting participants from the authors' professional networks. As shown in Table 3, two of the six participants work for OEM companies, conducting TARAs on a vehicle level; the remaining four participants work for a product supplier, conducting TARAs on a component level. To facilitate open discussions without restricting the range of possible responses, we conducted semi-structured expert interviews [2,15]. The interview guide was iteratively developed through several rounds of discussion among the authors. Before the main study, we conducted a test interview with one expert to refine the guide. The results of this test interview were not included in the final analysis. The finalized interview guide comprised three phases:

1. **Introduction.** The session began with mutual introductions and an overview of the project. Interviewees were first asked to describe how they typically determine risk treatment within the TARA process.
2. **Description of the framework.** Participants were presented with the framework through a series of slides and the sample use case introduced in Sect. 5.1 to illustrate its application.
3. **Evaluation of the framework.** Interviewees were given the opportunity to ask clarifying questions about any aspect of the framework. They were then asked whether they found the problem the framework addresses to be relevant, and whether the framework itself represented a valid approach. Finally, they were invited to suggest modifications or adaptations to improve the framework.

Table 3. Interview Participants

Role	Number of Participants	Scope	Avg. Years of Experience
Cybersecurity Manager	4	component level	8
Cybersecurity Consultant	2	vehicle level	14

The interviews were conducted in February 2025 and had an average duration of 43 min. One author conducted all six interviews, while at least one additional author participated in each session, enabling further questions and brief discussions after the participant had left. The interviews were conducted remotely via an online conferencing tool and held in either English (n=3) or German (n=3). Participants were informed that their data would be anonymized before analysis and published in an aggregated format. With their consent, the interviews were recorded with a digital voice recorder and subsequently transcribed. For data analysis, we applied inductive coding as described by Corbin and Strauss [7]. The first round of coding was conducted by the author who led the interviews, identifying recurring patterns based on predefined themes. The findings were then discussed in several iterative rounds among the authors, leading to inductive conclusions based on expert insights.

Results. In the following, we present the key findings from the expert interviews. First, we summarize the feedback received. Then, we discuss the identified limitations of the process and derive key areas for future research.

The respondents predominantly concurred with the identified gap, emphasizing that insufficient guidance exists for selecting appropriate cybersecurity controls. They widely acknowledged that, in practice, control selection relies heavily on expert judgment and is often conducted in an ad hoc manner, lacking a structured evaluation of alternatives. A key reason cited for this is the complexity of real-world projects, where numerous interdependent factors and constraints influence the selection process in ways that cannot always be controlled. This not only limits the available range of control options from the outset but also makes it difficult to derive generalized and universally applicable methods for control selection.

Several factors were identified as contributing to this issue, including regulatory requirements, decisions imposed by other stakeholders (e.g., clients), and strong dependencies on hardware and software constraints inherent to the component or project. Therefore, most participants emphasized that, in order to ensure practical applicability, the decision-support framework should be flexible, easily configurable, and adaptable to different use cases to accurately capture and manage real-world complexities.

Another aspect discussed in this context was the potential benefit of using the decision-support process to account for different implementation variants of the same controls. This insight led to the recognition that the framework must incorporate additional control specifications and upfront filtering mechanisms during the generation of control sets to ensure that only practically applicable control combinations proceed to further assessment, eliminating invalid sets early in the process. Consequently, the corresponding step of the framework *generating control sets* was updated accordingly.

Despite highlighting these challenges, all interview participants expressed strong endorsement for a process that provides more data-driven insights and key indicators for evaluating implementation alternatives. The structured and transparent nature of the approach was particularly well received, as even experienced field experts sometimes find it difficult to fully retrace past decisions. This further reinforces the value of a structured decision-support process, ensuring that reproducible results strengthen the rationale behind control selection.

While some respondents raised concerns about the extent to which cost considerations should influence decision-making in the context of cybersecurity, the chosen approach–which provides targeted information and suitable cost-benefit indicators to promote cost-awareness–was generally seen as beneficial. However, interviewees explicitly pointed out the challenges in accurately estimating costs, given the involvement of multiple stakeholders and various influencing factors. As a result, costs should remain a secondary factor in cybersecurity-related decision-making rather than a primary driver of control selection.

Although this aspect was simplified in Sect. 5.1 for illustrative purposes, two experts recommended keeping risk values derived from different impact categories separate rather than mixing them, as the scales of these values typically cannot be directly or unequivocally translated into one another in practice. Instead, they suggested conducting the decision-support process individually for each impact category to further enhance transparency and improve the information gained.

The topic of whether budget constraints should be integrated as a preselection criterion was also frequently discussed during the interviews. However, due to the additional uncertainty associated with such an approach, it was generally recommended that budget considerations be provided in the form of an additional indicator in the final output rather than as a strict filtering criterion (e.g., "percentage of budget used by the set").

Several participants further suggested incorporating additional metrics and indicators to better assess the risk reduction capability of a given control set. Among the proposed additions were the relative risk reduction achieved by the set and an evaluation of the number of risks that remain completely unaddressed by a given control combination. Incorporating such indicators would not only enhance the information displayed in the output but could also be leveraged for more precise preselection methods, further refining the decision-support process.

Conclusions from the Interviews. The interviews generally confirmed the need for a more structured and transparent approach to cybersecurity control selection within the automotive industry. While challenges such as project complexity, dependencies, and external constraints were acknowledged, participants strongly welcomed the idea of a flexible and data-driven framework to support and foster more informed decision-making. Insights gained from the expert interviews were used to iteratively enhance and refine the proposed decision-support process. Overall, the participants viewed the approach as a promising step toward addressing existing gaps, and they encouraged further development and refinement of the concept.

6 Discussion and Future Work

While the proposed decision-support process contributes to a more structured and transparent selection of security controls, certain limitations should be acknowledged. One of the key factors influencing both the applicability and accuracy of the decision-support process is the quality of input data, particularly the data derived from TARA. Since TARA fundamentally relies on expert judgment and assumptions, a degree of inherent uncertainty and subjectivity remains unavoidable. However, this dependency further underscores the necessity of ensuring that TARA is as precise and systematic as possible.

A closely related issue, also raised during expert interviews, concerns the accuracy of cost estimations. The framework assumes that cost values for implementing controls are both available and sufficiently accurate. However, in practice, cost estimation is inherently complex, as it depends on numerous factors such as deployment environments, labor costs, and unforeseen integration challenges. To further enhance the framework, future research could focus on developing standardized cost estimation models applicable across various organizational contexts and use cases to ensure more reliable cost projections aligned with real-world conditions.

The framework also operates on the basis of a predefined list of available security controls, which facilitates a structured evaluation of existing alternatives but does not inherently support the identification or generation of new controls. Exploring methods for the identification of security controls could therefore be a promising direction for future research.

Another significant aspect is scalability. Since all possible control combinations are evaluated systematically, the computational complexity increases exponentially with each additional control (following the formula $2^n - 1$). Future work could focus on optimizing the selection process through heuristic filtering mechanisms, prioritization techniques, or more efficient algorithms.

While these outlined limitations present persistent challenges, they also create promising opportunities for future research. Addressing these challenges will not only refine the proposed framework, but will also enhance its practical utility. By embracing these challenges, future research can pave the way for the next generation of decision support solutions, offering greater transparency, efficiency, and ultimately more resilient security strategies.

7 Conclusion

In this paper, we introduce a framework for a decision support process that enhances transparency and reproducibility in TARA-based control selection for automotive cybersecurity, thereby addressing a lack of guidance within ISO 21434. The proposed approach provides a systematic methodology for evaluating available controls, aiming to balance risk reduction capabilities with cost considerations while accounting for the specific constraints and complexities of product cybersecurity environments. Through multiple iterative refinements and expert evaluations, the framework has been systematically validated and tailored to practical needs, establishing a strong foundation in real-world challenges while ensuring its applicability across diverse organizational contexts. While absolute objectivity in cybersecurity control selection remains challenging due to inherent uncertainties in risk estimations, this framework contributes to a more structured, transparent, and automated approach to control selection. Moreover, its modular design not only enhances adaptability but also provides multiple entry points for future research and further refinements to improve decision-making for cybersecurity risk treatment.

References

1. Iso/iec 21434:2022(e). road vehicles cybersecurity engineering (2022)
2. Adams, W.C.: Conducting Semi-Structured Interviews. In: Handbook of Practical Program Evaluation, pp. 492–505. Wiley (2015)
3. Akbar, M.A., Naseem, A., uz Zaman, U.K., Petronijevic, J.: Integrated-decision support system (dss) for risk identification and mitigation in manufacturing industry for zero-defect manufacturing (zdm): a state-of-the-art review. Int. J. Adv. Manuf. Technol. **135**(5-6), 1893–1931 (2024)
4. Decision support for selecting information security controls: Almeida, L., Resp cio, A. J. Decis. Syst. **27**, 173–180 (2018)
5. Benyahya, M., Lenard, T., Collen, A., Nijdam, N.A.: A systematic review of threat analysis and risk assessment methodologies for connected and automated vehicles. In: Proceedings of the 18th International Conference on Availability, Reliability and Security, pp. 1–10. ARES 2023, ACM (2023)
6. Benyahya, M., Lenard, T., Collen, A., Nijdam, N.A.: A systematic review of threat analysis and risk assessment methodologies for connected and automated vehicles. In: Proceedings of the 18th International Conference on Availability, Reliability and Security. ARES 2023, ACM (2023)

7. Corbin, J., Strauss, A.: Basics of qualitative research (3rd ed.): techniques and procedures for developing grounded theory (2008), https://methods.sagepub.com/book/basics-of-qualitative-research
8. Fran ois, M., Arduin, P.E., Merad, M.: Classification of decision support systems for cybersecurity. In: MCIS 2023 Proceedings, No. 11 (2023), https://aisel.aisnet.org/mcis2023/1
9. Gangi, M.D., Belcore, O.M., Polimeni, A.: An overview on decision support systems for risk management in emergency conditions: present, past and future trends. Int. J. Transp. Dev. Integrat. **7**, 45–53 (2023)
10. Gordon, L.A., Loeb, M.P.: The economics of information security investment. ACM Trans. Inf. Syst. Secur. (TISSEC) **5**(4), 438–457 (2002)
11. Gordon, L.A., Loeb, M.P., Zhou, L.: Integrating cost benefit analysis into the nist cybersecurity framework via the gordon loeb model. J. Cybersecurity **6**(1) (2020)
12. Ingoldsby, T.R.: Attack tree-based threat risk analysis. Amenaza Technologies Limited (2013), https://api.semanticscholar.org/CorpusID:231854288
13. Kiesling, E., Ekelhart, A., Grill, B., Strauss, C., Stummer, C.: Selecting security control portfolios: a multi-objective simulation-optimization approach. EURO J. Decis. Process. 85–117 (2016). https://doi.org/10.1007/s40070-016-0055-7
14. Lautenbach, A., Almgren, M., Olovsson, T.: Proposing heavens 2.0 an automotive risk assessment model. In: Proceedings of the 5th ACM Computer Science in Cars Symposium. CSCS 2021, Association for Computing Machinery, New York, NY, USA (2021)
15. Leech, B.L.: Asking questions: techniques for semistructured interviews. PS: Polit. Sci. Polit. **35**(4), 665–668 (2002), publisher: Cambridge University Press
16. L veill , D., Jaskolka, J.: A game-theoretic approach for security control selection. Electron. Proc. Theor. Comput. Sci. **409**, 103–119 (2024)
17. Mohamed, I., Hefny, H.A., Darwish, N.R.: Enhancing cybersecurity defenses: a multicriteria decision-making approach to mitre att&ck mitigation strategy (2024)
18. Nowey, T., Federrath, H., Klein, C.: Pl l, K.: Ans tze zur evaluierung von sicherheitsinvestitionen. In: Sicherheit 2005. Sicherheit Schutz und Zuverl ssigkeit, pp. 15–26. Gesellschaft f r Informatik e.V, Bonn (2005)
19. Pal, S.S.: MCDM for selection of cybersecurity technologies used in cybersecurity education. Ph.D. thesis (2022)
20. Sein, M.K., Henfridsson, O., Purao, S., Rossi, M., Lindgren, R.: Action design research. MIS Q. **35**(1), 37–56 (2011)
21. Stouffer, K., et al.: Guide to operational technology (ot) security. Technical Report, NIST Special Publication 800-82 Revision 3, National Institute of Standards and Technology, Gaithersburg, MD (2023)
22. Vielberth, M., Raab, K., Glas, M., Grümer, P., Pernul, G.: Elevating tara: a maturity model for automotive threat analysis and risk assessment. In: Proceedings of the 19th International Conference on Availability, Reliability and Security, pp. 1–9 (2024)
23. Weish upl, E., Yasasin, E., Schryen, G.: Information security investments: an exploratory multiple case study on decision-making, evaluation and learning. Comput. Secur. **77**, 807–823 (2018)
24. Yevseyeva, I., Basto-Fernandes, V., Emmerich, M., van Moorsel, A.: Selecting optimal subset of security controls. Procedia Comput. Sci. **64**, 1035–1042 (2015)

A Data-Driven Approach for Cyber Security Assessments of SMEs

Nico Mexis(✉) and Stefan Katzenbeisser

University of Passau, Innstraße 43, 94032 Passau, Germany
{nico.mexis,stefan.katzenbeisser}@uni-passau.de

Abstract. This paper presents a novel framework for assessing the cyber security of Small and Medium-sized Enterprises (SMEs) and identifying the specific problematic security controls. The combination of dimensionality reduction and clustering techniques with logistic regression results in a data-driven, non-linear scoring system that provides more information about the current state and possible improvements, including "the best way of improvements." The state of the art in the context of assessments is a linear scoring system, which is most often subjective due to manually determined weights in the corresponding linear combination. Our unsupervised methodology addresses not only this issue through the application of unsupervised algorithms, but also the unique challenges faced by SMEs in terms of limited resources, lack of expertise and inadequate cyber security measures. To validate our approach, we acquired a variety of data sets from SMEs across different industries and geographies. These data sets include organisational characteristics, cyber security controls and incident response measures. Our analysis shows that the proposed framework accurately provides actionable recommendations for improvement, while remaining highly configurable and extensible.

Keywords: Cyber Security · Assessment · Small and Medium-sized Enterprise (SME) · Score · Principal Component Analysis (PCA) · Logistic Regression (LR) · Cluster · Risk Management · Survey

1 Introduction

In today's interconnected world, organisations face a constantly evolving cyber threat landscape [16,17,23,24]. A single breach can cripple operations, damage reputations and cause significant financial loss. As described in ENISA's 2024 Threat Landscape report, the frequency as well as the impact of cyber attacks is growing rapidly [9]. In the past, mainly large companies have been the focal point of these attacks. Today, however, Small and Medium-sized Enterprises (SMEs) are also becoming targets of these attacks due to their unawareness and inability to deal with these kinds of attacks [15,16,20]. As SMEs represent 99.8% of businesses in Europe, employ 64.4% of people and add 52.5% of value [7],

B. Coppens et al. (Eds.): ARES 2025 Workshops, LNCS 15997, pp. 23–39, 2025.
https://doi.org/10.1007/978-3-032-00639-4_2

tailored solutions should be developed to secure them and their entire supply chain adequately. To this end, we assume the definition of a SME that has been proposed by the European Commission [6]. It states that an SME is defined as a company that employs less than 250 people and has either an annual turnover that does not exceed EUR 50 million or has an annual balance sheet total that does not exceed EUR 43 million.

In order for SMEs to improve their cyber security, they need a quantitative way to assess it appropriately. For this, certifications and assessment questionnaires have proven to be rather promising solutions. A countless number of papers follow a methodology that calculates a one-dimensional score that is simply a linear combination of various security control responses [13,19,21]. This approach, however, offers only limited insight into the actual needs of the corresponding companies. Because of this, newer assessment technologies such as the GEIGER toolbox [11] offer more sophisticated, threat-based approaches to identify the most pressing cyber security issues. However, also these approaches still need manually and hence subjectively determined weights in order to function properly. An objective scoring system offers significant improvements over traditional approaches due to its ability to resist bad influences and corruption. This stems from the fact that the results stem from a solid mathematical and logical foundation. It also helps companies understand better what their actual cyber security needs are.

In contrast, works such as Brodny's and Tutak's [1] use Principal Component Analysis (PCA) in conjunction with other technologies, such as in this case the EDAS method [10]. The authors have applied these algorithms in order to analyse the digital maturity of European SMEs in relation to specific properties of them, such as their geographical location. Our literature review reveals that data-driven methodologies have not yet been applied to assess the cyber security of SMEs in an empirical and objective way. Building on this, this paper explores a novel approach to cyber security assessments, particularly for SMEs, by applying PCA, identifying clusters using algorithms such as DBSCAN and k-means with a final identification step using logistic regression. To this end, we make the following contributions:

- To the best of our knowledge, this is the first work to use non-linear scoring systems in the context of security assessments.
- Furthermore, we propose a data-driven and completely objective approach to assess the cyber security of SMEs.
- Our approach is also extensively evaluated on six data sets, and a robust methodology based on a two-dimensional scoring system is selected.
- Finally, schemes using more dimensions are briefly discussed to determine their applicability.

The rest of this work is structured as follows: In Sect. 2, we explain this paper's most important definitions and aspects. Then, Sects. 3 and 4 describe the implementation and the results of our study, respectively. Finally, Sect. 5 concludes the work and points out possible routes for future work.

2 Background

First of all, PCA is a technique that is used to reduce the dimensionality of a given set of vectors. In our specific application, each vector corresponds to the answers of an SME to a fixed set of questions. The amount of questions thus indicates the dimensionality of the vectors. In general, PCA is an efficient way to transform the input vectors in such a way that their variance is illustrated optimally. This means that vectors that are close will still be close, and those that are very different will end up far apart. However, this is done in such a way that not as many dimensions are needed in order to illustrate their (dis)similarity. In general, the number of extractable principal components is equal to the dimensionality of the input vector, but the amount of explained variance is decreasing, which makes many of the principal components rather redundant. The number of principal components to extract can be determined using techniques from the field of Exploratory Factor Analysis (EFA), which contains, e.g., Cattell's scree plot, the Kaiser criterion, or Horn's parallel analysis [3].

DBSCAN [5] is an efficient data clustering algorithm that is used to determine clusters within given data. One of the main spotlights of DBSCAN is the ability to distinguish clustering points from noise. Next to a set of vectors, DBSCAN takes two parameters as input. ϵ is the maximum distance between points within a cluster and `minPts` is the minimum amount of points that should be considered as a start point for a cluster. Methods have been proposed to determine the parameters automatically [2,22]. In our use case, we have opted for simpler and more lightweight ways as described in Sect. 4.1. The output is the resulting cluster "ID" for each of the vectors.

Another popular choice for data clustering is the k-means algorithm. It takes a parameter k and the vector data set as an input. Here, k is the amount of clusters that the data should be divided into. The algorithm works by iteratively assigning each data point to the nearest k cluster centres (*centroids*). These centroids are then recomputed as the mean of all data points assigned to each cluster, and the process repeats until the assignments no longer change or a maximum number of iterations is reached. The main drawback of k-means is that it has problems correctly identifying clusters of different densities and non-spherical shapes, a problem that DBSCAN addresses by identifying clusters based on density connectivity. Finally, it should be mentioned that the optimal value for k can be determined through, e.g., the elbow method.

LR is a statistical model that, in its basic form, uses a logistic function (or sigmoid function) to model the probability of a binary outcome. It is a supervised learning classification algorithm used to predict the probability of a categorical target variable, most commonly binary. LR predicts a probability between 0 and 1 that represents the likelihood that an observation belongs to a particular category. It is often debated whether LR counts as a machine learning technique because it can be used as a more lightweight replacement. Once trained, the model can be used to predict the probability of an outcome for new, unseen data.

3 Data-Driven Security Assessment

In this section, we describe the general methodology, prerequisites and implementation of our approach.

3.1 Overview of the Approach

Our approach follows a completely objective, data-driven and empirical flow. First, SMEs are asked to complete a survey about their cyber security, which serves as a self-assessment. The answers to the questions are converted to numbers, which are then arranged in a n-dimensional vector for further processing. Intuitively speaking, clusters (i.e., sets of SMEs with similar responses) are determined, which represent various "security classes." The evaluation of a new enterprise is done using the same process. The ID of the cluster that the organisation belongs to is used to identify problematic cyber security categories and/or controls.

In order to obtain the best results, we chose to use PCA as the decomposition algorithm and compare the results from various methodologies in order to determine the best clustering algorithm. Six data sets will be determined, as described in detail in Sect. 3.2. Each data set can be clustered using two different clustering algorithms, namely DBSCAN and k-means, as described earlier. Finally, LR is used as a cluster identifier for new inputs/companies.

The amount of principal components stemming from the PCA process can be adjusted for each setup. For this, we apply Kaiser's criterion and Cattell's scree plot, which results in at most two different methodologies per configuration. Various configurations are analysed in Sect. 4, in each sub-section.

3.2 The Data Set

As part of this work's methodology, a data set was acquired, which is used to infer information about the current state of cyber security within SMEs. Inspired by the work of Brodny and Tutak [1], the EUROSTAT database was scanned and a relevant data set was identified, namely *Security policy, measures, risks and staff awareness by size class of enterprise* [8]. Alas, it was deemed unfitting for the purposes of this work as it only correlates the various countries of the EU with an average cyber security score across the enterprises within them. For this reason, the data does not represent an individual enterprise and can not be used to derive useful information about any company on its own.

The CYSSME project offers a self-assessment survey for SMEs [4]. Preferably, IT-specialised personnel or other employees who are proficient with cyber security and the digital structure of the company are asked to complete the survey. Whilst the data set is not publicly accessible, we have been given access to the anonymised data by the project members. They offer a standard and a basic assessment survey. The former consists of 25 questions divided into 7 categories and the latter is a subset of it that only has 13 questions divided into 6 categories, as shown in Appendix A. Enterprises can answer either with "Yes,"

"No," "Partly," or "Don't know." Only question 14 allows also for "N/A" as an answer. These answer options are converted to scalars as 1.0, 0.0, 0.5, -1.0, and -2.0, respectively.

A total of 96 SMEs completed either the basic or standard survey, 46 of which answered only the basic questions, leaving 50 SMEs that answered all the questions of the standard assessment. 29 SMEs have used neither "Don't know" nor "N/A" as the answer to any question, meaning their results can be easily interpreted as answers on a 3-point Likert scale [14]. This smaller data set is called `data-only-scaled`.

In order to form bigger data sets, "Don't know" and "N/A" can be included to form the `data` data set or instead be interpreted as 0.5 and 1.0, respectively. This results in the `data-scaled-conv` data set. We have chosen these values because "Don't know" should not introduce bias and "N/A" should not penalise the corresponding enterprise. In the same way, the data sets `basic-data`, `basic-data-scaled-conv`, and `basic-data-only-scaled` are created with the data from the basic assessment.

3.3 Implementation

We have implemented the assessment in Python 3 and use the PCA, DBSCAN, k-means and LR algorithms from `scikit-learn` [18]. Our novel approach first removes the mean and scales all the values to unit variance by using the `StandardScaler`. This is required to properly apply `PCA` to the data afterwards. We have opted to extract only two principal components in order to be able to visualise an enterprise's cyber security rating in a simple 2D plane. Also, as seen in Fig. 1, Cattell's scree plot exhibits an "elbow" at two principal components for all the data sets. Kaiser's criterion also indicates that two principal components should be sufficient in the case of the basic data sets. For the detailed analysis, we hence chose to use two principal components for all the data sets. The results of this process are discussed in detail in Sect. 4. Further experiments involve extracting more principal components and interpreting the results as more sophisticated multi-dimensional shapes and the results are described in Sect. 4.7.

After extracting the desired value of principal components, a clustering algorithm is applied on them. We have identified `DBSCAN` and `KMeans` as the most popular choices. As described earlier, both approaches have their pros and cons and a comparison of their results in the context of this work is done in Sects. 4.1,4.2 and 4.4. Finally, `LogisticRegression` is used to easily identify areas/shapes, which correspond to the identified clusters. Since DBSCAN is also able to identify noise, the fitting for the LR model is only applied to core points and reachable points. The resulting shapes from the LR fitting process yield cluster assignments for outliers such that no point is left unassigned.

The clusters themselves do not carry any information and need to be manually analysed and interpreted first in order to be able to assess the cyber security of enterprises. This is done by comparing the answers to the evaluation questions of the companies behind each point within a cluster and across clusters. The best way for an enterprise to improve its cyber security is then to improve its posture in the categories or questions which point best into the direction of either a "better" cluster or the point which corresponds to a theoretical enterprise that answered the best to all the questions. This is achieved in our implementation using a similarity measure, as described in Sect. 4.4 and illustrated in Fig. 6.

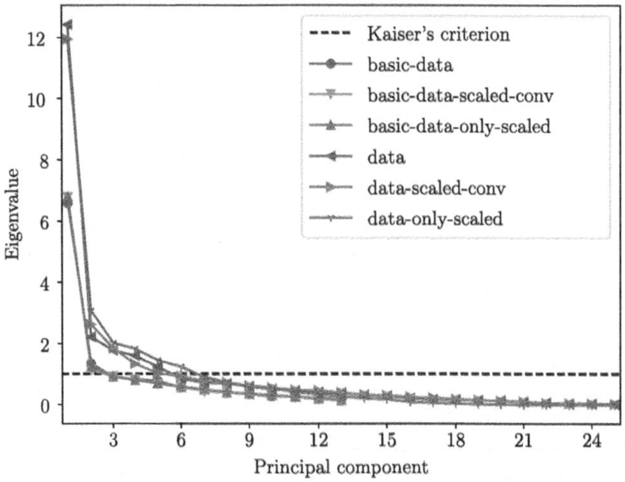

Fig. 1. Cattell's scree plot for all the six data sets. The threshold of Kaiser's criterion is marked with a dashed line. The elbows of all the plots are at two principal components.

4 Key Findings and Evaluation

In this section, we describe various approaches and their key findings. The analysis then yields the best fitting methodology.

4.1 Clustering Using DBSCAN

As explained in Sect. 2, DBSCAN needs two parameters in order to work correctly, namely `minPts` and ϵ. Due to the limited number of data points, we have opted for fixing `minPts` = 1. This has the side-effect of not marking any data point as an outlier. In order to determine the "perfect" amount of clusters, various values for ϵ have been tested on every data set, as illustrated in Fig. 2.

Obviously, the clusters are rather unstable for most of the data sets when $\epsilon < 0.8$. The stability is discussed in detail in Sect. 4.6. We also avoided smaller values for ϵ because of the large amount of clusters. Most of them only contain a very limited number of points and thus do not indicate any useful information. After trying out various values and inspecting the resulting clusterings, we identified a sweet spot for all the data sets, individually, whose clusters can be interpreted in a meaningful way. The number of clusters amounts to ≈ 7 for each data set. After applying logistic regression and plotting the resulting shapes, every input that was not in the training data set can also be classified accordingly. The areas for all the clusters are depicted in Fig. 3.

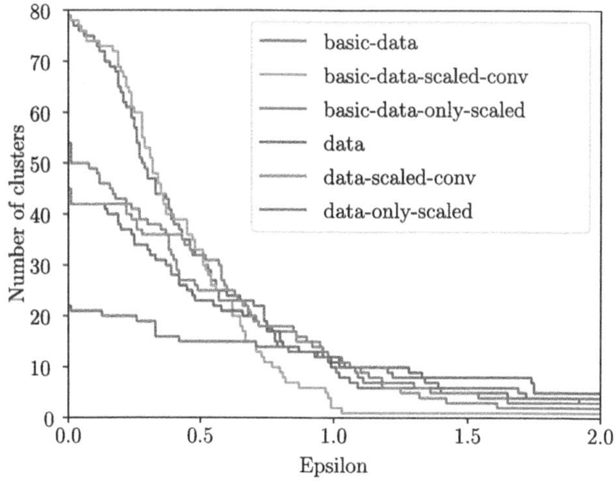

Fig. 2. Amount of clusters when applying DBSCAN to the data points of the six data sets after PCA with `minPts` = 1.

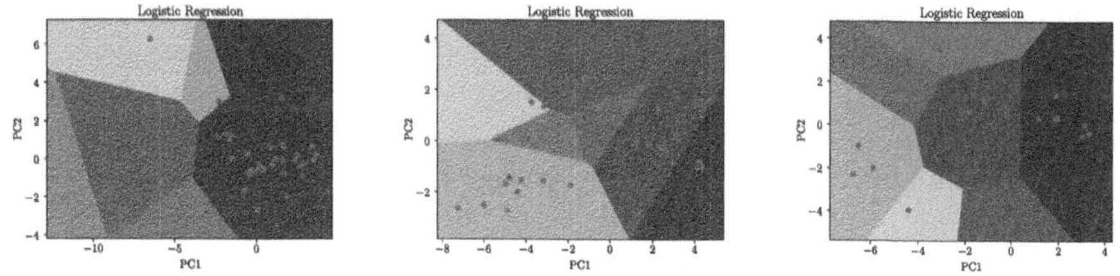

(a) (b) (c)

Fig. 3. The various clusterings using DBSCAN on the data set (a) `data`, (b) `data-scaled-conv`, and (c) `data-only-scaled`.

4.2 Clustering Using k-means

The clustering process using the k-means algorithm does not yield as many clusters that can be separated in a meaningful way. We believe that k-means is not applicable to our data sets because they contain enterprises that can definitely be considered outliers, which leads k-means to overestimating their impact on the overall result. Furthermore, as seen in Fig. 3, the clusters are far from spherical, which is the shape what k-means assumes. As a result, the resulting clusters are not very informative and cannot be interpreted in the same way as the clusters using DBSCAN. Nevertheless, we still illustrate the "best" clusterings using the k-means algorithm in Fig. 4.

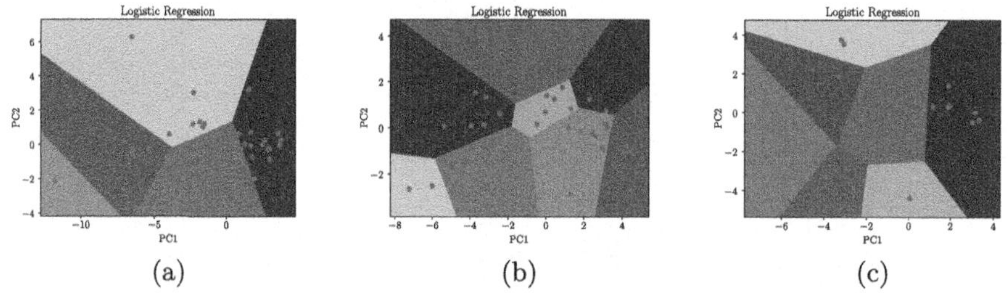

Fig. 4. The various clusterings using k-means on the data set (a) `data`, (b) `data-scaled-conv`, and (c) `data-only-scaled`.

4.3 Analysis of the Basic Assessment Data Sets

We have applied the procedure using DBSCAN also to the `basic-*` data sets and the results are shown in Fig. 5. It is obvious that the amount of clusters decreased significantly in general in comparison to the standard data sets. Many of the clusters also only consist of only a single or only two points. The same applies to the standard data sets, but this is more evident with the basic ones.

Furthermore, there is always a single "big" cluster, which contains most of the points. Because of this, most enterprises are not distinguishable any more and no meaningful conclusion can be drawn. Because of this, we have tried to include more principal components in order to include more variance. The detailed results for this are presented in Sect. 4.7.

4.4 Chosen Methodology

Comparing the different results from Sects. 4.1,4.2 and 4.3, we have identified the third approach from Sect. 4.1 (DBSCAN on the data set `data-scaled-conv`) as the most promising for further analysis. This is due to the fact that the clusters are rather well formed, properly separated and well interpretable.

The rightmost data point from Fig. 3(c) corresponds to an enterprise that answered every question with a "Yes" and hence should be considered as the desired state. Other points hence correspond to enterprises with non-optimal cyber security. The best suggestions, or rather the quickest way to improve cyber security, can be determined by finding a quick path from the latter points

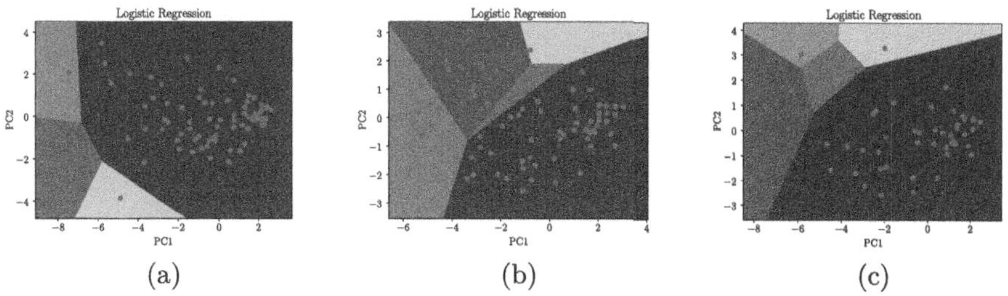

Fig. 5. The various clusterings using DBSCAN on the data set (a) `basic-data`, (b) `basic-data-scaled-conv`, and (c) `basic-data-only-scaled`.

to the former point, according to the question vectors. Figure 6(a) shows the directions in which the marked point would move if it were to improve in the corresponding questions. As already described in Sect. 3.3, a similarity measure is being used to find the vectors that model the quickest way to the ideal point, which is depicted in Fig. 6(b). To determine the best next vector, we simulate an enterprise which answers 1 to a question which it has not answered with 1 before and determine the new point's distance to the ideal point. We do this for all the applicable questions and choose the one with the minimal distance as the next improvement. Another applicable similarity measure would be simple cosine similarity. However, it does not take into account the length of the vectors, which lead to longer/less optimal improvement paths in our simulations. As soon as the path enters a new cluster, the search is cancelled and the path is considered final, because the enterprise has entered a new cluster area, which indicates that the SME has an improved assessment score.

It should be noted that none of the question vectors has a negative x-value (none points even slightly to the left). Hence, the eigenvector for x describes yet another linear way of scoring the cyber security of SMEs, where the weights correspond to the values within the eigenvector. Since the eigenvector is calculated solely from the data, it can be argued that the weights are hence derived automatically/unsupervised and are completely objective, which is not the case in previous scoring systems.

4.5 Cluster Assessments

The various clusters need to be manually interpreted in order to identify scores for each. Since no question vector points to the left, it is obvious that the leftmost clusters should have the lowest scores and the rightmost clusters should have the highest scores. Comparing the answers of the SMEs to the 25 questions from the questionnaire, we ended up with the following scores and cluster names (the cluster IDs correspond to those from Fig. 6):

1. very good posture overall, score: 4
2. fairly good with sporadic minor problems, score: 3
3. organisational security and identity & access management lacking, score: 2
4. major problems in Data Security, Network Security, D&R, and minor problems in system security and organisational security, score: 1
5. major problems in D&R, but also minor problems overall, score: 1
6. major problems everywhere, score: 0
7. minor problems in most areas, score: 0

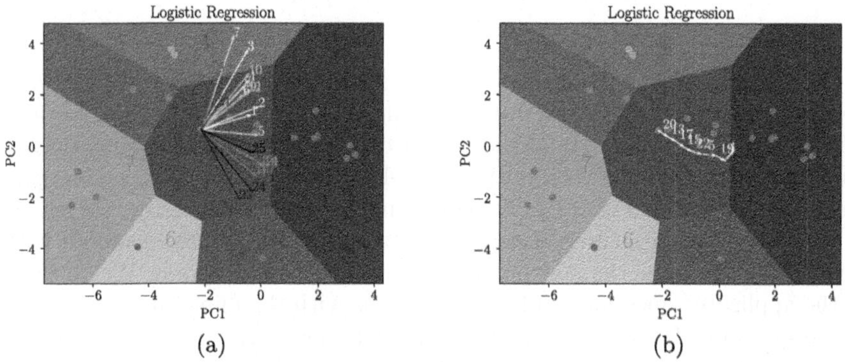

Fig. 6. The clusters and their corresponding IDs when using DBSCAN on the data set `data-only-scaled` with (a) all the question vectors (9× scale) and (b) the "best" way from a random enterprise to the "best" cluster (1× scale).

4.6 Stability of the Clusters

As described earlier and illustrated in Fig. 2, the stable and hence suitable values for ϵ can be found for $\epsilon > 0.8$. However, `basic-data-scaled-conv` is an outlier and shows stable behaviour only for a very small range around $\epsilon \approx 0.9$, which yields the five clusters shown in Fig. 5 (b). For values $\epsilon > 1.1$, all points form a single cluster. The other data sets exhibit rather large plateaus with $\epsilon > 1.2$, which makes these values particularly suitable as a threshold.

Ultimately, we decided to choose a value of ϵ for each data set, which guarantees stability while still allowing a meaningful interpretation of the various clusters.

4.7 Beyond Two Dimensions

In contrast to Cattell's scree plot, Kaiser's criterion indicates that six principal components should be extracted in order to properly analyse the `data-only-scaled` data set. The other two standard assessment data sets should be analysed with five principal components. For the basic data sets, two principal components are sufficient according to both criteria. However, visualisations of four dimensions (using different marker shapes and colours etc.) and beyond might turn out too abstract for SMEs. Because of this, numerical scores instead of graphs would probably be better in this case.

Also, due to our previous analysis, we have decided to only apply DBSCAN in the multi-dimensional approach. As seen in Fig. 7, a value of $\epsilon = 4.5$ results in 6, 5, and 2 clusters for the standard data sets, respectively. For other values of ϵ, the data set `data-only-scaled` yields rather unstable clusters and hence should not be used. However, the amount of information that two clusters can describe is rather limited. Because of this, the multi-dimensional approach does not seem to be appropriate for this particular data set. However, the other two data sets yield enough clusters to be analysed properly.

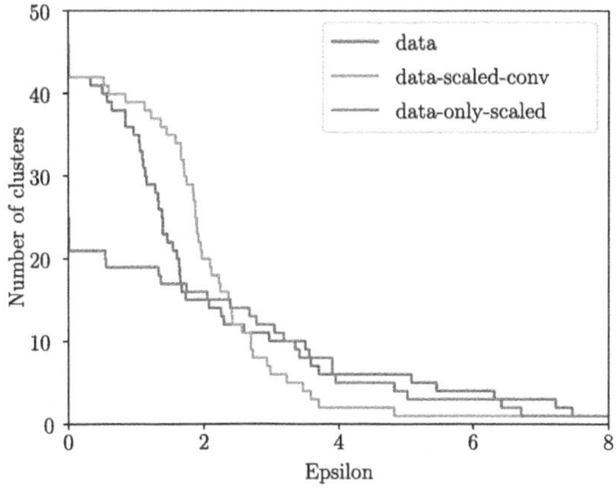

Fig. 7. Amount of clusters when applying DBSCAN with `minPts` = 1 to the data points of the data sets `data`, `data-scaled-conv`, and `data-only-scaled` after PCA using 5, 5, and 6 principal components, respectively.

The data set `data` yields clusters that are hugely dependent on the amount of -1 values within the raw assessment vectors, which makes them suboptimal for proper analysis. However, the data set `data-only-scaled` is exactly as interpretable using this methodology as in the two-dimensional approach. The first cluster again corresponds to the "best" SMEs and subsequent clusters indicate various problems in specific categories. Also, again a category exists each for enterprises with sporadic and major problems in each category.

4.8 Where Are the Main Problems in SMEs?

SMEs in general are very heterogeneous. Not only in regards to their inner structure [12] or size, but also in terms of business sector. All of these factors influence the specific digital needs of an SME and hence also the relevant cyber security controls. The clusterings derived earlier may also be the result of this diversity. However, this does not invalidate their existence or the information they contain, as objective and informative scoring systems were still derived from them. The companies might just choose to ignore certain issues if they are not applicable or relevant in their current structure.

Most of the companies in our selected data set performed quite well, placing them in clusters **1** and **2**, as seen in Fig. 6. The general tendency of the outliers is towards the upper and left clusters, namely **4**, **5**, and **7** since **3** and **6** contain only a single point, each. This indicates major problems in data security, network security and especially D&R, and minor problems especially in system security and organisational security, but also sporadic problems in most other areas. The same issues were identified using the clusters derived from the other data sets, in a similar fashion. The authors would like to mention that these areas are merely the most problematic areas within the framework of the CYSSME data set and that they may not be generalisable.

Since the `data-scaled-conv` data set is rather compatible with our chosen `data-only-scaled` data set, we also ran the assessment on all its points. Figure 8 shows that most of the "new" points fall into either cluster **1**, **2** or **7**, which indicates that they are either rather good enterprises to begin with or exhibit the same problems described earlier.

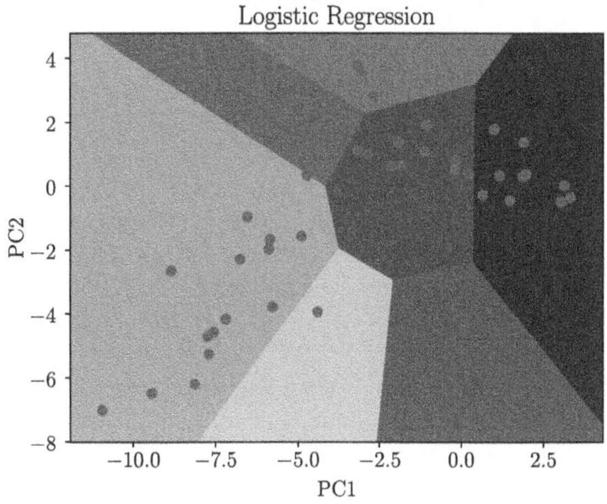

Fig. 8. The clusters when fitting DBSCAN and LR on the data set `data-only-scaled`. The visualised points are from the super set `data-scaled-conv` and transformed using the same process.

4.9 Limitations

Although this paper presents a novel and empirical way of assessing the cyber security of SMEs, there are various limitations that leave room for improvement.

First and foremost, our evaluation is based on a rather limited data set. Further analysis should be carried out in a similar manner using larger and more complete samples of SME assessments to fully capture the heterogeneity of SMEs. This might also result in different clusters and hence different scoring systems. In addition, the data used could be biased because the participating SMEs had to assess their own cyber security. Assessments from an objective external perspective would remove this limitation.

The cluster interpretation process in Sect. 4.5 is also based on a manual and rather subjective approach. Formalising this step of the assessment setup would be crucial to ensure that the actual cyber security needs of the assessed SMEs are reflected. Ongoing machine learning innovations in the area of large language models may offer a promising way to improve the objectivity of this process, although they are neither fully transparent nor objective.

Additionally, there is a lack of external validation of the clusters against actual security incidents or breaches. In general, it is unclear whether the clusters reflect the actual security postures of SMEs, or at least ones that correlate with real-world outcomes.

Finally, the "best way of improvements" as described in Sect. 4.4 assumes that all security controls are equally implementable for all SMEs, which is not the case in practice. Due to the heterogeneity of SMEs, some cyber security measures may be easier or less costly to implement or even applicable to some companies than others.

5 Conclusions and Future Work

In this paper, we have developed a novel methodology to assess cyber security, specifically of SMEs, using PCA, cluster analysis and LR. The results show that our approach works at least as well as existing approaches, while being more objective and informative. Our final combination of data set and parameters results in seven clusters that can be interpreted in a meaningful way, together with a simple procedure capable of identifying the "best way" to quickly improve the cyber security posture of any given organisation.

Our novel approach to assessing the cyber security of SMEs also offers significant opportunities for future research. First and foremost, the limitations mentioned in Sect. 4.9 should be addressed. Also, other questionnaires that take operational technology and supply chain more into account might yield even more informative clusters. In general, other algorithms instead of PCA (for example, Sparse Dictionary Learning (SDL)) or DBSCAN and k-means (for example, hierarchical clustering or even fuzzy clustering) should be inspected for their applicability to this methodology. Instead of LR, general machine learning algorithms can be used as well, which might also result in more sophisticated cluster shapes other than simple Voronoi cells. Finally, we plan to transform novel approaches such as the one developed in this paper into freely accessible and open-source online tools. This would immediately benefit SMEs by allowing them to assess their cyber security in a more accurate, objective and less abstract or obscure way.

Acknowledgments. This work is co-funded by the European Union through INTERREG VI-A Germany/Bavaria-Austria 2021–2027 – INTERREG VI-A Bayern-Österreich 2021–2027, as part of the Project "CySeReS-KMU: Cyber Security and Resilience in Supply Chains with focus on SMEs" (project number BA0100016).

We would also like to thank the European CYSSME project for providing us with the necessary data sets to evaluate our approach.

Disclosure of Interests. The authors have no competing interests to declare that are relevant to the content of this article.

A Appendix: Cyber Security Questionnaire

This section lists the questions divided into the categories as presented in the cyber security survey. The letters B and S indicate that the question is present in the basic and standard self-assessment survey, respectively.

I. Organisational Security
1. Do you have an information security policy? [B,S]
2. Do you train your employees with regards to information security? [B,S]
3. Is there one or more designated people in your company who are responsible for information security? [B,S]
4. Do you have a documented inventory of all your IT assets and services? [S]
5. Do you manage your suppliers and third-party partners according to a defined supply chain risk assessment process? [S]

II. Identity & Access Management
6. Do you manage access to your systems according to the least privilege principle? [B,S]
7. Do you require your employees to use secure passwords? [B,S]
8. Do you use multi-factor authentication (MFA) at least when accessing externally accessible systems? [S]

III. System Security
9. Do you configure your systems in a secure way? [B,S]
10. Do you regularly update all IT systems and applications with security updates? [B,S]
11. Do you have and store log files of your systems? [B,S]
12. Do you monitor your IT systems for malware by using up-to-date Anti-virus, -spyware, and other -malware programs? [B,S]
13. Do you have implemented a vulnerability management process that includes identifying, analysing and remedying vulnerabilities? [S]

14. Do you have a documented and tested Secure Software Development Lifecycle implemented? [S]
15. Do you conduct penetration tests in your system landscape? [S]

IV. Data Security
16. Do you encrypt sensitive data when transmitted over the Internet? [B,S]
17. Do you have protection against data leakage implemented? [S]

V. Network Security
18. Do you use firewalls to protect your network from outside? [B,S]
19. Do you monitor your system landscape for unusual activities and anomalies? [S]
20. Do you collect and correlate event data from multiple sources and sensors? [S]

VI. Backup & Recovery
21. Do you regularly conduct backups of your relevant data and systems? [B,S]
22. Do you have Incident Response, Business Continuity and IT recovery plans as well as suitable corresponding resilience measures established, maintained, and tested? [S]

VII. Detection & Response
23. Do you have implemented automatic response capability with pre-defined security safeguards when integrity violations are discovered (e.g. blocking not explicitly allowed processes)? [S]
24. Do you have a SOC to continuously monitor systems and network to detect cybersecurity breaches? [S]
25. Do you have access to qualified resources including IT forensics in the case of a security event? [S]

References

1. Brodny, J., Tutak, M.: Digitalization of small and medium-sized enterprises and economic growth: evidence for the eu-27 countries. J. Open Innov. Technol. Market Complex. **8**(2), 67 (2022). https://doi.org/10.3390/joitmc8020067
2. Bushra, A.A., Kim, D., Kan, Y., Yi, G.: Autoscan: automatic detection of dbscan parameters and efficient clustering of data in overlapping density regions. PeerJ Comput. Sci. **10**, e1921 (2024). https://doi.org/10.7717/peerj-cs.1921
3. Courtney, M., Gordon, R.: Determining the number of factors to retain in efa: Using the spss r-menu v2 0 to make more judicious estimations. Pract. Assess. Res. Eval. **18**(1), 8 (2013). https://doi.org/10.7275/9CF5-2M72
4. CYSSME: Cyssme self assessment – cyssme – cybersecurity for smes supported by the ec. https://cyssme.eu/getting-started/cyssme-self-assessment/, Accessed 02 Jan 2025

5. Ester, M., Kriegel, H.P., Sander, J., Xu, X.: A density-based algorithm for discovering clusters in large spatial databases with noise. In: Simoudis, E., Han, J., Fayyad, U.M. (eds.) Proceedings of the Second International Conference on Knowledge Discovery and Data Mining (KDD-96), pp. 226–231. AAAI Press, August 1996, https://cdn.aaai.org/KDD/1996/KDD96-037.pdf
6. European Commission: Directorate-general for internal market, industry, entrepreneurship and SMEs: user guide to the SME definition. Publ. Office (2020). https://doi.org/10.2873/255862
7. European Commission, Eurostat: key figures on European business 2024 edition. Publications Office of the European Union (2024). https://doi.org/10.2785/659794
8. European Commission: Eurostat: security policy, measures, risks and staff awareness by size class of enterprise. Publ. Office Eur. Union (2024). https://doi.org/10.2908/ISOC_CISCE_RA
9. European Union Agency for Cybersecurity, ENISA: Enisa threat landscape 2024 (2024) https://doi.org/10.2824/0710888
10. Ghorabaee, M.K., Zavadskas, E.K., Olfat, L., Turskis, Z.: Multi-criteria inventory classification using a new method of evaluation based on distance from average solution (EDAS). Informatica **26**(3), 435–451 (2015), https://journals.sagepub.com/doi/abs/10.3233/INF-2015-1070
11. van Haastrecht, M., Sarhan, I., Shojaifar, A., Baumgartner, L., Mallouli, W., Spruit, M.: A threat-based cybersecurity risk assessment approach addressing sme needs. In: Proceedings of the 16th International Conference on Availability, Reliability and Security, ARES 2021, pp. 1–12. ACM, August 2021. https://doi.org/10.1145/3465481.3469199
12. Karoui, L., Khlif, W., Ingley, C.: Sme heterogeneity and board configurations: an empirical typology. J. Small Bus. Enterp. Dev. **24**(3), 545 561 (2017). https://doi.org/10.1108/jsbed-12-2016-0197
13. Latsiou, A.C., Nyg rd, A.R., Katsikas, S., Lambrinoudakis, C.: Never trust - always verify: assessing the cybersecurity trustworthiness of suppliers in the digital supply chain. Procedia Comput. Sci. **254**, 98–107 (2025) https://doi.org/10.1016/j.procs.2025.02.068, International Conference on Digital Sovereignty (ICDS)
14. Likert, R.: A technique for the measurement of attitudes. Arch. Psychol. **22**(140), 5–55 (1932)
15. Lill, B., Sauerwein, C., Zeisler, A., Hochstrasser, C., Mexis, N.: Assessing cybersecurity readiness among SME. In: Proceedings of the 27th International Conference on Enterprise Information Systems - Volume 2: ICEIS, pp. 253–263. INSTICC, SciTePress - Science and Technology Publications, Porto, Portugal, April 2025. https://doi.org/10.5220/0013353400003929,
16. Markakis, E. et al.: Acceleration at the edge for supporting smes security: the fortika paradigm. IEEE Commun. Mag. **57**(2), 41 47 (2019). https://doi.org/10.1109/mcom.2019.1800506
17. Mexis, N., Lill, B., Doleh, Y., Katzenbeisser, S.: Exposing the gaps: the state of supply chain coverage in current security standards. In: Information Security Education. Springer, Cham, Switzerland (submitted for publication)
18. Pedregosa, F., et al.: Scikit-learn: machine learning in Python. J. Mach. Learn. Res. **12**, 2825–2830 (2011), http://jmlr.org/papers/v12/pedregosa11a.html
19. Ponsard, C., Massonet, P., Grandclaudon, J., Point, N.: From lightweight cybersecurity assessment to sme certification scheme in belgium. In: 2020 IEEE European Symposium on Security and Privacy Workshops (EuroS&PW), pp. 75–78. IEEE, September 2020, https://doi.org/10.1109/eurospw51379.2020.00019

20. Renaud, K.: How smaller businesses struggle with security advice. Comput. Fraud Secur. **2016**(8), 10–18 (2016). https://doi.org/10.1016/s1361-3723(16)30062-8
21. Saripalli, P., Walters, B.: Quirc: A quantitative impact and risk assessment framework for cloud security. In: 2010 IEEE 3rd International Conference on Cloud Computing, pp. 280–288. IEEE, July 2010, https://doi.org/10.1109/cloud.2010.22
22. Sharma, A., Sharma, A.: Knn-dbscan: using k-nearest neighbor information for parameter-free density based clustering. In: 2017 International Conference on Intelligent Computing, Instrumentation and Control Technologies (ICICICT), pp. 787–792. IEEE, July 2017, https://doi.org/10.1109/ICICICT1.2017.8342664
23. U.S. Small Business Administration: Stay safe from cybersecurity threats (2021), https://www.sba.gov/business-guide/manage-your-business/strengthen-your-cybersecurity, Accessed 13 Dec 2024
24. World economic forum: global cybersecurity outlook 2022 insight report (2022), https://www3.weforum.org/docs/WEF_Global_Cybersecurity_Outlook_2022.pdf

A Viewpoint-Based Model of Data Protection Impact Assessments

Andreas Diepenbrock(✉) and Sabine Sachweh

IDiAL Institute, Dortmund, Germany
{andreas.diepenbrock,sabine.sachweh}@fh-dortmund.de

Abstract. The increasing complexity of software systems and the multidisciplinary nature of data protection obligations pose significant challenges to the effective conduction of Data Protection Impact Assessments (DPIAs). Despite regulatory mandates such as the GDPR, current DPIA practices often lack structured methods for integrating legal, technical, organizational, and privacy-related perspectives. This research addresses the gap by introducing a viewpoint-based model for DPIAs that systematically captures and interrelates stakeholder concerns. The objective is to enhance the transparency, traceability, and completeness of DPIAs across the lifecycle of data processing activities.

Grounded in the ISO 42010:2022 standard and principles of Model-Driven Engineering, we developed a conceptual model comprising found interlinked viewpoints: legal, engineering, application, and privacy. Each viewpoint is formalized using UML-based model kinds and is mapped to corresponding stakeholder roles and concerns identified through literature and regulatory analysis.

Our findings demonstrate that a viewpoint-based approach can improve interdisciplinary communication, clarify responsibilities, and support more structured and accountable DPIA processes. This model offers a foundation for future tool integration, empirical validation, and automated risk analysis. Ultimately, it contributes to a more robust, stakeholder-inclusive approach to privacy-by-design and regulatory compliance in software engineering.

Keywords: data protection · privacy · viewpoints · data protection impact assessment

1 Introduction

In an era of ubiquitous data collection and processing, the protection of personal data has emerged as a central concern for governments, organizations, and individuals alike [23]. To mitigate possible challenges arising from data collection and processing, the European Union introduced the General Data Protection Regulation (GDPR) [7] as a structured and risk-based approach to improve the level of data protection and privacy in general [3,22]. Therefore, GDPR propose the use of Data Protection Impact Assessment (DPIAs) for processing operations that

B. Coppens et al. (Eds.): ARES 2025 Workshops, LNCS 15997, pp. 40–56, 2025.
https://doi.org/10.1007/978-3-032-00639-4_3

are likely to result in high risks to the rights and freedoms of individuals. DPIAs are intended to identify, evaluate, and mitigate data protection risks throughout the lifecycle of data processing activities.

However, conducting an effective DPIA remains a complex and multidisciplinary challenge [5,16]. DPIAs intersect with multiple domains of expertise. They require input not only from legal professionals familiar with regulatory compliance, but also from software engineers, system architects, and domain experts. Each of these stakeholder groups brings a different perspective – what we refer to as a *viewpoint* – on the systems being evaluated. Additionally, these groups of stakeholders have different concerns and interests regarding the DPIA and are facing knowledge gaps in unknown domains and disciplines [16] or lacking a common understanding, which can lead to misinterpretations and communication issues [5].

Although several tools and guidelines exist to support the DPIA process, they often focus on isolated aspects, such as legal compliance or technical implementation, without providing a comprehensive framework that integrates the diverse perspectives of all stakeholders involved [16,22]. This siloed approach creates fragmentation and makes it difficult to trace how legal requirements are addressed in the technical implementation of a system or how business use cases impact privacy risks. Furthermore, existing methods often lack formalization and are difficult to adapt across domains, limiting their usefulness in practice [18]. To address these shortcomings, a holistic and systematic approach is needed that captures the interrelations between legal, technical, organizational, and data-subject concerns in a structured manner and promotes transparency and traceability throughout the system lifecycle [5].

The overall goal of this paper is to contribute towards a more systematic, transparent, and stakeholder-inclusive DPIA process. This viewpoint-based approach enables DPIAs to effectively reflect the interdisciplinary nature of modern software systems and the diverse concerns they must address in the context of DPIAs. Consequently, our research answers the following research questions (RQ):

RQ1 *Which stakeholder-centric viewpoints are necessary and sufficient to cover the legal, technical, organizational and data-subject concerns of a DPIA?*

RQ2 *How can those viewpoints be integrated into a coherent conceptual model that preserves traceability across views and aligns with DPIA information obligations?*

The remainder of this paper is structured as follows: In Sect. 2 we give an overview of work that is related to our research. The methodology of our research is described in Sect. 3, and the contributions of this paper are presented in Sect. 4. Section 5 will discuss our approach and its limitations. The conclusion of our paper is described in Sect. 6.

2 Related Work

In this section we present related work on DPIAs in general and related challenges (Sect. 2.1). Section 2.2 covers how Model-Driven Engineering (MDE) can be applied in the context of data protection and privacy. Furthermore, in Sect. 2.3 related work regarding viewpoints in the context of software engineering.

2.1 Data Protection Impact Assessments

DPIAs are a central instrument under the GDPR for assessing and mitigating privacy risks in software systems. However, their practical application remains a challenge due to the complexity of the process itself, its interdisciplinary nature, and the diverse perspectives involved. Furthermore, conducting a DPIA is currently primarily a manual, paper- and interview-based process, which is often time-consuming and error-prone.

Several studies highlight that privacy is often treated as an afterthought in software engineering. Tahaei et al. [24] and Diepenbrock et al. [5] demonstrates that developers frequently lack the tools, knowledge, and support to integrate privacy effectively into the development and assessment lifecycle of a software system. Similarly, Ferreyra et al. [8] emphasize that software engineers often lack formal training in implementing privacy-preserving software, which may leads to vulnerabilities and non-compliant software systems. Netto et al. [18] conducted a qualitative study on how the software industry incorporates data protection law into requirements engineering, revealing inconsistent practices and a lack of formalization.

Additionally, tool-based approaches have been proposed to mitigate these challenges. Riemann et al. [22] present "DPIA click&go", an open-source tool designed to streamline the creation of DPIAs in medical research contexts. Their approach addresses the inherent complexity and resource demands of conducting DPIAs by providing a semi-automated platform where users can efficiently select predefined risks and tailored mitigation strategies based on institutional requirements. Khedkar et al. [16] introduce "Assessor View", a tool designed to support cross-disciplinary collaboration between developers, DPOs, and legal experts. The tool bridges the communication gap between these stakeholders by translating static program slices into multiple abstraction levels based on the Data Protection Vocabulary (DPV) [19]. The resulting visualizations enable technical and non-technical stakeholders to comprehend privacy-relevant behaviors in source code, e.g., data collection, sharing, and storage. These approaches show promise, but tend to focus on specific domains or stakeholder roles, lacking generalizability and structured integration across perspectives.

Furthermore, domain-specific challenges have been studied in contexts such as smart cities. Diepenbrock et al. [6] emphasize the need for systematic DPIA methods that can address heterogeneous data sources, multiple stakeholders, and evolving infrastructures.

Altogether, this body of work highlights a recurring theme: DPIAs demand coordination between various stakeholders, each with their own expertise and concerns, but existing tools and approaches often fail to bidge these gaps. Our work addresses this limitation by providing a unified, viewpoint-based model that explicitly structures stakeholder concerns and interrelates them within a single conceptual framework.

2.2 Model-Driven Engineering and Data Protection

Torre et al. [25] propose a UML representation with a set of OCL rules to model the GDPR and its requirements. Their study shows how MDE can be applied to turn dense legal text into machine-readable models. Furthermore, they discuss the challenges met while formalising an entire regulation. However, our legal viewpoint builds on the same MDE foundations but shifts the focus from modelling the regulation itself to integrate those formal obligations with other relevant viewpoints of a DPIA. Their presented OCL rule set could, however, be reused as a traceable rules repository for our legal model kinds, enabling automated consistency checks between regulatory clauses and the risks expressed in the privacy viewpoint.

In their study, Pedroza et al. [20], introduces a model-driven privacy-by-design approach that covers different lifecycle phases including personal-data identification, data modelling and privacy-risk assessment using strategies proposed by Hoepman [13]. Their goal is to support engineers by embedding GDPR requirements during the design phase of software systems. However, in our work we complements their approach with our engineering and application viewpoints by providing the cross-stakeholder perspective that their approach leaves to later compliance activities.

Agarwal et al. [1] presents a compliance-assessment framework that decouples legislation models from questionnaire-style tooling by extending the W3C ODRL information model to capture duties, soft obligations and expectations, then instantiating it for the GDPR. Their approach supports multiple regulations and dynamically tailors questions through a preliminary assessment step and keeps assessments in sync with evolving legal texts. While our research targets DPIAs rather than self-assessment checklists, the ODRL profile offers a promising foundation for representing legal obligations in our legal viewpoint.

2.3 Viewpoints in Software Engineering

The concept of viewpoints is well-established in software engineering and architectures as a means to manage complexity and addresses the diverse concerns of involved stakeholders. The ISO 42010:2022 standard [14] defines a viewpoint as a specification of the conventions for constructing and using a view, including the stakeholders it serves and the concerns it addresses.

Heithoff et al. [12] and Rademacher [21] show how integrated multi-viewpoint modeling can be used to build consistent architectural representations from heterogeneous modeling languages. These works emphasize the importance of making stakeholder-specific views explicit and formally connected. Similarly, Mohagheghi et al. [17] demonstrate the value of MDE in managing complexity through viewpoint abstraction in large-scale industrial systems. They argue that multi-view modeling enhances traceability and interdisciplinary communication – objectives that are directly aligned with DPIA needs.

In related research, Bedjeti et al. [2] apply viewpoint modeling to represent context in architectural descriptions, highlighting how abstract model kinds can be used to improve decision-making and compliance in regulated environments. Their work, though not focused on privacy, illustrates the power of conceptual modeling for integrating diverse concerns.

While these contributions demonstrate the potential of viewpoint modeling for system analysis and stakeholder communication, none of them directly address DPIAs or privacy-specific concerns. To our knowledge, no approach has yet applied ISO 42010:2022 or viewpoint-based modeling principles to the DPIA process in a systematic and stakeholder-aligned way.

3 Methodology

In this section we present our methodology for identifying relevant viewpoints for DPIAs and the development of our DPIA-model that captures these viewpoints. The goal of this section is to provide a comprehensive overview of the processes and principles that guided our research.

The development of the DPIA-model was aligned by the principles of MDE [9] and the ISO 42010:2022 standard [14]. Although, the ISO 42010:2022 standard is primarily focused on the description of system architectures, we used it as a guideline for the development of our model and the viewpoints, respectively. However, the standard proposes the use of model kinds, which we adopted on a comparatively high level of abstraction by means of conceptual models, similar to Bedjeti et al. [2] and Rademacher [21]. By adopting this abstraction level, it allows us to emphasize the semantic intent of each viewpoint without being bound to a specific modeling language or notation.

Therefore, we employed a systematic approach to develop the DPIA-model and its associated viewpoints.

1. **Identification of stakeholder concerns:** Based on a qualitative analysis of existing literature on DPIAs, regulatory guidelines, and empirical findings from previous studies, we elicited the key concerns and perspectives of stakeholders involved in the DPIA process.
2. **Definition of viewpoints:** For each identified stakeholder group, we defined a distinct viewpoint in accordance with ISO 42010:2022 [14]. Each viewpoint specifies its stakeholders, their concerns, and the corresponding model kind.
3. **Conceptual modeling of model kinds:** We derived high-level conceptual models to represent the model kinds for each viewpoint. These models capture the relevant concepts and relationships necessary to express and analyze the respective stakeholder concerns. We avoided concrete syntax at this stage to preserve the flexibility, generality, and tool independence. However, we used UML class diagrams to represent the model kinds and their relationships, as proposed by Gogolla [11].

4 A Viewpoint-Based Model for Data Protection Impact Assessments

In this section, we present our DPIA-model for the identified viewpoints depicted as UML class diagrams. The model serves as a framework that captures the essential elements and relationships within each viewpoint and their interrelations between them. Consequently, the viewpoints encompass the i) legal, ii) engineering, iii) application, and iv) privacy viewpoints.

4.1 Stakeholders and Concerns

As DPIAs are multidisciplinary, they require the involvement of stakeholders from various disciplines [16]. Each group of stakeholders contributes their specific expertise and has distinct concerns that should be addressed during the DPIA. In accordance to ISO 42010:2022 [14], a stakeholder is defined as an individual or group with interests in the system, and a concern refers to any interest which affects the system's acceptability or suitability. To systematically capture and represent the concerns of stakeholders involved in the DPIA process, we identified the stakeholder groups and elicited their primary concerns by a qualitative analysis of existing literature on DPIAs, regulatory guidelines, and empirical findings from previous studies.

In Table 1 we give an overview of the concerns of stakeholders involved in the DPIA process. Each concern is represented by a unique identifier, a brief description, and the corresponding stakeholder group.

Table 1. Concerns of stakeholders involved in the DPIA process.

No.	Concern	Primary Stakeholders
C1	Specification of legal frameworks and regulations.	Legal Experts
C2	Validation of legal compliance of a software system based on legal specifications.	
C3	Specification of the software system's structure, data flows, and other technical components.	Software Engineers
C4	Verification of compliance with technical and organizational measures, e.g., retention policies and data usage purposes adherence.	
C5	Specification of system functionalities and their interactions with personal data.	Domain Experts
C6	Identification, classification, and contextualization of personal data and its sources.	
C7	Identification and assessment of privacy risks from a data subject's perspective.	Data Protection Officers
C8	Evaluation of safeguards and transparency measures to uphold data subject rights.	

Legal Experts are responsible for the specification of legal frameworks and regulations that are relevant for the processing of personal data [6]. Their concerns center around the identification of lawful bases for processing, ensuring compliance with relevant legal obligations, and evaluating whether the system's behavior aligns with applicable regulations.

Software Engineers are responsible for the specification and implementation of the software system itself [26]. This includes the design of data flows, system operations, and security mechanisms. Their concerns focus on the technical feasibility of implementing legal requirements, ensuring secure and compliant data processing, and verifying that system behaviors adheres to specified constraints, such as retention policies, data usage purposes, or access controls.

Data Protection Officers act as intermediaries who ensure that data protection is embedded into the system by design and by default [4]. Based on the specifications provided by legal experts and software engineers, Data Protection Officer (DPOs) are responsible for evaluating privacy risks, assessing safeguards, and ensuring that data subject rights, e.g., access, rectification, and deletion, are upheld. Their concerns span both legal and technical aspects and include the verification of compliance with privacy principles, adequacy of safeguards, and transparency measures [18].

Domain Experts contribute specific knowledge about the application context in which the software system operates [10]. They are responsible for specifying business processes, use cases, and contextual factors that influence how personal data is collected and processed. Their concerns relate to aligning system behavior with domain-specific requirements, ensure functional adequacy, and supporting appropriate interpretations of data processing purposes and risks within the operational environment.

4.2 Legal Viewpoint

The legal viewpoint captures the regulatory and normative foundations that govern the processing of personal data. In the context of a DPIA, this viewpoint plays a central role by ensuring that all data processing activities are justified under applicable legal bases, e.g., consent, contractual necessity, or legitimate interests. The primary group of stakeholders involved in this viewpoint are legal experts and use it to specify, trace, and validate the legal compliance of a system's data processing activities. This viewpoint addresses the concerns C1 and C2 (cf. Sect. 4.1) by providing a structured representation of legal frameworks, regulations, and their interrelations with the technical and organizational aspects of a software system.

The legal viewpoints focuses primarily on the specification of entities and legal bases, which are essential for specifying the legal framework within which the data processing activities occur. In Fig. 1, the conceptual model of legal viewpoint is shown.

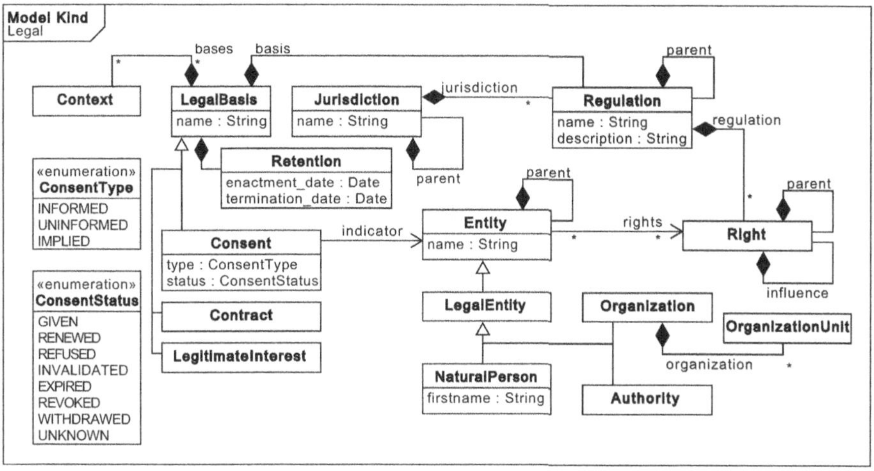

Fig. 1. Conceptual model of the legal viewpoint as a UML diagram.

At the core of the legal viewpoint is the notion of a `LegalBasis`, which captures the justification for data processing activities. These bases can be further specialized in specific representations, e.g., `Consent`, `Contract`, or `Legitimate-Interest`. By using the `LegalBasis` concept, we ensure that we can extend the model in the future to include additional legal bases or specify other legal bases that are only relevant in specific contexts, i.e., only applicable in a certain viewpoint. Each `LegalBasis` may be associated to specific `Regulation` and is additionally contextualized by a `Jurisdiction`, reflecting the territorial applicability of different legal norms.

Furthermore, data processing activities are associated to an organizational or institutional `Entity`, which can be distinguished into a `LegalEntity` or `Organization`. A `LegalEntity` can further be specialized into a `NaturalPerson` or an `Authority`. The `NaturalPerson` represents an individual, while the `Authority` represents a public authority or agency. The `Organization` concept is used to represent any other type of organization, such as a company or non-profit organization.

Finally, a `Regulation` specify the rights via `Right` which an `Entity` has in the context of a `LegalBasis`.

4.3 Engineering Viewpoint

The engineering viewpoint represents the technical perspective on a software system's data processing activities. Its primary purpose is to provide software engineers with a structured means to specify, analyze, and trace the technical implementation of privacy and data protection requirements. In doing so, this viewpoint addresses stakeholder concerns C3 and C4 (cf. Section 4.1). Figure 2 illustrates the conceptual model of the engineering viewpoint.

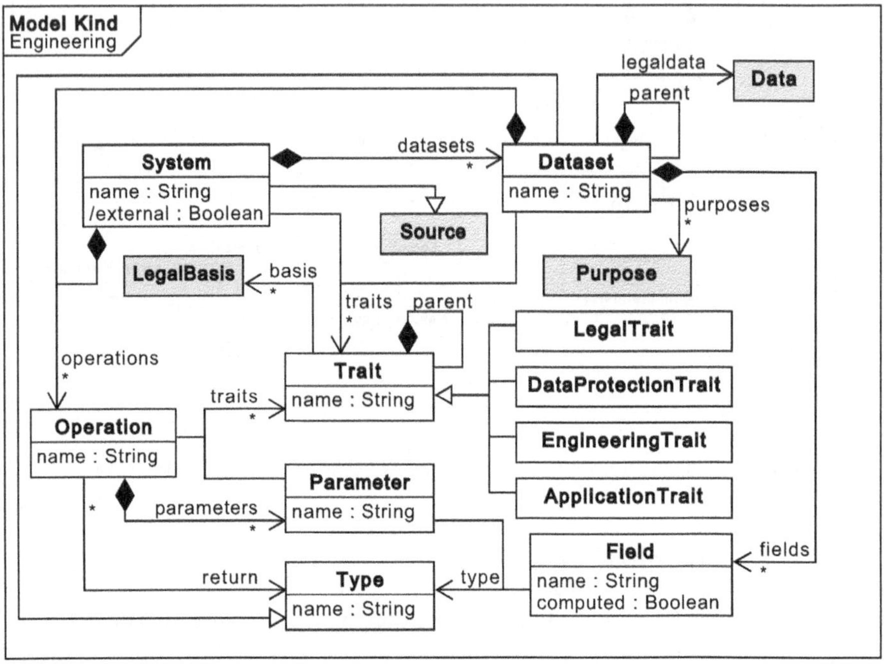

Fig. 2. Conceptual model of the engineering viewpoint as a UML diagram. Referenced concepts are colored in gray. (Color figure online)

At its core, the engineering viewpoint models the structural elements of a `System`, which may be either internal or external to the primary processing context, i.e., it is controlled or managed by the respective assessor or not. Each `System` encompasses `Datasets`, which define logical groupings of data relevant to a specific processing purpose or functionality. Additionally, a `Dataset` consists of `Fields` or `Operations`. The `Field` concept represents an individual data elements within a dataset, while the `Operation` concept represents the actions, transformations, and transmittion of data that can be performed on the data. `Fields` and `Operations` are associated with a specific `Type`, which defines the nature of the data being processed, such as text, number, or date. By specifying the respective `Type`, the traceability from technical functionality to data they represent can be achieved. Furthermore, this level of detail supports the identification of privacy-relevant operations and their potential impact on data subjects. Additionally, each `Field` can be marked as computed or directly collected, supporting the identification of derived or inferred information that may impact data sensitivity and privacy assessments.

Crucially, the engineering viewpoint facilitates the specification of concrete characterictics relating to aspects of other viewponts via assigned `Traits`. These traits act as semantic annotations that link technical elements to legal, application-specific, or privacy-related concerns. For instance, a `Field` may be annotated with traits such as the `DataProtectionTrait` to indicate its basis for processing. By supporting such cross-viewpoint annotations, the engineering model becomes an anchor for traceability and compliance verification throughout the system architecture and the DPIA. Additionally, this allows to add custom traits in the future, which can implement specific rules and validations for the respective system.

4.4 Application Viewpoint

The application viewpoint models the operational and contextual perspective of data processing, focusing on how personal data is handled in real-world scenarios. It captures the alignment between functional system behavior, organizational processes, and data protection obligations, thereby supporting domain experts and business stakeholders in representing and validating the intended purposes of processing. The viewpoint directly addresses concern C5, which relates to ensuring that system functionalities are appropriately contextualized and traceable in the DPIA process. The conceptual model of the application viewpoint is depicted in Fig. 3.

The core of this viewpoint is the representation of `Activities`, which represent discrete processing steps performed by or involving various entities. These activities can be further spezialized into `Processes`, but are not limited to them. Each `Process` belongs to a specific `OrganizationUnit`, reflecting the organizational structure in which data processing occurs. Each activity is linked to a specific `LegalEntity` responsible for its execution, and is associated to one or more `Entities` categorized as participants. This enables the representation of responsibilities and supports accountability. Additionally, processing activities can be represented within a particular `Environment`, which may be physical, virtual, or a combination of both.

An `Activity` may be triggered by `Events`, which represent external or internal event such as user interactions, sensor inputs, or other kinds of events within a processing activity. Furthermore, `Events` are hierarchically organized and may also reflect temporal or logical dependencies between activities. To support the representation of common usage flows, activities are aggregated into `Scenarios`. Each `Scenario` is associated with a specific `Purpose`, which defines the intended goal of respective scenario. `Scenarios` and `Purposes` can be cross-referenced with legal justifications from the legal viewpoint and privacy risks from the privacy viewpoint.

Furthermore, an `Activity` can be associated with relevant `Datasets`, which represent the data processed during the activity. This association allows for

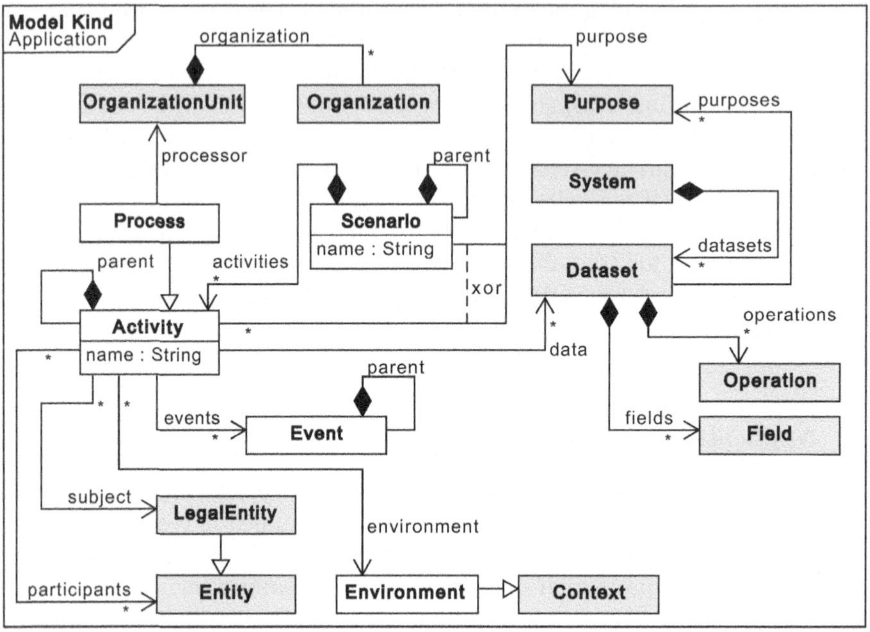

Fig. 3. Conceptual model of the application viewpoint as a UML diagram. Referenced concepts are colored in gray. (Color figure online)

a clear mapping between the activities and the data they involve, facilitating traceability and accountability.

4.5 Privacy Viewpoint

The privacy viewpoint focuses on evaluating data protection risks from the perspective of the data subject. It supports the identification of sensitive processing activities, the evaluation of appropriate safeguards, and the validation of compliance with fundamental privacy principles such as transparency, data minimization, and purpose limitation. This viewpoint is primarily used by DPOs, who act as intermediaries between legal, technical, and organizational domains. It addresses the stakeholder concerns C7 and C8 (cf. Section 4.1). Figure 4 depicts the conceptual model of the privacy viewpoint.

The core of this viewpoint is the representation of `Data`, which can be specialized into `PersonalData` and `NonPersonalData` handled by the software system. Each `Data` is characterized by its `Sensitivity`, distinguishing between different levels of sensitivity, as proposed by the GDPR Art. 9 [7]. To assess the origins and potential risks of data, the model introduces the concept of `Source`, with several specialized subtypes that reflect different modes of data collection. To support the extension of possible supported sources, we use the `Source` concept as a generalization for all possible sources of data. Furthermore, the model

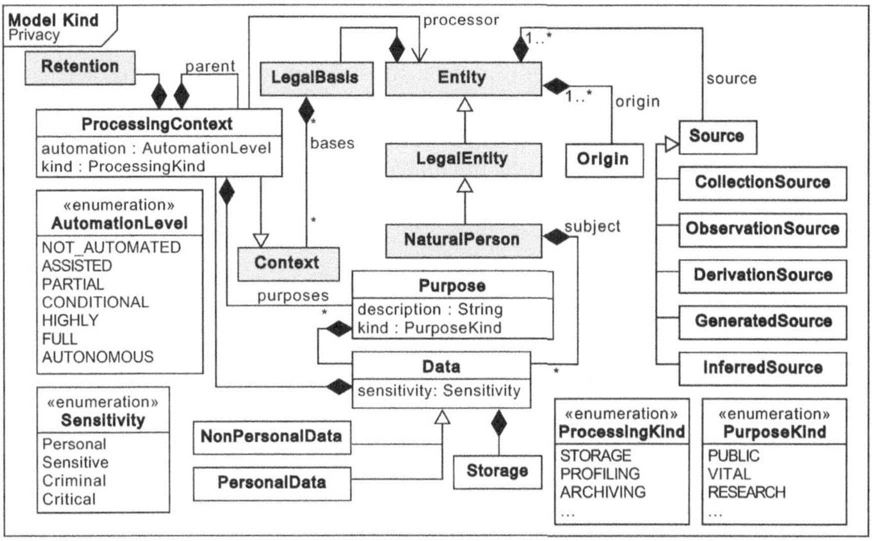

Fig. 4. Conceptual model of the privacy viewpoint as a UML diagram. Referenced concepts are colored in gray. (Color figure online)

includes the specification of an `Origin`. Similar to DPV [19], we distinguish between `Source` and `Origin` and rely on the same rational for this. An `Origin` refers the specific entity or artifact, which produced or created the respective data. A `Source` refers to the direct or indirect place, entity, or other concept from which the data was collected. For example, a `Source` could be a user, a device, or an external system, while the `Origin` could be the specific action or event that generated the data, such as a user input or a sensor reading. Each `Data` can be assigned to a `Storage`, which represents the location or medium where and how the respective data is stored.

Consequently, the `NaturalPerson` concept links the `Data` to its respective subject, making the viewpoint explicitly grounded in the rights and expectations of individuals. Each data subject may be associated with one or more data instances, reflecting the multiplicity of data flows that pertain to a single individual. Additionally, the viewpoint incorporates `LegalBasis` and `Purpose` as a cross-viewpoint reference to ensure that privacy assessments are not isolated from legal justifications or functional goals. By linking data to its lawful basis and processing purpose, DPOs and auditors can assess whether the processing aligns with the principles of necessity and proportionality.

Lastly, the processing activities are associated with a `ProcessingContext`, which provides a comprehensive overview of the data processing activities and their implications for data subjects. The `ProcessingContext` concept serves as a container for all relevant information related to the processing activities, including the purpose, legal basis, and involved stakeholders. This allows for a holistic view of the data processing activities and their impact on data subjects. Furthermore, each `ProcessingContext` is associated with a specific `AutomationLevel`, which indicates the degree of automation involved in the processing activities. The `AutomationLevel` can be classified into three categories: i) fully automated, ii) semi-automated, and iii) manual processing. This classification helps to identify the level of human involvement in the processing activities and the potential risks associated with each level, as proposed by ISO 22989:2022 [15].

4.6 Mapping of Viewpoints to Stakeholders

Each viewpoint in our DPIA-model is designed to reflect the distinct concerns, responsibilities, and knowledge domains of specific stakeholder groups involved in the DPIA process. To ensure that the model aligns with the ISO 42010:2022 [14] principle of stakeholder-centered viewpoint design, we explicitly associate each viewpoint with the primary stakeholder group it serves. In Table 2 this mapping is summarized.

Table 2. Mapping of viewpoints to their primary stakeholder groups.

Viewpoint	Stakeholder group	Description
Legal	Legal experts	Legal experts use the legal viewpoint to specify the legal framework and obligations that govern the data processing activities. This includes identifying relevant laws, regulations, and standards that apply to the software system.
Engineering	Software engineers	Software engineers use the engineering viewpoint to specify the technical aspects of the software system, including data structures, data flows, and system operations.
Application	Domain experts	Domain experts use the application viewpoint to specify the application context of the software system, including the purpose of data processing, the involved stakeholders, and the intended use cases. This viewpoint focuses on the practical implications of data processing activities and their impact on users and other stakeholders.
Privacy	Data protection officers	Data protection officers use the privacy viewpoint to assess the privacy implications of data processing activities and ensure compliance with privacy regulations. This includes identifying potential privacy risks, evaluating data protection measures, and assessing compliance with relevant privacy regulations.

The legal viewpoint is primarily intended for legal experts. It supports the articulation of regulatory frameworks, lawful processing grounds, consent structures, and jurisdictional obligations. Legal experts use this viewpoint to ensure that all processing activities are backed by appropriate legal bases and to validate whether system behaviors conform to the principles and obligations defined by applicable laws and regulations.

The engineering viewpoint addresses the needs of software engineers and system architects. It captures the technical structure of the system, including its data flows, operations, and data models. By annotating these elements with relevant traits from other viewpoints, engineers can ensure that legal and privacy requirements are implemented accurately and traceable within the system architecture.

The application viewpoint is tailored to domain experts and business stakeholders who possess detailed knowledge of the system's functional and operational context. This viewpoint captures the purposes for which data is processed, the stakeholders involved in specific use cases, and the contextual dependencies that influence processing decisions. It ensures that the system behavior aligns with real-world usage scenarios and sector-specific requirements.

The privacy viewpoint is centered on the responsibilities of DPOs. It provides the means to assess privacy risks from a data subject's perspective, evaluate the adequacy of safeguards, and ensure compliance with privacy principles. By linking data to its source, sensitivity level, and automation context, the viewpoint enables DPOs to perform structured, comprehensible, and evidence-based risk assessments.

5 Discussion and Limitations

The viewpoint-based DPIA-model presented in this paper offers a structured and stakeholder-aligned approach to conducting DPIAs. By explicitly organizing the DPIA process into four distinct but interconnected viewpoints – legal, engineering, application, and privacy – the model supports the integration of diverse stakeholder concerns and enables traceable reasoning across regulatory, technical, and organizational domains.

A strength of this approach lies in its alignment with ISO 42010:2022, which emphasizes the importance of making stakeholder concerns explicit in system architecture modeling. Our model operationalizes this principle by capturing stakeholder-specific perspectives and establishing conceptual connections between them. For example, legal justifications defined in the legal viewpoint are traceable to specific system operations in the engineering viewpoint, and risks identified in the privacy viewpoint can be evaluated against purposes defined in the application viewpoint. This interconnected structure enhances the comprehensibility, consistency, and transparency of the DPIA process in general.

Moreover, the abstraction level of the model – realized through conceptual modeling rather than implementation-specific details – ensures broad applicability across domains and technologies. The use of traits as cross-cutting annotations further supports extensibility and tool integration in the future.

However, several limitations must be acknowledged. First, while the model was designed based on a qualitative analysis of existing literature and empirical findings, it has not yet been validated in real-world DPIA scenarios or by practitioners. As such, the practical usability, comprehensibility, and completeness of the model in operational contexts remain to be assessed. Second, the current model emphasizes conceptual clarity over operational tooling. Although UML class diagrams were used to visualize model kinds, no accompanying implementation or tooling support has been developed to date. For the model to be effectively utilized in practice, it will require integration with modeling tools or DPIA platforms. Additionally, the model currently covers the core concerns of key stakeholder groups but does not capture the full diversity of roles involved in specific sectors, e.g., health care or finance. Further refinement and stakeholder engagement may reveal additional viewpoints or concern areas that requires formalization.

The presented DPIA-model serves as a conceptual framework for integrating the identified viewpoints into a coherent representation of the DPIA process. However, it is important to acknowledge that the DPIA-model is not exhaustive and may require further refinement and validation through practical application and feedback from stakeholders involved in DPIAs. Additionally, the DPIA-model does not address the specific implementation details or tools that may be used to support the DPIA process.

6 Conclusion

In this paper, we presented a viewpoint-based model for conducting DPIAs that systematically integrates the concerns of legal, technical, and organizational stakeholders. Based on the ISO 42010:2022 standard and realized through conceptual UML models, our approach provides a structured, traceable, and stakeholder-oriented framework for analyzing and documenting the privacy implications of software systems. The model introduces four distinct viewpoints – legal, engineering, application, and privacy – each tailored to the responsibilites and information needs of a specific stakeholder group. By capturing the interrelations among these viewpoints through shared concepts and semantic traits, the model fosters interdisciplinary collaboration and enhances the clarity, consistency, and transparency of the DPIA process.

While the model currently exists at a conceptual level, its structure offers a foundation for future operationalization. In ongoing and future work, we plan to refine the model through empirical validation in real-world DPIA scenarios and by engaging with practitioners from various domains. Furthermore, we aim to implement the model in a software tool to enable automated conduction and validation of DPIAs.

References

1. Agarwal, S., Steyskal, S., Antunovic, F., Kirrane, S.: Legislative compliance assessment: framework, model and GDPR instantiation. In: Medina, M., Mitrakas, A., Rannenberg, K., Schweighofer, E., Tsouroulas, N. (eds.) APF 2018. LNCS, vol. 11079, pp. 131–149. Springer, Cham (2018). https://doi.org/10.1007/978-3-030-02547-2_8
2. Bedjeti, A., Lago, P., Lewis, G.A., De Boer, R.D., Hilliard, R.: Modeling context with an architecture viewpoint. In: 2017 IEEE International Conference on Software Architecture (ICSA), pp. 117–120. IEEE, April 2017. https://doi.org/10.1109/icsa.2017.26

3. Bieker, F., Friedewald, M., Hansen, M., Obersteller, H., Rost, M.: A process for data protection impact assessment under the European general data protection regulation, pp. 21–37. Springer (2016). https://doi.org/10.1007/978-3-319-44760-5_2
4. Ciclosi, F., Massacci, F.: The data protection officer: a ubiquitous role that no one really knows. IEEE Secur. Priv. **21**(1), 66–77 (2023). https://doi.org/10.1109/msec.2022.3222115
5. Diepenbrock, A., Fleck, J., Sachweh, S.: An analysis of stack exchange questions: Identifying challenges in software design and development with a focus on data privacy and data protection. In: Proceedings of the 18th International Conference on Availability, Reliability and Security, ARES 2023, Association for Computing Machinery, New York, NY, USA (2023). https://doi.org/10.1145/3600160.3605465
6. Diepenbrock, A., Sachweh, S.: Towards a conceptual framework for data protection impact assessments of smart city data ecosystems. In: 2025 IEEE European Technology and Engineering Management Summit (E-TEMS), IEEE, May 2025
7. European union: regulation (EU) 2016/679 of the European parliament and of the council of 27 April 2016 on the protection of natural persons with regard to the processing of personal data and on the free movement of such data, and repealing Directive 95/46/EC (General Data Protection Regulation), https://eur-lex.europa.eu/legal-content/EN/TXT/?uri=CELEX:32016R0679, official Journal of the European Union, L vol. 119, pp. 1–88, April 2016
8. Ferreyra, N.E.D., Khelifi, S., Arachchilage, N., Scandariato, R.: The good, the bad, and the (un)usable: a rapid literature review on privacy as code (2024). https://doi.org/10.48550/ARXIV.2412.16667
9. France, R., Rumpe, B.: Model-driven development of complex software: a research roadmap. In: Future of Software Engineering (FOSE 07), p. 37–54. IEEE, May 2007, https://doi.org/10.1109/fose.2007.14
10. Friedewald, M., Schiering, I., Martin, N., Hallinan, D.: Data protection impact assessments in practice: experiences from case studies, pp. 424–443. Springer (2022). https://doi.org/10.1007/978-3-030-95484-0_25
11. Gogolla, M.: UML and OCL in conceptual modeling, pp. 85–122. Springer, Berlin, Heidelberg (2011) https://doi.org/10.1007/978-3-642-15865-0_4
12. Heithoff, M., Jansen, N., Kirchhof, J.C., Michael, J., Rademacher, F., Rumpe, B.: Deriving integrated multi-viewpoint modeling languages from heterogeneous modeling languages: An experience report. In: Proceedings of the 16th ACM SIGPLAN International Conference on Software Language Engineering, SLE 2023, pp. 194–207. ACM, October 2023, https://doi.org/10.1145/3623476.3623527
13. Hoepman, J.H.: Privacy design strategies, pp. 446–459. Springer, Berlin, Heidelberg (2014) https://doi.org/10.1007/978-3-642-55415-5_38
14. International organization for standardization, international electrotechnical commission, Institute of electrical and electronics engineers: ISO/IEC/IEEE 42010:2022 – systems and software engineering architecture description. Standard 42010:2022, ISO/IEC/IEEE (2022), https://www.iso.org/standard/74374.html
15. International organization for standardization and international electrotechnical commission: ISO/IEC 22989:2022 information technology artificial intelligence artificial intelligence concepts and terminology. Standard ISO/IEC 22989:2022, ISO/IEC JTC 1/SC 42, July 2022, https://www.iso.org/standard/74296.html, first edition
16. Khedkar, M., Schlichtig, M., Bodden, E.: Advancing android privacy assessments with automation. In: Proceedings of the 39th IEEE/ACM International Conference

on Automated Software Engineering Workshops, ASEW 2024, pp. 218–222. ACM, October 2024, https://doi.org/10.1145/3691621.3694953
17. Mohagheghi, P., Gilani, W., Stefanescu, A., Fernandez, M.A., Nordmoen, B., Fritzsche, M.: Where does model-driven engineering help? experiences from three industrial cases. Softw. Syst. Model. **12**(3), 619 639 (2011). https://doi.org/10.1007/s10270-011-0219-7
18. Netto, D.P.D.S., Silva, C., Ara jo, J.: How software industry specifies requirements compliant with data protection laws: a survey-based study. In: Proceedings of the XXIII Brazilian Symposium on Software Quality, SBQS 2024, pp. 242– 252. ACM, November 2024, https://doi.org/10.1145/3701625.3701663
19. Pandit, H.J., Esteves, B., Krog, G.P., Ryan, P., Golpayegani, D., Flake, J.: Data privacy vocabulary (dpv) – version 2 (2024). https://doi.org/10.48550/ARXIV.2404.13426
20. Pedroza, G., Muntes-Mulero, V., Martin, Y.S., Mockly, G.: A model-based approach to realize privacy and data protection by design. In: 2021 IEEE European Symposium on Security and Privacy Workshops (EuroS&PW), pp. 332–339. IEEE, September 2021, https://doi.org/10.1109/eurospw54576.2021.00042
21. Rademacher, F.: A Language ecosystem for modeling microservice architecture. Ph.D. thesis (2022). https://doi.org/10.17170/KOBRA-202209306919
22. Riemann, L.T., Hähner, F.P.S., Schmitz, A.K., Ataian, M., Jaster, M., Ückert, F.: An open-source software tool to facilitate data protection impact assessments. Appl. Sci. **13**(20), 11230 (2023). https://doi.org/10.3390/app132011230
23. Shelake, V.M., Shekokar, N.: A survey of privacy preserving data integration. In: 2017 International Conference on Electrical, Electronics, Communication, Computer, and Optimization Techniques (ICEECCOT), pp. 59–70 (2017). https://doi.org/10.1109/ICEECCOT.2017.8284559
24. Tahaei, M., Vaniea, K., Saphra, N.: Understanding privacy-related questions on stack overflow. In: Proceedings of the 2020 CHI Conference on Human Factors in Computing Systems, CHI 2020, pp. 1–14. ACM, April 2020.https://doi.org/10.1145/3313831.3376768
25. Torre, D., Alferez, M., Soltana, G., Sabetzadeh, M., Briand, L.: Modeling data protection and privacy: application and experience with GDPR. Softw. Syst. Model. **20**(6), 2071–2087 (2021). https://doi.org/10.1007/s10270-021-00935-5
26. Wijesundara, T., Warren, M., Arachchilage, N.A.G.: Sok: enhancing privacy-preserving software development from a developers' perspective (2025). https://doi.org/10.48550/ARXIV.2504.20350

Cybersecurity Vulnerability Prioritisation via Risk Assessment

Steve Taylor[1(✉)], Panos Melas[1], Mike Surridge[1], Paolo De Lutiis[2], Manuel Leone[2], Martin Gilje Jaatun[3], and Ravishankar Borgaonkar[3]

[1] University of Southampton, Southampton, UK
{S.J.Taylor,pmelas,ms8}@soton.ac.uk
[2] Security Engineering and Threat Management, TIM S.p.A, Torino, Italy
{paolo.delutiis,manuel.leone}@telecomitalia.it
[3] Software Engineering, Safety and Security, SINTER Digital Trondheim, Trondheim, Norway
{Martin.G.Jaatun,Ravi.Borgaonkar}@sintef.no

Abstract. The Common Vulnerabilities and Exposures (CVE) database lists a large number of vulnerabilities that are present in specific versions of software libraries and applications, but although there is a severity ranking, it does not immediately follow that an identified vulnerability with high severity will be particularly important for a specific application. This paper presents the motivation for CVE Prioritization for a given case and describes an outline process for evaluating the priority of CVEs via risk assessment simulations.

Keywords: Vulnerabilities · CVE · SBOM · Risk · Software

1 Introduction

A Common Vulnerabilities and Exposures (CVE) instance describes a specific security issue in software or hardware, assigning it a globally unique identifier (e.g., CVE-2025-12345). It helps security professionals track and address security risks effectively in a standardized manner. The CVE initiative was launched at the beginning of 2000 by the US MITRE organization [1] and is today commonly used by the cybersecurity expert community and industry: many tools, such as scanners and (cyber) threat intelligence platforms, use CVE to identify and track vulnerabilities.

The total count of CVEs increases significantly every year. In 2025, more than 45.000 published vulnerabilities are expected [2]. This high number clearly highlights the complexity of vulnerability management, requiring security experts and companies to invest significant effort and resources to effectively safeguard their networks and mitigate potential risks. In fact, addressing this large number of vulnerabilities is often impractical due to market-driven time pressures, limited budgets, or the constrained remediation capabilities of device manufacturers. For instance, the Fraunhofer Institute reported between 348 and 579

B. Coppens et al. (Eds.): ARES 2025 Workshops, LNCS 15997, pp. 57–69, 2025.
https://doi.org/10.1007/978-3-032-00639-4_4

high-severity CVEs per device [3]. Therefore, it is important to have tools and methodologies that help prioritize vulnerability remediation to achieve effective risk reduction at reasonable effort cost.

2 Related Work

2.1 Current Approaches

The Common Vulnerability Scoring System (CVSS) [4] uses a scoring approach, where the score ranges from 0 to 10, higher numbers indicating more critical security risks. The value represents the severity of a cybersecurity vulnerability based on the related impact and exploitability. The score does not represent the likelihood of an attack, although some parameters can be used indirectly to evaluate such aspects (e.g., if a CVE can be exploited via network, its exploitability likelihood is greater than a CVE that requires physical access to the device to be exploited). CVSS values (in particular CVSSv3, but partially also CVSSv4) are global and static values bound to the CVE intrinsic characteristics, without considering real-world factors like attacker motivation, availability of Proof of Concept (PoC) or public exploits, the target device's configuration and its positioning within the network architecture, the presence of additional security mechanisms, such as firewalls, Intrusion Prevention System (IPS), etc. To overcome these limitations, Security teams typically consider additional sources of information. A key source is Cyber Threat Intelligence feeds that take into consideration the actual threats/risks the device containing the CVE is exposed to.

The Exploit Prediction Scoring System (EPSS) proposed by the FIRST organization in 2019 [5] is a framework based on Machine Learning algorithms, that estimates the probability of a CVE being exploited in the wild, thus helping organizations prioritize patching by focusing on vulnerabilities that are more likely to be actively attacked.

The Vulnerability Priority Rating (VPR), proposed and maintained by Tenable [6], is designed as an enhancement over the traditional CVSS scores and incorporates threat intelligence, vulnerability age, exploit availability, and asset context to prioritize vulnerabilities and to help organizations to focus on vulnerabilities that are most likely to be exploited in real-world attacks. The Known Exploited Vulnerabilities (KEV) catalog [7], maintained by the Cybersecurity and Infrastructure Security Agency (CISA), aims to identify vulnerabilities that are actively being exploited by cybercriminals. These vulnerabilities have been confirmed to be used in real-world attacks, making them high-priority targets for patching. While KEV primarily strengthens the security posture of U.S. government agencies, it also serves as a valuable resource for organizations worldwide.

Several initiatives on this topic have also been registered in the commercial domain. Among these, we mention Cisco Vulnerability Management (formerly Kenna.VM [8]), whose primary goal is providing a prioritized list of vulnerabilities analyzing data ingested from several sources (such as vulnerability scanners) and combining them with real-world exploit activity.

2.2 Main Limitations

The proposed methods for CVE prioritization have their own advantages and limitations. As correctly stated by Spring et al. [9], CVSS is primarily designed to assess the technical severity of a vulnerability; but it is often misused for vulnerability prioritization and risk assessment. While CVSS measures severity, even with the inclusion of Temporal and Environmental scores, it does not assess risks. Consequently, its effectiveness for vulnerability prioritization remains limited. Moreover, it is not suitable for handling deployment in complex scenarios, nor can it be used to aggregate scores across multiple vulnerabilities [10]. EPSS, VPR and partially KEV enhance severity measurement through the contribution of Threat Intelligence. However, their support for multiple vulnerabilities remains limited, and like CVSS, they do not account for specific characteristics of the device under test and the system into which it is deployed.

3 Case Study: Residential Gateway

The case study for this work concerns a Residential Gateway (RGW). The RGW is a commodity device that provides connections for domestic subscribers of broadband services to the Widea Area Network (WAN) provided by the Internet Service Provider, which in this case study is a telecommunication company (TC). TC provides various communication services, including mobile telephony and residential data services. TC has defined rigorous security testing processes and a risk-based methodology to manage and maintain the cybersecurity of its infrastructures. Every device, prior to deployment in the field, must be tested within specialized labs to verify its actual security posture.

The RGW is a special kind of device from the cyber security point of view. Although it is based on a low-cost architecture, it is a key element for the interconnection (and security) between the internal LAN of the residential customers (where it is common to have IPTV, PC, and other user devices) and the Internet, which provides at the same time digital services but also cyber threats and risks. The patch management of such devices is also complex, especially considering that the number of devices deployed can be several million. Therefore, the efficient patching of the devices is a key requirement, and for this the assessment of exploitability and severity for CVEs affecting the RGW is needed to determine priorities for patching.

The conditions required to exploit vulnerabilities in a Residential Gateway can be highly specific to that device, potentially limiting the impact of the Threat Intelligence in accurately assessing the actual risk. The environment into which the RGW is deployed is also a key factor - the fact that a specific vulnerability is actively exploited in the wild may be irrelevant for a Residential Gateway due to its particular access model, which could prevent actual exploitation. Conversely, detecting that a specific device has been successfully targeted may occur too late. This challenge is especially evident for RGW devices, where the software or the device configuration is often customized by the Telco operator, further complicating traditional threat intelligence assessments. Moreover, in such a situation, these solutions provide limited assistance to executive management in understanding the real risk posture and how to mitigate a potential future security disaster.

In short, none of the methods considered are truly tailored to the target devices. While this is reasonable for general-purpose approaches, more specialized strategies could be applied in specific use cases or when the target device is well known, as in the RGW use case. These strategies should rely on more detailed models capable of accurately assessing the real exploitability of vulnerabilities and combining them with the effectiveness and power of the risk analysis approach.

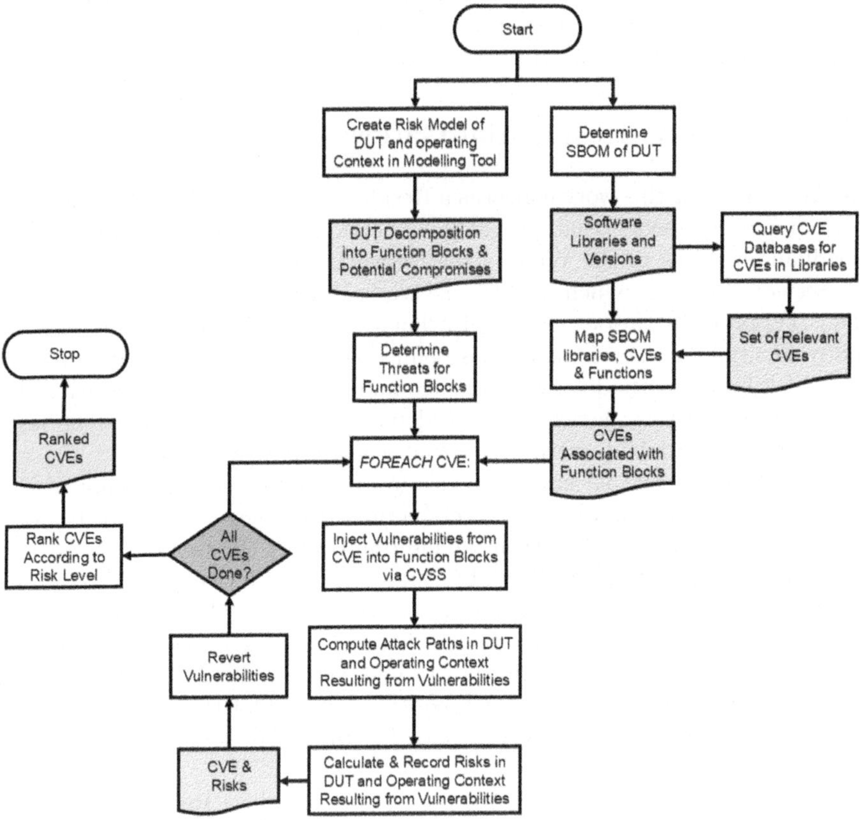

Fig. 1. CVE Prioritization Approach

4 Approach

Our approach to addressing these limitations is to use risk simulation to assess the compromises, along with their impacts and likelihood (key components of risk assessment), potentially caused by each CVE in the Device Under Test (abbreviated DUT). The overall approach is shown in the process diagram of Fig. 1 and detailed steps of this process are discussed in the next subsections.

Risk assessment typically maps threats to consequences, where a consequence has a severity (the degree of the damage were the consequence to occur) and a likelihood (how probable the consequence is). Vulnerabilities are weaknesses that threats exploit, and thus risk assessment enables mapping of vulnerabilities in CVEs to consequences of importance to the stakeholders undertaking the analysis.

In this work, we have used the Spyderisk tool[1] (Phillips et al. [11]), a tool for risk simulation via a knowledge-based modelling approach. Here the user builds a model of their System Under Test (SUT) using predefined ICT elements such as computers, software processes, data, networks, routers plus the socio-technical environments and actors they operate in such as people and physical spaces.

In the Case Study, a model (shown in Fig. 2) is built of the RGW under test (the DUT), crucially in its deployment environment (the SUT), which enables relating risks in the deployment environment to vulnerabilities associated with CVEs. The deployment environment is a domestic situation containing typical elements on the private home network (e.g. computers, TVs, smart devices), users (e.g., the subscriber and their family), data (e.g., documents, music, photos, all of which are likely to be important to the subscriber and thus need protecting) plus the connection to the WAN provided by the ISP and the bridge to the Internet. In parallel, a Software Bill of Materials (SBOM) is generated from the DUT's binary firmware, which provides software packages and versions, and using this information, CVEs can be determined via lookup. The risk model is used to evaluate the CVEs associated with the RGW in simulation of the effects caused by the CVE under realistic expected usage conditions.

4.1 Attack Paths

A key concept from Phillips et al. [11] that underpins the approach described here is that of *attack paths*. These are chains of vulnerability-threat-consequence patterns, where a vulnerability (e.g. represented by a CVE) in a system component exposes it to a threat, which leads to a consequence (e.g., degradation of a key property of a component), which may also lead to a new vulnerability, which may lead to another threat, and so on. The consequences can be measured as risks, which comprise the severity of the consequence occurring, which is a subjective judgement and dependent on the stakeholder(s) involved or affected, and the likelihood, which is determined by the potential for exploitation of the vulnerability, the difficulty of executing the threat, any controls in place to manage threats, etc. Thus, from this repeating pattern of vulnerability-threat-consequence, attack paths can be formed that link vulnerabilities in one system component to consequences in it, or other connected entities. Via this mechanism, our approach is to evaluate CVEs by determining their simulated

[1] https://spyderisk.org.

resulting risk levels, to identify which vulnerabilities lead to the highest-level risks and thus which CVEs should be prioritized.

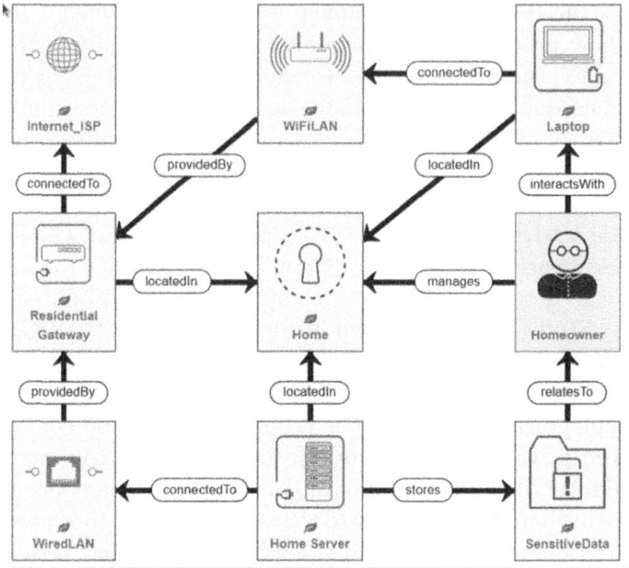

Fig. 2. Residential Gateway (router) in Context

An illustrative example of an attack path is provided in Fig. 2 and Table 1 showing a Residential Gateway (RGW) in a domestic context. The RGW provides: access to the Internet, a wired and wireless network, to which a laptop and a home server are connected. The home server stores sensitive personal data relating to the Home owner.

Here, a key consequence is: Loss of Confidentiality (or low Confidentiality) at SensitiveData, which is defined as: *"Disclosure of data to unauthorised parties, or a state where prevention or detection of such a disclosure cannot be ensured"*. Here, because the data is sensitive, the impact (or severity) of the unauthorized disclosure is high, and its likelihood is calculated to be very high. An Attack Path to this consequence is shown in Table 1.

The table illustrates that the consequence in one row leads to the vulnerability in the row beneath it. Here the root vulnerability is the assumed (low) trustworthiness (TW in the table) of everyone in the world leading to an intrusion into the Home. This leads to the consequence of theft of the Home Server and thence to the exposure of the Sensitive Data stored within it. This is a trivial example because the simple control of locking the door of the Home addresses it (by restricting access to trusted individuals), but it serves to describe the link between vulnerabilities, threats and consequences in an attack path. Because the risk model is constructed of the RGW in the domestic situation in which it is

Table 1. Attack Path to Loss of Confidentiality of Sensitive Data

Vulnerability	Threat	Consequence	Distance	Likelihood
Occupant TW at *World*	Physical intrusion into private space *Home* from *World*	Loss of Occupant TW at Home	5	Very High
Loss of Occupant TW at *Home*	Theft of device *Home Server* from *Home*	Loss of Possession at *Home Server*	3	Very High
Loss of Possession at *Home Server*	Physical access to data *SensitiveData* on stolen host *Home Server*	Loss of Confidantiality of *SensitiveData*	1	Very High

deployed, it represents the relationship between vulnerabilities in the DUT and the consequences they cause in the environment in which the DUT is deployed. This method of attack path analysis therefore considers the effects of chains of vulnerabilities and also considers the relationship between the DUT and its deployment environment, overcoming limitations of current approaches.

4.2 Functional Decomposition and Modelling

Figure 2 illustrates a model of the RGW in context, and to map CVEs to the router, a functional decomposition of the core functionality of the RGW is undertaken. This entails examining the core functions of the router and building a risk model of these core functions, how they are configured and mapping this to software packages from the SBOM. The complete Spyderisk model for the RGW is shown in Fig. 3 and its core functionality is decomposed as shown in Fig. 4.

A basic residential gateway has a connection to the Internet, wired ethernet ports and a wireless access point. The RGW under test is based on OpenWrt[2], whose networking relies on the Linux kernel networking subsystem which provides packet processing and routing functionalities. Kernel modules interact with device drivers that handle WAN, LAN, and WiFI interfaces, or hardware accelerators. Packet filtering and network address translation (NAT) are managed by the kernel's Netfilter framework. User-space services and tools such as ppp, dhcp, fw3, and hostapd manage various router networking functionalities including the WiFi access point. Their behaviour is configured through /etc./config files which can be modified via the unified configuration interface (LuCI/uhttpd) via a web browser.

The orange connections in Fig. 4 depict flows of control or management, from managing to managed component, and each path of configuration or management represents a potential attack path, since any exploitable vulnerability at a point on this path can affect the components downstream. For example, if there

[2] https://openwrt.org.

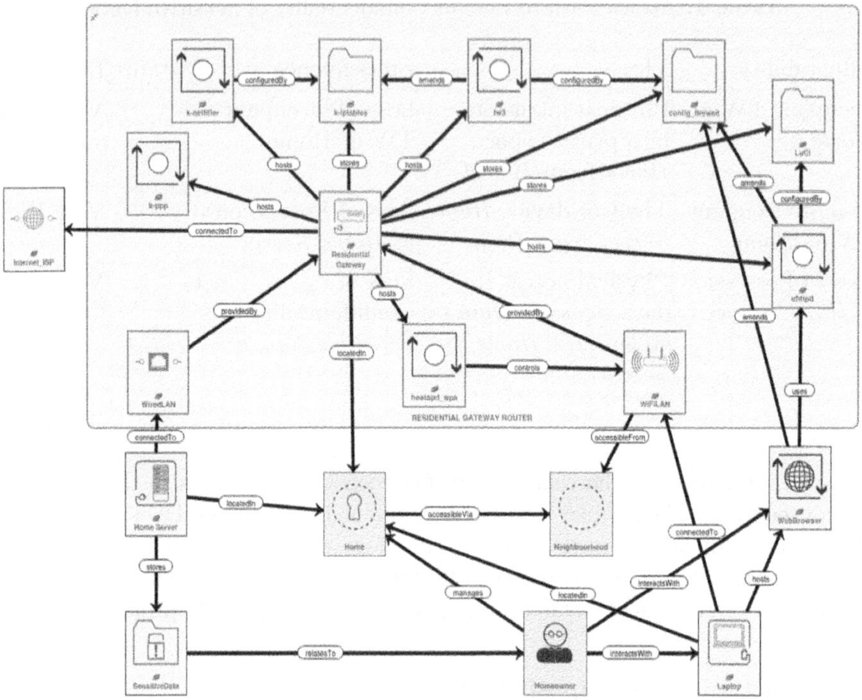

Fig. 3. RGW Spyderisk model

is a vulnerability in uhttpd, this can have potentially far-reaching effects, since it is the means by which all the downstream processes are configured, and which eventually controls the hardware networks provided by the RGW.

Using this functional decomposition, a risk model of the RGW is constructed in the simulation tool described by Phillips et al. [11]. The model uses "process" elements to describe the software processes (blue elements in Fig. 4) and "data" elements to describe configuration files (orange elements in Fig. 4), as well as specific elements for the hardware Internet, LAN and WiFi interfaces. These are connected as described in Fig. 4, thus modelling the software processes that control the networking elements, the config files that control them and the software processes that enable the config files to be updated. The resulting model is shown in Fig. 3 and is an expanded model of the RGW element of Fig. 2 (the RGW in context) with the topology of Fig. 4 (the software/hardware structure of the RGW).

Each of the processes in the RGW decomposition is a potential source of vulnerabilities, and determining which vulnerabilities may be applicable requires SBOM generation for the packages that provide that process.

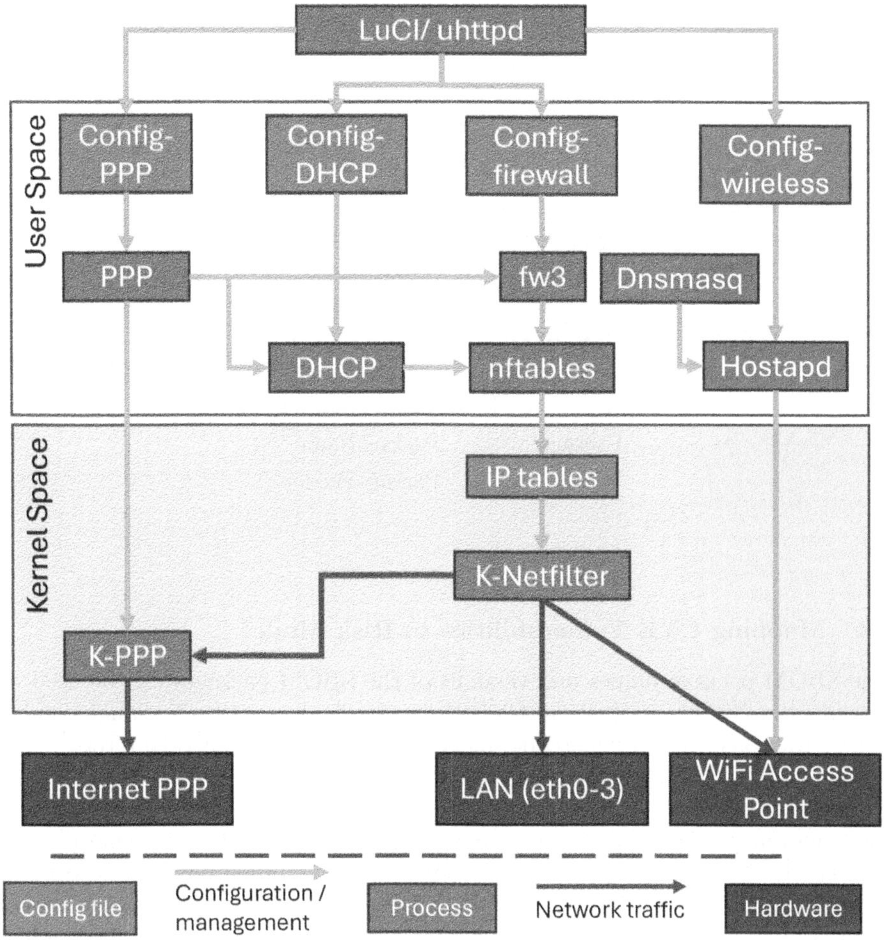

Fig. 4. RGW Functional Decomposition

4.3 SBOM Generation

In an ideal world, all vendors would include an up-to-date SBOM with their software/devices, but this is often not the case. If an unencrypted, un-obfuscated version of the binary firmware is available, tools can be used to extract library names and version strings directly from the firmware [12,13]. This can then be used to construct a (partial or complete) SBOM for further analysis.

An SBOM in the Software Package Data Exchange (SPDX) format may be generated using the Open Package Manager (OPKG) system. OPKG is a lightweight package management system that is used in OpenWrt without needing access to source code. OPKG can be used to provide a list of the installed software packages including package details such as:

- Package name
- Version name
- Depends list
- Architecture name
- Installed-Time
- List of installed files

This information is enough to construct an SPDX SBOM file with minimal mappings as shown in Table 2.

Table 2. Mapping OPKG to SPDX

OPKG Attribute	SPDX Attribute
Package	PackageName
Version	PackageVersion

4.4 Mapping CVE Vulnerabilities to Risk Model

The SBOM package names and versions of the SBOM packages can be used as arguments to queries to look up CVEs from databases such as National Vulnerability Database[3] using client-side query tools such as the CVE Bin Tool[4]. The result is a set of CVEs associated with the SBOM.

Each CVE returned by the query has associated CVSS vectors, and these vectors contain metrics that enable mapping into the risk model, via a mechanism named "Trustworthiness Attributes" (TWA). The mapping between CVSS and TWA is described by Phillips et al. [11], but briefly TWA describes attributes such as Confidentiality, Integrity, Availability (CIA) for data; and access vector, authentication requirements, user trustworthiness, availability, intrinsic trustworthiness, reliability, timeliness, malware, overloading and control for processes. CVSS vectors contain attributes covering access vectors to processes and data, e.g., whether it is remote or local, the attack complexity and the authentication required to exploit the vulnerability; plus impact in terms of Confidentiality, Integrity and Availability (CIA) on data and processes, which can be mapped to the TWA. Example mappings are described in Sect. 5.

4.5 Risk Assessment Per CVE

The risks resulting from each CVE are computed via an iterative loop. Each iteration performs the following actions:

1. Adjust the relevant TWAs associated with the CVE's CVSS vector.

[3] https://nvd.nist.gov/.
[4] https://github.com/intel/cve-bin-tool-action.

2. Calculate the attack path and resulting risks, thus determining the risks due to the CVE.
3. Record the risks associated with the CVE.
4. Reset the risk model to a known state.

The result is a set of attack paths and risks for each CVE in the SUT where the DUT is deployed. These results can be then ranked to show the CVEs with the highest level risks.

5 Example

Initial tests have been undertaken by mapping vulnerabilities into the risk model in Fig. 3 representing the RGW structure of Fig. 4 in the context of a domestic environment of Fig. 2. Appropriate controls were applied to the model to simulate a realistic environment (e.g. physical locks on the Home, encrypted communication in the wireless network, firewall blocks at the interface between the RGW and the Internet). The RGW under test is running OpenWrt, an open-source GNU/Linux distribution firmware for embedded devices. An SBOM was generated for OpenWrt and using queries based on the libraries and versions in the SBOM, CVEs were retrieved from the NVD database. These were successively applied to the risk model and risks calculated. An example CVE is discussed next.

CVE-2020-8597[5] describes a buffer overflow vulnerability in the pppd (Point-to-Point Deamon) process with the CVSS vector:

```
AV:N/AC:L/Au:N/C:P/I:P/A:P
```

The vector indicates a remote code execution network based attack (AV:N) of low complexity (AC:L) that does not require authentication (Au:N). This results in partial compromise of Confidentiality, Integrity and Availability of data in the affected processes (C:P/I:P/A:P), which is interpreted as user-level access, according to scoring tip#9 of the CVSS v2.0 guide[6]. The vector is mapped to TWAs in the k_ppp model process as described in Table 3.

Table 3. Trustworthiness Attributes changes

Trustworthiness Type	From	To	Basis
Extrinsic-AU-TW	`''Safe''`	`''Low''`	No authentication needed (`Au:N`)
Extrinsic-U-TW	`''Safe''`	`''Low''`	User-level access trustworthiness from `CIA:P`
Extrinsic-VN-TW	`''Safe''`	`''Low''`	Remote network access trustworthiness from `AV:N`

In each of the TWAs, the value "Low" is determined by the attack complexity AC:L, meaning a low-complexity attack, therefore low trustworthiness results.

[5] https://nvd.nist.gov/vuln/detail/CVE-2020-8597.
[6] https://www.first.org/cvss/v2/guide.

The risk calculation is run and the resulting risk level becomes Very High, due to the significant rights potential gained from a low-complexity remote attack.

6 Conclusion

This paper presents an outline process for assessment of vulnerability (CVE) priority in Devices Under Test via linking CVEs in devices to system-level risks and using risk levels at system-level to determine the CVE priority. The outline addresses challenges of incorporating the DUT's deployment environment and the propagated effects of vulnerabilities in the DUT to risks that affect important assets at system level. The approach enables analysts to declare their priorities in terms of risk severity, then use attack path analysis to determine the likelihood that the vulnerabilities lead to compromise of these priorities. Future work is aimed at running extensive tests on the use case, plus addressing the following sub-challenges.

1. Model resolution. The RGW is a complex system, including multiple packages in addition to the core gateway/routing functionality. Further work is needed to determine the appropriate fidelity of the risk model, including modelling the critical and non-critical functions of a given router (even if functions are non-critical to the operation of the router, they may still provide entry points to attack paths to critical functions).
2. CVSS versions. CVSS is continually evolving and in many cases later versions are not backwards compatible with earlier versions because semantics of the vector has changed across the version. Thus it is challenging to support mapping from CVSS as it evolves to risk assessment and further work is needed to determine a robust mapping scheme.
3. Function to Software Package Mapping. It is often the case that a core element of RGW function is delivered via multiple software packages, or that the same package delivers multiple RGW functions. Thus the mapping between the functions and actual packages is not straightforward and careful analysis of both the functional breakdown and the packages that support it is needed, requiring significant domain knowledge of hardware, software, networking etc.
4. Exploitability of vulnerabilities in realistic system-level situations. Understanding under what circumstances a vulnerability becomes exploitable is needed via consultation with experts to build risk models that enable simulation of realistic scenarios where the RGW may be employed including different domestic environments, taking into account factors such as the types of smart devices connected to the private network, default configuration of such devices and different levels of cybersecurity awareness of domestic subscribers. In addition, understanding of the relative importance of different elements in the system (i.e., what is important to protect) is a key consideration. Evaluating the factors above to determine such scenarios is an immediate item of further work.

Acknowledgment. This work is performed within the Horizon Europe TELEMETRY (Trustworthy mEthodologies, open knowLedgE & autoMated tools for sEcurity Testing of IoT software, haRdware & ecosYstems) project, supported by EC funding under grant number 101119747, and UKRI under grant number 10087006.

References

1. MITRE: Mitre corporation. https://www.mitre.org/
2. Ireann Leverett: Vulnerability forecast for 2025. https://www.first.org/blog/20250607-Vulnerability-Forecast-for-2025 (2025) FIRST
3. Weidenbach, P., vom Dorp, J.: Home router security report 2020. Technical report, Fraunhofer Institute for Communication, Information Processing and Ergonomics FKIE (2020)
4. CVSS Special Interest Group: Common vulnerability scoring system version 3.1: Specification document (2019), Accessed 2025
5. Roytman, M., Jacobs, J.: Predictive vulnerability scoring system. In: Black Hat USA, Las Vegas, August 2019
6. Tenable: vulnerability priority rating. https://docs.tenable.com/vulnerability-management/best-practices/security/Content/VulnerabilityPriorityRating.htm
7. Cybersecurity infrastructure security agency (CISA): known exploited vulnerabilities catalog. https://www.cisa.gov/known-exploited-vulnerabilities-catalog
8. Cisco: cisco vulnerability management. https://www.cisco.com/site/us/en/products/security/vulnerability-management/index.html
9. Spring, J., Hatleback, E., Householder, A.D., Manion, A., Shick, D.: Towards improving CVSS. Carnegie Mellon University - Software Engineering Institute, White paper (2018)
10. FIRST: EPSS - frequently asked questions. https://www.first.org/epss/faq
11. Phillips, S.C., Taylor, S., Boniface, M., Modafferi, S., Surridge, M.: Automated knowledge-based cybersecurity risk assessment of cyber-physical systems. IEEE Access **12**, 82482–82505 (2024)
12. Messner, M., Kuehne, B., Eckmann, P., Hoxha, E.: Emba - the security analyzer for firmware of embedded devices. https://github.com/e-m-b-a/emba (Multiple other contributors)
13. Linux: strings(1) - linux man page. https://linux.die.net/man/1/strings

Proceedings of the Second International Workshop on Emerging Digital Identities (EDId 2025)

EDId 2025 Preface

The identity environment has evolved into a complex and dynamic ecosystem that demands seamless interoperability, stronger security measures, and user-centric experiences in an increasingly interconnected digital world. As digital transformation accelerates across sectors, the challenges surrounding digital identity systems have grown in scope and complexity. The rise of decentralized architectures, cross-border data flows, and mounting concerns over surveillance, data misuse, and exclusion have made identity management a focal point for innovation and critical inquiry.

One significant development in this space is the introduction of the European Digital Identity (EUDI) Wallet, which aims to provide EU citizens and residents with a trusted, secure, and interoperable solution for managing their digital identity across borders. The EUDI Wallet exemplifies the shift toward user-controlled identity models. It also raises critical questions around standardization, governance, and inclusion—issues beyond the European context. Addressing these questions requires a collaborative effort that bridges disciplinary boundaries.

The 2nd International Workshop on Emerging Digital Identities (EDId) aimed to foster dialogue, share emerging research, and catalyze innovative solutions. EDId explores the evolving digital identity landscape by engaging with various topics—from implementing secure authentication protocols and interoperability standards to the legal and regulatory dimensions of data protection, privacy, and digital rights.

This workshop accepted 6 manuscripts out of a total of 13 submissions. At least three reviewers followed a double-blind approach to peer review the manuscripts. The reviewers, who were part of the Program Committee, were composed of 19 experts in digital identities. Based on their valuable reviews, 6 papers were accepted to be published in the LNCS volume by Springer and presented at the workshop.

We thank all the participants, including the authors, the reviewers, the invited keynote speaker, and the attendees, for their valuable work and significant efforts, which contributed to the workshop's success. We hope that this workshop will advance the development of emerging digital identities.

August 2025

Nils Gruschka
Daniela Pöhn
Amir Sharif

EDId 2025 Organization

Workshop Chairs

Nils Gruschka	University of Oslo, Norway
Daniela Pöhn	Universität der Bundeswehr München, Germany
Amir Sharif	Fondazione Bruno Kessler, Italy

Program Committee

Hamed Arshad	Cegal, Norway
Diana G. Berbecaru	Politecnico di Torino, Italy
Tamas Bisztray	University of Oslo, Norway
Julien Bringer	Kallistech, France
Francesco Buccafurri	Università degli Studi Mediterranea di Reggio Calabria, Italy
Andre Büttner	University of Oslo, Norway
Roberto Carbone	Fondazione Bruno Kessler, Italy
Lothar Fritsch	OsloMet, Norway
Michael Grabatin	Universität der Bundeswehr München, Germany
Wolfgang Hommel	Universität der Bundeswehr München, Germany
Meiko Jensen	Karlstad University, Sweden
Sandra Kostic	FU Berlin & Fraunhofer AISEC, Germany
Sara Lazzaro	Università degli Studi Mediterranea di Reggio Calabria, Italy
Stefan More	Graz University of Technology, Austria
Cecilia Pasquini	Fondazione Bruno Kessler, Italy
Marco Pernpruner	Fondazione Bruno Kessler, Italy
Silvio Ranise	Fondazione Bruno Kessler & University of Trento, Italy
Guido Schmitz	Lancaster University Leipzig, UK
Giada Sciarretta	Fondazione Bruno Kessler, Italy

Additional Reviewer

Tahir Ahmad

Attestation of Electronic Identification Schemes Based on Secure Channels Through Security Microcontrollers

Stefan Genchev(✉), Lars Wüstrich, and Georg Carle

Chair of Network Architectures and Services, Technical University of Munich, Boltzmannstr. 3, 85748 Garching near Munich, Germany
{genchev,wuestrich,carle}@net.in.tum.de

Abstract. This paper presents AttApp, a novel mechanism for attestation in Authenticated Key Exchange + Secure Channel (AKE+SC) electronic identification (eID) schemes. AttApp enhances auditability and enables the use of AKE+SC in scenarios that require proof of authentication, such as Know Your Customer compliance. By leveraging a Trusted Execution Environment, AttApp ensures the integrity of authentication attestations while mitigating insider threats. Furthermore, it is specifically designed for deployment on resource-constrained Security Microcontrollers (ICCs). We implement AttApp as a JavaCard applet, demonstrating its feasibility and evaluating its performance on commercially available ICCs. The key contributions of this work include (i) a novel attestation framework for eID schemes based on Extended Access Control as an instance of AKE+SC, (ii) a JavaCard-based implementation compatible with existing ICCs, (iii) a security analysis of the proposed approach, and (iv) an empirical assessment of its performance on real-world hardware.

Keywords: Electronic Identification · Attestation · Smart Cards · TEE

1 Introduction

Electronic Identification (eID) solutions are the cornerstone of trustworthy business processes in the digital world. eID solutions represent a mechanism to remotely authenticate human users and provide information about a user's real-world identity. Especially with an anticipated rise in fraud that AI can facilitate [6], there is an increased necessity for reliable eID technologies.

eID solutions based on cryptographic protocols are being rolled out throughout the world as means of strong user authentication across various domains. Examples include European ID [12] and U.S. PIV [5] cards with an embedded security microcontroller (Integrated Circuit Cards/ICCs), storing an authentication certificate and protecting a corresponding private key.

B. Coppens et al. (Eds.): ARES 2025 Workshops, LNCS 15997, pp. 75–92, 2025.
https://doi.org/10.1007/978-3-032-00639-4_5

Several widespread user authentication protocols [10] [13] rely on signature-based challenge-response authentication. One instantiation of this pattern is TLS with mutual authentication [13]. In contrast, other eID schemes rely on an Authenticated Key Exchange + Secure Channel (AKE+SC) construction [8]. Here, a device authenticating a person and a Relying Party (RP) perform a key agreement based on public keys that they have authenticated respectively to establish a shared secret. They then use the shared secret to derive session keys and establish a Secure Channel to exchange trusted information. The underlying assumption is that only an entity with access to an authenticated key can derive the keys for the Secure Channel and appropriately authenticate exchanged messages.

An important privacy characteristic of AKE+SC eID schemes is that authentications suffice to establish a high level of trust while remaining repudiable. Users can deny having authenticated to an RP in case of a data breach and RPs can use decoy data sets to conceal real records. While RPs can record signatures in signature-based schemes (e.g., by recording the handshake messages for TLS), AKE+SC eID schemes leave no (cryptographic) evidence that an authentication has taken place. There are, however, use cases in which such proof may be necessary to show compliance with regulations. For example, banks in the U.S. are required to keep records of all information obtained as part of their identity verification procedures (*cf.* 31 CFR 1020.220(a)(3) [11]). Such requirements represent a barrier to the adoption of AKE+SC eID schemes.

In this work, we propose and evaluate a mechanism for attesting authentication for an AKE+SC construction called `AttApp`. Attestations produced by `AttApp` protect the information obtained during an authentication through a cryptographic signature and thus enable auditability. To protect the privacy of authenticated individuals, `AttApp` binds authentications to a specific context and can restrict the verifiability of attestations to authorized entities. `AttApp` also enables extensibility of the underlying eID scheme to support new use cases or act as a polyfill solution for older eID tokens. This enables the use of AKE+SC in scenarios that require proof that an authentication has taken place.

To guarantee the integrity of the attestation process, our design utilizes a Trusted Execution Environment (TEE). A TEE enables us to defend against insider attacks in which the operator of an attestation system can falsify proofs. Our approach can be implemented on a security microcontroller with limited computational resources such as an ICC. Thus, our attestation mechanism can be deployed in decentralized way without the need for expensive hardware. We prove this statement by implementing our approach as a JavaCard applet. Our evaluation provides insights into the performance implications of running `AttApp` on a commercially available ICC. To the best of our knowledge, this work provides the first public report on using a real-world ICC as a trust anchor for attestations.

As a concrete protocol instantiation, we discuss how `AttApp` can enable RPs to attest eID based on Extended Access Control (EAC) [2]. This formally verified [8] AKE+SC scheme is supported by more than 75 million ICCs in the field in

Germany as of October 2024 [7]. Furthermore, considering the maturity of this scheme, we believe that its investigation as a privacy-preserving alternative to signature-based approaches such as SD-JWT and as a more leightweight and conservative alternative to zero-knowledge proofs is particularly interesting in the context of the planned EU Digital Identity Wallet.

In summary, our paper has four main contributions:

1. We present a novel concept for attesting eID based on EAC as an instantiation of an AKE+SC eID scheme. In contrast to an eID Server [2], we investigate a solution with a minimal Trusted Computing Base.
2. To prove its feasibility, we implement our attestation mechanism as a JavaCard applet that is compatible with existing ICCs. We report on our approach to solving challenges arising from the use of an ICC in a server setting.
3. We discuss the security characteristics of our proposed solution by providing security arguments. We specifically show that our solution mitigates relevant Denial of Service (DoS) attacks and protects the integrity of attested data.
4. We report on experiments assessing the performance of our implementation on a commercially available ICC. We find that a single ICC can handle up to 5 parallel simulated sessions at the same time and estimate that the determined performance meets the need of distributed small-to-medium setups.

2 Requirements

The problem our work seeks to address is the cryptographic attestation of repudiable authentications. In the following, we define requirements that attestations must fulfill in order to meet our functional goals while preserving privacy.

The main goal of our work is the attestation of an authentication that an RP can use as proof to third parties. Thus, the core requirement is the issuance of such a statement for an authentication (R1). We additionally define three specific functional requirements related to attestations that support our targeted use cases. **(i)** First, attestations must protect the temporal context of authentications (R1.1) - e.g., by indicating the time of authentication through a timestamp. This enables RPs to implement different security policies based on the age of attestations. **(ii)** User authentication is not a standalone service but instead happens in the context of a business process. Therefore, the attestation should bind an authentication to a specific transaction (R1.2). This binding prevents RPs to abuse an attestation for other purposes by presenting it as proof for a different process. **(iii)** Finally, the attestation needs to be verifiable by at least one designated entity (R1.3). This ensures that the attestation can be used to proof that an eID authentication took place - e.g., for external audits by oversight agencies.

In addition, we aim to increase the expressiveness of attestations by including application-specific logic. We consider this goal an extension of existing authentication protocols - implemented on the RP's side (R2). By incorporating additional logic in the attestation component, we create a stronger binding with authentications that this logic is executed on. This mechanism can also be used as a bridge between different eID schemes by perfoming a protocol "translation".

Finally, we aim to establish a method that requires low computational and memory overhead (R3). This reduces the requirements for the used hardware when implementing and using our mechanism, facilitating distribution.

3 Threat Model

Before we present our attestation mechanism, we introduce our threat model. Our threat model is specific to the envisioned deployment scenario.

The main goal of an attacker is to forge an authentication attestation. In particular, the attacker aims to either generate arbitrary proof of an authentication or falsify details of a legitimate one. This goal includes obtaining an attestation both for attacker-supplied data and for real data in an invalid context (e.g., with a wrong indication of the issuance date). In relation to the extensibility requirement (R2), we define an additional attack goal - the ability to execute the extension functions without a binding to a genuine authentication factor.

We assume a powerful attacker that operates outside of TEEs. We make the following assumptions that will guide the design of our system:

- T1 **TEE application:** We assume that an application loaded on a TEE implements the logic described in this work correctly.
- T2 **TEE hardware:** We assume that TEEs effectively protect the integrity of on-chip computations and the confidentiality and integrity of processed data.
- T3 **Attacker access:** We assume that an attacker can gain unrestricted access to components other than TEEs on the attestation side. In particular, we note that the operator of the system can be mapped to an attacker.

In this work, we do not explicitly discuss the confidentiality of extracted personal information as a security goal. We argue that confidentiality can be achieved trivially through the TEE hardware protections (T2) and encryption of an attestation's payload with a preconfigured key.

4 Concept

This section introduces the design of our solution for authentication attestation - `AttApp`. We first present our generic approach to attesting authentications for AKE+SC schemes in Sect. 4.1. Our goal is to define a design that can apply to different AKE+SC schemes in this section. Afterward, we apply our generic design to the selected protocol instantiation - EAC-based eID - in Sect. 4.3.

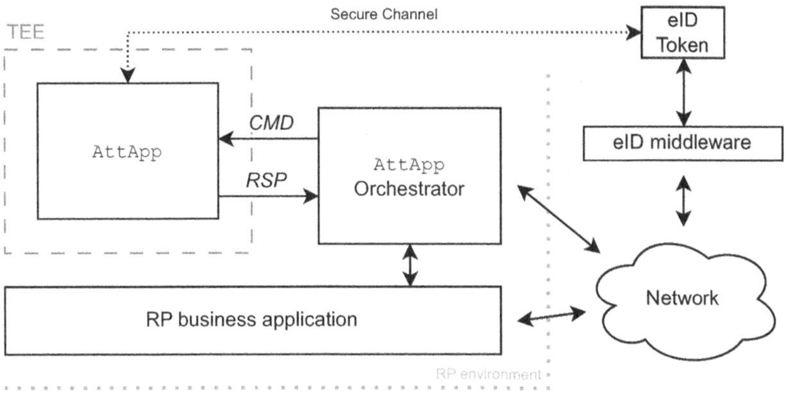

Fig. 1. Overview of the systems involved in an attestation that reflects the deployment of AttApp. The dashed line around AttApp indicates TEE boundaries. The fine dotted line between AttApp and the eID Token represents a logical Secure Channel. The structured dotted lines represent the boundaries of an RP.

4.1 Generic Construction

At the center of our approach is establishing a Trusted Computing Base, AttApp, for authentication attestation in a TEE. Specifically, this system must handle the authentication protocol of the target eID scheme and the attestation logic.

Deployment. AttApp processes authentications with eID Tokens (ICCs without loss of generality) and certifies the results through an attestation (R1). AttApp is part of an RP's infrastructure and is controlled by an orchestration service. Applications implementing business logic on the RP's side interact with the orchestrator to request and retrieve an attestation. The orchestration service further interacts with remote ICCs through a middleware component. We provide a visual representation of the involved systems and their communication relationships in Fig. 1.

Attestation Issuance. Each AttApp instance uses an attestation key pair that is generated within the TEE boundaries and that authenticates attestations. The public keys of trusted AttApp instances are distributed out-of-band. In order to enforce verifiability by authorized entities (R1.3), AttApp implements a mechanism for protecting the confidentiality of attestation signatures. We propose two concrete methods for this purpose. AttApp can encrypt an attestation's signature using a known key of an authorized entity. Without access to the corresponding key, an attacker cannot establish the authenticity of attestations, providing repudiation to authenticated users. Alternatively, a designated-verifier signature scheme [14] can be used. With such a scheme, attestation signatures can only be verified using the private key of an entity specified during signature generation.

Secure Channel Termination. In the context of eID schemes based on Secure Channels, AttApp must terminate the Secure Channels with ICCs. Without this property, the integrity of data received from an ICC cannot be established directly. Per Assumption T2, we assume that a TEE provides two guarantees to applications hosted on it - integrity of an application's logic and confidentiality of processed data. `AttApp` relies on these guarantees in order to terminate a Secure Channel and issue attestations in a trustworthy manner. Specifically, the integrity guarantee ensures that the application's logic cannot be modified to certify attacker-supplied data. The confidentiality guarantee, in turn, provides the following protection required by `AttApp`:

- **Attestation provenance:** An attacker cannot extract the attestation key and use it to sign attestations without `AttApp`'s control of the logic.
- **Session keying secrecy:** An attacker cannot extract the session key material for an authentication and tamper with an ICC's responses. We explicitly assume an untrusted channel between the ICC and the TEE.
- **Data privacy**: An attacker cannot access the information from an ICC if it is not shared explicitly (e.g., in the attestation).

Extensibility. By terminating Secure Channels within a TEE, `AttApp` can be understood as an extension of an ICC's environment, forming a single logical entity supported by the Secure Channel. For this reason, `AttApp` can extend the eID scheme or an ICC's implementation of an eID scheme (R2). For example, BSI TR-03110 [2] specifies a mechanism called *Pseudonymous Signatures* which allows an RP to request a signature, which is linked to the SP's identity, from an ICC. However, this mechanism is not yet available in German EAC-enabled documents. `AttApp` can transparently provide this functionality to RPs. Hence, `AttApp` can act also as a polyfill adding support for legacy cards.

In addition, `AttApp` can implement auxiliary logic based on the information received from an ICC, benefiting from the TEE's security boundaries. For example, `AttApp` can derive keys bound to an ICC's holder identity or the ICC being used. In the former case, an approach suggested by Schwarz et al. [15] can be used to derive keys from the personal information retrieved from an ICC. In the latter case, the Sector ID computed in EAC-based eID schemes can support the derivation. An initialization of `AttApp` with a long-lived secret as an input keying material is required in both cases.

Minimal Attestation Data Set. Independent from a protocol instantiation, an attestation issued by `AttApp` must include, as a minimum:

1. **Identity of `AttApp` instance:** In order to identify the instance that produced the attestation, its identity should be included.
2. **Time of issuance:** In compliance with R1.1, `AttApp` must protect the time of issuance of the attestation.
3. **External Transaction ID:** An RP application can supply an External Transaction ID to be included in an attestation. This ID both serves as an external nonce and bounds the authentication to a specific context (R1.2).

4.2 Abstract Operational Model

For the purposes of this paper, we define an abstract model for the operation of `AttApp` in a TEE. We describe this model in this section.

In order to allow diverse TEE implementations to host `AttApp`, we assume minimal I/O interaction capabilities between `AttApp` and orchestration applications. Concretely, we solely expect a reliable, ordered communication channel with `AttApp` which enables bidirectional communication. We do not assume any other form of connectivity (such as internet connectivity), a data persistence mechanism or an (accurate) clock. To accommodate smaller buffer sizes, we also assume available buffer space of up to 2 KiB.

Similar to ISO 7816-4, we base our protocol on commands dispatched to `AttApp` and responses produced by `AttApp`. A command executes a specific function (deterministically except when randomness is explicitly required). Importantly, the execution happens in the context of a session.

4.3 Application to EAC-Based eID Schemes

In this paper, we select eID based on EAC (such as the German eID solution [3]) as a concrete protocol instantiation for `AttApp`. We explain our approach to attesting authentications based on this particular scheme in this section.

Functions. In the previously defined model, we define the following functions that `AttApp` exposes to its environment:

- **Perform TA:** As the first step in an authentication, `AttApp` performs Terminal Authentication given an ICC's challenge and compressed ephemeral public key from PACE. The environment also supplies a reference date for Document Validity Verification, the operations to be performed by `AttApp` (e.g., through a CHAT) and an External Transaction ID. `AttApp` generates an ephemeral key pair for Chip Authentication and signs the public key together with the reference date for Document Validity Verification as Authenticated Auxiliary Data. This function initializes the session state shared between different functions for this authentication. All inputs as well as computed variables are added to the state. We note that this function creates a unique binding between an ephemeral key pair and an External Transaction ID.
- **Perform CA:** The involved middleware transmits `AttApp`'s signature to the ICC and performs Chip Authentication. With the ICC's *CardSecurity* file, `AttApp` performs Passive Authentication and extracts a certified public key. `AttApp` also performs Chip Authentication with the ICC's nonce and authentication token. The derived session key material is added to the state.
- **Get next command**: This function determines the next command to be sent to the ICC and wraps it for transmission over the Secure Channel established with the ICC. `AttApp` executes this function multiple times during an authentication. We discuss our proposed set of commands and transmission sequence later on. The function updates the state to reflect which commands were already produced.

- **Process response**: For each command produced by `AttApp`, a matching response must be supplied. `AttApp` ensures that each response has a valid Message Authentication Code and indicates the expected status word. The progress is similarly tracked through the state. The state is also augmented by the read out information.
- **Get attestation**: Finally, after all required responses were processed, `AttApp` can issue an attestation based on the session state. First, a serialization of the attestation payload is computed. Then, `AttApp` computes a signature over the serialization. Both artifacts are then forwarded to the initiating RP.

Further functions in this model can be defined to support the extensibility requirement R2.

Command Sequence. The function *Get next command* iteratively prepares the next command to be sent to an ICC over a Secure Channel. However, the behavior of this function is ambiguous since different command configurations and sequence are possible to retrieve the required information from an ICC. We propose the following configuration of commands, presented as to be prepared in the *Get next command* function and sent in sequence:

1. `Select`: Select the eID application.
2. `Verify`: Perform Document Validity Verification with a reference date.
3. `MSE: Set AT`: Prepare execution of Restricted Identification.
4. `General Authenticate`: Retrieve the ICC's Revocation ID.
5. `MSE: Set AT`: Prepare execution of Restricted Identification.
6. `General Authenticate`: Retrieve the ICC's Sector ID.
7. `Read Binary`: For each requested Data Group, read out its contents. For standard Data Groups, selection through a Short File ID is possible and an explicit `Select` is not necessary. Furthermore, most Data Groups are expected to fit into an ICC's APDU buffer and only one `Read Binary` command is required per Data Group.

Attestation Contents. Upon conclusion of an authentication, the command *Get attestation* prepares and signs an attestation. In addition to the general information for inclusion in an attestation, we propose the following protocol-specific information to be included:

1. **Document Validity Verification reference date:** This is the date for which the involved ICC reported being valid.
2. **`AttApp`'s ephemeral public key:** Since an ephemeral key pair is generated for each authentication (each Terminal Authentication challenge is unique to a protocol run), the public key can be used as a unique transaction ID.
3. **ICC static public key:** This public key allows RPs to perform Passive Authentication.
4. **Revocation ID:** This ID enables RPs to check an ICC's revocation status.
5. **Sector ID and DGs:** All the personal information requested by an RP should also be protected by the attestation.

5 AttApp on an ICC

We require a TEE for the execution of AttApp in order to protect the integrity of the attestation logic and the confidentiality of the needed key material. Programmable ICCs represent, in our opinion, a form factor of special interest for highly decentralized TEEs. For this reason, we focus our investigation on the use of an ICC as a TEE for AttApp. We argue that TEEs in general-purpose chipsets fit the functional profile of ICCs. Consequently, focusing on ICCs as a TEE should not restrict the generality of our approach. In this section, we provide considerations needed for mapping our concept from Sect. 4 to an application on a security microcontroller.

Limited RAM. Since an applet cannot use the comparatively large persistent memory during runtime (due to memory wear in flash storage), the session information of all authentication handled by the applet must be stored in RAM. However, only very limited RAM is available to applets on current ICCs. To nevertheless enable AttApp to process multiple sessions at the same time, we propose an auxiliary mechanism for exporting a session's state. Each instance of AttApp should generate a set of non-exportable, symmetric encryption and message authentication keys during applet initialization. When a session's state is to be exported, AttApp can serialize it, encrypt the result and authenticate the ciphertext. To then install exported state to AttApp, the process is reversed. By using instance-specific keys, we bind an exported state to its instance of origin.

Reference Date Tampering. ICCs do not have an independent source of power and therefore do not maintain a clock. To prevent back dating of the reference date for Document Validity Verification, AttApp must persist every new date passed to it and ensure that it is after the last known persisted date. In the other direction, in order to mitigate the risk of an operator supplying a date in the future, we propose an approach based on attestation linking. Each attestation should contain a digest over the previous issued attestation. The operator of AttApp can provide a history of all issued attestation as proof of correct operation.

Batch Processing. No command in the proposed configuration and sequence (see Sect. 4.3) requires feedback from an ICC's response. Hence, all commands can be prepared in a single run (by increasing the Send Sequence Number by 2 for each command) and sent in a single round trip to the middleware. In this work, we suggest such batch processing to prevent excessive state changes.

Trust Management. ICCs typically operate in untrusted environments following a trusted initialization process. We propose the reuse of existing, ICC-related infrastructure and policies for AttApp. In this way, AttApp can benefit from tighter security bounds concerning the trust management through the use of well-established and mature practices. For example, PACE-PP [1] is a relevant Common Criteria Protection Profile. Specific to AttApp's functionality, we expect that providers of ICCs hosting an `AttApp` instance generate the attestation key material on-device and certify the public part during a trusted initialization procedure. The trust anchors of such providers can be later distributed through a metadata service.

6 Implementation

To prove the feasibility of our construction and to use as a basis for performance measurements, we implemented `AttApp` as a smart card applet. In this section, we shortly report on our implementation.

We target JavaCard version 3.0.5 as this is the first version to provide native support for CMAC and German identity documents currently deploy Secure Messaging with CMAC for authentication [3]. Our applet exclusively uses one-shot implementations of cryptographic primitives, where available. They avoid writing state to persistent memory which is of great importance for durability. We also exclusively use operations utilizing the RAM (such as transient arrays) for processing commands.

During applet installation (i.e., in the constructor of the applet class), we instantiate and initialize all cryptographic mechanisms used during runtime in order to enable reuse. We also generate an attestation key pair and symmetric keys for encryption and authentication of exported state.

Our implementation only supports the set of cipher suites (including domain parameters) currently used in German eID-capable cards. We initialize `AttApp` with BrainpoolP256r1 domain parameters. For both Terminal Authentication and Chip Authentication we support version 2 of the protocols. `AttApp` supports Secure Messaging with AES-128 and CMAC. We note that the applet is subject to extension without loss of generality.

For the attestation, we use CBOR as a compact format for data serialization. CBOR allows for indefinite lengths of maps and arrays which enable us to not count bytes when serializing an attestation. We sign the serialized attestation using ECDSA with the attestation key generated during initialization.

7 Security Evaluation

Our motivation for the use an attestation mechanism reflects the fact that other business processes rely on the result of authentications, emphasizing the need for a trustworthy authentication process. In this section, we provide arguments for the security of our construction. We first define a set of security goals in Sect. 7.1 and later discuss to which extent our design meets these goals in Sect. 7.2.

7.1 Security Goals

We already outlined an attacker's goals in Sect. 3. Based on these high-level goals, we define a refined set of requirements that also reflect our design decisions.

1. **Data integrity:** An attacker cannot obtain an attestation over attacker-supplied data.
2. **Temporal context:** An attacker should not be able to change the temporal context of an authentication by changing an attestation's date to the past or the future.
3. **Consistent state installation:** An attacker cannot mix-and-match data from different authentication sessions. We define this goal in response to `AttApp`'s functionality to export from and install authentication state.
4. **DoS protection:** The construction should provide Denial of Service (DoS) mitigations by design. The use a specialized hardware for the TEE enables an attacker controlling the orchestration to perform DoS attacks by blocking access to the TEE. We therefore focus on remote DoS attacks.
5. **Ephemeral key reuse:** An attacker cannot obtain two distinct attestations claiming the same ephemeral public key. When this goal is met, the ephemeral public key in an attestation can serve as a unique identifier (ticket) for an authentication to RP business application.

7.2 Fulfillment of Security Goals

Given our security goals, we now proceed with arguments of their fulfillment.

Data Integrity. To show that the integrity of attested data is guaranteed, we need to show that (i) an attacker cannot tamper with a Secure Channel with an eID Token and that (ii) the usage of the attestation key is controlled.

`AttApp` terminates the Secure Channel with an eID Token through a set of functions executed within a TEE. Based on our Assumption T2, the execution environment ensures the confidentiality of processed data. Hence, no sensitive key material is accessible to an attacker and an attacker cannot forge ICC responses with key material obtained from `AttApp`. An `AttApp` instance's attestation key is similarly used from a function executed within a TEE. With confidentiality provided by the TEE, an attacker cannot extract this key from the instance.

The integrity guarantees from Assumption T2 further ensure that an attacker cannot tamper with the data in memory (including the read out data) or program logic. In combination with the Assumption T1 that `AttApp` implements the correct logic, an attacker cannot obtain an attestation for data not originating from logic in `AttApp`.

It follows that the integrity of the attested data is guaranteed throughout the authentication and issuance process.

DoS Protection. We consider two DoS attacks: (i) an attacker blocking `AttApp` by not completing a valid authentication and (ii) an attacker initiating many authentication attempts without a valid eID Token (resource exhaustion).

Our design, through the capability for exporting a session's state, provides (partial) mitigation to both attacks. `AttApp`'s orchestrator can remove an attacker's blocking session after any function execution, completely mitigating the first attack. The state export mechanism also enables parallel processing of many authentication attempts. However, the trusted hardware providing the

TEE still represents a bottleneck. The limited computational resources on an ICC can lead to a severe service degradation with many parallel authentication attempts. Our design therefore considers a mitigation to the second attack but is fundamentally vulnerable to load-based DoS attacks.

Ephemeral Key Reuse. `AttApp` generates an ephemeral key and a Terminal Authentication signature in an atomic function. TA signatures require a challenge from an ICC. A generated ephemeral key is therefore bound to a single challenge through the Terminal Authentication signature given the signing key's confidentiality.

Assuming a compliant implementation, eID Tokens generate a random challenge for each execution of Terminal Authentication. Hence, an attacker cannot use an existing ephemeral key unless an attacker can find an ephemeral key generated for the same challenge. Currently, BSI TR-03110 [2] mandates 64-bit challenges, resulting in a $1/2^{64}$ probability of finding a collision.

Consistent State Installation. The functions defined in Sect. 4.3 represent atomic operations in our construction. Hence, state can be restored only between execution of these function. We further propose a grouping of (i) the Chip Authentication execution function and the command preparation functions as well as of the (ii) response processing functions and the attestation function. If `AttApp` enforces this grouping of functions technically, a restore is only possible before performing Chip Authentication and before processing an ICC's responses in a session. TA and Chip Authentication are linked through the Terminal's ephemeral key material. We have shown that an ephemeral key pair cannot be reused for a second authentication. Therefore, an attacker cannot mix session states. Prior to the second attack window, Chip Authentication establishes a Secure Channel that is unique to an ICC (through the ICC's nonce). This prevents the association of an ICC's responses with a session different from the session that initialized the Chip Authentication function.

Temporal Context. An attacker can record a session's exported state and replay it at a later point in time. We use the reference date for Document Validity Verification as a main mitigation to prevent the issuance of attestations for authentication performed in a past temporal phase. Since the reference date for Document Validity Verification is protected through the Terminal Authentication signature, the same argument as for the Terminal's ephemeral key applies to the reference date. Consequently, an attested authentication is bound to a single reference date - the date used at the time of session initiation.

In case `AttApp` has access to a trusted clock (e.g., when executed in an HSM), `AttApp` can ensure that the reference date corresponds to the current date. In this case, attestations can report exact times of initiation and attestation production. As discussed in Sect. 5, we can also ensure that the Document Validity Verification fits in an expected time window even without access to a clock. In this case, `AttApp` achieves a granularity on the level of a calendar date. Through attestation chaining, the granularity can be increased if a sufficient number of trusted authentications are performed as trusted boundaries. Such trusted authentications can be performed regularly by an independent party with proof of execution time.

8 Performance Evaluation

In order to assess the performance of our attestation mechanism in terms of processing delays on an ICC, we performed several experiments. We outline our experiments in Sect. 8.1 and report on our results in Sect. 8.2.

8.1 Experiments

We perform several experiments with a variable number of concurrent authentications handled by an `AttApp` running on a single ICC. Our goal is to assess the suitability of a single ICC for different RP workloads. Concretely, we consider three deployment scenarios - sequential processing as well as processing of 5 and 10 concurrent sessions at any point in time. In the case of sequential processing, a new authentication is performed only after a previous one was terminated. This type of processing should support smaller deployments with mostly discrete authentications. In the case of concurrent sessions, several authentications are active at the same time and we utilize the capability to replace the state of an identification to accommodate to the ICC's native single-threaded processing. This setup targets applications handling larger authentication workloads. We use a constant number of simulated sessions at any point of time.

Simulator. For our tests, we provide a simulation of an eID Token. Each simulated eID instance is personalized during initialization. We do not enforce processing delays expected from an ICC in our simulation in order to also consider virtual eID tokens hosted in the cloud. We also do not consider delays introduced by communication over a network due to the plethora of possible access paths.

Scheduling. For parallel processing, our test driver performs random scheduling between the active authentication sessions based on a pseudo-random number generator. The scheduler can perform a context switch upon completion of each set of non-blocking operations for a session: This approach ensures minimal blocking of the execution due to the single-thread nature of `AttApp`. Upon a context switch, the state of the old session is exported and the state of the new session installed. Once an authentication session is completed, the test driver starts a new simulated session in its place.

Setup. Our test driver is a Java application targeting JDK 17 running on a Raspberry Pi 4 Model B with 8 GB RAM with Ubuntu 22.04.5 as an OS. For interaction with the ICC, the test driver uses the Java Smart Card I/O API. We use the `System.nanoTime()` method to obtain a (relative) timestamp with nanosecond precision. We use a JCOP model J3R180 ICC to execute our attestation application. This ICC provides a JavaCard 3.0.5 runtime environment.

8.2 Results

In this section, we report on the results of our measurements. First, we analyze the end-to-end duration of a simulated eID session for the three deployment scenarios and present our results. Second, we discuss the measurements in the context of `AttApp` intended usage context.

End-to-End Delay. We define the end-to-end processing delay/duration as the time elapsed between a session entering the pool of sessions and the time an attestation for this session is available. Under the assumption that a user receives access to a service upon presentation of an attestation, the user will experience this delay in addition to local (e.g., processing delays on an ICC and PACE) and network overhead. Hence, measurement of the end-to-end processing delay is important to assess the usability of our solution for different workloads.

To analyze this duration, we simulate at least 1000 sessions for each deployment scenario. Figure 2 depicts our measurements for sequential processing as well as parallel processing of 5 and 10 sessions as a violin plot diagram.

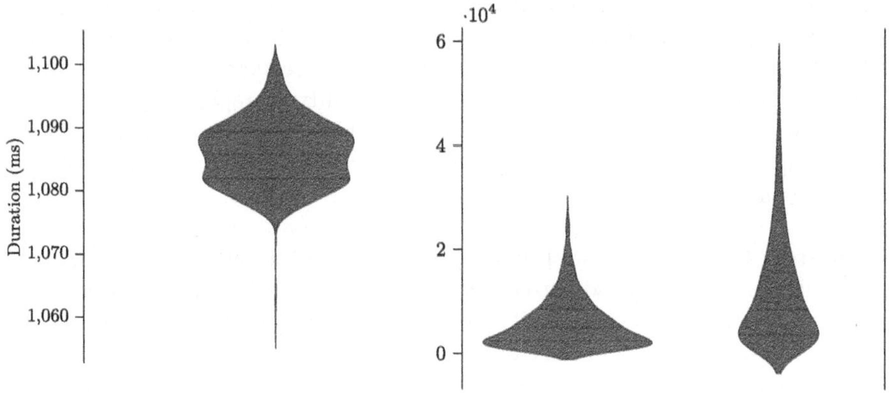

Fig. 2. Violin plot representing the measured end-to-end delay for sequential processing (left) as well as parallel processing of 5 (middle) and 10 (right) sessions, respectively, 99th percentile.

With sequential processing, 75% of the sessions can be completed within 1 s and 90 milliseconds. In contrast, processing of 5 and 10 parallel sessions requires significantly more time for completion. Processing of 5 parallel sessions takes 2.4 s in the 25th percentile and 8.5 s in the 75th percentile, with a 99th percentile of 27.8 s. Processing of 10 parallel sessions takes 3.6 s in the 25th percentile and 17 s in the 75th percentile. In 6.4% of the cases, however, processing can take more than 30 s.

Discussion. Holders of ICC-based eID token must maintain contact between the ICC and their NFC-enabled device until all responses are returned by the ICC. We argue that our measurements for the processing of 10 parallel sessions break the psychological barrier for usage of an authentication method of average users.

We performed our measurements on a single ICC. Based on the obtained results, we argue that certain RPs can use a single ICC for 5 or less parallel sessions. Specifically, we estimate that this throughput addresses the needs of small and medium organizations. We also note that these results reflect constant utilization. In reality, for such organizations, varying utilization in time with individual peaks is anticipated.

A cluster of ICCs with individual scheduling could handle the workloads of larger deployments. For a description of a possible cluster setup, we refer to the work of Pascal Urien [17]. Due to the relatively low cost of ICCs (e.g., compared to HSMs), a cluster solution is also accessible to small organizations.

When considerably higher throughput is required, an HSM may be an appropriate alternative to ICCs. HSMs similarly provide a specialized environment protecting the storage and usage of cryptographic key material. In this case, the logic of `AttApp` could be implemented as a custom firmware extension. We were not able to perform measurements on an HSM due to licensing issues.

Overall, we show that implementing `AttApp` on an ICC is feasible. For smaller workloads, a single ICC is sufficient. Especially for sequential processing, we measure a delay that is negligible in the context of user authentication. A cost-effective cluster solution could handle a larger number of parallel sessions. These results support our goal for a decentralized deployment of `AttApp` - each instance can handle local authentications and setting up an instance is highly accessible.

9 Related Work

To the best of our knowledge, there is no other work directly related to attesting eID schemes based on an AKE+SC construction using an ICC. In this section, we provide an overview of works related to our goals and methodology.

The German implementation of eID based on EAC [3] uses standardized interfaces for communication between the subsystems involved in an authentication. One such subsystem implements the authentication-related functionality on an RP's side. BSI TR-03130 [4] encapsulates this functionality in a component called an eID Server. RP business applications can interact with an eID Server through two well-defined interfaces - an *eID Interface*, based on SOAP, and SAML. Importantly, for both protocols, the eID Servers applies a signature over the result of an authentication. The resulting signed messages are functionally equivalent to an attestation in the context of this paper. However, we argue that the reliability of there messages is limited due to the environment they were created in. eID Servers require, as a minimum, a TLS stack, an HTTP stack, an XML library with support for digital signatures and an implementation of EAC. These components introduce complexity and increase the attack surface significantly - even if an eID Server is executed in a TEE. Instead, our approach is limited to EAC as the core authentication protocol. In addition, without a TEE and on-device key generation (that are a core part of the design of `AttApp`), the use of an eID Server's attestation key is not constrained on a technical level. Hence, an attacker could issue false attestations only given control of the attestation key.

Schwarz et al. [15] propose the use of eMRTDs as a possession factor in a Web Authentication setting. Their construction, *FeIDo*, uses an application operated in a TEE to derive a credential. This application uses the personal information obtained from an eMRTD and a long-lived key for the derivation process. In order to ensure the authenticity, the TEE-hosted application performs Passive and Chip Authentication with eMRTDs. *FeIDo* and `AttApp` are similar in that they both implement EAC and use a TEE as a security foundation. Apart from the different goals of our works, we note one significant technical difference - eMRTDs use EAC version 1 while eID uses EAC version 2. *FeIDo* does not perform Terminal Authentication, leading to a fundamentally different security model. Furthermore, we investigate the use of an ICC as a TEE for `AttApp`, while Schwarz et al. discuss Intel SGX.

TLSnotary is a project enabling users to obtain proof that a TLS server has sent specific data over a TLS-protected channel [16]. In *TLSnotary*'s operational model, a *prover* and a *verifier* share a TLS client's session key material and must cooperate to send and receive data over a TLS channel with a server. On a cryptographic level, this cooperation is realized through Secure Multi-Party Computation. The *prover* can prove properties on the session's plaintext to the *verifier* and the *prover* can use a trusted party, a *Notary*, to receive a signature for the plaintext's provenance. For the purposes of *post factum*, offline auditability targeted by our work, we assume an interactive *verifier* infeasible. On the other side, we assume a deployment with a *Notary* an alternative to our attestation mechanism. Our goal, however, is to achieve security based on hardware guarantees. Implementing the *Notary* in a TEE to protect the usage of the notarization private key represents a subject of possible future work.

BSI TR-03130 [4] specifies an extension enabling eID Servers to transmit a custom attestation statement. In a setup in which an `AttApp` complements an eID Server by terminating Secure Channels, an attestation statement produced by `AttApp` can be transmitted to an eService through this extension. Governikus proposes an attestation format based on JWT [9]. While this format could be used for `AttApp`, JSON and JWT introduce a large overhead for an ICC. We note that Governikus only proposes the format, while `AttApp` also provides the means to produce an attestation statement in a trustworthy manner.

We provide a comparison of `AttApp` with selected related work in Table 1. *TLSnotary* uses computationally intensive operations and does not scale as well as classical solutions. TEEs based on general-purpose chipsets may require protections against "lab attacks" or timing attacks, preventing a deployment in a completely untrusted environment. We consider the local deployment costs for BSI TR-03130 and *TLSnotary* to be high as providers require a server with a specific chipset.

Table 1. Comparison with related work

	AttApp	BSI TR-03130	*FeIDo*	*TLSnotary*
Target	EAC v2	EAC v2	EAC v1	TLS
Protocol stacks in TCB	EAC	EAC, TLS, HTTP, XML, XML-DSig	EAC, FIDO	TLS
Scalability	Low	High	High	Medium
Required environment	Untrusted	Somewhat Trusted	Somewhat Trusted	Untrusted
Local deployment costs	Low	High	High	Medium
Confidence in confidentiality protections	High	Medium	Medium	N/A

10 Conclusion

The paper introduces `AttApp` - a secure solution for attesting Electronic Identification (eID) for protocol schemes based on Secure Channels, addressing the increasing need for reliable identity verification in digital transactions. `AttApp` employs a Trusted Execution Environment (TEE) to ensure the integrity and confidentiality of the attestation process and can be implemented on resource-constrained security microcontrollers, facilitating adoption in a distributed deployment. A JavaCard applet demonstrates the feasibility of this approach on widely used Integrated Circuit Cards (ICCs).

The security evaluation of `AttApp` confirms the successful mitigation of Denial of Service attacks and that the integrity of the data in attestations is guaranteed. Furthermore, we show that an implementation of `AttApp` on a commercially available ICC suffices to meet the needs of small-to-medium setups.

In conclusion, `AttApp` provides a practical and secure method for attesting eID authentications. The TEE ensures attestation integrity and confidentiality and the JavaCard implementation demonstrates feasibility on ICCs. The design addresses potential DoS attacks and performance evaluations offer insights for real-world applications and potential optimizations.

Acknowledgements. This work was supported by the EU Horizon Europe programme, projects SLICES-PP (10107977) and GreenDIGIT (101131207), by the German Federal Ministry of Education and Research (BMBF), projects 6G-life (16KISK002) and 6G-ANNA (16KISK107), by the German Research Foundation, project HyperNIC (CA595/13-1), and by the Bavarian Ministry of Economic Affairs, Regional Development and Energy, project 6G Future Lab Bavaria.

References

1. Machine Readable Travel Document using Standard Inspection Procedure with PACE (PACE PP), BSI-CC-PP-0068-V2-2011. Protection profile, Federal Office for Information Security, Bonn, DE (2011)
2. Technical Guideline TR-03110 - Advanced Security Mechanisms for Machine Readable Travel Documents and eIDAS Token. Technical guideline, Federal Office for Information Security, Bonn, DE (2016)
3. Technical Guideline TR-03127 - eID-Karten mit eID- und eSign-Anwendung basierend auf Extended Access Control. Technical guideline, Federal Office for Information Security, Bonn, DE (2020)
4. Technical Guideline TR-03130 - eID-Server. Technical guideline, Federal Office for Information Security, Bonn, DE (2020)
5. FIPS 201-3 - Personal Identity Verification (PIV) of Federal Employees and Contractors. Federal information processing standards publication, National Institute of Standards and Technology (2022)
6. Blake Hall: How AI-driven fraud challenges the global economy and ways to combat it. World Economic Forum Annual Meeting (2025). https://www.weforum.org/stories/2025/01/how-ai-driven-fraud-challenges-the-global-economy-and-ways-to-combat-it/. Accessed 8 Mar 2025
7. Bundesministerium des Innern und für Heimat: Diensteanbieter werden (2025). https://www.personalausweisportal.de/SharedDocs/faqs/Webs/PA/DE/Dienstanbieter-werden/Diensteanbieter-werden.html. Accessed 8 Mar 2025
8. Dagdelen, Ö.: The cryptographic security of the german electronic identity card. Ph.D. thesis, Technische Universität, Darmstadt (2013)
9. Governikus GmbH & Co. KG: JSON-Schema for a special identification report. https://github.com/Governikus/IdentificationReport. Accessed 8 Mar 2025
10. Lonvick, C.M., Ylonen, T.: The Secure Shell (SSH) Authentication Protocol. RFC 4252 (2006). https://www.rfc-editor.org/info/rfc4252
11. Office of the Federal Register: Code of Federal Regulations - Title 31 (2025). https://www.ecfr.gov/current/title-31. Accessed 8 Mar 2025
12. Police and Border Guard Board, Republic of Estonia: Estonian eID scheme: ID card (2019). https://ec.europa.eu/digital-building-blocks/sites/display/EIDCOMMUNITY/Estonia?preview=/62885749/218763054/EE%20eID%20LoA%20mapping%20-%20ID%20card%20v1.1.pdf. Accessed 8 Mar 2025
13. Rescorla, E.: The Transport Layer Security (TLS) Protocol Version 1.3. RFC 8446, RFC Editor, August 2018
14. Rjako, M., Stanek, M.: On designated verifier signature schemes. Cryptology ePrint Archive, Paper 2010/191 (2010). https://eprint.iacr.org/2010/191
15. Schwarz, F., Do, K., Heide, G., Hanzlik, L., Rossow, C.: FeiDo: recoverable FIDO2 tokens using electronic IDs. In: Proceedings of the 2022 ACM SIGSAC Conference on Computer and Communications Security, CCS 2022, pp. 2581–2594. Association for Computing Machinery, New York, NY, USA (2022)
16. TLSNotary: TLSNotary Documentation created with mdBook. https://github.com/tlsnotary/docs-mdbook. Accessed 8 Mar 2025
17. Urien, P.: Demonstration of performance for low cost personal HSM. In: 2023 IEEE 20th Consumer Communications & Networking Conference (CCNC), pp. 879–880 (2023)

A High-Level-of-Assurance EUDI Wallet with a Remote WSCD Supporting Biometrics and Passkeys

Claudia Franco(✉), Carlos Lancha, Daniel Flores, Rosario Arjona, and Iluminada Baturone

Instituto de Microelectrónica de Sevilla (IMSE-CNM), University of Seville-CSIC, Seville, Spain
{cfranco,clancha,marjona,lumi}@us.es, danflode@alum.us.es

Abstract. The European Digital Identity (EUDI) Wallet is a user-controlled digital environment that is being developed to be used by all citizens of the European Union. The Architecture and Reference Framework (ARF) of the EUDI Wallet is a set of specifications designed to ensure their interoperability and security. Among specifications, a Wallet Secure Cryptographic Device (WSCD) with a high Level of Assurance must be used. A high LoA is achieved through the multifactor authentication of the Wallet User and the use of secure hardware for implementing the needed cryptographic and biometric algorithms. Also, EUDI Wallets should include a functionality to generate and manage user-chosen pseudonyms, to authenticate Users when accessing online services. This paper describes a high LoA EUDI Wallet using a remote WSCD, which is the most inclusive, user-friendly and scalable type of WSCD. User authentication is done through something you know (a password), something you have (a smartphone), and who you are (with facial biometrics). As secure hardware for the remote WSCD, we use an Intel SGX enclave. The WSCD allows the generation and management of Passkeys, which are a kind of pseudonyms following the W3C WebAuthn specification. A demonstrator has been developed using a Samsung Galaxy A52 as User device with the Wallet Instance, and a laptop with an Intel® Core ™ i7-10750H at 2.60 GHz and 16 GB RAM with Ubuntu 20.04.6 LTS, Intel SGX1 and disabled hyper-threading to implement the remote WSCD. The experimental results show that the WSCD needs 128MB of RAM and takes 374.2 ms to be bound to a User, 375.2 ms to authenticate the User and create a new Passkey, and 373.8 ms to authenticate the User and sign with an already existing Passkey.

Keywords: Digital Identity Wallets · Multifactor Authentication · Biometrics · Hardware Secure Module · Intel SGX · Passkeys

1 Introduction

The European Digital Identity (EUDI) Wallet is a secure, user-controlled digital environment that will enable Users to manage and present their Person Identification Data (PID) and attestation of attributes to public and private services in the European Union (EU)

B. Coppens et al. (Eds.): ARES 2025 Workshops, LNCS 15997, pp. 93–110, 2025.
https://doi.org/10.1007/978-3-032-00639-4_6

[1]. The Wallet Unit obtains PID/attestation of attributes from PID/attestation providers. The Relying Parties are entities such as businesses, government agencies, or service providers that need to authenticate Users securely. The Wallet can be used to register the User to different Relying Parties and/or present PID/attestations to said Relying Parties. Member States will have to offer their citizens a Wallet solution, and public and private services will be mandated to recognize the Wallet as a valid identification method [2].

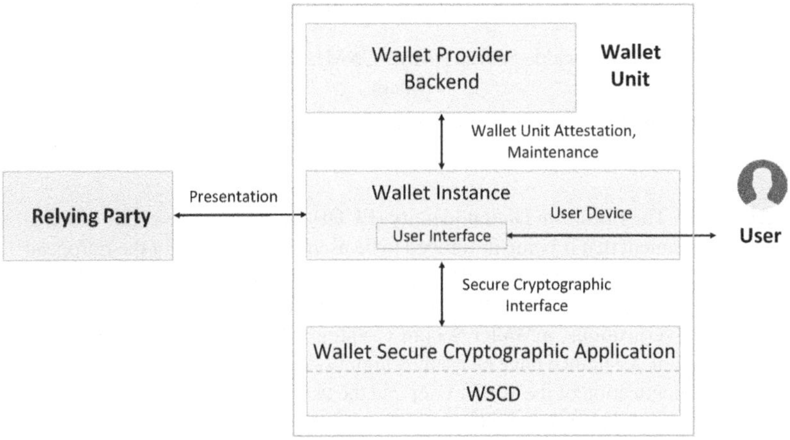

Fig. 1. High-level architecture of the EUDI Wallet

The Architecture and Reference Framework (ARF) explains the architecture of the EUDI Wallet ecosystem and all its components, as well as how these components interact with each other. The goal of ARF is to create uniform conditions for the implementation of the EUDI Wallet throughout Europe [1]. One of the conditions is that the Wallet must achieve a high Level of Assurance (LoA), which refers to the degree of confidence in the claimed identity of a person [3]. A high LoA is achieved, among other factors, by using secure hardware for key management, sensitive data and cryptographic functions and implementing multi-factor authentication [4], which means using more than one factor when authenticating the User. The different authentication factors are what the User has (device possession), what the User knows (password) and who the User is (biometrics).

The high-level architecture of the EUDI Wallet is shown in Fig. 1. The Wallet Unit is formed by: the Wallet Instance, that is, the App or browser running inside the User device (which is typically a mobile phone); the Wallet Secure Cryptographic Device (WSCD), that is, a secure hardware element that stores cryptographic keys, sensitive data and performs cryptographic functions in a secure environment; the Wallet Secure Cryptographic Application, that is, an application that manages the functions inside the WSCD and connects the WSCD with the Wallet Instance; and the Wallet Provider Backend, responsible for offering support to Users, performing maintenance and issuing Wallet Unit Attestations that define the properties of that specific Wallet solution [1]. The Wallet Provider is also responsible for attesting the correctness of the WSCD and ensuring that all users have access to a WSCD secure enough to achieve a high LoA.

The ARF considers several WSCD architectures: native, local internal, local external and remote [1]. A native WSCD is hardware belonging to the User device, such as processors with ARM TrustZone or the iPhone's Secure Enclave. A local internal WSCD is hardware within a User device, such as an eSE (embedded Secure Element) or SIM card. A local external WSCD is a device outside the User device but connected by a short-ranged connection like NFC or Bluetooth. A remote WSCD is generally achieved by a Hardware Secure Module (HSM) in a remote server. Also, a hybrid model combining different types is also accepted as a solution.

A WSCD should be scalable (easily deployed and implemented), inclusive (accessible to Users with old or low-end smartphones), and user-friendly (comfortably integrated into the User experience) [5]. Native WSCDs are very user-friendly because they are already integrated into the device, but they are not scalable or inclusive. A study [6] on the Italian market revealed that only 10.5% of mobile phones had a certified native solution secure enough for the EUDI Wallet requirements. Local internal WSCDs are not easily scalable because the development of applications for them is restricted and controlled by the device manufacturer or issuer [7]. Local external solutions can be problematic regarding user-friendliness since they require Users to buy and carry a new secure token, such as a smart card or a USB key. Hence, we focus in this paper on remote WSCDs, because they are inclusive (they do not depend on the User device hardware), easy to use (they do not change the interface between the User and the Wallet), and easily scalable, as they are a cloud-based service.

Relying Parties should not be able to identify the User unless it is necessary for their services. One of the functionalities of the Wallet established on the ARF is the generation and use of pseudonyms for authentication [1]. Pseudonyms avoid malicious Relying Parties from tracking the interactions of a User with multiple Relying Parties, which could lead to an identification of the User. The WebAuthn API for Public Key Credentials by W3C [8] defines the technical specifications for Passkeys, which are a type of pseudonyms. Passkeys are public-private key pairs created when registering a User into a new service and used for authentication. During the registration phase, the User generates a new key pair, stores it in a secure device and sends the public key to the Relying Party. In the authentication phase, the Relying Party sends a challenge to the User, who uses the private key stored at registration to sign the challenge and sends it back to the Relying Party. If the Relying Party verifies the signature correctly with the public key saved at registration, the User is considered authenticated.

The secure device used to manage the User's Passkeys is called an authenticator by the WebAuthn API. Before the introduction of Passkeys and pseudonyms in the ARF, the use of FIDO Authenticators (authenticators manufactured or certified by the FIDO Alliance) were already proposed as a solution for the EUDI Wallet [9]. The FIDO Alliance also published a whitepaper on the use of FIDO Authenticators and WebAuthn in the Wallet [10]. FIDO Authenticators are mostly native or local internal or external [11]. In the context of the EUDI Wallet, the authenticator is the WSCD. Before using a Passkey saved on the WSCD, the WSCD needs to authenticate the User [1].

In this paper we present the implementation of a high-LoA EUDI Wallet with a remote WSCD, following the specifications of the ARF. The WSCD, exploiting the hardware security of the Intel SGX Trusted Execution Environment, authenticates the

User by device possession, password knowledge, and facial biometrics. Hence, the User's identity is securely linked to their digital Wallet, which is known as User binding. Also, the WSCD generates and manages Passkeys securely, allowing the User registration and authentication in several Relying Parties, without revealing their identity. We constructed an example implementation using an Android phone, a Relying Party server and an Intel SGX enclave running on a desktop. The experimental results obtained show that it is a feasible solution.

The paper is structured as follows. In Sect. 2 the necessary background about Passkeys and Intel SGX is introduced. Section 3 explains the implementation proposed, describing the protocols between the Wallet Instance and the WSCD for User binding and between the Wallet Unit and the Relying Parties for User registration and authentication using Passkeys. Section 4 presents the demonstrator constructed and the experimental results. Finally, Sect. 5 concludes our work.

2 Background

2.1 WebAuthn API for Public Key Credentials

The WebAuthn API for Public Key Credentials [8] defines the use and lifecycle of Passkeys. Four different parties are defined. Following the nomenclature used in the ARF [1], the parties are:

- Relying Party Server: the Relying Party that wishes to offer a service for which it needs to authenticate the User.
- Relying Party Client: program that runs in the Client of the User (at the User device) and communicates with the Relying Party Server.
- Client: the client that the User uses to interact with the Relying Party client and with the Authenticator. In the EUDI Wallet, this is part of the Wallet Instance at the User device.
- Authenticator: secure environment or device controlled by the User to create, store and manage Passkeys. In the EUDI Wallet, it is the WSCD.

The WebAuthn API establishes a model defining the responsibilities or actions of every party, without defining how the Authenticator and Client must communicate. The WebAuthn API defines multiple IDs that are necessary so that the protocol works:

- Relying Party ID (RP ID): a unique identifier for the Relying Party. The Authenticator will learn which Relying Party is asking for authentication and if a Passkey exists for said Relying Party.
- Credential ID: a unique identifier for each Passkey.
- User ID: a unique identifier for each User and Relying Party, assigned by the Relying Party and provided to the Authenticator. The Authenticator will keep track of the User IDs for each Relying Party.
- User Name: an alias assigned to a specific User ID. It allows the User to easily decide which Passkey to use.

To ensure that the Authenticator has created and saved the Passkeys during registration, an attestation of the attributes of the Authenticator can be included. In the WebAuthn API there are multiple types of attestations mentioned:

- Basic Attestation: the Authenticator stores an Attestation key pair and employs it to sign every newly created public Passkey. A certificate on the Attestation key is included in every registration. To avoid tracking by malicious Relying Parties, multiple Authenticators should have the same attestation keys (for example, the same models by a certain manufacturer would have the same attestation keys and certificates).
- Attestation CA: the Authenticator stores a master key pair and uses them to communicate with a Certification Authority (CA). This CA would issue certificates on multiple attestation key pairs. A malicious Relying Party could partially track the movements of the Passkeys that used the same attestation key.
- Anonymization CA: same as the Attestation CA but the CA certificates a new Attestation key pair every time a Passkey is generated. Only the CA that certifies the Authenticator could track the User movements.
- Self Attestation: the attestation is signed with the private key of the new Passkey pair. This does not give any guarantees to the Relying Party that a valid Authenticator is being used.
- No Attestation: no attestation is presented. This does not give any guarantees either to the Relying Party.

Given the security properties of the EUDI Wallet, Self Attestation and No Attestation are not valid options for the WSCD.

2.2 Intel SGX

Intel SGX (Software Guard Extensions) is a Trusted Execution Environment (TEE) included in some Intel processors. It creates secure containers called enclaves that provide integrity and confidentiality to all code and data inside, protecting its contents from the rest of the server/desktop [12]. A measurement hash of all the code and data loaded into the enclave during its creation is calculated and used for future identification/attestation of the enclave.

Two secrets are embedded into the processor using efuses, a type of One Time Programmable (OTP) memory. These secrets are used together with the enclave measurement hash to derive unique Enclave Sealing Keys (k_{Seal}) for each enclave.

Attestation of the platform and code is performed to ensure a remote party that it is communicating with the correct enclave. An attestation report containing the enclave's measurement hash is signed with an SGX Attestation Key and sent to the remote party. The SGX Attestation Key is verified by a chain of certificates, including an Intel signature [12].

To securely communicate with the enclave and send private data, a Transport Layer Security (TLS) handshake can be performed [13]. TLS is an industry standard for secure communications. TLS allows for the authentication of one or both parties by exchanging X.509 certificates that include the public TLS key of one party and are signed by a Certification Authority [13]. It protects the integrity and confidentiality of the data by establishing a common symmetric session key between the two parties with a protocol called TLS handshake. Enclaves can perform a TLS with a remote party for secure loading of secret information.

Figure 2 shows an overview of a TLS handshake between a remote party and an enclave. First, the remote party sends a "ClientHello" which includes a random nonce. The server answers with a "ServerHello" (similar to the ClientHello) and its X.509 certificate. The remote party encrypts a secret with the public key ($TLSpk$) included in the certificate and sends it to the server. The enclave is the only party that can decrypt said secret. Lastly, both enclave and remote party compute a session key (K) from both random nonces and the last sent secret. All future messages in the session will be sent encrypted with K [13].

RA-TLS [13] is a type of TLS that includes the attestation report of an enclave in the X.509 certificate. The attestation report includes the public TLS key which ensures to the other party that the keys were created inside the enclave. To verify an attestation report, Intel offers quote libraries [14] which are not compatible with some architectures of mobile processors.

Although several vulnerabilities of Intel SGX security have been discovered throughout the years [15], such as side-channel attacks that extract private data by studying timing information, power consumption, instruction counts, etc., several measures have also been given to avoid them, such as disabling hyper-threading on the processor, using memory safe languages, updating Intel SGX microcode (that provides patches to certain attacks) and using external libraries with no known vulnerabilities.

3 Proposed Scheme

We propose the use of an enclave to host remote WSCDs in a remote server. The enclave has an Enclave Sealing key (k_{Seal}) from which the WSCD of the User would derive a unique Sealing key (Wk_{Seal}), ensuring that no User can access another User's WSCD. The private data saved on the WSCD, such as the Passkeys ($PASSpk$, $PASSsk$) or enrolment data, are encrypted with the WSCD Sealing key and saved in the long-term memory of the remote server.

A multi-factor authentication scheme is used by the WSCD to authenticate the User before doing any cryptographic operation. The authentication is based on what the User knows (a password), what the User has (a secret key stored inside the mobile device) and who the User is (face biometrics). Once the WSCD authenticates the User, the User can employ the EUDI Wallet to enroll/authenticate in a Relying Party using the Passkeys created and stored at the WSCD.

The Wallet Provider is responsible for attesting the WSCD (as indicated in the EUDI Wallet ARF). Since the User mobile device cannot verify an Intel attestation report, we propose that the Wallet Provider acts as a Certification Authority and provides the enclave with a signed TLS certificate.

A secure communication channel is established between the Wallet Instance at the User device and the remote WSCD by a TLS handshake. Sensitive data are sent to the enclave encrypted with the ephemeral session key (K) and decrypted inside. Since all the data inside an enclave is confidential, the enclave can handle it as plaintext without the remote server seeing or learning any information. The authentication information (such as the face image, the password or the mobile device secret) is deleted at the end of the protocol. Since the enclave cannot deviate from the code loaded at creation, it cannot act maliciously and save any private information.

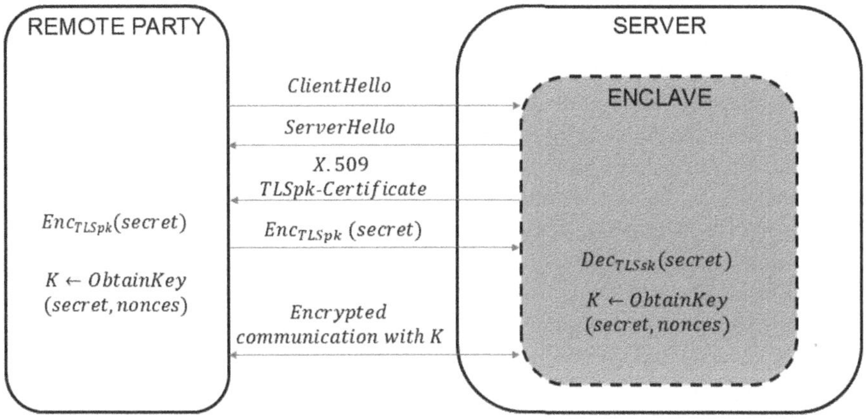

Fig. 2. TLS handshake between an enclave and a remote party

The Wallet Provider also signs a certificate for the Passkey Attestation Keys (*ATTpk*, *ATTsk*) created inside the enclave. Since multiple WSCDs are handled by the same enclave, the Attestation is based on Basic Attestation. These Attestation Keys are different from the SGX Attestation Key mentioned in Sect. 2; while SGX Attestation Keys are certified by Intel, our Attestation Keys are certified by the Wallet Provider (because they attest the WSCDs of the provided wallets).

Table 1 shows the keys used on the WSCD.

Table 1. Keys used on the WSCD

Key	Key Function
Enclave Sealing Key (k_{Seal})	Sealing key of the Intel SGX Enclave based on the enclave measurement hash
WSCD Sealing Key (Wk_{Seal})	Sealing key of a specific WSCD, derived from the Enclave Sealing Key and the User secret
SGX Attestation Key Pair (*SGXATTpk*, *SGXATTsk*)	Attestation Key Pair used for attesting the enclave and certified by Intel
Enclave TLS Key Pair (*TLSpk*, *TLSsk*)	Key Pair generated inside the enclave and used to establish a secure communication channel with the User
Ephemeral session Key (K, K_{RP})	Keys established by the TLS handshake to establish a secure communication channel
Passkey Attestation Key Pair (*ATTpk*, *ATTsk*)	Attestation Key Pair used for attesting the WSCD to Relying Parties and certified by the Wallet Provider
Passkey (*PASSpk*, *PASSsk*)	Key pair used to authenticate a User to a Relying Party

3.1 User Binding

When initiating the Wallet, the User needs to establish multiple authentication factors with the WSCD for future multi-factor authentication. We show in Fig. 3 the binding process between the User through the Wallet Instance (inside the User device) and the WSCD. First, a secure communication channel is established between them with a TLS handshake. In the process, the WSCD presents a certificate signed by the Wallet Provider to prove its identity. A secure session key K is established and the following communications are encrypted with said symmetric key K. Then, a new *WalletID* is generated inside the WSCD.

The User device takes a sample of the User face ($sample_E$) for biometric authentication, introduces a password which is hashed ($hpass_E$) for what the User knows, and presents a secret key stored inside the device for possession authentication ($secret_E$). The three factors are encrypted with K and sent to the WSCD. Inside the enclave, the three factors are decrypted and used to create the enrolment data as follows:

1. The $secret_E$ and the Enclave Sealing Key k_{Seal} are used to derive a unique sealing key for the User WSCD, Wk_{Seal}.
2. The binary biometric embeddings are extracted from the face sample $bio_E \leftarrow FeatureExtraction(sample_E)$. Details about this process are given in Sect. 4.
3. The password hash and the binary biometric embeddings are XORed to create the enrolment data $mf_E \leftarrow hpass_E \oplus bio_E$.
4. The enrolment data are symmetrically encrypted with the enclave's sealing key as $\widetilde{mf_E} \leftarrow AES.Enc_{Wk_{Seal}}(mf_E)$. We employ the AES algorithm.

The *WalletID* is sent to the Wallet Instance where it is stored. The WSCD stores the *WalletID* and the encrypted enrolment data $\widetilde{mf_E}$ and deletes all other information: $sample_E, hpass_E, secret_E, Wk_{Seal}, bio_E, mf_E$.

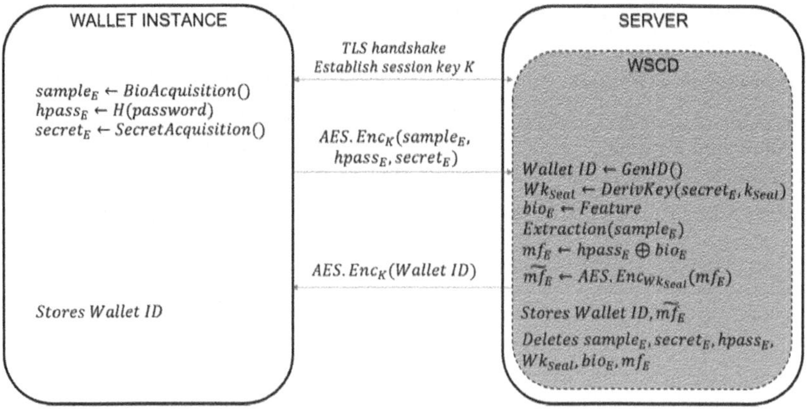

Fig. 3. Protocol between the Wallet Instance and the WSCD for User binding

3.2 User Registration at a Relying Party

When registering for a new Relying Party service, a new Passkey needs to be generated. Figure 4 shows the User registration process with a Relying Party.

First, a secure communication channel is established between the Wallet Instance and the Relying Party; we assume the protocol used is TLS and a session key K'_{RP} is established to encrypt the communications. The Wallet Instance asks to register with a new *UserName* and Passkey. The Relying Party generates a challenge (Ch) and a *UserID* and sends them to the Wallet Instance with its Relying Party ID ($RPID$). Then, the Wallet Instance verifies that the received RP ID corresponds to the RP HTTPS Origin. This ensures no registration/authentication data is communicated to a wrong RP.

To use the WSCD as an Authenticator, the User must be authenticated by the WSCD. Before sending any private data, the Wallet Instance and the WSCD create a secure communication channel using TLS and establish a new ephemeral session key K'. The Wallet Instance acquires a face sample ($sample_A$), performs the password hash ($hpass_A$) and acquires the secret key stored in the device ($secret_A$) and sends them to the WSCD with the *WalletID* encrypted with K'. The Wallet Instance also sends the necessary data for creating the Passkey: $UserID$, $RPID$, Ch and the $UserName$.

The WSCD calculates the multifactor authentication data (mf_A) to compare it with the enrolment data (mf_E). First, the WSCD Sealing Key (Wk_{Seal}) is derived again using the secret $secret_A$ and the Enclave Sealing Key (k_{Seal}). Then, the authentication data mf_A are calculated as $mf_A \leftarrow hpass_A \oplus bio_A$.

The enrolment data are decrypted as $mf_E \leftarrow AES.Dec_{Wk_{Seal}}(\widetilde{mf_E})$. To compare the enrolment and authentication data, their Hamming Distance dis is calculated by XORing them and calculating the Hamming Weight (number of 1s) of the result: $dis \leftarrow HW(mf_E \oplus mf_A)$. To decide the authentication result, the Hamming Distance dis is compared with a threshold value TH.

If $secret_A == secret_E$ the enrolment data are decrypted correctly and the distance corresponds to $dis = HW(hpass_E \oplus bio_E \oplus hpass_A \oplus bio_A)$. If $hpass_A == hpass_E$, the distance calculated is the distance between the biometric embeddings $dis = HW(bio_E \oplus bio_A)$. If the distance is bigger than the threshold value TH, the authentication fails and the RP registration is finished. If the distance is smaller than or equal to TH, the authentication succeeds and the RP registration can continue.

Once the authentication finished successfully, the WSCD creates a new Passkey ($PASSpk$, $PASSsk$) and a *CredentialID* to identify it. Then, the challenge Ch and the new *PASSpk* are signed using the Attestation Key *ATTsk* ($Attestation \leftarrow Sign_{ATTsk}(Ch||PASSpk)$). The $PASSpk$, the *CredentialID*, the *Attestation* and the *ATTpk* certificate (*ATTpkCert*.) signed by the Wallet Provider are sent to the Wallet Instance who sends it to the Relying Party.

Then, the Relying Party verifies the *Attestation* and *ATTpkCert*. If the verification is positive, the Relying Party stores the new Passkey *PASSpk* with its *UserID*, *UserName* and *CredentialID*.

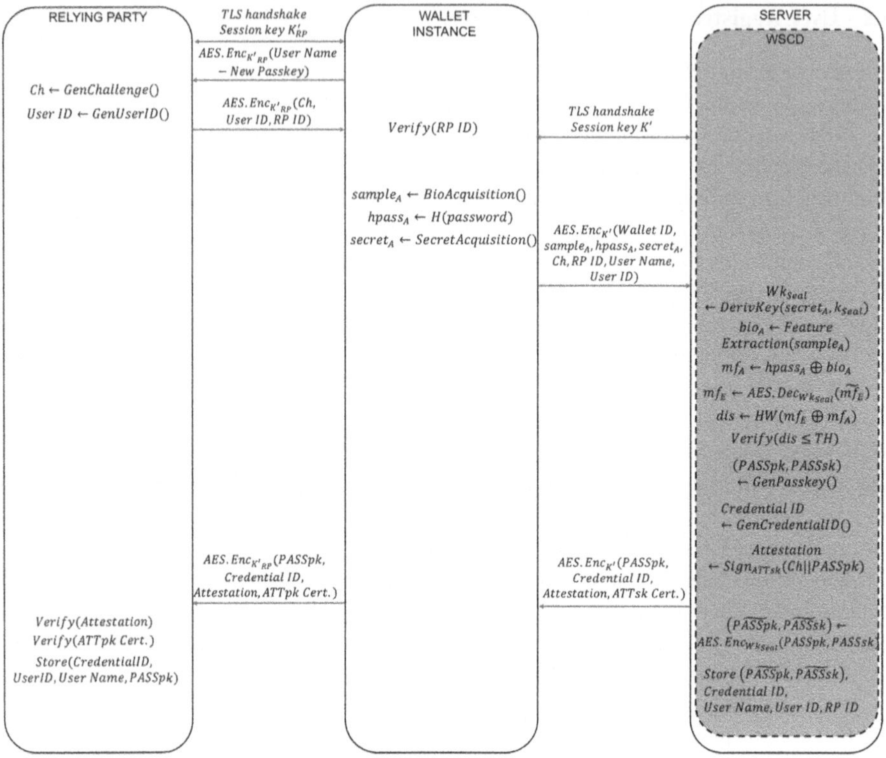

Fig. 4. User Registration at a Relying Party

3.3 User Authentication in a Relying Party

Users will employ the created Passkeys to authenticate themselves with Relying Parties. The User authentication process is shown in Fig. 5.

First, the Wallet Instance and the Relying Party create a secure communication channel. We assume a TLS handshake is performed and a new session key K''_{RP} is created.

The Wallet Instance asks the Relying Party to authenticate the User with the User Name and Passkey associated. The Relying Party creates a new challenge *Ch* and sends it with its Relying Party ID (*RPID*) to the Wallet Instance. Then, the Wallet Instance verifies that the RP ID corresponds to the corresponding RP.

To continue, the WSCD must authenticate the User with the multi-factor information. The process is the same as in the User Registration process. If the authentication is successful, the Passkey presentation process continues.

The Wallet Instance sends to the WSCD the challenge *Ch*, the Relying Party ID (*RPID*) and the *UserName* associated to the Passkey to use. The WSCD retrieves the secret Passkey *PASSsk* linked to the received *UserName* and decrypts it with the WSCD Sealing key $PASSsk \leftarrow AES.Dec_{Wk_{Seal}}\left(\widetilde{PASSsk}\right)$. Then, it uses the Passkey to sign the

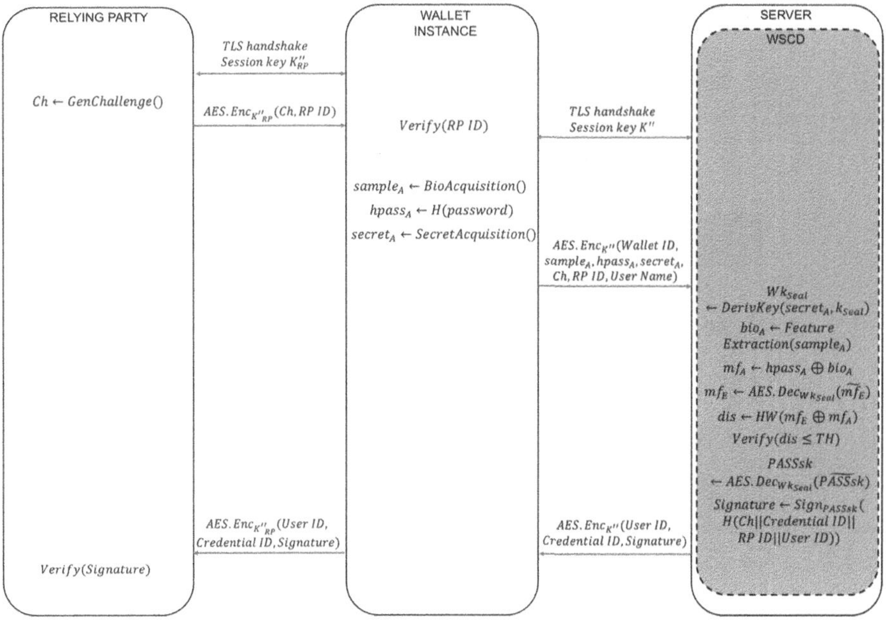

Fig. 5. User Authentication at a Relying Party

received challenge *Ch* together with other information such as the *CredentialID*, the *UserID* and the *RPID*.

The WSCD sends the *Signature* to the Wallet Instance and the Wallet Instance resends it to the Relying Party. The Relying Party verifies the *Signature* with the stored public key for this *UserID* and *CredentialID*. If all the verifications are correct, the Relying Party authenticates the User.

4 Demonstrator of the Proposal

To test our proposal, we have developed a demonstrator using the EUDI Wallet Android reference application offered by the official GitHub Organization of the European Digital Identity project [16]. A Samsung Galaxy A52 was used as User device with the Wallet Instance (WI). We have employed two servers, one running on Intel SGX to act as the remote WSCD and the other acting as a simulated Relying Party. A laptop with an Intel® Core ™ i7-10750H at 2.60 GHz and 16 GB RAM with Ubuntu 20.04.6 LTS and Intel SGX1 with hyper-threading disabled was used to implement the remote WSCD. The enclaves were programmed using Gramine (previously named Graphene-SGX) [17], a

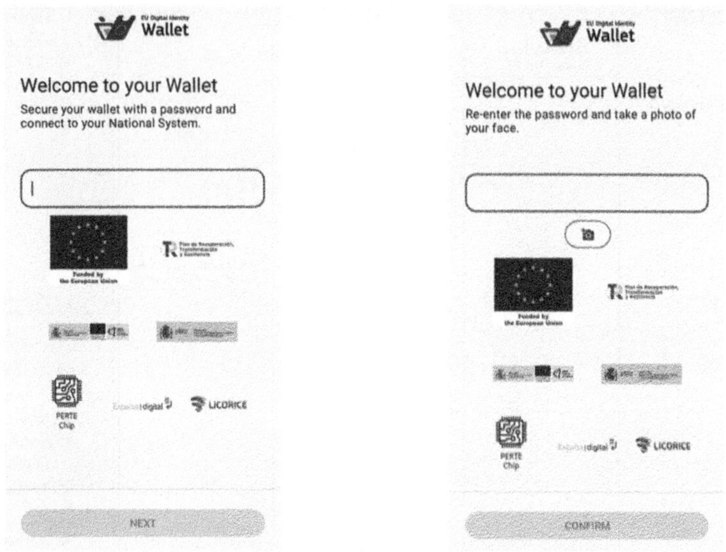

a) b)

Fig. 6. EUDI Wallet reference App with: a) the use of password and b) the use of password and face photo

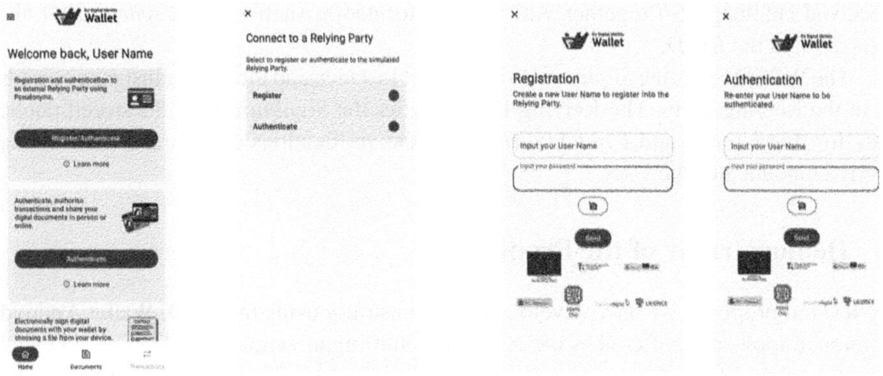

a) b) c) d)

Fig. 7. App steps for User Registration and Authentication in a Relying Party: a) Selection of Registration and Authentication to an external RP using Pseudonyms; b) Selection of Register or Authenticate actions; c) Introduction of User Name, password and face photo for Registration; d) Introduction of User Name, password and face photo for Authentication

libraryOS used to implement complex applications inside an Intel SGX enclave. The same laptop was used to run the simulated Relying Party server.

We have changed the PIN authentication implemented by the EUDI Wallet reference application to allow for the introduction of a password and a face sample while the secret

Starting server on port 4433
Using certificate: ssl/server.crt
Using private key: ssl/server.key
Waiting for a connection...
Performing TLS handshake...
Successful TLS handshake. Respoding to the requests...
INFO: Created TensorFlow Lite XNNPACK delegate for CPU.

USER BINDING
WSCD output:
{"id":"6/qc3XrAYwo=","public_key":"BAVrH6jTkCvRabVIO8ZZDZOWBlCuEqHGJQdKeoI1gtH8SpO4HczSapDEMuq1DVAOg77mza5AFINhA/7pWHOLgCo="}
Waiting for a connection...
Performing TLS handshake...
Successful TLS handshake. Respoding to the requests...

USER AUTHENTICATION AND PASSKEY CREATION
WSCD output:
{"Attcert":"MIIBUzCB+gIUeSLgj/p6OadAOV16OZ5G3/YKWLYwCgYIKoZIzj0EAwIwFDESMBAGA1UEAww3TX1FQ0RTQUNBMB4XDTI1MDQzMDEzMjMyMVoXDTI2M
DQzMDEzMjMyMVowRTELMAkGA1UEBhMCQVUxEzARBgNVBAgHCLNvbWUtU3RhdGUxITAfBgNVBAoMGEludGVybmV0IFdpZGdpdHMgUHR5IEx6ZDBZMBMGByqGSM49Ag
EGCCqGSM49AwEHA0IAB3lbAK3d+sJo9puz2L9xEOaFsFuVJ8TtnrFqGMTjAIlxzNmDOSXTzaqNU1FF7dky1c/A7kf+FqrH78R1cF9QkCgwCgYIKoZIzj0EAwIDSAA
wRQIgVnH39Q/vc+ZzokoFuDvrCynjwCZiaZHA8wSSYzBS4RwCIQCgc4NXPkRR9LqlxlIfh29tSwmkkT1rWXthPSYjQtE+2Q==","attestation":"MEYCIQC0MnC
xzdGho81+1UukNOvTHwpAG2b5T7p1Xck6gOxeUATHAL5E3n/w5/vmJHy4PZHwXvvTmQa+4jV5uv13jupHYdB","credentialID":"0FBSXDLot4U=","public_
key":"BG2J3slXj65Lwf/1bHcnjwDf3x2UuNBzx0v/X59Y2z7DtVBjXxvIb6D3ICwA74KqBaf6ufvXpZnUQ3AmqqMQpnB="}
Waiting for a connection...
Performing TLS handshake...
Successful TLS handshake. Respoding to the requests...

USER AUTHENTICATION AND PASSKEY PRESENTATION

WSCD output:
{"credentialID":"0FBSXDLot4U=","signature":"MEUCIQCFiSqT7Ta43/mgZo1Ugzu5ymwByaW6bNoO1cV1gdMgIwIgC/VPDLzDAunkHFpt/kmWnPOGEbxwd
sFbzeVX9eyMtc="}
Waiting for a connection...

Fig. 8. WSCD server terminal during User Binding, User Registration to a Relying Party and User Authentication to a Relying Party

is simply generated in the application assuming that it is stored securely in the mobile phone [18]. This change is shown in Fig. 6 with a picture of the EUDI Wallet reference App. In Fig. 7 we also show the steps for the User registration/authentication with the Relying Party. To communicate with the Relying Party using Passkeys, a new button has been included in the home page of the App (Fig. 7a) and a new page has been developed to choose between registration and authentication (Fig. 7b). The two screens for registration and authentication are shown in Fig. 7c and 7d, respectively. At both, the User Name, the Wallet password and the face photo are required.

The WSCD and Relying Party server terminals are shown in Fig. 8 and Fig. 9, respectively.

Starting server on port 4330
Using certificate: ssl/server.crt
Using private key: ssl/server.key
Waiting for a connection...
TLS handshake completed...

USER REGISTRATION
RP output:
{"RPID":"AAAAAAAAAAA=","challenge":"30k3K8ZNmjDLfDG7MsLpIpclkVOIqCjEufBLRrIHWGw=","user
ID":"Qjwk8D8OrDY="}
RP output:
{"result":"Enrolment successful"}

Waiting for a connection...
TLS handshake completed...
USER AUTHENTICATION
RP output:
{"RPID":"AAAAAAAAAAA=","challenge":"sCQ7baZ5dHE7g7WW/dJdkFbG5FCvW5ptGOqhXLd+/lM="}
RP output:
{"result":"Authentication Successful"}

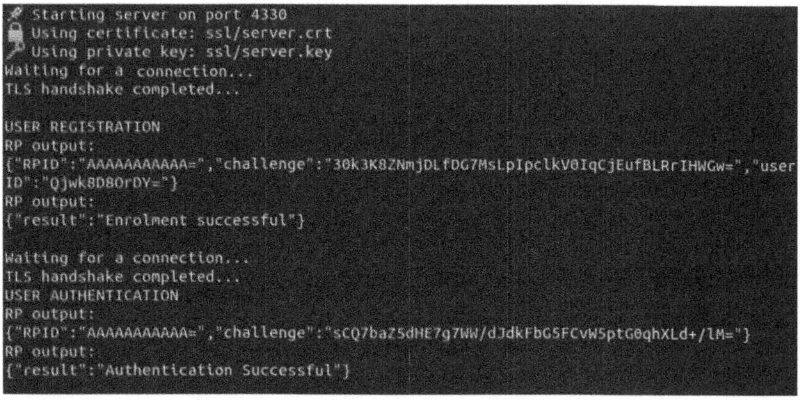

Fig. 9. Relying Party server terminal during User Registration to a Relying Party and User Authentication to a Relying Party

The model BlazeFace for short range face detection from Google Mediapipe library [19] is included in the app to cut the face image to the appropriate size (160×160 pixels). In the WSCD, a Facenet Tensorflow-Lite model was used, obtained from the original Facenet model [20], to implement the feature extractor. The resulting Facenet embeddings were binarized using a linearly separable subcode (LSSC) [21] with the codes 000, 001, 011 and 111 and applying a segmentation of the feature space with the intervals $(-\infty, -0.1)$, $[-0.1, 0.0)$, $[0.0, 0.1)$ and $[0.1, +\infty)$. The resulting binary embeddings were composed of 384 bits. The False Accept Rate (FAR) or False Match Rate (FMR) measure the number of impostors that are wrongfully recognized while the False Rejection Rate (FRR) or False Non-Match Rate (FNMR) measure the number of genuine users that are not correctly recognized; the Equal Error Rate (EER) is the point where both measures are the same and it is typically used to measure the recognition performance of a system [22]. In [23] the biometric performance of combining FaceNet and LSSC was evaluated with the FERET and LFW databases. In the FERET database, they achieved an EER of 1.69% with an accuracy of 98.9%. In the LFW database, they achieved an EER of 1.18% with an accuracy of 99.2%.

Concerning the main cryptographic operations, a padding of 128 bits is added to the binary embeddings before XORing them with a 512-bit hash of the password calculated with SHA-512. The result is encrypted in four blocks since AES encrypts 128-bit blocks. The signing method for the challenges and attestation was ECDSA with a 256-bit curve as defined by FIPS 186-4 [24].

In Table 2, we present the execution times for User binding, registration and authentication at the WSCD and at the Relying Party, and the total execution time which includes communication times. These results prove that the operations can be executed at reasonable times. Table 3 shows execution times for the main operations considered inside the enclave. Compared to the execution times of these operations outside the enclave, it can be determined that the addition of the enclave does not imply much cost. Lastly, Table 4 shows the communication overhead in bytes between the different parties without including the necessary bytes for the regular TLS handshakes; the face images $sample_E$ and $sample_A$ are 307200 bytes each. This proves that the information required is minimal, even between the Wallet Instance and the WSCD.

Table 2. User binding, registration and authentication times (in ms)

	User binding	Registration	Authentication
Relying Party	-	9.9	5.0
WSCD	374.2	375.2	373.8
Total	1705.5	2326.8	2219.0

Table 3. Execution times inside and outside the enclave (in ms)

	Feature Extraction	Hamming Weight	XOR	Credential ID Generation	Key Generation	Signing
Inside enclave	368.9148	0.0056	0.0048	0.0106	0.3546	0.4400
Outside enclave	245.6366	0.0004	0.0003	0.0026	0.3555	0.4473

With Intel SGX1, the WSCD enclave needs 128 MB of RAM to be executed properly. In Intel SGX2 processors, the enclaves can have a maximum SGX RAM (Enclave Page Cache) of 512 GB [25], allowing the parallel execution of around 4000 enclaves at the same time.

Table 4. Communication overhead (in bytes)

	RP → WI	WI → RP	WI → WSCD	WSCD → WI
User binding	-	-	307280	8
User Registration	48	489	307336	489
User Authentication	40	89	307328	89

5 Conclusions and Future Work

Among the Wallet Secure Cryptographic Devices (WSCDs) considered by the Architecture and Reference Framework (ARF) of the European Digital Identity (EUDI) Wallet, we propose the use of a remote WSCD since it is the most inclusive, user-friendly and scalable. Its implementation is done with an Intel SGX enclave that provides integrity and confidentiality to all the cryptographic and biometric code and data processed by it, including the generation and management of Passkeys, which are a kind of pseudonyms defined by the W3C WebAuthn specifications. The paper describes the steps of the multifactor User authentication between the Wallet Instance and the WSCD for User binding. Also, the steps between the Wallet and a Relying Party offering an on-line service are described for User registration and authentication using Passkeys. The proposal has been tested with a demonstrator that uses the EUDI Wallet Android reference application offered by the official GitHub Organization of the European Digital Identity project. A Samsung Galaxy A52 was used as User device with the Wallet Instance and two servers were employed, one running on Intel SGX1 to act as the remote WSCD and the other acting as a simulated Relying Party. The execution times at the WSCD for User binding, registration and authentication at the Relying Party are 374.2, 375.2 and 373.8 ms, respectively. The RAM employed by the WSCD is 128 MB. The communication overhead between the Wallet instance and the remote WSCD for User binding, registration and authentication are 307.288, 307.825 and 307.417 kB, respectively, from which 307.200 kB correspond to the sample image for face recognition.

When binding the Wallet Unit to the User, saving the secret and/or password in a distributed backup system could be selected by the User. In the case of the User Device being lost or the password being forgotten, the distributed backup system would allow the User to recover its Wallet Unit. The development and distribution of this backup system is a future line of work. Another future development is the inclusion of solutions for countering presentation and injection attacks to the face authentication [26].

Acknowledgements. This work has been funded by Grants PDC2023–145873-I00, CPP2022–009796, and PID2023-150809OB-I00 by MICIU/AEI/10.13039/ 501100011033 and by the European Union–NextGenerationEU/PRTR; it has received funding from the European Union's Horizon Europe research and innovation programme under Grant Agreement No. 101168311 (LICORICE Project), and it has been funded by grant USECHIP (TSI-069100-2023-001) project by the Secretary of State for Telecommunications and Digital Infrastructure, Ministry for Digital Transformation and Civil Service and by the European Union–Next GenerationEU/PRTR.

References

1. European Digital Identity Wallet Architecture and Reference Framework (2025). https://eu-digital-identity-wallet.github.io/eudi-doc-architecture-and-reference-framework/latest/. Accessed 3 June 2025
2. European Digital Identity (EUDI) Regulation. https://digital-strategy.ec.europa.eu/en/policies/eudi-regulation. Accessed 3 June 2025
3. European Commission. eID Documentation: eIDAS Levels of Assurance. https://ec.europa.eu/digital-building-blocks/sites/display/DIGITAL/eIDAS+Levels+of+Assurance. Accessed 3 June 2025
4. Commission Implementing Regulation (EU) 2015/1502 of 8 September 2015 on setting out minimum technical specifications and procedures for assurance levels for electronic identification means pursuant to Article 8(3) of Regulation (EU) No 910/2014 of the European Parliament and of the Council on electronic identification and trust services for electronic transactions in the internal market. http://data.europa.eu/eli/reg_impl/2015/1502/oj2015. Accessed 14 May 2025

5. Ubiqu. The 4 main Wallet Secure Cryptographic Device/Application options compared. https://ubiqu.com/the-4-main-wallet-secure-cryptographic-device-application-options-compared/. Accessed 2 Apr 2025
6. Ansaroudi, Z.E., Sciarretta, G., De Maria, A., Ranise, S.: Navigating secure storage requirements for EUDI Wallets: a review paper. EURASIP J. Inf. Secur. **2025**(2) (2025)
7. GlobalPlaform. Card Specification Version 2.3.1. GlobalPlatform (2018)
8. Web Authentication: An API for accessing Public Key Credentials Level 2 W3C Recommendation, 8 April 2021. https://www.w3.org/TR/webauthn-2/#sctn-intro. Accessed 15 May 2025
9. Fehrensen, B., Hiltgen, A., Lindemann, R.: Fido Core for Eid-Wallets. https://ssrn.com/abstract=5009534. Accessed 3 June 2025
10. Elfors, S.: FIDO Alliance White Paper: Using FIDO for the EUDI Wallet (2023)
11. Domingues, P., Frade, M., Negrao, M.: Digital forensic artifacts of FIDO2 passkeys in windows 11. In: Proceedings of the 19th International Conference on Availability, Reliability and Security (ARES 2024), pp. 1–10. Association for Computing Machinery, New York, NY, USA, Article 34 (2024)
12. Costan, V., Devadas, S.: Intel SGX explained. IACR Cryptology ePrint Archive, 86 (2016)
13. Knauth, T., et al.: Integrating Intel SGX remote attestation with transport layer security. Intel Labs. https://arxiv.org/pdf/1801.05863. Accessed 3 June 2025
14. Intel® Software Guard Extensions (Intel® SGX) Data Center Attestation Primitives: ECDSA Quote Library API (2022). https://www.intel.com/content/www/us/en/content-details/734437/intel-software-guard-extensions-intel-sgx-data-center-attestation-primitives-ecdsa-quote-library-api.html. Accessed 25 Apr 2025
15. Kisand, A., Randmets, J.: An overview of vulnerabilities and mitigations of Intel SGX and Intel TDX applications. Cybernetica research report D-2-116 v1.4 (2025). https://cyber.ee/uploads/report_2025_sgx_19b89d79ed.pdf. Accessed 11 June 2025
16. EUDI Android Wallet reference application. https://github.com/eu-digital-identity-wallet/eudi-app-android-wallet-ui. Accessed 28 Apr 2025
17. Tsai, C., Porter, D.E., Vij, M.: Graphene-SGX: a practical library OS for unmodified applications on SGX. In: 2017 USENIX Annual Technical Conference, USENIX Association, CA, USA (2017)
18. Flores, D.: Analysis of the European digital identity wallet reference implementation and integration of a multifaction authentication solution. Computer Science Engineering Bachelor's thesis, University of Seville (2025)
19. Google AI for Developers. Face detection guide. https://ai.google.dev/edge/mediapipe/solutions/vision/face_detector. Accessed 5 May 2025
20. Facenet. https://github.com/davidsandberg/facenet. Accessed 10 Jan 2025
21. Lim, M.H., Teoh, A.B.J.: A novel encoding scheme for effective biometric discretization: linearly separable subcode. IEEE Trans. Pattern Anal. Mach. Intell. **35**(2), 300–313 (2013)
22. Jang, J., Kim, H.: Performance measures. In: Li, S.Z., Jain, A.K. (eds.) Encyclopedia of Biometrics. Springer, Boston, MA (2015)
23. Arjona, R., Franco, C., Román, R., Baturone, I.: Combining CRYSTALS-Kyber homomorphic encryption with garbled circuits for biometric authentication. In: International Conference of the Biometrics Special Interest Group (BIOSIG), pp. 1–5 (2024)

24. FIPS 186-4 Digital Signature Standard (DSS) (2013). https://doi.org/10.6028/NIST.FIPS.186-4. Accessed 25 Apr 2025
25. Intel® Processors Supporting Intel® SGX. https://www.intel.com/content/www/us/en/architecture-and-technology/software-guard-extensions-processors.html. Accessed 29 Apr 2025
26. Encina, M.: Study and realization of biometric systems implemented in smartphones and robust against presentation attacks. Computer Sciencer Engineering Bachelor's thesis, University of Seville (2025)

Pseudonymity for Personal Data Stores: Pseudonymous WebIDs and Decentralized Identifiers

Gertjan De Mulder(✉) and Ben De Meester

IDLab, Department of Electronics and Information Systems, Ghent University – imec, Technologiepark-Zwijnaarde 122, 9052 Ghent, Belgium
{gertjan.demulder,ben.demeester}@ugent.be

Abstract. Personal Data Stores like Fedora and Solid let users become data holders, controlling their personal data and Web interactions through interoperable standards. Pseudonyms protect privacy during data sharing while still allowing holders to later prove their true identity, making them key privacy-enhancing tools. However, pseudonyms are rarely tackled in existing decentralized personal data sharing standards. In this paper, we present, analyze, and evaluate pseudonymity methods within Solid – a maturing set of personal data sharing standards – applied to a job application use case. This use case consists of three flows: a pseudonym generation flow, a diploma verification flow using that pseudonym and data minimization using the Verifiable Credential standard, and a Proof of Ownership identity binding between the pseudonym and the user's true identity. We compare two pseudonym generation solutions: a Solid-native solution that depends on an external party to lease (Web-resolvable) pseudonyms, and a solution that leverages a static resolving method (DID:Key) to generate ephemeral pseudonyms. The data flow diagrams, and STRIDE and LINDDUN analysis indicate that static identifiers are better for pseudonymous use cases, as they avoid reliance on external parties. The requirement validation show both solutions meet most needs, though the WebID solution remains observable and the DID:Key solution lacks support for deleting or managing pseudonyms. With this pseudonymity work, we aim to provide a next step to combine personal data storage incentives with Wallet incentives (such as those put forward by the EUDI).

Keywords: DID · Personal Data Stores · Pseudonymity · Solid · Verifiable Credentials · WebID

1 Introduction

The amount of control centralized platforms exhibit emphasizes the need and importance for users to regain their control and, thus, their privacy [17,18]. This resulted in an uprise of **personal data stores (PDS)**: interoperable decentralized ecosystems where **users become data *holders***, exercising control over

B. Coppens et al. (Eds.): ARES 2025 Workshops, LNCS 15997, pp. 111–129, 2025.
https://doi.org/10.1007/978-3-032-00639-4_7

their personal data and their interactions on the Web. Maturing PDS standards are the Fedora Repository[1] and the Solid protocols [2].

This decentralization effort has expanded to the term Self-Sovereign Identity (SSI) [32], where users are in control of their digital identity without depending on a (central) authority. This technically implies that **all interactions between a data holder and a data *verifier*** (i.e., the actor that the holder interacts with) **should also be decentralized**, i.e., both holder and verifier have a choice in how they identify and authenticate themselves, and how to authorize other parties (this as opposed to, e.g., the OIDC de facto industry standard [1], where the verifier specifies which identity provider(s) can be used by the holder). This has given rise to the European Digital Identity (EUDI) Wallet [15]: a set of specifications and (reference) implementations to manage personal credentials such as driving license and diploma from your personal device.

PDS standards are related to SSI and EUDI Wallets, but not the same: PDS is use-case agnostic, focussed on interoperability and meant to store and share any kind of data (not only credentials, not only about the holder), whereas the EUDI Wallet is focussed on specific holder credentials, used within authentication flows.

Both Fedora and Solid propose a Web-resolvable identity to represent a holder. Specifically, the identifier (i.e., a *WebID*) is an HTTP URL that resolves to an identity document on the Web (i.e., a WebID Profile Document) describing the holder. A WebID can be obtained by registering one at an Identity Provider (IDP), or by directly leasing a domain name from a Domain Name Space (DNS) registrar.

Being able to globally and uniquely identify entities enables attribution (by associating claims), reputation building, and accountability [9]. However, using the same identifier for different purposes, within different contexts, and across various services increases the risk of tracking and profiling [28].

Pseudonymity is an important privacy-enhancing technology [16]. Holders can protect their privacy when interacting on the Web by using a *pseudonym* that reveals no identifying information, unless disclosure is required [13, 30]. However, pseudonymity is rarely tackled in existing PDS standards.

We consider the following motivating use case.

Alice, a data holder who controls her diploma data, is interested in a job requiring a Master's degree. Being aware of gender bias in the hiring process, the recruiter allows applicants to prove their degree without revealing further personal information. Alice wants to avoid using her public identifier (e.g., her public WebID https://id.flanders.be/Alice), as it may expose more data than necessary[2]. *To minimize bias, she chooses to apply using a pseudonym.*

[1] https://fedorarepository.org/.

[2] This example uses gender-based bias for clarity although one can assume that gender-based information is rarely encoded in an identifier. However, in an international setting, one could imagine a similar kind of bias towards applicants of very different origin – and thus using very different domain names in their identifier. Similarly, the presented use case abstracts away additional data interactions typically needed for applicant background checks.

In this paper, we address the following research question: "How can we introduce pseudonymous interactions in a WebID-based system, and how does this affect a user's privacy?".

After introducing our background in Sect. 2 and related works in Sect. 3, we introduce the process flows for the use case: a pseudonym generation flow, a diploma verification flow using that pseudonym and data minimization using the Verifiable Credential standard, and Proof of Ownership method to prove the binding between the pseudonym and the user's true identity (Sect. 4). In Sect. 5, we compare two pseudonym generation solutions: a WebID-native solution that depends on an external party to lease (Web-resolvable) pseudonyms, and a solution that leverages a statically resolvable identifier using the DID:Key method to generate ephemeral pseudonyms. We present the implementation in Sect. 6. We then evaluate and compare these solutions based on a functional, a security, and a privacy evaluation in Sect. 7. We conclude in Sect. 8.

2 Background

In this section, we introduce the entities and concepts relevant for the discussion of this paper. The relationship between those entities is visualized in Fig. 1.

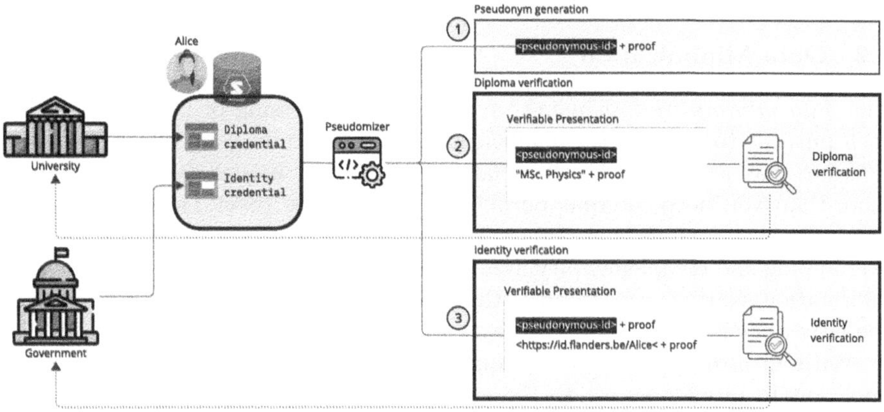

Fig. 1. Pseudonymous job application use case, involving three process flows. First, holder Alice creates a pseudonym. Second, Alice discloses a minimal set of required attributes (i.e., her diploma title) under that pseudonym, to apply for a job. The verifying recruiter can validate with the issuing university that the diploma is genuine. Third, assuming that Alice's pseudonym was selected for the job, Alice proves her governmentally issued identity and the binding with the pseudonym that was selected for the job. The recruiter can validate the pseudonym locally and the identity with the issuing government.

2.1 Entities

We adhere to the following definitions of More et al. [27], unless explicitly stated otherwise:

- **Issuer**: Issuers issue signed credentials to users, e.g., the *university* and *government* are Issuers of diploma Credentials and identity Credentials, respectively.
- **Credential**: A digital and cryptographically verifiable set of claims that is issued by an Issuer to a Holder [36].
- **Holder/User**: A user that manages credentials, which it can use to present verifiable sets of claims to a Verifier, e.g., *Alice* is a Holder that manages her diploma and identity Credentials.
- **Pod**: A personal data store on which users can store digital documents such as diploma and identity Credentials.
- **Pseudomizer**: A service or application that allows Holders to create and use a pseudonym when interacting with a verifier. We assume the Pseudomizer to run on the Holder's personal device.
- **Verifier/Service Provider/Relying Party**: An actor in the network that typically provides a service to a Holder if that Holder can prove specific claims, e.g., the *recruiter* verifies Alice's diploma when she applies for a job.

2.2 Data Minimization

The *data minimization principle*[3] requires the processing of personal data for each purpose to be *adequate* (sufficient to properly fulfil your stated purpose), *relevant* (has a rational link to that purpose), and *limited* (you do not hold more than you need for that purpose). Our use case (Sect. 1) shows the relevance of pseudonymity, based on the data minimization principle and multiple overlapping and complementary use cases stemming from Flemish career-related information sharing via Athumi[4] (the Flemish data utility company) and from the DID use cases[5].

Without a data minimization approach in place, a recruiter can request an applicant to provide access to the entire diploma. Not only does this increase the risk for outsider attacks (e.g., when the entire degree document has been compromised) but also the risk for attacks from the inside: for example, the recruiter can use the information for purposes for which the applicant did not agree (e.g., discovering more information about the applicant by looking up their name, university, etc.).

[3] GDPR Article 5(1)(c).

[4] https://athumi.be/en/personal-smart-data-spaces/my-career.

[5] https://www.w3.org/TR/did-use-cases/#featureBenefitGrid.

2.3 Selective Disclosure

Selective disclosure is the ability to reveal individual claims from a credential [27]. This minimizes the risk of privacy breaches and prevents unauthorized access to sensitive data. For example, to be adequate and relevant for the purpose of selecting an applicant for a job that is known to suffer from gender bias, the recruiter requires applicants to selectively disclose only the degree title (e.g., "Master of Physics"), rather than an entire diploma. *Zero-knowledge proofs* can be used to take selective disclosure a step further to only request *predicates* on an attribute (e.g., age > 18), which allows to demonstrate the validity of a statement without revealing the actual value of the attribute [27].

3 Related Work

We first discuss decentralized identity standards on the Web (sometimes coined as *user-centric* identity standards[6]), and their relation to (existing and new) authentication protocols (Sect. 3.1). We focus on open standards and relevant technologies are highlighted in bold. Then, we discuss privacy-related state-of-the-art of these standards, focusing on pseudonymity (Sect. 3.2).

3.1 Decentralized Identity

There are currently two main decentralized identity standards: WebID, and Decentralized Identifiers (DID).

The Solid Protocol [2] leverages Web standards governed by multiple W3C working and community groups, each focusing on different aspects of the ecosystem: identity using WebID [3], authentication using Solid-OIDC [12], and storage using the Linked Data Platform (LDP) [10]. A server implementation that provides the storage component is called a *pod*. **A WebID is a Web-resolvable URI** that resolves to a WebID Profile Document [3]. Thus, WebIDs require a domain registrar to register and look up the identifier over HTTP(S).

The Decentralized Identity Foundation (DIF)[7] develops the technical foundations to establish Self-Sovereign Identity (SSI) [32] where holders are in control of their digital identity, without depending on a (central) authority. To this end, Decentralized Identifiers (DIDs) [35] are standardized. Different DID methods exist[8] to resolve DIDs to DID documents, e.g., `did:ethr`-identifiers resolve to entries on the Ethereum blockchain, while `did:web`-identifiers can be transformed into Web-resolvable URIs, making them closely related to WebIDs.

Many DID methods rely on registries based on distributed ledger technologies (e.g., blockchain, distributed hash tables, etc.), but **static DID methods**[9] avoid the need for complex infrastructures, external dependencies, and network

---

[6] To keep consistency with Sect. 2, we will consistently refer to users as holders.

[7] https://identity.foundation/.

[8] https://w3c.github.io/did-spec-registries/#did-methods.

[9] https://w3c-ccg.github.io/did-method-key/.

operations, as they contain sufficient information to construct the corresponding DID Document. When used as short-lived identifiers, static DID methods are particularly suitable for pseudonymity use cases[10]. `did:peer`[11] and `did:key`[12] are common static DID methods. While `did:peer` allows for embedding multiple keys and service endpoints, `did:key` is minimized, only allowing for embedding a single public key in the identifier. Creating a `did:key` DID requires generating a new cryptographic key pair: the DID is a specific encoding of the public key of that generated key pair.

DIDs are typically used in conjunction with W3C recommended **Verifiable Credentials (VC)** [36]: a data model for cryptographically verifiable digital credentials. Within the VC standard, the term Verifiable Presentation (VP) is introduced as a package selectively created by the holder to present one or more VCs to a verifier, possibly with **proof of authenticity and selective disclosure of only the necessary claims**. For the scope of this paper, we focus on the VC open standards and not other (compatible) digital credential formats such as JSON Web Tokens (JWTs), and [36].

The European Digital Identity (EUDI) Wallet is a European Union initiative that aims to solve **(high-level) requirements for decentralized identity**, part of the eIDAS 2.0 regulation (Regulation (EU) 2024/1183) [15]. The EUDI Wallet is typically implemented as a secure mobile application that allows individuals to store, manage, and selectively disclose digital credentials and attributes. It uses DIDs and VCs as interoperable standards for identifiers and verifiable credentials.

Authentication protocols currently proposed in these decentralized identity standards typically rely on a trusted third party (typically called an Identity Provider or IDP), and are often aligned with the OpenID-Connect (OIDC) standards [1]. WebID authentication currently uses Solid-OIDC: an OIDC extension that allows holders to choose their own IDP[13]. The EUDI wallet uses OIDC for Verifiable Presentations (OIDC4VP)[14]: an OIDC extension that allows verifiers to request specific VPs from holders.

Initial WebID authentication was based on mutual TLS (mTLS) [8], however, this requires X.509 certificates for both server and clients, for which (browser-)support is limited. Other related authentication protocols are typically peer-oriented (e.g., based on DIDComm[15]), which makes them fit less in a Web-based context.

[10] https://ref.gs1.org/docs/2025/VCs-and-DIDs-tech-landscape#layerComparison.

[11] https://identity.foundation/peer-did-method-spec.

[12] https://w3c-ccg.github.io/did-method-key/.

[13] In OIDC, IDPs must be preregistered by the verifier, e.g., many applications allow logging in via Google, Facebook, or Microsoft, but you are not able to choose your own IDP to log in with.

[14] https://openid.net/specs/openid-4-verifiable-presentations-1_0.html.

[15] https://identity.foundation/didcomm-messaging/spec/.

3.2 Pseudonyms in Decentralized Identity

A security and privacy threat analysis of Solid's identification, authentication, and authorization protocols using LINDDUN [13] shows that the Solid protocols mitigate 54% of the security threats and only 4% of the privacy threats [26].

In general, privacy is an open issue for the WebID specification [38]. *Anonymous WebIDs* via a trusted third party (TTP) has been studied by Heitmann et al. [21], however, this is not suitable for pseudonymity, as it excludes proving the association between the original WebID and an anonymous WebID [20].

Meanwhile, DIDs and VCs are put forward as important technological specifications to have a secure decentralized (authentication) protocol [6].

Selective disclosure is extensively applied and tested in decentralized identity, typically for privacy-preserving (WebID) authentication [7,21,39]. Sharing a minimal set of attributes protects the privacy of the holder, however, the WebID of the VC's holder still needs to be disclosed for authentication. In recent VC standardization efforts, selective disclosure has been natively supported in crypto suites, i.e., selectively disclosed VCs can be locally verified via cryptographic means and without need for additional interactions with the issuer, holder, or other third party. Examples for such crypto suites are those using Elliptic Curve DSA (ECDSA) [23] or an extension of Boneh âĂŞ Boyen âĂŞ Shacham (BBS) [5] that allows for selective disclosure and zero-knowledge proofs (BBS Cryptosuite) [4].

The EUDI presents a set of *pseudonymity requirements*[16] on top of GDPR, and general privacy requirements have been posed by More et al. [27].

Typical pseudonymization approaches involve a TTP or some form of distributed ledger that generates and manages the pseudonyms [14,25,29,37], of which pairwise pseudonymous identifier flow is integrated in OIDC (requiring trusting a TTP), and where the European Blockchain Services Infrastructure (EBSI) provides a Key Attestation specification[17] (requiring trusting an EBSI Key Attestation issuer). TTPs typically keep track of the mapping between the original identifier and the generated pseudonymous identifier [16,19], enabling them to re-identify pseudonyms. To combat potential insider attacks, "data-owner based pseudonymization" – in which the data owner creates the pseudonyms – is proposed [19].

3.3 Requirement Analysis

Based on the above related work, we derive minimal requirements for a digital pseudonym. On the legal side, we focus on the EU's GDPR and EUDI Wallet pseudonymity requirements. We extend these requirements with related work on pseudonymity [27].

[16] https://eu-digital-identity-wallet.github.io/eudi-doc-architecture-and-reference-framework/1.9.0/annexes/annex-2/annex-2-high-level-requirements/#a2311-topic-11-pseudonyms.

[17] https://code.europa.eu/ebsi/json-schema/-/tree/main/schemas/vcdm2.0/key-attestations.

- **R01: Purpose**: Personal data shall be collected for specified, explicit and legitimate purposes (GDPR, [27]: LREQ1).
- **R02: Data Minimization**: Personal data collected shall be limited to what is necessary in relation to the purposes for which they are processed (GDPR, [27]: LREQ2)
- **R03: Consent**: No credentials should be disclosed or shown unless a holder explicitly operates the wallet software for that purpose (GDPR).
- **R04: Pseudonym generation** is possible (EUDI Wallet: PA_01).
- **R05**: **Pseudonym generation is independent** of the verifier or pod provider (EUDI Wallet: PA_03).
- **R06**: **Multiple pseudonyms can be generated** for the same verifier (EUDI Wallet: PA_04).
- **R07**: **Attach information to a pseudonym** (e.g., an alias) (EUDI Wallet: PA_05).
- **R08: Delete a pseudonym** (EUDI Wallet: PA_07).
- **R09: Manage pseudonyms.** Inform users about when and which verifier used their pseudonyms (including canceled or unsuccessful transactions) (EUDI Wallet: PA_08).
- **R10: Overview of pseudonyms.** Users can see all existing pseudonyms, including the associated verifiers (EUDI Wallet: PA_09).
- **R11: Unlinkability** between the identity and (between) its pseudonym(s) (GDPR, [27]).
- **R12: Unobservability**: Only the user and the verifier learn that a showing takes place. Neither the issuer nor any other authority (e.g., the government) should learn where the user is using their credentials, or even that the user is using their credentials (GDPR, [27]).

4 Process Flows

Alice can protect her privacy in a job application use case by controlling what information she shares: her identity and diploma data. This is achieved by i) using a pseudonym to hide her true identifier, and ii) disclosing only the minimum verifiable degree information, signed with that pseudonym. If selected, she can later prove the link between her pseudonym and real identity.

The use case has three process flows. *Flow 1: Pseudonym Generation*: Alice uses the Pseudomizer to generate her pseudonym for the next flows. *Flow 2: Diploma Verification*: Alice hides her true identity using a pseudonym and provides the minimal set of diploma attributes required by the recruiter. *Flow 3: Identity Verification*: Alice proves the binding between her true and pseudonym to the recruiter. In Flow 2 and 3, we rely on crypto suites to attest and locally verify the claims. We provide a high-level Data Flow Diagram representing the entities, interactions, and assets needed to handle these flows (Fig. 2).

We assume the following: i) Alice has a pod linked to her governmentally issued WebID; ii) Alice obtained her government-issued identity credential and

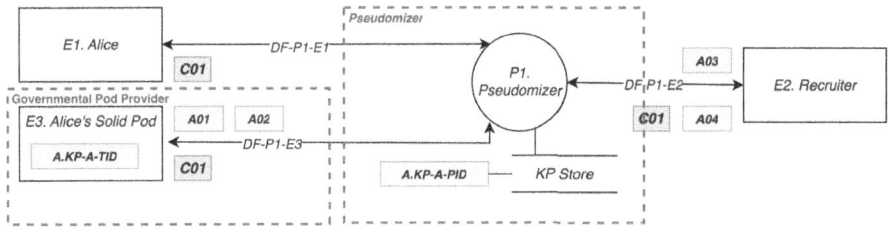

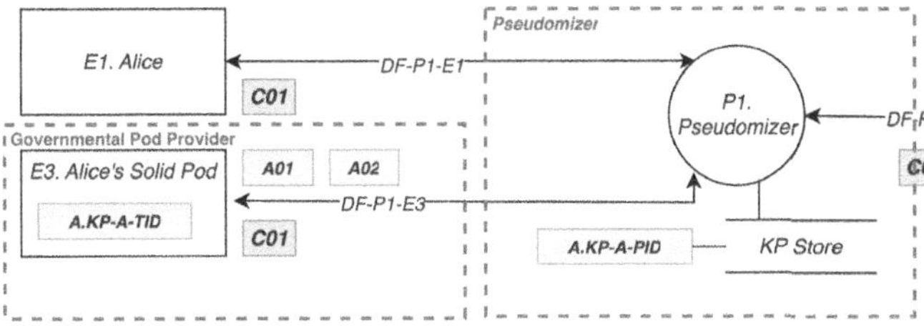

Fig. 2. High-level Data Flow Diagram. Rectangular boxes represent entities, and circles represent processes. The edges between them resemble data flows. Green labels indicate *security controls* that apply to a particular data flow, yellow labels represent *assets*, at rest, or transferred over a data flow. (Color figure online)

university-issued diploma credential and stored them in her pod; iii) all interactions occur over a secure channel (TLS, indicated by the green-colored tag `C01`); and iv) a new pseudonym is generated per job application.

The following assets are part of one or more flows.

- `A01`: a *diploma credential* containing sensitive and personally identifiable information.
- `A02`: an *identity credential* containing personally identifiable information.
- `A03`: a verifiable presentation (the *diploma VP*) that contains selectively disclosed attributes from the diploma credential (`A01`) as minimally required by the recruiter (e.g., only the "degree title").
- `A04`: a verifiable presentation to prove the binding between Alice's identity and her pseudonym (the *identity binding VP*).
- `A.KP-A-TID`: the key pair associated with Alice's identity, issued by her government and stored on her pod.
- `A.KP-A-PID`: the key pair associated with Alice's pseudonym, generated and managed by `P1. Pseudomizer`.

During the *pseudonym generation flow*, `E1. Alice` uses `P1. Pseudomizer` to generate a new pseudonym (and `P1. Pseudomizer` generates a new key pair in the process).

During the *diploma verification flow*, `E1. Alice` uses `P1. Pseudomizer` (`DF-P1-E1`) to apply for a job at `E2. Recruiter`. `P1. Pseudomizer` fetches `E1. Alice`'s *diploma credential* (`A01` over `DF-P1-E3`), creates a minimized diploma credential (using selective disclosure) under the previously generated pseudonym, and presents as a (pseudonym-signed) VP it to `E2. Recruiter` (`A03` over `DF-P1-E2`). `E2. Recruiter` can verify the diploma VP locally, using standardized VC cryptographic methods that support selective disclosure.

During the *identity verification flow*, `E1. Alice` uses `P1. Pseudomizer` (`DF-P1-E1`) to send an identity binding credential to `E2. Recruiter`. `P1. Pseudomizer` fetches `E1. Alice`'s *identity credential* (`A02` over `DF-P1-E3`), selectively discloses identifying attributes from the identity credential, binds them with the previously generated pseudonym, and sends that to `E2. Recruiter`

(A04 over DF-P1-E2). E2. Recruiter can verify the identity binding credential locally without additional interactions, using standardized VC cryptographic methods.

5 Solution

In this paper, we focus on a comparison of two pseudonym generation solutions: a WebID-native solution that depends on an external party to lease (Web-resolvable) pseudonyms, and a solution that leverages a statically resolvable identifier using the DID:Key method to generate ephemeral pseudonyms. Both solutions apply the same data minimization methods for the diploma data, and the pseudonym document only contains a public key to later prove the identity binding. The key difference is in creating and using the pseudonymous identifier.

Our first solution uses a third-party IDP that leases URIs to be used as pseudonymous WebIDs (Fig. 3): a new keypair is generated by P1. Pseudomizer of which the public key is subsequently forwarded to P1.2 IDP Pseudo (over DF-P1.PG-P1.2). P1.2 IDP Pseudo leases a URI that only discloses the newly generated public key when being resolved, effectively creating a pseudonymous WebID (A05). The recruiter resolves the identity document from that IDP (A05 over DF-P1.2-E2) to obtain the public key material needed to verify the digital signatures of both the diploma VP and identity binding VP identity document (cfr. DF-P1.2-E2).

Our second solution uses the static did:key method to generate a pseudonym: a new keypair is generated by P1. Pseudomizer of which the public key is encoded in the did:key identifier. Hence, no new dataflow is required for the DID:Key solution (Fig. 2): The recruiter does not need additional interactions to resolve the identity document and can locally verify the digital signatures of both the diploma VP and identity-binding VP.

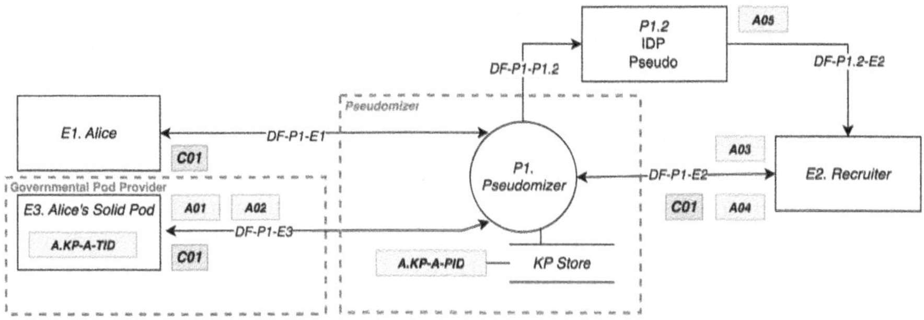

Fig. 3. Data Flow Diagram: WebID solution

We provide **identity binding** by enabling Alice to provide *Proof of Ownership* – a method that allows proving ownership over an asset by demonstrating control over the private cryptographic key associated with that asset [11] – for her governmentally issued identity, her generated pseudonym, and a self-asserted claim associating her identity with her pseudonym.

Alice creates two cross-signed VCs that both explicitly attest the link between the true identity and the pseudonym. However, one is fetched from Alice's pod, signed using the private key associated with Alice's true identity ($VC_1 = vc(sk_{true}, ID_{true}, ID_{pseudo})$) and the other is signed by `P1.Pseudomizer` using the private key associated with her pseudonym ($VC_2 = vc(sk_{pseudo}, [ID_{true}, ID_{pseudo}])$). These VCs are then encapsulated into a VP, together with a selectively disclosed identity credential that only discloses Alice's true identifier ($VP_{binding} = vp(sk_{true}, [VC_1, VC_2, vc(sk_{true}, ID_{true})])$). As this VP consists of VCs expressing the identity binding between two different key pairs, which is only possible by an entity that controls both key pairs, *Proof of Ownership* is provided.

6 Implementation

To showcase the feasibility of the proposed solutions, we implemented both pseudonymity solutions in TypeScript, MIT-licensed open source, and available at[18]. We designed a generic VC actor allowing to perform common operations of a credential lifecycle (i.e., creating, signing, deriving, and verifying). This actor also abstracts the cryptographic suites and the controlling identity (i.e., the identity used when performing credential operations), allowing us to create a variety of concrete class implementations, each employing different identity types (e.g., WebID, DID) and cryptographic suites (e.g., `eddsa-rdfc-2022`, `bbs-2023`).

We also performed a preliminary performance evaluation on a local machine[19], where we benchmarked the use case's credential operations and measured the execution time. The results are available online[20]. We ran an experiment simulating the steps of the proposed use case, averaging the results over 100 runs: when the recruiter verifies the diploma credential, the mean execution time is 91.15 ms for the WebID solution, and 44.35 ms for the DID:Key solution. This is because `did:key` identity documents can be directly resolved from the identifier, while WebID Profile Documents need to be fetched over the network. We can conclude that both solutions remain feasible on commodity hardware.

7 Evaluation

After validating which requirements our system adheres to, we perform an initial security (Sect. 7.2) and privacy threat analysis (Sect. 7.3) and discuss (Sect. 7.4).

[18] https://github.com/SolidLabResearch/pseudonymity-demo.
[19] MacBook Pro 16-inch (2021) with Apple M1 Max (10 cores) and 32GB of RAM.
[20] https://github.com/SolidLabResearch/pseudonymity-demo/blob/main/performance/PERFORMANCE-preliminary-analysis.ipynb.

7.1 Requirement Validation

Alice is in control when to engage with the recruiter (R03), and for which purpose (i.e., only for the purpose of job solicitation, R01). When doing so, she can select which part(s) of her diploma to share (R02), verifiable using a generated pseudonym (R04, R07). The pseudomizer is independent of the service provider or pod provider (R05), and does not limit Alice in how many pseudonyms she can generate, even for the same service provider (R06). In the case of a leased WebID, the IDP could allow for pseudonym deletion and management, which is not possible for the statically generated DID using the `did:key` method (R08, R09). In both cases, an overview of which pseudonym was generated for which service provider could be created (R10). The pseudomizer allows to create unlinkable pseudonyms, as only a uniquely generated public key is exchanged with each pseudonym (R11). In the case of a leased WebID, the IDP could observe which service provider is using which pseudonym, as resolving for the public key involves an HTTP request to the IDP (R12). Where both solutions cover most requirements, the leased WebID solution does not cover R12 due to the resolvance over HTTP, whereas the DID:Key solution does not cover R08 and R09 due to the ephemeral nature of the `did:key` method.

7.2 Security Analysis

To evaluate the security of our solution, we perform a STRIDE analysis [33] – one of the most widely used threat modeling approaches – where we identify possible attack scenarios and provide potential mitigations, based on the applicant's perspective (as other perspectives are deemed out of scope for this paper). We scope our security threat analysis to the application layer of the TCP/IP model, covering the session, presentation, and application layers of the OSI model), and assume all Web interactions are done over uncompromised HTTPS channels.

Spoofing. The risk of impersonation where an attacker attempts to act like someone else (e.g., authenticating as another user or using another user's credentials). On the one hand, this can happen by *acquiring control over the identity's key pair*, stored on the holder's PDS (`A.KP-A-TID`)[21]. In the WebID solution, this pseudonym key pair is stored by the Pseudomizer's Web service (which, due to its remote access possibilities, inhibits a larger threat). In the DID:Key solution, the key pair resides on the holder's local device. On the other hand, this can happen due to *first-party fraud*: Alice can create a derived diploma credential from a friend's (better matching) diploma credential. This can be **mitigated by relying on trusted issuers for these kinds of VPs, or by requesting proof of bound attributes**: assuming the identity document and diploma contain matching identifying data (e.g., both contain a social security number), the recruiter could request another zero-knowledge proof that the national identifier

[21] Either logically, i.e., at software-level, e.g., through ransomware; or physically, i.e., via physical access to the holder's device.

of the identity credential equals the national identifier of the diploma credential, without disclosing the national identifier.

Tampering. The risk of unauthorized alteration of data (e.g., an applicant altering a diploma credential to better match the desired vacancy) [24]. **Tampering is inherently mitigated by using Verifiable Credentials** as a collection of cryptographically verifiable claims of which the associated digital signatures prevent unauthorized alteration. Even when a VC is tampered with upstream, local verification upon receipt will unveil any kind of tampering.

Repudiation. The risk that an entity can deny performing an action. For example, Alice performs a Sybil attack in which a large number of pseudonyms are created to flood the recruiter with requests or present (minimized) diploma credentials that do not match the vacancy's requirements. Even when an audit log is provided [31][22], a holder could i) intentionally disclose its secret key to deny malicious actions, or ii) delete its pseudonyms so that requests can no longer be verified or bound to the holder. On the one hand, **disclosure of the secret key should be prevented by the keypair managing hardware or software**[23]. On the other hand, **deleting malicious pseudonyms remains a risk to the WebID solution** but is not an issue for the DID:Key solution, as the ephemeral nature of the `did:key` method makes it impossible to remove any DID pseudonym [24].

Information Disclosure. The risk that more information is disclosed than intended. The proposed solutions mitigate threats to information disclosure using: i) a pseudonym which prevents exposing an applicant's true identity; and ii) selective disclosure which allows applicants to present a minimized version of their data to requesting parties. However, the recruiter may discover Alice's identity by tracking her pseudonym. This is a threat specific to the WebID solution as resolving an identifier over a network discloses domain information. Furthermore, responses to probing requests for a particular WebID can disclose information (e.g., status code) from which more information can be inferred (e.g., whether a particular WebID still exists). In contrast, the DID:Key solution's identifier contains no identifiable information and can be resolved locally. For the WebID solution, this can be partially mitigated using herd privacy: a Pseudo IDP can choose to mint many WebID pseudonyms under the same HTTPS URI (e.g., by minting a new WebID using a hash identifier, similar to the VC's revocation list[24]: https://pseudo.com/webids/#1, https://pseudo.com/webids/#2, etc.).

Denial of Service. The risk of attempting to disrupt an actor's functioning. Related to the Sybil attack mentioned in the Repudiation discussion, attacks may involve sending intentionally large, invalid, or inefficiently structured credential payloads to exceed the memory/computation resources of a verifier. **Mit-**

[22] In which special attention should be given to make sure these audit logs cannot create binding data between pseudonyms and true identities.
[23] For example, https://www.ledger.com/.
[24] https://w3c-ccg.github.io/vc-status-rl-2020/.

igations for such a scenario typically require countermeasures at network and application levels (e.g., firewall rules, preemptive validity checks, rate limiting, throttling, appropriate error handling, and Challenge-Response mechanisms (e.g., CAPTHCA)).

Elevation of Privilege. The risk of gaining privileged access to compromise the system, which in our case coincides with the Spoofing risk: Alice providing a falsified diploma credential to get the job.

7.3 Privacy Analysis

We apply the LINDDUN methodology [34] to perform the privacy threat analysis, complemented with a detailed linkability analysis. LINDDUN categorizes threats in seven threat types: *Linking* (associating data items or user actions to learn more about an individual or group), *Identifying* (Learning the identity of an individual, through leaks, deduction, or inference), *Non-repudiation* (being able to attribute a claim to an individual), *Detecting* (deducing the involvement of an individual through observation), *Data disclosure* (excessively collecting, storing, processing or sharing personal data), *Unawareness & Unintervenability* (insufficiently informing, involving or empowering individuals in the processing of their personal data), and *Non-compliance* (deviating from security and data management best practices, standards and legislation). In our analysis, we assume that the pseudomizer i) sufficiently informs its users about how their personal is being processed; and ii) is compliant with the GDPR legislation. Therefore, we consider both solutions to yield no threats to type *Unawareness & Unintervenability* and *Non-Compliance*. Below, we discuss the differences between the two solutions that were not yet covered in the STRIDE analysis[25].

Linking. `L.1.1` (*Unique identifier*) is a threat for the WebID solution: the leased pseudonymous WebIDs' domain name can be linked with the Pseudo IDP, increasing its risk of becoming a target for hackers.

Identifying. Similar to `L.1.1`, `I.2.3` (*Distinguishable attributes*) is a threat for the WebID solution: although a new pseudonymous WebID is being used for every job application, these pseudonymous WebIDs can be distinguished based on the URI domain.

Non-repudiation. `Nr.1` (*Attributable data evidence*) is a threat in both solutions once a derived credential (e.g., the diploma VP) arrives at the recruiter. A credential is cryptographically tied to the holder's private key. Assuming this private key has not been compromised, only the legitimate holder can create a derived credential. Therefore, a user cannot deny having created a derived credential.

Detecting. D.1-3 (*Observed communications*, *Application side effect*, and *System responses*) are threats in the WebID solution: this solution needs flow `P1.2` where the recruiter needs to interact with the pseudonymous IDP, Fig. 3).

[25] The more detailed analysis can be found at https://github.com/SolidLabResearch/pseudonymity-demo/blob/main/performance/LINDDUN-analysis.xlsx.

Linkability Analysis. To properly discuss the pseudonymity potential, we performed a linkability analysis of data items (Table 1), allowing us to discuss which data links can be made by which actors. The following acronyms and symbols are used. /: Not applicable. ∅: Empty set. P: Pseudomizer. R: Recruiter. PP: Pod provider. T_ID: True identifier. P_ID: Pseudonymous identifier. D: DNS service. The asset identifiers (Axx) are reused from Sect. 4.

Table 1. Which data items can be linked by an actor (column "Link(A,B)", reflexive and transitive relation) considering following scenarios: i) status quo, i.e. users employ their true identity (column: "No-solution"); ii) pseudonymous WebID solution; iii) DID:Key solution. The following acronyms and symbols are used. /: Not applicable. ∅: Empty set. P: Pseudomizer. R: Recruiter. PP: Pod provider. T_ID: True identifier. P_ID: Pseudonymous identifier. D: DNS service. The asset identifiers (Axx) are reused from the LINDDUN analysis.

Link(A,B)	WebID	DID:Key
Link(T_ID, A01)	PP	PP
Link(T_ID, A02)	PP	PP
Link(T_ID, A03)	/	/
Link(P_ID, A03)	P or R	P or R
Link(P_ID, A05)	P or R	P or R
Link(P_ID, A05a)	P or R	∅
Link(T_ID, P_ID)	P or (R, P_IDP, D)	P

- *Link(T_ID, A01) and Link(T_ID, A02)*: In all cases, PP is able to link T_ID with A01 andA02. Hence, a vast amount of trust is required in PP.
- *Link(T_ID, A03)* In the "no solution" scenario, both PP and R can directly link T_ID with A03. For the other two pseudonymous scenarios, PP and R can only create a link between P_ID and A03.
- *Link(P_ID, A05a)* The WebID solution allows R to discover more information, A05a, i.e. information about the *party hosting the pseudonym document* (A05), for example, through DNS probing. This is not the case for the DID:Key solution, as R can algorithmically generate A05.
- *Link(T_ID, P_ID)* P allows users to create and use P_ID. This service is thus able to associate one's T_ID with a created P_ID. As the WebID solution also involves the IDP leasing the pseudonymous IDs and the DNS service(s) handling requests to the corresponding domain, this introduces additional attack vectors that can lead to link T_ID with a P_ID.

7.4 Discussion

The requirement validation showed that both solutions cover most requirements (although the WebID solution remains observable, and the DID:Key solution does not allow deleting or managing deleting pseudonyms). The STRIDE analysis showed a couple of threats for both the WebID and DID:Key solution, that can be (partially) mitigated by the suggested countermeasures. The LINDDUN privacy analysis results, however, indicate that the WebID solution has an increased risk of linking, identifying, non-repudiation and detecting, due to its reliance on an external IDP to host the pseudonym.

8 Conclusion

Users can protect their privacy using a pseudonym. In this paper, we show how we can combine Solid and DID standards to provide pseudonymity, and which (partial and open) threats were identified.

As demonstrated with our use case, both WebIDs and DIDs can be used as pseudonymous identifiers. However, WebIDs cannot be created autonomously, as they inevitably depend on other actors (i.e., IDPs and DNS Registrars), and require the pseudonym document to be resolved from the Web. Using the `did:key` method, we can build completely self-standing pseudonymous DID identifiers.

We did not tackle the trust that is needed from the issuers or pod providers in our case. Indeed, a lot of trust is needed in the pod provider or pod providing software, as this is the holder's storage for all its credentials, and the pod has the required functionality to sign credentials (e.g., to create the cross-signed VC during identity binding). Furthermore, our STRIDE analysis was only performed from the viewpoint of the holder. Alternative viewpoint analyses (e.g., the recruiter's) are needed to make our analysis more complete.

The EUDI Wallet regulations are an incentive to improve personal data sharing while maintaining privacy. With this pseudonymity work, we hope to provide a next step to combine personal data storage incentives with Wallet incentives.

In future work, we aim to advance our threat analyses by leveraging specialized threat-analysis tooling (e.g., SPARTA), and further investigate alternative deployments, e.g., by hosting a pod (proxy) on the holder's local device.

Acknowledgements. The described research activities were supported by SolidLab Vlaanderen (Flemish Government, EWI and RRF project VV023/10). imec ICON project SHARCS (Agentschap Innoveren en Ondernemen project nr. HBC.2022.0543), and Interreg project SecuWeb (0100085). The authors thank Vincent Naessens, Ruben Verborgh, and Pieter Colpaert for their valuable feedback.

Declarations. The authors declare no conflict of interest.

References

1. OpenID Connect Protocol. https://auth0.com/docs/authenticate/protocols/openid-connect-protocol
2. Solid Technical Reports (2021). https://solidproject.org/TR/

3. Balseiro, V., Turdean, T., Zucker, J.: Solid WebID Profile (2023). https://solid.github.io/webid-profile/
4. Bernstein, G., Sporny, M.: BBS cryptosuite v2023 (2023). https://www.w3.org/TR/2023/WD-vc-di-bbs-20231218/
5. Boneh, D., Boyen, X., Shacham, H.: Short Group Signatures (2004). https://doi.org/10.1007/978-3-540-28628-8_3
6. Braun, C.H.J., Horne, R., Käfer, T., Mauw, S.: SSI, from Specifications to Protocol? Formally verify security! In: ACM Web Conference (2024). https://doi.org/10.1145/3589334.3645426
7. Braun, C.H.J., Käfer, T.: Attribute-based access control on solid pods using privacy-friendly credentials. In: Poster and Demo Track of the 18th International Conference on Semantic Systems (SEMANTiCS) (2022). https://ceur-ws.org/Vol-3235/paper1.pdf
8. Campbell, B., Bradley, J., Sakimura, N., Lodderstedt, T.: OAuth 2.0 Mutual-TLS Client Authentication and Certificate-Bound Access Tokens. RFC 8705 (2020). https://doi.org/10.17487/RFC8705
9. Capadisli, S.: Linked Research on the Decentralised Web (2019). https://csarven.ca/linked-research-decentralised-web
10. Capadisli, S., Berners-Lee, T., Verborgh, R., Kjernsmo, K.: Solid Protocol (2022). https://solidproject.org/TR/protocol
11. Chaum, D., Larangeira, M., Yaksetig, M., Carter, W.: W-OTS+ up my sleeve! A hidden secure fallback for cryptocurrency wallets (2021). https://doi.org/10.1007/978-3-030-78372-3_8
12. Coburn, A., Pavlik, E., Zagidulin, D.: Solid-OIDC (2022). https://solidproject.org/TR/oidc
13. Deng, M., Wuyts, K., Scandariato, R., Preneel, B., Joosen, W.: A privacy threat analysis framework: supporting the elicitation and fulfillment of privacy requirements. Requir. Eng. (2011). https://doi.org/10.1007/s00766-010-0115-7
14. Deng, X., Tian, C., Chen, F., Xian, H.: Designated-verifier anonymous credential for identity management in decentralized systems. Mob. Inf. Syst. **2021** (2021). https://doi.org/10.1155/2021/2807395
15. European Commission: EU Digital Identity Wallet – Architecture and Reference Framework (2025). https://eu-digital-identity-wallet.github.io/eudi-doc-architecture-and-reference-framework/2.0.0/
16. European Network and Information Security Agency: Pseudonymisation techniques and best practices: recommendations on shaping technology according to data protection and privacy provisions (2019)
17. Fallatah, K.U., Barhamgi, M., Perera, C.: Personal data stores (PDS): a review. Sensors (3) (2023). https://doi.org/10.3390/s23031477
18. Florea, M., Esteves, B.: Is automated consent in solid GDPR-compliant? An approach for obtaining valid consent with the solid protocol. Information (12) (2023). https://doi.org/10.3390/info14120631
19. Gabel, A., Schiering, I.: Privacy Patterns for Pseudonymity (2019). https://doi.org/10.1007/978-3-030-16744-8_11
20. Hackett, M., Hawkey, K.: Security, privacy and usability requirements for federated identity. In: Workshop on Web (2012)
21. Heitmann, B., Kim, J.G., Passant, A., Hayes, C., Kim, H.G.: An architecture for privacy-enabled user profile portability on the web of data. In: 1st International Workshop on Information Heterogeneity and Fusion in Recommender Systems (2010). https://doi.org/10.1145/1869446.1869449

22. Hofmeier, M., Pöhn, D., Hommel, W.: DistIN: analysis and validation of a concept and protocol for distributed identity information networks. In: 19th International Conference on Availability, Reliability and Security (2024). https://doi.org/10.1145/3664476.3669930
23. Johnson, D., Menezes, A., Vanstone, S.: The elliptic curve digital signature algorithm (ECDSA). Int. J. Inf. Secur. **1**(1), 36–63 (2001). https://doi.org/10.1007/s102070100002
24. Kersic, V., Vidovic, U., Vrecko, A., Domajnko, M., Turkanovic, M.: Orchestrating digital wallets for on-and off-chain decentralized identity management. IEEE Access (2023)
25. Kim, T., Seo, D., Kim, S.H., Lee, I.Y.: A comprehensive approach to user delegation and anonymity within decentralized identifiers for IoT. Sensors **24**(7) (2024). https://doi.org/10.3390/s24072215
26. Mirzamohammadi, O., Jannes, K., Sion, L., Van Landuyt, D., Abidin, A., Singelée, D.: Security and privacy threat analysis for solid. In: IEEE Secure Development Conference (SecDev) (2023). https://doi.org/10.1109/SecDev56634.2023.00033
27. More, S., Heher, J., Fasllija, E., Mathie, M.: Service provider accreditation: enabling and enforcing privacy-by-design in credential-based authentication systems. In: 19th International Conference on Availability, Reliability and Security. ARES 2024 (2024). https://doi.org/10.1145/3664476.3669934
28. Mourby, M., Mackey, E.: Identity, profiles and pseudonyms in the digital environment, chap. 14 (2024). https://doi.org/10.2307/jj.12124947.16
29. Niu, Y., Wei, L., Zhang, C., Liu, J., Fang, Y.: Towards anonymous yet accountable authentication for public Wi-Fi hotspot access with permissionless blockchains. IEEE Trans. Veh. Technol. **72**(3) (2023). https://doi.org/10.1109/tvt.2022.3218528
30. Pfitzmann, A., Köhntopp, M.: Anonymity, unobservability, and pseudonymity - a proposal for terminology. In: Designing Privacy Enhancing Technologies, Intl. Workshop on Design Issues in Anonymity and Unobservability (2000). https://doi.org/10.1007/3-540-44702-4_1
31. Pillitteri, V.Y.: Assessing security and privacy controls in information systems and organizations (2022)
32. Schardong, F., Custódio, R.: Self-sovereign identity: a systematic review, mapping and taxonomy. Sensors (15) (2022). https://doi.org/10.3390/s22155641
33. Shostack, A.: Threat Modeling: Designing for Security (2014)
34. Sion, L., Wuyts, K., Yskout, K., Van Landuyt, D., Joosen, W.: Interaction-based privacy threat elicitation. In: IEEE European Symposium on Security and Privacy Workshops (EuroS&PW) (2018). https://doi.org/10.1109/EuroSPW.2018.00017
35. Sporny, M., Guy, A., Sabadello, M., Reed, D.: Decentralized identifiers (DIDs) V1.0 (2022). https://www.w3.org/TR/did-core/
36. Sporny, M., Jr, T.T., Jones, M., Cohen, G., Herman, I.: Verifiable credentials data model V2.0 (2025). https://www.w3.org/TR/2025/CRD-vc-data-model-2.0-20250225/
37. Sucasas, V., Aly, A., Mantas, G., Rodriguez, J., Aaraj, N.: Secure multi-party computation-based privacy-preserving authentication for smart cities. IEEE Trans. Cloud Comput. **11**(4) (2023). https://doi.org/10.1109/tcc.2023.3294621

38. Verborgh, R.: End-user identity in Solid: the interoperability problem space (2023). https://solidlab.be/wp-content/uploads/2023/04/End-user-identity-in-Solid-the-interoperability-problem-space.pdf
39. Wild, S., Wiedemann, F., Heil, S., Tschudnowsky, A., Gaedke, M.: ProProtect3: an approach for protecting user profile data from disclosure, tampering, and improper use in the context of WebID. In: Hameurlain, A., Küng, J., Wagner, R., Bianchini, D., De Antonellis, V., De Virgilio, R. (eds.) Transactions on Large-Scale Data- and Knowledge-Centered Systems XIX. LNCS, vol. 8990, pp. 87–127. Springer, Heidelberg (2015). https://doi.org/10.1007/978-3-662-46562-2_4

Identity and Access Management for Dataspaces Using the European Business Wallet and eIDAS-Based Credentials

Tobias Wich, Detlef Hühnlein(✉), Tina Hühnlein, Mike Prechtl, Michael Rauh, Neil Crossley, Florian Otto, and Marina Artis

ecsec GmbH, Sudetenstr. 16, 96247 Michelau, Germany
{tobias.wich,detlef.huhnlein,tina.huhnlein,
mike.prechtl,michael.rauh,neil.crossley,florian.otto,
marina.artis}@ecsec.de
https://ecsec.de

Abstract. The European Commission recently announced the "European Business Wallet" (EUBW) as business-oriented companion to the human-centric and smartphone-based "European Digital Identity Wallet" (EUDIW) in order to boost the competitiveness of European enterprises. While a very important use case of the EUBW is the trustworthy data exchange in industrial Dataspaces using a suitable "Dataspace Protocol" (DSP), the currently available identity and access management approach based on the "Eclipse Decentralized Claims Protocol" (DCP) is unfortunately limited to self-issued identity tokens and decentralized identifiers lacking a clear trust framework and proprietary protocols for the issuance and presentation of credentials, which completely ignore existing standards in the web authorization domain, such as the "OAuth 2.0 Authorization Framework", but instead resemble an existing patent, which is held by Microsoft Technology Licensing LLC.

This is extremely unfortunate for participants within European Dataspaces, because there is the well established and recently amended eIDAS Regulation (EU) No. 910/2014 in place and one may expect that most European enterprises will soon become "Wallet-Relying Parties" (WRP) in the sense of Art. 2 (1) of (EU) 2025/848, which are equipped with X.509-based "Wallet-Relying Party Access Certificates" (WRPAC) according to Art. 2 (12) of (EU) 2025/848. These certificates can not only be used for requesting credentials and claims from the EUDIW, but they can also be used for the automation of many other sensitive business processes using the EUBW and especially the trustworthy identity and access management in industrial Dataspaces across Europe and beyond.

Against this background, we propose an alternative identity and access management architecture utilizing the widely accepted OAuth 2.0 framework and introduce the "Open Identity Protocol" (OIP), which can use the functionality of the EUBW together with standardized credentials including WRPACs, which seems to be much better aligned with the foreseeable European developments driven by the eIDAS Regulation and the forthcoming EUBW.

B. Coppens et al. (Eds.): ARES 2025 Workshops, LNCS 15997, pp. 130–147, 2025.
https://doi.org/10.1007/978-3-032-00639-4_8

Keywords: Decentralized Identifiers (DIDs) · Eclipse Decentralized Claims Protocol (DCP) · European Business Wallet (EUBW) · European Digital Identity Wallet (EUDIW) · Open Authorization (OAuth) · Open Identity Protocol (OIP) · Verifiable Credential (VC)

1 Introduction

On the 29th of January 2025 the president of the European Commission, Ursula von der Leyen, presented the so called "Competitiveness Compass" [10,11], which aims at turning Europe into a place where future technologies, services, and clean products are invented, manufactured, and put on the market. It serves as roadmap and sets out the strategic course the European Commission will follow in the next five years. Among the announced "Flagship Actions enablers" for the year 2025 is the "European Business Wallet" (EUBW), which will build upon the amended eIDAS-Regulation (EU) No. 910/2014 and is envisioned to be "the cornerstone of doing business simply and digitally in the EU, providing a seamless environment for companies to interact with all public administrations."

As outlined in Sect. 2.1 and discussed in [17] in more detail, the EUBW will typically[1] be a server-based system, which complements the human-centric and smartphone-based "European Digital Identity Wallet" (EUDIW) according to Article 3 (42) and 5a of (EU) No. 910/2014 in order to enable automated yet trustworthy electronic business and government processes across Europe. The technical characteristics of the EUDIW is outlined in a high-level manner within the "Architecture and Reference Framework"(ARF) [12], which is part of the common "Union Toolbox" recommended in (EU) 2021/946 and bindingly specified in detail within the growing set of implementing acts[2] and the technical standards referenced therein.

As explained in the recent paper "Towards the European Business Wallet" [17], there are many application scenarios and use cases for the forthcoming EUBW, whereas a particular important one is the trustworthy automated data exchange in industrial "Dataspaces", for which the main concepts and characteristics are about to be standardized in ISO/IEC 20151 [21], using a suitable "Dataspace Protocol" (DSP), such as [19,28] for example, together with the corresponding identity, access and trust management mechanisms as discussed in the present paper.

For this purpose there is in particular the "Eclipse Decentralized Claims Protocol" (DCP) [2], which is unfortunately not based on widely accepted industry standards for web authorization and established trust frameworks, but rather

[1] In addition to the obvious server-based realization, one could imagine a large variety of different implementations, which also include tiny device wallets in form of embedded systems, which communicate with other smart devices using "Machine-to-Machine" (M2M) protocols or other EUBWs in order to realize a "Digital Product Passport" according to Art. 9 of (EU) 2024/1781 for example.

[2] See (EU) 2024/2977, (EU) 2024/2979, (EU) 2024/2980, (EU) 2024/2981, (EU) 2024/2982, (EU) 2025/846, (EU) 2025/847, (EU) 2025/848 and (EU) 2025/849.

utilizes self-issued identities, decentralized identifiers (DIDs) [40] together with potentially arbitrary DID-methods [42] and last but not least proprietary protocols for the issuance and presentation of credentials, which completely ignore existing and widely used and well analyzed standards in the web authorization domain, such as the "OAuth 2.0 Authorization Framework" specified in **RFC 6749** [15] and related standards, but instead seems to resemble the **patent** "Decentralized attribute-based access control" **US20230388287A1** [27], which has been granted on the 10th of December 2024 and which is currently held by **Microsoft Technology Licensing LLC**.

Therefore using DCP in industrial Dataspaces does not only impose a serious threat with respect to sovereignty, but potentially also creates additional security risks, because this set of protocols is not based on existing and well analyzed[3] standards such as OAuth 2.0 and well defined trust frameworks, such as the one defined by the eIDAS-Regulation. Therefore it is very hard to reason about the overall security of such a system in a serious manner. Consequently, it is, unfortunately, currently rather unclear, whether one can finally put trust in an industrial Dataspace built on such uncertain grounds.

Against this background, the present paper proposes to utilize the widely accepted "OAuth 2.0 Authorization Framework" specified in **RFC 6749** [15] and related standards in order to end up with a set of protocols for the identity, access and trust management in Dataspaces, which we collectively call the "Open Identity Protocol" (OIP). This approach leverages the capabilities of the forthcoming EUBW in combination with standardized credentials, such as the X.509 [22] and **RFC 5280** [7] based "Wallet-Relying Party Access Certificates" (WRPACs) and optionally additional electronic attestations, and aligns more closely with upcoming European developments driven by the amended eIDAS Regulation and the advent of the EUBW.

In addition to these obvious advantages for "Business-to-Business" (B2B) and "Business-to-Government" (B2G) processes, our approach also allows to easily integrate natural persons into the emerging Dataspaces in order to implement efficient "Business-to-Consumer" (B2C) and in a similar manner also "Government-to-Citizen" (G2C) processes. Note, that this feature does *not* require any additional effort, if one assumes that the EUBW is also acting as "Wallet-Relying Party" (WRP) according to Art. 2 (1) of (EU) 2025/848 in order to communicate with EUDIWs using the "OpenID for Verifiable Presentations" (OID4VP) protocol [41]. We assume that this feature may turn out to be crucial for Dataspaces in which natural person play a central role, such as in the recently enacted "European Health Data Space" (EHDS) according to (EU) 2025/327 for example.

The rest of the paper is structured as follows: Sect. 2 provides an overview of the system architecture in Sect. 1 and then recalls the most relevant existing related work. This includes a short summary of the existing versions of the DSP [19,28] in Sect. 2.2, for which the latter is envisioned to be submitted to ISO

[3] See RFC 6819 [29] and RFC 9700 [30] for OAuth 2.0 related security considerations and recommended practices.

in the near future, the most important existing web authorization standards in Sect. 2.3, which may be used to realize an authentication and authorization layer for DSP, the most relevant aspects of DCP in Sect. 2.4 and the necessary background on the "OpenID for Verifiable Presentations" (OID4VP) protocol, which is used by WRPs to access the EUDIW which stimulated the creation of the present paper. Section 3 is the main part of the present paper in which we present our alternative "Open Identity Protocol" (OIP) based on the widely used "OAuth 2.0 Authorization Framework" according to **RFC 6749** [15] and eIDAS-based credentials, which may be expected to be available all over Europe soon. Section 4 discusses the advantages and disadvantages of the two approaches and we conclude the paper in Sect. 5 with a brief summary of the main results and an outlook with respect to possible further developments.

2 Background

2.1 Overview and System Architecture

As outlined in Fig. 1 we concentrate on the typical setting of a Dataspace as described in [19,21,28] for example, in which there are at least two "Participants", which are acting as "Provider" and "Consumer" of data and services, which are collectively called "Datasets", and which are equipped with a "Participant Agent" or "Connector"[4], which is a technical system that is registered within the Dataspace and acts on behalf of the Participant.

A practical implementation of such a Connector is the "Eclipse Dataspace Connector" (EDC), which has been designed and developed within the "Eclipse Dataspace Components" project and extended in related downstream projects, such as "Tractus-X" for example.

In line with the classical ISO OSI reference model defined in ISO/IEC 7498-1 [20] it is commonly assumed, that such a Connector has a "Control Plane", which supports the DSP [19,28] as summarized in Sect. 2.2, and a "Data Plane", which takes care about the data transport using some wire protocol, which is less relevant for the present paper.

Furthermore, we suggest to assume that there is an additional plane separate from the Control Plane, which takes care about the identity, access and trust management and is therefore called "Trust Plane" in Fig. 2 of [17] and also within the present paper.

In this layer lives the DCP [2], which will be briefly summarised in Sect. 2.4 and our alternative proposal OIP, which will be presented in Sect. 3 in more detail.

[4] Note, that the term "Connector" is only used in DSP [19,28], but not in DCP [2], as there is a slightly different focus of the two not yet completely finalized specifications. We do *not* distinguish between these two terms here and rather treat them as synonymous.

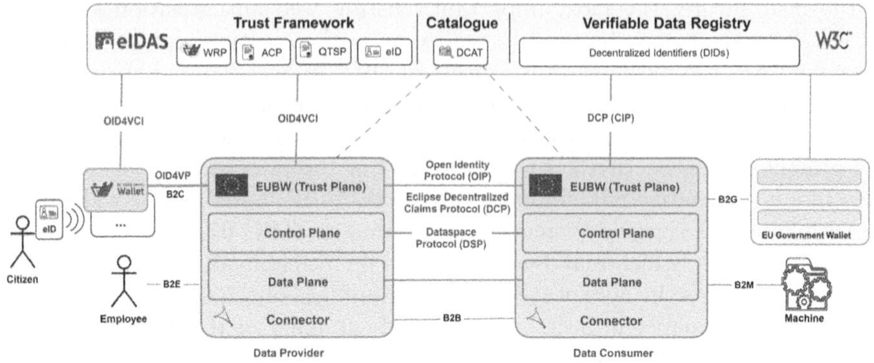

Fig. 1. System Architecture with EUBW in Dataspace

2.2 Dataspace Protocol

The DSP [19,28] lives on the Control Plane of the Connector and specifies a set of protocols and HTTPS[5] bindings for

- the publication of metadata about "Resources" including Datasets available within a Dataspace using a "Catalog" based on the "Data Catalog Vocabulary" (DCAT) [1] for example, which may include or refer to "Policies" expressed within the "Open Digital Rights Language" (ODRL) [18] using the *"Catalog Protocol"* [28, Section 5 and 6],
- the negotiation of "Agreements" for the use of Datasets, which combine a concrete Policy associated with a specific Dataset that has been signed by both the Provider and Consumer using the *"Contract Negotiation Protocol"* [28, Section 7 and 8] and
- the transfer of data using the *"Transfer Process Protocol"* [28, Section 9 and 10], which features both a `push` and `pull` message exchange pattern with `finite` and `non-finite` data [28, Section 9.1.1.2].

While it is clear from a security perspective that there needs to be some sort of "Authentication"[6] of the involved Connectors and the "Authorization"[7] of the different web service requests from some client system within the sphere of the Consumer to some server system on the Provider side, it is important to understand, that DSP does not specify the details with respect to authentication and authorization, but leaves such details to the components within the "Trust Plane". Therefore the DSP specification [28] only contains a rather short Sect. 4.1 on authorization, which reads as follows:

[5] "Hypertext Transfer Protocol" (HTTP) according to RFC 9110 [14] over "Transport Layer Security" (TLS) according to RFC 8446 [37].

[6] See [4] for an overview of protocols for authentication and key establishment.

[7] See [33] for a systematic literature review for authorization and access control.

"All requests to HTTPS endpoints should use the `Authorization` *header to include an authorization token. The semantics of such tokens are not part of these specifications. The* `Authorization` *HTTP header is optional if the Connector does not require authorization."*

As there is no reference in DSP [28] to any of the existing HTTP specifications including the latest one in **RFC 9110** [14], it is unfortunately not entirely clear, what "the `Authorization` header" and the mentioned "authorization token" exactly means here, but one may guess that the `Authorization` header according to the HTTP specification could be meant here.

The corresponding definition in the latest HTTP specification in **RFC 9110** [14, Section 11.6.2] is as follows:

"The "Authorization" header field allows a user agent to authenticate itself with an origin server – usually, but not necessarily, after receiving a 401 (Unauthorized) response. Its value consists of credentials containing the authentication information of the user agent for the realm of the resource being requested."

Note, that in this basic web model, there is a **HTTP Client**, called "user agent" in **RFC 9110** [14, Section 11.6.2], which is in a straightforward setting part of the Consumer sphere, and a **HTTP Server**, which is typically part of the Provider system. The HTTP Server is hosting some Resource and the HTTP Client wants to access this Resource and therefore needs to authenticate itself by providing some "credential" within the `Authorization` header mentioned above.

2.3 Authorization in the Web and the Dataspace Protocol

For the "credentials containing the authentication information" mentioned in **RFC 9110** [14, Section 11.6.2] there are numerous existing and widely used standards including

- the *"HTTP Digest Access Authentication"* according to **RFC 7616** [35], in which a `nonce` is offered by the server and the client responds with an unkeyed digest of the `username`, the `password`, the given `nonce` value, the HTTP method, and the requested URI,
- the *"Basic HTTP Authentication Scheme"* according to **RFC 7617** [36], in which the credentials are simply transmitted as Base64 encoded `user-id` / `password` pairs,
- the *"The OAuth 2.0 Authorization Framework"* with so called "Access Tokens" (AT) according to **RFC 6749** [15, Section 4], which are issued by an "Authorization Server", which has previously authenticated the Client in the sense of **RFC 6749** and validated a so called "Authorization Grant"[8],

[8] Note, that **RFC 6749** [15, Section 1.3] specifies four different grant types (`authorization code`, `implicit`, `resource owner password credentials`, and `client credentials`) and in addition even provides an extension mechanism [15, Section 4.5 and 8], which allows to define additional grant types. Note, that the **client credentials** grant type is utilized in our proposed OIP in conjunction with **RFC 7523** [23].

- the *"The OAuth 2.0 Authorization Framework"* with opaque "Bearer Tokens"[9] according to **RFC 6750** [26],
- the *"Assertion Framework for OAuth 2.0 Client Authentication and Authorization Grants"* according to **RFC 7521** [6], which is an abstract framework, which needs to be considered together with its specific instantiations, such as
  - SAML according to [34] within the *"Security Assertion Markup Language (SAML) 2.0 Profile for OAuth 2.0 Client Authentication and Authorization Grants"* according to **RFC 7522** [5] and
  - JSON Web Tokens (JWT) according to **RFC 7519** [25] within the *"JSON Web Token (JWT) Profile for OAuth 2.0 Client Authentication and Authorization Grants" according to* ***RFC 7523*** [23], which plays a central role in our proposed OIP.

It is important to note, that despite the impressive number and great variety of existing standards for web authorization within the OAuth 2.0 family and the huge set of related Open Source tools and freely available enterprise solutions, such as Keycloak for example, the editor and key authors of DCP deliberately decided **not** to use any of these existing standards, but rather created something "new", which seems to resemble their patent **US20230388287A1** [27].

Note, that the authors of DCP do not only seem to be negligent here, but even go one step further and "turn around" the commonly used, and well analyzed[10], web authorization and related trust patterns, as in the "Presentation Flow" in [2, Section 5.1] there is an Access Token issued *within the sphere of the "Client"*, which is then shipped to the "Verifier" within the request to access the protected Resource in step (3), such that a corresponding verifiable presentation can later on be fetched by the Verifier in step (6).

2.4 Eclipse Decentralized Claims Protocol (DCP)

The "Eclipse Decentralized Claims Protocol" (DCP) [2] aims at complementing the DSP [19,28] by defining "a set of protocols for asserting participant identities, issuing verifiable credentials, and presenting verifiable credentials using a decentralized architecture for verification and trust."

DCP is using "Verifiable Credentials" (VC) according to the "W3C Verifiable Credentials Data Model" (VCDM) (Version 1.1) [39] with "Self-Issued ID Tokens" and "Decentralized Identifiers" (DIDs) according to [40].

While the DID-Method [42], which is envisioned to be used in DCP is not precisely specified, the examples within the DCP specification [2] mention `did:web` [8].

[9] Note, that there is the "OAuth 2.0 Demonstrating Proof of Possession (DPoP)" mechanism according to **RFC 9449** [13], which provides a cryptographic binding of the token to a key pair for enhancing security beyond bearer tokens and that there is a somewhat related internet draft for "OAuth 2.0 Attestation-Based Client Authentication" [32], which could provide even more security by providing a current attestation of the trustworthiness of the involved platform.

[10] See **RFC 9700** [30] and the references therein.

DCP emphasizes to follow the classical role model with an "Issuer", "Holder" and "Verifier" depicted both in [2, Figure 1] and [39, Figure 1] and the detailed internal structure of the Holder is shown in [2, Figure 1], which is included here for the convenience of the reader (Fig. 2).

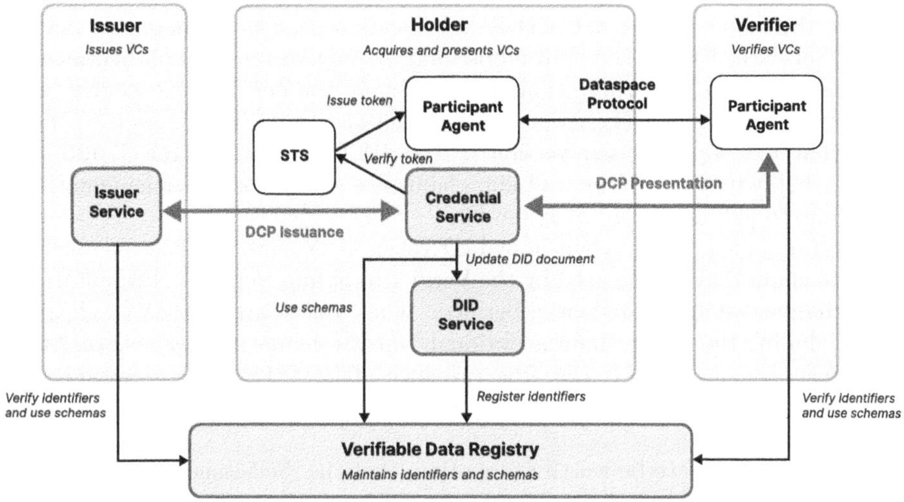

Fig. 2. Information Flow Architecture (from DCP [2, Figure 2])

The Holder contains a so called "Participant Agent", which communicates with another Participant Agent within the "Verifier" via the DSP. These agents correspond to the Control Plane of the Connector in Fig. 1 above. Furthermore, the Holder also contains the following identity-related agents, which essentially have the same purpose as the EUBW in the Trust Plane of the Connector in Fig. 1 (see [2, Section 2.1.2]):

- *"Security Token Service* (STS) – The STS creates self-issued authorization tokens that contain identity claims used by participant agents under the control of the same participant.
- *Credential Service* (CS) – The CS manages Verifiable Credentials. This includes read and write endpoints for Verifiable Presentations and Verifiable Credentials.
- *DID Service* (DIDS) – The DIDS creates, signs[11] and publishes DID documents.

[11] It seems to be questionable, whether this is indeed correct, because signing DID documents to create a VC seems to be among the tasks of an Issuer in a VC-based system according to [39].

As explained in [2, Section 4.3] the Participants use Self-Issued ID Token to authenticate themselves and present self-attested claims to a Verifier. A Self-Issued ID Token is represented as a JWT according to **RFC 7519** [25], which is signed with a private key under the Participant's control. The value of self-attested claims in industrial business processes seems to be worth to discussed and clarified in the definition of a governing trust framework, which seems to be beyond the scope of the current DCP specification [2]. Furthermore, the details of the Self-Issued ID Tokens are unfortunately only sketched in [2, Section 4.3] and leave room for interpretation, which may in the end impose security and interoperability issues. The format of the Self-Issued ID Tokens seem to be a somewhat less sophisticated version of the JWT specified in **RFC7523** [23, Section 3.2], whereas the `iss` and `sub` claims are equal to the participants DID according to [40] and likely `did:web` [8].

As stated in [2, 4.3.1] "a Self-Issued ID Token MAY contain an access token as a `token` claim that can be used by the Verifier to obtain Verifiable Presentations from the participant's Credential Service." The capital letter "MAY" indicates, that including the `token` claim is optional, but it remains unclear, whether this is correct, because in this case the presence of the STS in DCP would also be optional, which does not seem to make sense in any realistic production environment.

Finally, it seems to be worth to mention, that the "Self-Issued ID Tokens" in DCP are handled in a completely different fashion as the equally named tokens mentioned in the "Self-Issued OpenID Provider" (SIOP) specification [43], as the later are issued by an OAuth based OpenID Provider, whereas the tokens in DCP are issued by the STS in an "implementation-specific" way (see [2, Section 4.3.2]), which may be based on the OAuth 2.0 *"Client Credential Grant"* according to **RFC 6749** [15, Section 4.4] (see [2, Section 4.3.2.1.]).

The following figure takes a closer look at the presentation flow of the DCP, where the Holder, which is referred to as Client here, interacts with a Verifier to present a Verifiable Credential (Fig. 3).

The presentation flow begins with the issuance of a Self-Issued ID Token including an Access Token in step (1) and (2), which is sent to the Verifier in step (3). This token contains the DID of the Holder/Client as well as the DID of the Verifier. The Verifier resolves the Holder's DID and retrieves the Credential Service endpoint address from the DID in the steps (4) and (5). Using the Self-Issued ID Token, the Verifier then requests a "Verifiable Presentation" (VP) from the Holder's Credential Service in step (6). Upon validating the ID Token, the Holder responds with the requested VP in step (7), which contains the requested claims. The Verifier can validate the received VP and check it against suitable policies. If the validation passes, the requested resources are returned to the Holder by the Verifier in step (8). More details with respect to the presentation flow can be found in the DCP protocol specification [2, Section 5.1].

The *"Credential Issuance Protocol"* specified in [2, Section 6] as part of DCP also uses the STS to issue Self-Issued ID Token, which are then sent to the *Issuer Service*. The Self-Issued ID Token contains the DID of the Holder, which

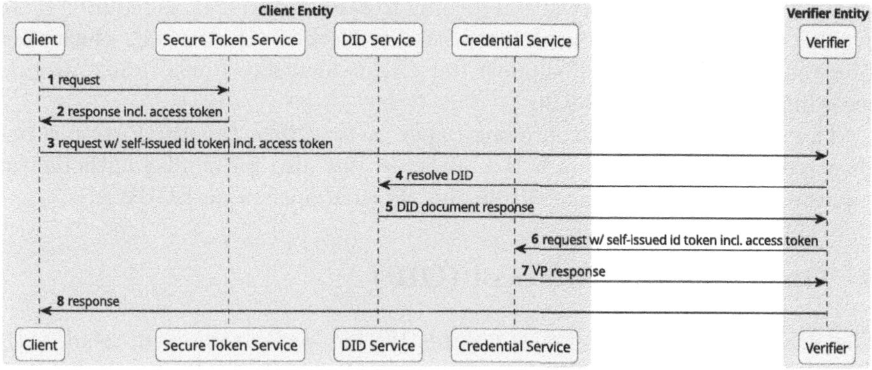

Fig. 3. Presentation Flow (from DCP [2, Figure 4])

is verified and resolved by the Issuer Service. Based on this verification, the request is either approved or rejected. If approved, the Issuer Service generates the Verifiable Credential (VC) and delivers it to the Holder's Credential Service. Further information about this process can be found in the specification of the DCP protocol [2, Section 6.1].

We do not go into more details here, as the functionality provided by the Credential Issuance Protocol is already available in a more mature fashion within the widely used *"ÒpenID for Verifiable Credential Issuance"* (OID4VCI) protocol [31].

2.5 Access Certificates for Wallet-Relying Parties

Art. 5a of the amended eIDAS Regulation (EU) No. 910/2014 has triggered various activities in all European Member States to design, implement, certify and roll-out the "European Digital Identity Wallet" (EUDIW) as technically outlined in the "Architecture and Reference Framework" (ARF) [12] until the end of 2026. As the EUDIW will in particular enable the user to use strong authentication and identification on a high level of assurance, sign by means of qualified electronic signatures by default and free of charge, while providing interesting security and privacy features, such as authenticating the accessing "Wallet-Relying Parties" (WRP)[12] using their X.509-based "Wallet-Relying Party Access Certificates" (WRPAC)[13], it seems to be reasonable to assume that such certificates will be broadly available in Europe after 2027.

These certificates are not only based on X.509 [22] and **RFC 5280** [7], but further profiled in ETSI TS 319 411-8 [9] to foster security and interoperability. The WRPAC in particular allows to create advanced electronic signatures or seals on the `Authorization Request` within OID4VP [41, Section 5] in form of a

[12] See Art. 2 (1) of (EU) 2025/848.
[13] See Art. 2 (12) of (EU) 2025/848.

"JSON Web Signature" (JWS)[14] according to **RFC 7515** [24], as required by the "OpenID4VC High Assurance Interoperability Profile" (HAIP) [44], which stipulates that the EUDIW shall support the "Client Identifier Prefix" `x509_san_dns` according to [41, Section 5.9.3].

The central idea of the present paper is to utilize the WRPAC not only for accessing the EUDIW in a B2C process, but also for similar authorization requests in a B2B Dataspace within the "Trust Plane" of an EUBW.

3 Open Identity Protocol (OIP)

The DSP [19,28] uses the standard HTTP `Authorization` header [14, Section 11.6.2] for authentication against a Connector endpoint. It does not specify further requirements with respect to the authentication and authorization scheme, which allows to combine the DSP [19,28] with a wide variety of authentication and authorization mechanisms. OAuth 2.0 based on **RFC 6749** [15] and the related family of standards (see Sect. 2.3) is nowadays the de facto standard for authentication and authorization in web-based environment using Bearer tokens to authenticate requests and authorize web endpoints, making it an ideal fit for the DSP [19,28].

Therefore our proposed "Open Identity Protocol" (OIP) is consciously designed to utilize the well established and widely accepted standards from the OAuth 2.0 family, whenever possible, to realize the required authentication and authorization functionality to be plugged into DSP and ideally allow to use existing stock components, which are sometimes even available as enterprise-grade Open Source. This makes our OIP fit very well into the modern web and allows the solution to utilize existing and freely available "Authorization Server" (AS) and "Client" components, such as Keycloak for example.

As Dataspace environments are inherently decentralized and federated, typically each participant and Connector maintains its own AS in order to control access to its endpoints in the Control plane and its provided resources, such as its Datasets, which are typically registered in the local Catalog of the Connector and shared with the central Catalog of the Dataspace. The AS authenticates and authorizes the foreign party on behalf of the accessing Connector and issues an "Access Token" (AT), which is then used to access the Connector API on the Control Plane. The accessed Connector therefore realizes the role of a "Resource Server" (RS), while the accessing Connector is the Client in the sense of **RFC 6749** (see [15, Section 1.1]). The accessed Connector can then validate the provided AT and extract further information about the accessing subject with "Token Introspection" according to **RFC 7662** [38], or alternatively evaluate the standardized JWT-based Access Tokens according to **RFC 9068** [3], which may even simplify the overall message flow and integration (Fig. 4).

Note, that the identity within the `sub` claim of the JWT within the client authentication and possibly further claims about the authenticated client may

[14] Note, that a JWS according to **RFC 7515** [24] is by definition also a JWT according to **RFC 7519** [25].

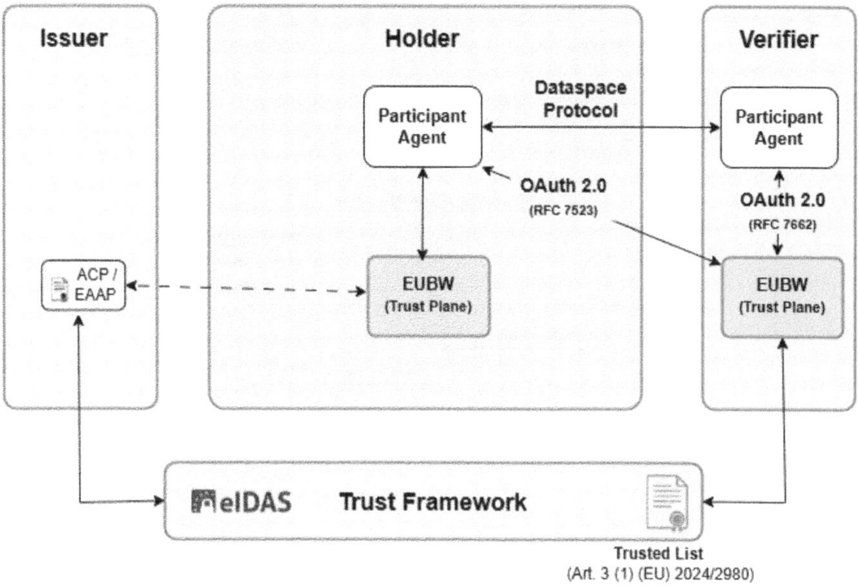

Fig. 4. Overview of the Open Identity Protcol using EUBW

be evaluated by an external "Policy Engine", as explicitly depicted within the overview diagram in the previous version of the DSP [19].

3.1 Basic JWT-Based Token Request Using the EUBW

OAuth is in general very unspecific with regard to the actual authentication means. This allows to plug in any method, which fulfils the applicable policy and security requirements of the environment. The EUBW may be expected to also act as WRP and consequently has an X.509-based WRPAC, which can be used to identify the legal entity owning the wallet. It can therefore be easily used to register and authenticate a participant in a Dataspace. Although registration of an OAuth Client in the context of Dataspaces is not discussed further in this paper, it should be noted, that the WRPAC can be used to identify the Participant there, too. It is further assumed that the registration of the OAuth Client is established beforehand.

The basic JWT-based Token Request, as shown in Fig. 5, starts by creating a JWT signed by the EUBW using the WRPAC. This JWT is signed by the key registered for this Client in the AS of the Data Provider. The Client can then directly use the JWT to authenticate itself while invoking directly the token endpoint using a JWT-based authentication according to **RFC 7523** [23] using a simple "Extension Grant"[15] according to Sect. 4.5 of **RFC6749** [15].

[15] When performing machine-to-machine based Client authentication, a preceding Authorization Request makes no sense, and is indeed not necessary as explained

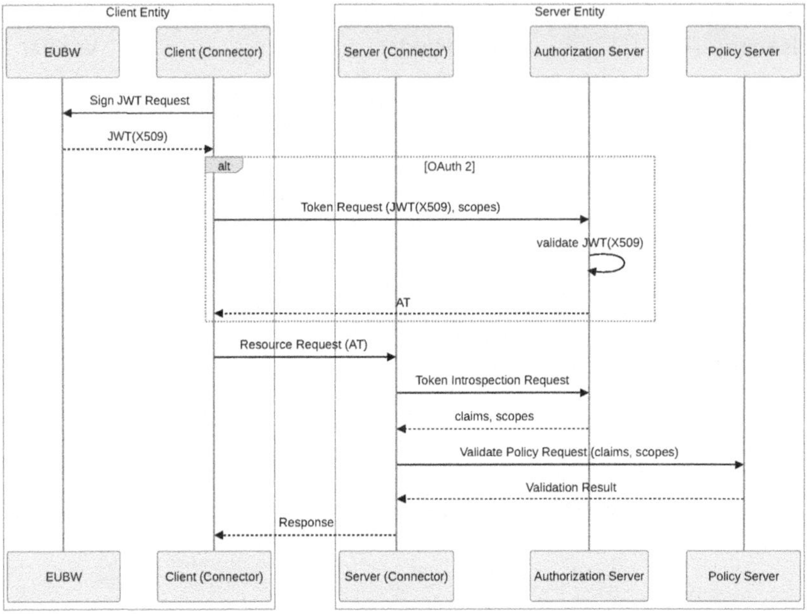

Fig. 5. Basic JWT-based Token Request using the EUBW

The AS of the Data Provider then validates the JWT with the used X.509-based WRPAC and determines whether the requestor is allowed to receive an AT for the Control Plane of the Connector. Optionally provided scope values may further specify the operations the Client intends to use with the AT. Once the request is validated, the Client receives the AT for further use within the Control Plane of the Connector within the DSP.

Note, that the previous version of the DSP from 2024 [19] contained an explicit step in which the eligibility of the request is determined by performing a policy evaluation. In the OAuth 2.0 variant discussed here, the right place to perform this policy evaluation seems to be after the resource request has been issued and further information has been retrieved for the authentication and authorization of the requestor. This may include claims, scope values, and other metadata, which are available either in the AT itself, as specified in **RFC 9068** [3], or by performing an additional token introspection call according to **RFC 7662** [38] against the AS.

3.2 Using Additional Electronic Attestations

Although using the WRPAC of the EUBW provides a very simple mechanism, that can be realized with widely available standard components and services,

in the description of the closely related "Client Credential Grant" (see Sect. 4.4 of **RFC 6749** [15]).

since only finalized and widely accepted standards from the OAuth 2.0 family are utilized in our OIP, the information available to the AS during authentication may be quite limited depending on the detailed content of the WRPAC, which is currently specified ETSI TS 119 411-8 [9].

In order to overcome this potential limitation and harness the full power of the EUBW and the trust framework of the eIDAS-Regulation, it would be desirable to have the option to include additional self-asserted claims and further electronic attestations issued by some trusted third party in the JWT, which is used for requesting the AT at the Token Endpoint of the AS. Fortunately, this possibility for including additional claims and attestations his already been considered in [23, Section 3, Nr. 8], which clearly states that "The JWT MAY contain other claims."

Furthermore, it is clear that corresponding credentials and electronic attestations from trusted third parties can simply be obtained using the widely accepted OID4VCI protocol [31], and the initial step in Fig. 5 may use a simplified[16] profile of the standardized OID4VP protocol [41] between the EUBW and the Connector, which in this case acts as relying party for the EUBW here.

Finally, it seems to be worth to be noted here, that – depending on the specific policy and security requirements within the Dataspace – one may instead or additionally utilize the "OAuth 2.0 Attestation-Based Client Authentication" [32] in order to utilize attestation mechanisms in order to ensure and attest the trustworthiness of the involved platforms, which may in particularly be useful in so called "Compute-to-Data" scenarios as outlined in [45].

4 Discussion

The DCP [2] uses Verifiable Credentials for authentication and authorization within the DSP. Issuing these credentials can be seen as the registration step necessary for the participation in a Dataspace, or to apply for access to a specific Connector. These credentials are then used as claims data sources for the access decision after a resource request has been issued. Unfortunately, this construction makes it necessary to deviate from mainstream architectural web authorization patterns and invent a non-standard protocol flow, where VPs can be retrieved with an AT issued within the wallet of the Holder. It also deviates from the well-established methodology that an Access Token for a Resource Server is issued by the entity owning the Resource, such as a Dataset for example. Instead, the AT is intended for the issuer of the resource request and can be used to retrieve the asserted information about the requestor.

On the other hand, our strictly OAuth 2.0 based OIP proposed in this paper, does not invent a new method for registration, authentication and authorization, but simply utilizes well-established standards from the OAuth 2.0 family. This has the important benefit, that the required components and services for the

[16] Note, that the Connector and the EUBW are typically operated in the same environment, there is no need to utilize Access Certificates ad the security enhanced HAIP [44] here.

base variant can be realized with unmodified standard components from the OAuth 2.0 domain.

Our approach also allows to include additional self-attested claims or electronic attestations issued by a trusted third party in the JWT-based authentication request to meet additional policy and security requirements.

Finally, a nice and noteworthy side-effect of our OAuth-based proposal is, that at the core it only deals with Access Tokens. It is therefore very easy to remove all parts regarding the internal details of the JWT and policy based claims validation, thus massively simplifying test and development setups.

As already mentioned, the registration for the participation in a specific Dataspace, or for the individual access to a specific Connector in a Dataspace, is a mandatory part of the DCP approach, but in our OAuth-based proposal this is not necessarily the case, because the registration to participate within the eIDAS ecosystem has already happened within the registration process at the "national register of wallet-relying parties" according to Art. 2 (10) of (EU) 2025/848 as a prerequisite to obtain the WRPAC, which is later on used for identity and access management within the Dataspace or for other use cases of the EUBW.

If an explicit registration within a specific Dataspace or with an individual business partner is necessary, this can easily be achieved using standard means and protocols. For example, the EUBW uses a WRPAC, and possibly further electronic attestations can be obtained using standard protocols such as OID4VCI [31]. Finally, it is needless to say that the existing and legally endorsed trust framework, according to the amended eIDAS-Regulation (EU) No. 910/2014 can easily be combined with other contractual agreements and identity management mechanisms, such as those detailed by decentralized identifiers [40] or OpenID Federation [16].

5 Conclusion and Outlook

In the present paper we have presented a standard-based alternative to DCP for the identity and access management in industrial Dataspaces based on the DSP [19,28], which we call the "Open Identity Protocol" (OIP). It utilizes the X.509-based WRPAC, which are assumed to be broadly available in 2027 and beyond. As discussed in the present paper, our OIP has several advantages compared to the previously existing DCP – especially in European Dataspaces in which one may expect, that there will soon be a large population of European enterprises, which also act as WRP and hence already have a governmentally trusted and endorsed WRPAC at hand. Our OIP has also important advantages within international Dataspaces, as this protocol is not touched by the patent **US20230388287A1** [27], which seems to closely resemble DCP.

We intend to present our novel approach to interested stakeholders within the European and international Dataspace communities. Further steps may follow after the initial discussions with relevant communities and stakeholders around the Eclipse, Gaia-X, Catena-X, Tractus-X, Manufacturing-X, and sphin-X for example.

We kindly acknowledge that the present paper has greatly benefited from the fruitful exchange of thoughts with numerous Dataspace and identity management experts including Christian Bormann, Werner Folkendt and Torsten Lodderstedt for example.

Finally, we gratefully acknowledge, that the present work has been supported by the German Federal Ministry of Economics and Energy within the partially funded research projects TEAM-X and moveID and last but not least by the Free State of Bavaria within the GRANIT project.

References

1. Albertoni, R., Browning, D., Cox, S.J.D., Beltran, A.G., Perego, A., Winstanley, P.: Data catalog vocabulary (DCAT) - version 3. W3C Recommendation (2024). https://www.w3.org/TR/vocab-dcat-3/
2. Bertagnolli, A., et al.: Eclipse decentralized claims protocol v1.0-RC3, March 2025. https://eclipse-dataspace-dcp.github.io/decentralized-claims-protocol/v1.0-RC3/
3. Bertocci, V.: JSON Web Token (JWT) Profile for OAuth 2.0 Access Tokens. IETF RFC 9068. https://www.rfc-editor.org/rfc/rfc9068
4. Boyd, C., Mathuria, A., Stebila, D.: Protocols for Authentication and Key Establishment. Springer (2020)
5. Campbell, B., Mortimore, C., Jones, M.: Security Assertion Markup Language (SAML) 2.0 Profile for OAuth 2.0 Client Authentication and Authorization Grants. IETF RFC 7522. https://www.rfc-editor.org/rfc/rfc7522.html
6. Campbell, B., Mortimore, C., Jones, M., Goland, Y.: Assertion framework for OAuth 2.0 client authentication and authorization grants. IETF RFC 7521. https://www.rfc-editor.org/rfc/rfc7521.html
7. Cooper, D., Santesson, S., Farrell, S., Boeyen, S., Housley, R., Polk, W.: Internet X.509 public key infrastructure certificate and certificate revocation list (CRL) profile. IETF RFC 5280 (2008). https://www.rfc-editor.org/rfc/rfc5280
8. DID: Web Method Specification. Unofficial Draft, 31 July 2024. https://w3c-ccg.github.io/did-method-web/
9. ETSI TS 119 411-8: Electronic Signatures and Infrastructures (ESI); Trust Service Providers issuing certificates; Part 8: Common Access Certificate Policy for EUDI Wallet Relying Parties. Draft (2025). https://portal.etsi.org/webapp/WorkProgram/Report_WorkItem.asp?WKI_ID=74431
10. European Commission presents its compass to boost Europe's competitiveness in the next five years (2025). https://ec.europa.eu/commission/presscorner/detail/en/ac_25_385
11. European Commission: Competitiveness Compass for the EU. Communication from the Commission to the European Parliament, the European Council, the Council, the European Economic and Social Committee and the Committee of the Regions (2025). https://commission.europa.eu/document/download/10017eb1-4722-4333-add2-e0ed18105a34_en
12. European Digital Identity Wallet Consortium: Architecture and Reference Framework (ARF) (2025). https://eu-digital-identity-wallet.github.io/eudi-doc-architecture-and-reference-framework/2.1.0/architecture-and-reference-framework-main/

13. Fett, D., Campbell, B., Bradley, J., Lodderstedt, T., Jones, M., Waite, D.: OAuth 2.0 Demonstrating Proof of Possession (DPoP). IETF RFC 9449. https://datatracker.ietf.org/doc/html/rfc9449
14. Fielding, R., Nottingham, M., Reschke, J.: HTTP Semantics. IETF RFC 9110. https://www.rfc-editor.org/rfc/rfc9110
15. Hardt, D.: The OAuth 2.0 Authorization Framework. IETF RFC 6749. https://www.rfc-editor.org/rfc/rfc6749
16. Hedberg, R., Jones, M., Solberg, A., Bradley, J., Marco, G.D., Dzhuvinov, V.: OpenID Federation 1.0 - draft 42 (2025). https://openid.net/specs/openid-federation-1_0.html
17. Hühnlein, T., Hühnlein, D., Stöcker, C., Schwalm, S.: Towards the European Business Wallet. Proceedings of Open Identity Summit 2025 (2025). https://dl.gi.de/items/c1d7ff4a-374a-4c11-a81e-64c5cc607e04
18. Iannella, R., Villata, S.: ODRL Information Model 2.2. W3C Recommendation (2018). https://www.w3.org/TR/odrl-model/
19. International Data Spaces Association: Dataspace Protocol 2024-1 (2024). https://docs.internationaldataspaces.org/ids-knowledgebase/dataspace-protocol
20. ISO/IEC: Information technology—Open Systems Interconnection—Basic Reference Model: The Basic Model. ISO/IEC 7498-1 (1994)
21. ISO/IEC: Information technology—Cloud computing and distributed platforms—Dataspace concepts and characteristics. ISO/IEC DIS 20151 (2025)
22. ITU-T: Information technology - Open Systems Interconnection - The Directory: Public-key and attribute certificate frameworks. Recommendation X.509 (2019). https://www.itu.int/rec/T-REC-X.509-201910-I/en
23. Jones, M.: JSON Web Token (JWT) Profile for OAuth 2.0 Client Authentication and Authorization Grants. IETF RFC 7523. https://www.rfc-editor.org/rfc/rfc7523.html
24. Jones, M., Bradley, J., Sakimura, N.: JSON Web Signature (JWS). IETF RFC 7515. https://www.rfc-editor.org/rfc/rfc7515
25. Jones, M., Bradley, J., Sakimura, N.: JSON Web Token (JWT). IETF RFC 7519. https://www.rfc-editor.org/rfc/rfc7519
26. Jones, M., Hardt, D.: The OAuth 2.0 Authorization Framework: Bearer Token Usage. IETF RFC 6750. https://www.rfc-editor.org/rfc/rfc6750
27. Koen, P., Jahromi, B.G., Dingle, P., von der Wiele, S.M., Marino, J., Latzelsberger, P.: Decentralized attribute-based access control. US patent, US20230388287A1, December 2024. https://patents.google.com/patent/US20230388287A1/en
28. Koen, P., Kollenstart, M., Marino, J., Pampus, J., Turkmayali, A., Steinbuss, S.: Dataspace Protocol 2025-1-RC1, February 2025. https://eclipse-dataspace-protocol-base.github.io/DataspaceProtocol/2025-1-RC1/
29. Lodderstedt, T.E., McGloin, M., Hunt, P.: OAuth 2.0 Threat Model and Security Considerations. IETF RFC 6819. https://www.rfc-editor.org/rfc/rfc6819
30. Lodderstedt, T., Bradley, J., Labunets, A., Fett, D.: Best current practice for OAuth 2.0 security. IETF RFC 9700. https://datatracker.ietf.org/doc/html/rfc9700
31. Lodderstedt, T., Yasuda, K., Looker, T.: OpenID for Verifiable Credential Issuance (2024). https://openid.net/specs/openid-4-verifiable-credential-issuance-1_0.html
32. Looker, T., Bastian, P., Bormann, C.: OAuth 2.0 Attestation-Based Client Authentication. IETF Draft draft-ietf-oauth-attestation-based-client-auth-05 (2025). https://www.ietf.org/archive/id/draft-ietf-oauth-attestation-based-client-auth-05.html

33. Mohamed, A., Auer, D., Hofer, D., Küng, J.: A systematic literature review for authorization and access control: definitions, strategies and models. Int. J. Web Inf. Syst. **18**(2/3), 156–180 (2022)
34. OASIS: Assertions and Protocols for the OASIS Security Assertion Markup Language (SAML) V2.0. OASIS Standard (2005). https://docs.oasis-open.org/security/saml/v2.0/saml-core-2.0-os.pdf
35. Shekh-Yusef, E., Ahrens, D., Bremer, S.: HTTP Digest Access Authentication. IETF RFC 7616. https://www.rfc-editor.org/rfc/rfc7616
36. Reschke, J.: The 'Basic' HTTP Authentication Scheme. IETF RFC 7617. https://www.rfc-editor.org/rfc/rfc7617
37. Rescorla, E.: The Transport Layer Security (TLS) Protocol Version 1.3. IETF RFC 8446. https://www.rfc-editor.org/rfc/rfc8446
38. Richer, J.: OAuth 2.0 Token Introspection. IETF RFC 7662. https://www.rfc-editor.org/rfc/rfc7662
39. Sporny, M., Longley, D., Chadwick, D.: Verifiable Credentials Data Model v1.1 (2022). https://www.w3.org/TR/vc-data-model/
40. Sporny, M., Longley, D., Sabadello, M., Reed, D., Steel, O., Allen, C.: Decentralized Identifiers (DIDs) v1.0 (2022). https://www.w3.org/TR/did-core/
41. Terbu, O., Lodderstedt, T., Yasuda, K., Looker, T.: OpenID for Verifiable Presentations (2025). https://openid.net/specs/openid-4-verifiable-presentations-1_0.html
42. W3C: DID Methods. W3C Group Note (2025). https://www.w3.org/TR/did-extensions-methods/
43. Yasuda, K., Jones, M., Lodderstedt, T.: Self-Issued OpenID Provider V2 - draft 13 (2023). https://openid.net/specs/openid-connect-self-issued-v2-1_0.html
44. Yasuda, K., Lodderstedt, T.: OpenID4VC High Assurance Interoperability Profile - draft 03 (2025). https://openid.net/specs/openid4vc-high-assurance-interoperability-profile-1_0-03.html
45. You, J., Wu, J., Jin, X.X., Chowdhury, M.: Ship compute or ship data? Why not both? In: Proceedings of the 18th USENIX Symposium on Networked Systems Design and Implementation, 12–14 April 2021

Guardians of the Registry: Certificate Transparency for Relying Party Authorization in eIDAS 2

Edona Fasllija[1,2](✉) and Stefan More[1,2]

[1] Graz University of Technology, Graz, Austria
{edona.fasllija,stefan.more}@tugraz.at
[2] Secure Information Technology Center Austria (A-SIT), Graz, Austria

Abstract. User-centric, privacy-preserving identity wallets—such as those defined under the EU Digital Identity (EUDI) framework—control access to their ecosystem by requiring Relying Parties (RPs) to authenticate and declare their data access permissions. Under eIDAS 2, this is realized through two certificates: Access Certificates (RPACs), which authenticate individual service instances, and Registration Certificates (RPRCs), which specify the attributes a service is permitted to request. However, in the absence of auditability, misissuance and silent revocation of these certificates remain undetectable—undermining user trust and regulatory oversight.

To address this gap, we propose RP Certificate Transparency (`RPCT`): a transparent logging architecture that records both issuance and revocation of RP certificates in an append-only, publicly auditable log. By adapting Certificate Transparency (CT) principles to the EUDI context, `RPCT` enables monitoring of issued certificates and detection of overly permissive authorizations. Our design addresses known CT limitations, such as lack of revocation transparency, privacy leakage, and monitoring overhead, and adds support for offline-verifiable proofs that preserve user unlinkability. We demonstrate that our architecture meets the regulation's accountability, auditability, and privacy goals. More generally, our architecture represents an efficient, general-purpose transparency service that can be applied to any user-centric credential system.

Keywords: EUDI Wallet · Certificate Transparency · Accountability

1 Introduction

The 2024 revision of the eIDAS regulation introduces the EU Digital Identity (EUDI) wallet ecosystem. In the EUDI ecosystem, Relying Parties (RPs) must register and state the intended use of user attributes. Further, RPs obtain two kind of certificates from RP Certificate Authorities (CAs): an **RP Access Certificate (RPAC)**, which authenticates the RP, and (optionally) an **RP Registration Certificate (RPRC)**, which enumerates the attributes the RP is

B. Coppens et al. (Eds.): ARES 2025 Workshops, LNCS 15997, pp. 148–165, 2025.
https://doi.org/10.1007/978-3-032-00639-4_9

authorized to request. During a transaction, the wallet authenticates the RP via the RPAC, and then checks that the requested user attributes are within the scope declared in the RPRC. This architecture supports the regulation's data minimization principle. Users are explicitly informed about which RP is asking for which attributes, and the wallet can warn the user if the requested attributes fall outside the registered scope.
Challenges: Despite this design, a corrupt or compromised CA could secretly issue an RPRC with excessive permissions that are not registered by the RP. Using such an overly permissive certificate, a rogue RP gains unauthorized access to user data. Similarly, a CA could issue a bogus RPAC that would allow an attacker to pose as a legitimate RP. Any such missisuance threatens user privacy and completely undermines data minimization and user consent. In the Web PKI, Certificate Transparency (CT) addresses the problem of misissued certificates [11]. CT requires CAs to publish every issued TLS certificate in a public, append-only log. However, applying the standard CT mechanisms to RPACs and RPRCs offers only a partial solution. In classic CT, a log records only certificate *issuance* and provides no built-in transparency for certificate *revocation*. Beyond revocation, in the current CT designs, verifiers rely on Signed Certificates Timestamps (SCTs) as proof of logging, but this shifts trust to log servers. Moreover, the SCT auditing process compromises user privacy by leaking the user's browsing history. Also, Certificate Transparency (CT) relies on Monitors to continuously process the log for misissued certificates. This process requires full log scans that are computationally and bandwidth intensive.
Contributions: We propose `RPCT`, a system that relies not only on cryptographic signatures on RPACs and RPRCs, but also a publicly verifiable append-only log of all issued certificates. Our solution is tailored for the EUDI Wallet ecosystem and achieves verifiable logging of both issuance and revocation of RPACs/RPRCs, and enforces binding among the two. `RPCT` is designed with offline proofs: a user's device can validate the authenticity of log proofs without leaking which RP is being checked. Finally, our system supports efficient monitoring through a scalable and optimized underlying data structure to ensure practicality at EU scale.

Outline: Sect. 2 outlines the existing systems and the foundational context required to design `RPCT`. Section 4 introduces this paper's architecture and formulates our goals. Also, we derive system requirements from legal texts and literature. Section 5 introduces our transparency framework `RPCT`. We further integrate RPCT into the EUDI Wallet architecture, and detail the extended EUDI protocols. In Sect. 6, we instantiate RPCT using a hybrid authenticated data structure that supports both chronological appends and efficient key-based lookups. Section 7 evaluates our proposal with regards to the requirements formulated in Sect. 4, and lists the several ways our system improves on standard CT. Finally, we discuss operational aspects and make recommendations for the eIDAS process in Sect. 8.

2 Background

Certificate Authorities (CAs) issue certificates that bind an entity's identity information to its cryptographic public key [1]. *Authorization Certificates* are a special type of certificates that bind entities to authorization policies [5]. *Credentials* or *Attestations of Attributes* bind an entity's identity information to attributes of that entity.

Certificate Transparency (CT) is a WebPKI framework that records all TLS certificates issued by CAs [11]. In CT, each CA submits every certificate it issues to one or more public servers called *logs*. Each log maintains a Merkle history Tree, and periodically publishes a Signed Tree Hash (STH). Upon certificate submission, the log returns a Signed Certificate Timestamp (SCT) which is a promise that the certificate will be included in the log within a fixed time window, the Maximum Merge Delay (MMD). Clients (i.e., web browsers) require that each certficate they accept is accompanied by a valid SCT. Domain owners and Monitors fetch log entries and check for misissued certificates, while Auditors ensure that the log grows in an append-only fashion and does not equivocate.

Key Transparency (KT) schemes are an extension of CT for public keys [13]. KT protocols treat a Key Directory as an append-only authenticated dictionary that maps usernames to public keys. Crucially, KT designs focus on efficient lookups: clients can query the directory for their keys without requiring a full scan. The Key Directory is organized as a Merkle Prefix tree based on the user identifiers. To preserve privacy, KT systems mask user identifiers and hide the directory structure through a Verifiable Random Function (VRF) before insertion.

Both CT and KT systems rely on authenticated data structures; typically variants of Merkle Trees. One important variant in KT-like systems is a *Merkle Patricia Trie (MPT)*. An MPT is a path-compressed and space-efficient variant of a Sparse Merkle Tree that is both prefix-indexed and cryptographically hashed. The basic idea is that each label is encoded as a path in a prefix tree, and every node is hash-linked into the Merkle root. It deterministically encodes all (label,value) bindings and the entire directory can be succinctly identified by a single root hash. Beyond Merkle Trees, *Hash Chains* can be used to record sequential history. As the name implies, in a Hash Chain, each new entry is hashed with the previous hash to form a chain. This allows for the verification of the full history by recomputing from a known anchor.

To reduce reliance on online proof checks and improve privacy, recent work [17] has introduced techniques and specifications for *offline verifiable proofs*. Broadly, these proof bundles are cryptographic attestations that can be verified independently of real-time queries, often using data fetched periodically. This offline approach preserves user privacy by not revealing the user's browsing history.

3 Related Work

CT Improvements: CTng [12] is a redesign of CT aimed at fixing its security gaps. Unlike RPCT, it retains the underlying Merkle Tree data structure but leverages new cryptographic tools (short-lived log keys, aggregate signatures, and a CRLite-inspired certificate revocation vector) to ensure that certificate issuance and revocation are all logged and verifiable without contacting online CAs. Sunlight CT[1] is a fresh CT log design that focuses on improving the scalability of CT by storing and serving certificate entries in fixed-size "tiles" that clients can download and verify offline. In Sunlight CT, SCTs are still used, but with some changes: submissions are batched in 1 s intervals and no SCT is issued until the certificate is actually merged into the tree. In contrast, CTng [12] does not use SCTs (similar to our proposal). After a CA submits a certificate, the log returns a signed tree head (STH) and an inclusion proof. The CA embeds these in the certificate, so the certificate itself proves it was logged. Monitors then sign the STH to vouch for consistency.

CT in EUDI ARF: The EU Architecture Reference Framework (ARF) [2] treats CT for Access Certificates as a requirement. While the ARF requires Access CAs to log all issued certificates in CT, it does not extend this requirement to RPRCs and does not provide any details on how CT should be integrated into the overall architecture. Some national drafts (Germany [7], Italy [8,9]) similarly discuss embedding SCTs or CT logs into wallet protocols. However, these usually follow the Web PKI model: global logs, SCTs, and separate revocation (CRL/OCSP) channels. The European Blockchain Services Infrastructure (EBSI) [15] acts as a decentralized, multi-purpose trust infrastructure. Its revocation is typically done by on-chain credential status registries or Verifiable Credentials status lists. These ensure tamper-evidence via blockchain, but are not searchable logs of all issued certificates.

4 Architecture & Goals

4.1 The Verifiable Credentials Framework and eIDAS 2.0

In the generic Verifiable Credentials (VC) framework, the core roles are typically (i) Issuer; who creates and issues credentials, (ii) Holder, who owns the credentials and can present them, and (iii) Verifier, who checks the authenticity and validity of credentials. In the EUDI context, we instantiate these roles with the following entities.

Issuer-related Entities: Issuers, called **PID Providers / Attestation Providers**, are responsible for issuing digital credentials (PID, Attestations) to users' wallets. The providers are accredited or designated by a Member State and their trust anchors are recorded in a Trusted List.

[1] https://sunlight.dev.

Holder-related Entities: The Holder, or **User**, is the subject of the digital credentials. A holder uses a **Wallet Unit** as a secure application that receives, stores, and manages credentials, and selectively discloses user attributes to verifiers.

Verifier-related Entities: A Verifier, called **Relying Party (RP)**, is the service provider that consumes credentials to authenticate users or validate certain user attributes. Each RP needs to register to access the EUDI ecosystem. The **RP Registrar** is a trusted party that verifies RPs during registration. The Registrar publishes the list of registered RPs and their intended use cases in the **RP Registry/Register**. Each RP, once registered, obtains one or more *RP Access Certificates (RPACs)* from a **RP Access Certificate CA** for its operational **RP Instances**. Each RP instance then uses their RPAC to authenticate to Wallet Units. Further, **RP Registration Certificate CAs** issue *RP Registration Certificates (RPRCs)*, which contains details on the attributes that the RP registered to request, and other regulatory metadata. These RPRCs can be used by the wallet to inform users about the legitimacy of a presentation request.

4.2 Goals

Our primary goal is the detection of RP certificate misissuance and overpermissive authorizations. For this, we establish a trustworthy and privacy-preserving authentication mechanism for RPs to interact with EUDI wallets. Conceptually, we want to enable wallets (and thereby users) to verify that the RP is authorized to request certain information. Since wallet authorization is not purely a technical problem, we want to enable competent entities such as data protection authorities to publicly monitor authorizations. In turn, our system ensures that the information observed by the authority matches the information presented to the wallet. For all of this we consider compliance with eIDAS 2.0 principles.

4.3 Requirements

In this section, we formalize our requirements. Based on the aforementioned goals, we explore legal aspects and derive requirements for RP authentication and authorization. We focus on the requirements on the handling of access and registration certificates.[2] We analyze the eIDAS regulation updated in 2024 [4], its corresponding implementing acts[3] (IAs) [3], and relevant literature [14].
Regulatory Requirements: The amended eIDAS regulation defines requirements on RPs in its Articles 5a and 5b.
REQ1 **RP Registration**: RPs must register in the Member State where they are established [4, Article 5b(1–2)].

[2] Other authorization means, e.g., eIDAS' Embedded Disclosure Policies [4, Article 5a], are not in the scope of this paper.

[3] At the time of writing in April 2025, several IAs are still under consultation and/or not published yet.

REQ2 **Purpose Registration**: RPs shall register the intended use of EUDI Wallets, including the data to be requested by the RP [4, Article 5b(1–2)].
REQ3 **RP Registration Transparency**: Member States must publish the registration information of relying parties in a register, suitable for automated processing [4, Article 5b(5)].
REQ4 **RP Authentication**: Relying parties must identify themselves to the user prior to accessing any credential data [4, Article 5b(8)].
REQ5 **Lawfulness**: Relying parties shall not request more data than was indicated during registration [4, Article 5b(3)]. We note that while the eIDAS regulation mentions this requirement as a basis for lawful processing, it does not require enforcement by the wallet. We discuss this aspect further in Sect. 8.2.
REQ6 **User Control & Consent**: Users must retain full control over the data in their European Digital Identity Wallets [4, Article 5a(14)]. Operations in the Wallet must require secure, explicit, and active user confirmation [4, Recital 31].
REQ7 **Privacy**: Wallets must prevent attestation providers or other third parties from tracking, linking, or observing user transactions after issuance, unless explicitly authorized by the user [4, Article 5a(5)(b), 5a(16)(a), Recital 32].

Regulatory Constraints: In addition to the eIDAS regulation itself, several implementing regulations further shape the EUDI wallet framework.[4] These implementing regulations, also called implementing acts (IAs), bridge the gap between legislatory framework and technical framework.

To realize the registration requirements stated by the eIDAS regulation, IAs introduce the concept of *RP Registrars* and *RP Registries*. Further, IAs introduce the concept of two types of certificates: First, *RP Access Certificates* (RPACs) tackle the authentication requirements. Second, (optional) *RP Registration Certificates* (RPRCs) are concerned with the intended purpose stated by a RP during registration (cf. Section 8.2). We discuss these entities in Sect. 4.1.

REQ8.1 **Access Certificates**: RPs shall acquire access certificates. Wallets must not present data to a RP without valid access certificate.
REQ8.2 **Access Information Consistency**: The contact information in the RPAC must match the information published in the RP register.
REQ8.3 **Registration Certificates**: RPs can acquire registration certificates that contain a description of the intended use of the attributes to be requested. Wallets can display that description to users.
REQ8.4 **Registration Information Consistency**: The intended use stored in the RPRC must match the intended use published in the RP register.
REQ8.5 **Certificate Validity**: RP Access and Registration Certificates must be valid and not revoked at time of use.

Additionally, the IA defines *"the obligation for the providers of wallet-relying party access certificates [RPACs] to log all wallet-relying party access certificates they have issued to ensure certificate transparency, in compliance mutatis mutandis with IETF RFC 9162"*, i.e., Certificate Transparency [11].

[4] The eIDAS committee voted on the IA concerning RP registration/authentication on April 9, 2025. However, as of the writing of this paper, the final text was not released; thus, we discuss the latest public draft from December 2024.

REQ9.1 **Certificate Transparency**: RP Access and Registration Certificates shall be publicly logged using certificate transparency.
REQ9.2 **Registration Log Consistency**: The information published in the Log must match the information published in the RP Register.
Additional Requirements: The IA only mandates RPRCs to include description of the intended use of the attributes but is not clear about the attributes itself. This information is needed to inform the user. We thus add an additional requirement.
REQ10 **Attributes in RPRC**: In addition to the description of the intended use, an RPRC must include a machine-readable list or policy of the attributes that the relying party intends to request.
Operational Requirements: We aim to support the system's adaptability to large-scale usage and evolving operational demands.
REQ11.1 **Scalability**: The system supports the EU-wide EUDI Wallet ecosystem. It must be feasible to operate server-side components on this scale. Operations potentially involving large datasets (e.g., monitoring, auditing) shall support efficient processing.
REQ11.2 **Performance**: Verification processes performed by the Wallet must have low latency to ensure a smooth user experience.

4.4 Threat Model

Misissuance of RPACs can allow an attacker to gain unauthorized access to the wallet ecosystem or impersonate a legitimate RP instance. Similarly, misissuance of RPRCs may enable an attacker to request attributes beyond the legally registered scope. We consider the following adversaries: **Malicious RP:** Attempts to claim more permissions than registered, tricking the user or wallet into disclosing more data than permitted. **Malicious CA:** Issues RPACs or RPRCs to fraudulent entities that are not properly registered, or includes unauthorized attributes. A malicious or compromised CA may also issue multiple certificates for the same RP identifier with conflicting attributes or intended use-cases. **Malicious RP Registry:** Silently omits publishing some RP certificates, or removes them after initially listing them. A malicious Registry can modify the recorded details of a certificate after publishing. Finally, the Registry can present different contents to different clients or at different times.

Assumptions: We assume CAs and Registrars use secure digital signatures and that clients have authentic CA/Registrar public keys (trust anchors). We assume trustworthy wallets that can detect certificate validation failures. Our system relies on competent entities to actively monitor the accuracy and legitimacy of information in the registry. We rely on the established security properties of Merkle trees and CT.

5 Design

We propose Relying Party Certificate Transparency (RPCT): a framework that extends the principles of CT to RP Certificates. The primary goal of RPCT is to *detect* and *deter* RP certificate misissuance—such as the unauthorized issuance of an RP Access Certificate (RPAC) to an illegitimate entity, or the issuance of an RP Registration Certificate (RPRC) that grants excessive or unjustified privileges. In addition, RPCT supports the detection of unauthorized attribute requests, where an RP attempts to access user data beyond what was formally registered and approved. To achieve this, RPCT records every issued RPRC and RPAC in a publicly-verifiable, *append-only*, *tamper-evident* log. The log periodically signs a *single public digest* that commits to the entire set of logged certificates to produce a verifiable log state. Based on these digests, the log supports inclusion proofs: a certificate can be cryptographically shown to be present in the log by referencing the latest digest. When a log state evolves from one digest to another, a *consistency proof* demonstrates that no prior entries were modified or removed. Moreover, RPCT extends CT by explicitly logging *revocations* of RP certificates and structurally incorporating them into the log structure. This ensures that proof of presence in the log also reveals whether a certificate is still valid and has not been revoked. As shown in Fig. 1, the RPCT ecosystem involves several entities, analogous to those in regular CT:

RP CAs (RPAC/RPRC CAs) submit each newly issued certificate to the log. **RP Instances** present their certificates and corresponding log proofs during credential presentation. **Wallet Units** verify the certificates that RPs present and their corresponding log proofs before releasing any attributes. The **Logger or Log Server** maintains the log, provides submission and query interfaces, and generates cryptographic proofs. **Monitors** continuously inspect the log for suspicious certificates and alert the affected parties. They further cooperate with competent entities (e.g., DPAs or NGOs) to detect overly permissive registrations. **Auditors** inspect the log to ensure it remains append-only and globally consistent.

Overall, RPCT guarantees that RP CAs are held accountable for every certificate they issue or revoke, and that wallets only trust certificates properly recorded in the log. Based on the goals defined in Sect. 4, the RPCT system exposes a compact set of algorithms for interacting with the log. Section 5.1 defines these algorithms as protocol primitives, together with the purpose and invoking actor(s) for each.

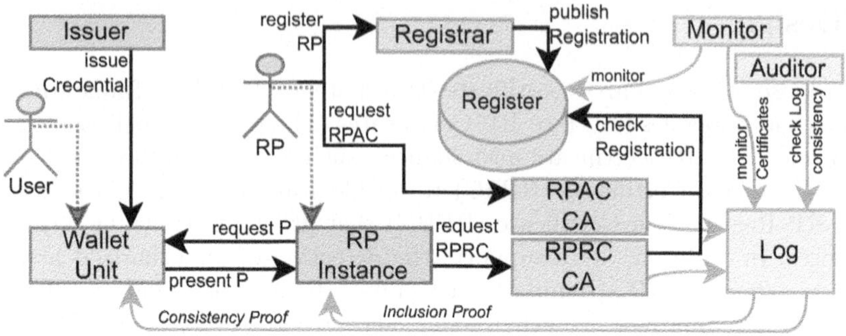

Fig. 1. RPCT: High-level Architecture

5.1 RPCT Definition

Let $\mathcal{E}$ denote the space of certificates (either RPRCs or RPACs). Each entry $e \in \mathcal{E}$ consists of a key-value pair (k, v). The key k encodes the identifier of the Relying Party and the value v consists of the certificate pertaining to the RP. The log maintains an internal state st that contains an ordered list of entries with a committed state digest d. An epoch T denotes a fixed-duration time window during which submitted certificate updates (issuance or revocation) are collected and batch-processed into the append-only log. We define the RPCT scheme as a set of algorithms that define both the *interface* layer exposed to external entities (such as RP CAs, Wallet Units, Monitors and Auditors) and the *internal* operations executed by the log to maintain the append-only log.

Internally, the **Logger** executes batched updates at the end of each epoch, maintains the underlying authenticated data structure, and generates the cryptographic proofs required to support transparency and verifiability:

$\mathsf{Setup}(1^\lambda) \mapsto (st_0, d_0)$ initializes the RPCT system. It sets up public parameters with security parameter λ and initializes an empty transparency log. It outputs an initial state st_0 and public digest (commitment) d_0.

$\mathsf{Update}(st_t, d_t, \mathcal{U}) \rightarrow (st_{t+1}, d_{t+1}, \pi_{incl\,i}, \pi_{cons})$ inserts a sequence of m certificate updates $\mathcal{U} = \{(e_i, T_i)\}_{i=1}^{m}$ at epoch T in the log state st. The log incorporates all pending submissions into the authenticated data structure. It outputs the updated state st_{t+1} and public digest d_{t+1}, inclusion proofs for each added entry $\pi_{incl\,i}$, as well as a consistency proof among the two, π_{cons}.

The following algorithms are used by the **Logger** to prove the transparency properties of the log:

$\mathsf{ProveInclusion}(st, d, e) \rightarrow \pi_{incl}$ is used by the **Logger** to convince a client that a given certificate e was indeed recorded in the log at a certain state st identified by the digest d.

$\mathsf{ProveConsistency}(st_i, st_j) \rightarrow \pi_{cons}$ generates a consistency proof between two states st_i and st_j (with $i < j$) to prove that nothing was removed or altered between these two log snapshots.

$\mathsf{ProveLookup}(st, d, k) \rightarrow (V, \pi_{look})$ outputs a lookup proof for the current value set V associated with k in state st. If a certificate exists for k, the proof π_{look} returns the set of current certificates V for k in the log. If no certificate is present (i.e., the RP is not registered), π_{look} serves as a non-membership proof showing k is absent.

$\mathsf{ProveHistory}(st, k, t_0) \rightarrow (H, \pi_{hist})$ verifies the history of certificate updates for a particular RP identified by key k. It outputs a history proof that links the sequence of certificate updates that have been associated with a RP-related key k starting from epoch t_0. The **Logger** returns the set of all entries matching a query (all certificate updates for key k) along with a proof that this set is complete and correct with respect to the log's current state.

The interface layer includes procedures for submitting certificate updates, retrieving proofs of inclusion or lookup, and verifying consistency over time.

$\mathsf{SubmitEntry}(e, t) \rightarrow (\pi_{incl}, d')$ is used by an **RP CA** to submit a RPRC/RPAC certificate issuance to the log. It first performs necessary validation checks (e.g., signature and policy checks) to ensure the submitter is authorized and the certificate chains to a trusted anchor. In turn, the **Logger** then invokes Update to append this entry (possibly batched with others) to the log. On success, it returns an inclusion proof for the newly added entry along with the log's updated digest to the submitting CA. Similarly, $\mathsf{RevokeEntry}(e, t) \rightarrow (d')$ is used by an RP CA to revoke a previously issued certificate e at epoch t. It creates a new entry in the log state indicating that e is no longer valid. The log appends this update and returns the updated digest of d' of the log state.

An **RP CA**, or the **RP Instance** gets an inclusion proof by running the interface algorithm $\mathsf{GetInclusionProof}(e, d)$. These entities, or the **Wallet Unit** verify the inclusion proof π_{incl} by running $\mathsf{VerifyInclusion}(e, d, \pi_{incl}) \rightarrow 0, 1$ and checking π_{incl} against the known digest d.

Auditors request consistency proofs via $\mathsf{GetConsistencyProof}(st_i, st_j)$ and verify the returned proof with $\mathsf{VerifyConsistency}(d_i, d_j, \pi_{cons}) \rightarrow \{1, 0\}$ to ensure the log did not omit any history. Similarly, $\mathsf{GetLookupProof}(st, d, k) \rightarrow (V, \pi_{look})$ and the verification algorithm $\mathsf{VerifyLookup}(k, V, \pi_{look}, d) \rightarrow \{1, 0\}$ is used by **Monitors** to perform periodic tracking of all certificates related to a specific RP identified by k. **Monitors** audit the full history of certificate updates from an epoch t_0 via $\mathsf{GetHistoryProof}(st, k, t_0)$, and ensure no relevant entries were omitted or falsified by verifying the returned proof by running $\mathsf{VerifyHistory}(k, H, \pi_{hist}) \rightarrow \{1, 0\}$.

5.2 Protocols Specification

We extend relevant EUDI protocols with RPCT to enable transparent, auditable issuance of RP Certificates (RPRCs and RPACs). We describe protocols for issuance of RP certificates (Protocol 1), and RP certificate verification during the interaction of an RP with a wallet (Protocol 2). Steps marked with + are newly introduced by our protocol. Further, we introduce protocols for revocation (Protocol 3) and auditing of RP certificates (Protocols 4 and 5). All protocols build on the RPCT interface (Sect. 5.1) and use an auditable, append-only structure. To omit issuing SCT-like inclusion promises— along with their associated complexity and privacy risks—we assume short epochs and return instead direct inclusion proofs after each update. A concrete instantiation follows in Sect. 6.

- Registration CA (for RPRC) or Access CA (for RPAC) creates a certificate e for the RP embedding the RP public key or the registered use cases for requested attributes.
+ The CA submits the certificate for logging using RPCT.SubmitEntry(e, t) to request logging of the new certificate.
+ The Logger stores e in the pending buffer $\mathcal{U}$. After MMD, the Logger incorporates the newly issued certificate by running RPCT.Update($s_t, d_t, \mathcal{U}$), where $e \in \mathcal{U}$. The log also issues an inclusion proof π_{incl_e}. The log's state is updated to st_{t+1} with new digest d_{t+1}.
+ The log returns (π_{incl_e}, d_{t+1}) to the RP CA. The RP CA attaches π_{incl_e} to e and returns the pair (e, π_{incl_e}) to the RP.

Protocol 1: RPAC/RPRC Issuance Process

+ The RP fetches a fresh inclusion proof for e w.r.t. the latest log digest d by running RPCT.GetInclusionProof(e, st, d) and obtains π_{incl_e}.
+ The RP includes (e, π_{incl_e}, d) for both RPAC and RPRC (if available) in its signed presentation request to a Wallet Unit.
+ The Wallet Unit checks for inclusion of the certificates e in the log by locally running RPCT.VerifyInclusion(e, d, π_{incl_e}) for each certificate. If the algorithm returns true, it confirms that e is part of the set of logged certificates identified by d.
- The Wallet verifies that the RP identifier in RPAC matches that in the RPRC it received, ensuring the RPAC is bound to the correct registration.
- The Wallet ensures all requested attributes in the presentation request comply with the RPRC's policy.
- If all checks pass, the Wallet asks the user's permission and then presents the requested attributes to the RP.

Protocol 2: Credential Presentation

+ Registration CA (for RPRC) or Access CA (for RPAC) prepare a revocation update for a previously logged certificate e by invoking RPCT.RevokeEntry(e, t)
+ The log treats revocations as ordinary append operations, updating the internal data structure, and returns a new state digest that does not include the revoked entry.

Protocol 3: RPAC/RPRC Revocation Process

In addition to the append-only checks in Protocol 4, third-party monitors can audit the certificates for a particular RP. A targeted audit protocol describes

- Each Auditor periodically fetches published roots d_t and $d_{t'}$ at epochs t and t' and requests a consistency proof via $\mathsf{RPCT.GetConsistencyProof}(d_t, d_{t'})$.
- The Log Server runs $\mathsf{RPCT.ProveConsistency}(d_t, d_{t'})$ to produce π_{cons}, the append-only proof that $d_{t'}$ extends d_t.
- Each Auditor runs $\mathsf{RPCT.VerifyConsistency}(d_t, d_{t'}, \pi_{cons})$, which succeeds only if no entries were removed or reordered between versions, ensuring the log's append-only integrity.
- A failure indicates a split-view or log equivocation, triggering an alert and potential delisting of the log.

Protocol 4: Append-Only Auditing Process

how competent third-party monitors in the EUDI Wallet context can verify the current status of the certificates, or optionally the whole history of certificates issued to a specific RP to detect misissuance or wrongful revocations.

- Each Monitor retrieves the most recent fingerprint d_t from the log.
- For each monitored RP with an identifier *rpid*, the monitor looks up the current set of certificates associated with that RP via $\mathsf{RPCT.GetLookupProof}(st, d, k)$.
- The Logger runs $\mathsf{RPCT.ProveLookup}(st, d, rpid) \rightarrow (V, \pi_{lookup})$.
- The monitor verifies the returned proof using $\mathsf{RPCT.VerifyLookup}(rpid, V, \pi_{lookup}, d)$ to confirm that V represents the currently active certificate set (both RPACs and RPRCs) for *rpid*. It also verifies that the query response matches the information in the RP Registry.
- The Monitor also optionally queries for the entire history of certificate updates for *rpid* by running $\mathsf{RPCT.GetHistoryProof}(st, rpid, t_0)$.
- The Log Server runs $\mathsf{RPCT.ProveHistory}(rpid, t_0) \rightarrow (H_{rpid}, \pi_{hist})$, where $H_{rpid} = [(t_i, e_i)]$ is the list of all certificate updates (issuance or revocation) from epoch t_0 to t, and π_{hist} contains inclusion proofs for each certificate update e_i.
- The Monitor checks that $\mathsf{RPCT.VerifyHistory}(rpid, H_{rpid}, \pi_{hist})$ returns true. It also verifies that the query response matches the information in the RP Registry.

Protocol 5: External Auditing Process

6 Instantiation

We now show a concrete instantiation of our RP Certificate Transparency system. The instantiation depends on a few design choices: selection of a suitable data structure for the log, placement of the log in the eIDAS architecture, and encoding of RP identifiers in the log. In addition, our instantiation includes support for offline verifiable proofs, consistent revocation transparency, and binding between RPRCs and RPACs.

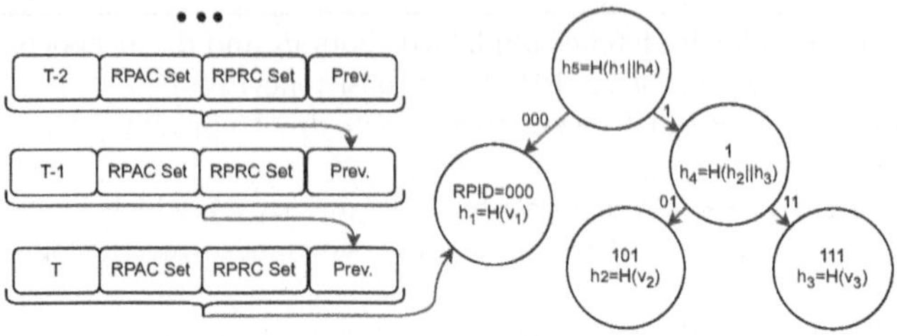

Fig. 2. MPT with per-key Hash Chains

6.1 Data Structure

To implement a tamper-proof, append-only log that supports efficient per-RP queries, RPCT employs a novel authenticated data structure recently proposed by [10]. The log is organized as a key-indexed Merkle Patricia Trie (MPT, depicted in Fig. 2) rather than a *history* tree. Each RP is identified by a unique identifier (*rpid*), serving as the key under which all certificates for that RP are logged. Encoding *rpid* results in a deterministic position in the tree for each RP. Each leaf node of the tree stores a hash chain $h_0, h_1, \ldots, h_t$ capturing the sequence of both RPAC and RPRC certificate updates for that RP.

Encoding of RP Identifiers: We consider several strategies for encoding *rpid*s as keys in the Merkle Patricia Trie. *Hashed Encoding* hashes RP identifiers (e.g., EORI, VAT) into fixed-length keys, producing a balanced but deep tree with longer proof paths. *Reverse Domain Encoding* encodes domain names right-to-left, resulting in shallow tries and short proof depths, though with wider proofs. A third option structures identifiers into segments such as country, type, and ID, producing a shallow, semantically organized trie that supports efficient grouping and queries by the register. Each of these method presents trade-offs in proof size, tree depth, and semantic structure. Selection thus depends on requirements such as proof locality, latency, or jurisdictional auditability.

Append-only RP History: We assume that each RP is assigned a leaf in the MPT, keyed by the cryptographic hash of *rpid*, interpreted as a bit string. The corresponding leaf value stores the current *head* of a per-RP hashchain. Each update (issuance or revocation) produces a new chain element $h_i = \mathsf{Hash}(T_i \parallel v_i \parallel h_{i-1})$, where T_i is the epoch, v_i the certificate set, and h_{i-1} the previous head. This forms an append-only hashchain per RP: as certificates are added or revoked, the chain grows, and each new head h_i implicitly commits to all prior certificates for that RP. Finally, the set of current chain heads $\{(k_i \mapsto h_i)\}$ is embedded in a MPT, which incrementally hashes from the leaves to the root. The MPT root $R = \mathsf{MPT.rootHash}()$ serves as a global commitment to the current state of all RPs.

Maintaining the Data Structure: When a new certificate is issued to or revoked for that RP, the leaf's stored value is updated to h_i, while the old h_{i-1} is cryptographically linked with h_i. h_{i-1} remains in the structure and is indirectly committed via the hash chain. $\mathsf{MPT.ProveIncl}(k, h_t)$ generates an *inclusion proof* for the (k, h_t) pair, i.e., the Merkle proof down this tree: the leaf's node label (key), its stored hash, and all sibling hashes along the path to the root. Verifying it means recomputing these hashes up to the root and checking that the result equals the known root commitment, confirming the pair is present. A *lookup proof* returns the current head h_t for a key k and its inclusion proof. If a key k is not present in the MPT, $\mathsf{MPT.proveAbs}(k)$ demonstrates that k does not exist in the trie. This is done by traversing the trie toward k and identifying a divergence point where the path for k would continue but no corresponding node exists. A *history proof* for or a key k provides the full sequence of heads $\{h_0, h_1, \ldots, h_t\}$, each linked via the hashchain. The verifier checks each link $h_i = \mathsf{Hash}(T_i \parallel v_i \parallel h_{i-1})$ and confirms inclusion of the current head in the MPT. $\mathsf{MPT.proveCons}(R_i, R_j)$ returns a *consistency* proof between two root hashes that shows that R_j extends R_i without deletion. It ensures every leaf of the old tree appears in the new tree and only new leaves were added. For *Revocation*, the CA submits a new value v_{t+1} that omits the revoked certificate, removing it from the set of active certificates. This update is appended like any other, preserving hashchain integrity and requiring no special revocation marker.

6.2 RPCT Instantiation

We now instantiate RPCT with the described data structure. We detail the implementation of RPCT Logger algorithms for certificate inclusion, lookup, inclusion, consistency, and historical queries. Figures 3 and 4 provide details for each of these operations.

Algorithm 1 RPCT.Setup

```
  Initialize empty MPT state st_0
  Generate signature keys (sk, pk)
  R_0 ← Hash(⊥)
  return (st_0, R_0, sk, pk)
```

Algorithm 2 RPCT.ProveConsistency

```
Input: R_a, R_b, with a < b
  π_cons ← MPT.proveCons(R_a, R_b)
  return π_cons
```

Algorithm 3 RPCT.Update

```
Input: State st_t, Root R_t, Updates U
  for all (k, v, T) ∈ U do
      h_prev ← latest head for k (or ⊥ if new)
      h_new ← Hash(T||v||h_prev)
      MPT[k] ← h_new
      π ← MPT.proveIncl(k, h_new)
      Append (k, h_new, π) to π_incl
  R_{t+1} ← MPT.rootHash()
  π_cons ← MPT.proveCons(R_t, R_{t+1})
  Update st_{t+1} ← new MPT state
  return (st_{t+1}, R_{t+1}, π_cons, π_incl)
```

Fig. 3. RPCT Instantiation Algorithms 1

Algorithm 4 RPCT.ProveInclusion

Input: Key k, Root R

```
if k in MPT then
    h ← MPT[k]
    π ← MPT.proveIncl(k, h)
    return (h, π)
else
    π ← MPT.proveAbs(k)
    return (π)
```

Algorithm 5 RPCT.ProveLookup

Input: Key k, Root R

```
if k ∈ MPT then
    h ← MPT[k]
    v ← value from history for head h
    π ← MPT.proveIncl(k, h)
    return (v, π)
else
    π ← MPT.proveAbs(k)
    return (⊥, π)
```

Algorithm 6 RPCT.ProveHistory

Input: Key k

```
H_k ← all entries (T_i, v_i) for key k
Initialize h_0 ← ⊥
for all (T_i, v_i) ∈ H_k do
    h_i ← Hash(T_i || v_i || h_{i-1})
π ← MPT.proveIncl(k, h_n)
return (H_k, π)
```

Fig. 4. RPCT Instantiation Algorithms 2

7 Evaluation

Requirements Evaluation:

RPs Registration: We require RPs to register and state their indented use of wallet attributes. Thereby we comply to REQ1 (RP Reg.) and REQ2 (Purpose Reg.). We then publish this information in a public register, enabling REQ3 (RP Reg. Transparency) and REQ5 (Lawfulness).

RP Certs: We issue access and registration certificates to RPs. Users can then approve or deny RP requests based on this information. This tackles REQ4 (RP Auth.), REQ8.1 (Access Certs), and REQ8.3 (Registration Certs). Wallets check the validity of those certs before answering requests from RPs, tackling REQ8.5 (Cert Validity). By directly sending the certs to wallets, we don't require a lookup and thus don't leak user information, compiling with REQ7 (Privacy).

Auditable Registration Consistency: To enable informed decisions, we include registered attributes in the registration certificate presented to wallets, tackling REQ6 (User Control & Consent) and REQ10 (Attributes in RPRC). We ensure consistency between the registered/published information and the information in the registration certificates. Also, adding registration certificates to the corresponding access certificate of the same RP binds both certificates. This enables compliance with REQ8.2 (Access Information Consistency) and REQ8.4 (Reg. Information Consistency). Issuance of certificates is logged in an append-only log. A log inclusion proof is retrieved by the RP and send to the wallet as part of the presentation request. This ensures that the information in the certificate corresponds to the information in the log, which is audited by competent entities. Competent entities can also monitor if the information in the log is consistent with the RP register (e.g., a subset of it). By also logging certificate revocations and providing (non-)revocation proofs, we support offline validation by wallets. We thus comply to REQ9.1 (Cert. Transparency) and REQ9.2 (Reg. Log Consistency).

Tailored Data Structure: RPCT yields smaller, structured proofs tied to a specific RP and its state. The tree size scales with the number of keys (RPs), not updates. This significantly reduces monitoring overhead by offering prefix-indexable keys and allowing history/lookup proofs per RP. This also ensures that RPCT can support the scale of an EU-wide EUDI deployment with low overhead for wallets and monitors, and tackles REQ11.1 (Scalability) and REQ11.2 (Performance).

Threat Model Evaluation:
Malicious RP: Wallets expect an RPAC and an RPRC and corresponding log inclusion proof from the RP. If those certificates are not valid and publicly logged, wallets deny the RP's presentation request. **Malicious Registrar or CAs:** RP registrations are published in the RP register, and issued RP certificates are publicly logged. This registers and logs are actively monitored by competent authorities, enabling detection of misissuance and inconsistencies. Wallets require an inclusion proof to validate RPACs and RPRCs. Inclusion proofs are only valid if the certificate is indeed logged in the public append-only log. **Malicious Log:** The log is append-only, meaning once a certificate is recorded, it cannot be removed or changed. Due to the cryptographic hashes, any tampering (insertion, deletion, modification) breaks the log's consistency. The log servers publish digests reflecting the entire history, and anyone can check them. Each digest is signed, preventing a malicious logger from presenting a fake root. This makes censorship or manipulation detectable (e.g. if a log tries to remove a certificate, it would change the Merkle root, which clients or auditors would notice). Signed digests and consistency proofs guarantee that if a split-view attack occurs, it can be detected by any party storing past snapshots and comparing these over time. Because the Wallet does not query the log directly to fetch an inclusion proof, its interactions with RPs remain unlinkable and unobservable to the log.

8 Discussion

8.1 Comparative Analysis

In classical CT, every certificate is a new entry (leaf). Monitoring updates to specific domains requires scanning the whole log. Instead, in RPCT, all updates for a specific RP are co-located. A single history proof covers all updates to that key, avoiding global scanning needs. Table 1 provides a comparative overview of the standard CT Merkle Tree and RPCT's MPT.

Moreover, the RPCT design omits SCTs entirely. Certificates carry instead a signed digest plus an inclusion proof, which replaces the log's promise. Finally, RPCT builds revocation/history tracking into the chain, eliminating the need for mechanisms like CRL or OCSP. Wallets can verify inclusion or exclusion proofs offline (without contacting a live log at presentation time), preserving privacy.

Table 1. Comparison of Standard CT Merkle Tree vs. RPCT Merkle Patricia Tree.

Operation	CT Merkle Hash Tree	RPCT (MPT + Chains)
Lookup by key	Not supported natively (must scan or index; $O(N)$)	Supported ($O(\log N)$ time, proof $O(\log N)$)
Inclusion proof	$O(\log N)$ hashes	$O(\log N)$ hashes + 1 chain link (current)
Consistency proof	$O(\log N)$ hashes (any two states)	$O(\log N)$ per update (batched proof possible)
History proof	Not native (multiple inclusion proofs needed)	Supported via chain ($O(L)$ links for L updates)

8.2 eIDAS Recommendations

While the amended eIDAS regulation is in effect, several IAs and the ARF remain under discussion or subject to future changes. We recommend the following:

REC1: According to the IA on RP registration [3, Appendix V], a Registration Certificate does not contain the "list of the attributes that the [RP] intends to request" (as defined in Appendix I, point 7). However, this information is needed to support an automated check of the RP registration by the wallet, and for the detection of misbehaving RPs. We therefore recommend to always include this list in machine readable form (e.g., DCQL [16, Sec. 6]) in the certificate.

REC2: The latest draft of the IA on RP registration states that member states *may require* issuance of Registration Certificates [3, Article 8]. However, if no RPRC is issued, wallets need to actively query the RP register, thereby leaking information about the user's behavior (leading to observability). This is in conflict with, e.g., Article 5a, point 16 (a), of the eIDAS regulation [4]. We thus recommend the issuing of RPRCs to be mandatory.

REC3: Article 5b, point 3, of the eIDAS regulation [4] states that RPs "shall not request users to provide any data other than that indicated" in the RP register. The regulation states this as requirement for the lawfulness of a data request. But, it does not require wallets to enforce this requirement. While we agree that the user should have the choice about sharing their data, we point to similar challenges, e.g., the web's *cookie consent problem* [6]. We recommend that IAs require wallets to properly inform users in case of over-asking RPs, and make it hard to share data in such situations. Further, we recommend to differentiate the sensitivity of data categories, and mandatory vs. optional attributes.

REC4: We recommend mandating transparency logs (i.e., CT) to enable auditability and ensure consistency between RP register and issued RP certificates.

Acknowledgments. This work was funded by the European Union's research and innovation programme under grant agreement № 101168311 (LICORICE).

References

1. Cooper, D., Santesson, S., Farrell, S., Boeyen, S., Housley, R., Polk, W.T.: Internet X.509 public key infrastructure certificate and certificate revocation list (CRL) profile. RFC **5280** (2008). https://doi.org/10.17487/RFC5280
2. EU Digital Identity Wallet Consortium: EUDI Architecture and Reference Framework (ARF) (2024). https://eu-digital-identity-wallet.github.io/eudi-doc-architecture-and-reference-framework, version 1.4.0
3. European Commission, Comitology: Draft: Commission implementing regulation (EU) ... laying down rules ... as regards the registration of wallet-relying parties ... (2024). https://eur-lex.europa.eu/legal-content/EN/TXT/?uri=PI_COM:Ares(2024)8509234
4. European Parliament, Council of the European Union: Regulation (EU) 2024/1183 ... of 11 April 2024 amending Regulation (EU) No 910/2014 as regards establishing the European Digital Identity Framework (eIDAS 2) (2024). https://eur-lex.europa.eu/eli/reg/2024/1183/oj
5. Farrell, S., Housley, R., Turner, S.: An internet attribute certificate profile for authorization. RFC **5755** (2010). https://doi.org/10.17487/RFC5755
6. Fassl, M., Gröber, L.T., Krombholz, K.: Stop the consent theater. In: CHI '21. ACM (2021). https://doi.org/10.1145/3411763.3451230
7. Germany, B.: Wallet-Relying Party Authentication and Certificate Transparency (2025). https://gitlab.opencode.de/bmi/eudi-wallet/eidas-2.0-architekturkonzept/-/blob/main/architecture-proposal/flows/Wallet-Relying-Party-Authentication.md
8. Italia Developers: X.509 Certificate Transparency – GitHub Issue #556 (2024). https://github.com/italia/eid-wallet-it-docs/issues/556
9. Italian Government: EID Wallet IT Documentation, Version 0.9.3 (2024). https://italia.github.io/eid-wallet-it-docs/v0.9.3/en/
10. Jackson, D.: The design space between CT and KT (2024). https://transparency.dev/pdfs/summit2024/The%20Design%20Space%20between%20CT%20and%20KT.pdf, lightning talk at Transparency.dev Summit 2024, London, UK
11. Laurie, B., Messeri, E., Stradling, R.: Certificate transparency version 2.0. RFC **9162** (2021). https://doi.org/10.17487/RFC9162
12. Leibowitz, H., Ghalwash, H., Syta, E., Herzberg, A.: CTng: secure certificate and revocation transparency. Cryptology ePrint Archive (2021)
13. Melara, M.S., Blankstein, A., Bonneau, J., Felten, E.W., Freedman, M.J.: CONIKS: bringing key transparency to end users. In: USENIX Security 15. USENIX Association (2015). https://www.usenix.org/conference/usenixsecurity15/technical-sessions/presentation/melara
14. More, S., Heher, J., Fasllija, E., Mathie, M.: Service provider accreditation: enabling and enforcing privacy-by-design in credential-based authentication systems. In: Proceedings of ARES 2024. ACM (2024). https://doi.org/10.1145/3664476.3669934
15. Tan, E., Du Seuil, D.: Services infrastructure (EBSI). Public Governance and Emerging Technologies: Values, Trust, and Regulatory Compliance, p. 83 (2025). https://doi.org/10.1007/978-3-031-84748-6
16. Terbu, O., Lodderstedt, T., Yasuda, K., Looker, T.: OpenID for Verifiable Presentations - draft 28 (2025). https://openid.net/specs/openid-4-verifiable-presentations-1_0.html
17. Valsorda, F.: Modern transparency logs. https://iacr.org/submit/files/slides/2024/rwc/rwc2024/68/slides.pdf (2024), presentation at Real World Crypto 2024

Authentication Inconsistencies Across Online Services: A Multi-Scenario Security Analysis

Andre Büttner[1(✉)], Nils Gruschka[1], Sverre Stafsengen Broen[1], and Daniela Pöhn[2]

[1] University of Oslo, Gaustadalléen 23B, 0373 Oslo, Norway
{andrbut,nilsgrus}@ifi.uio.no, s.s.broen@usit.uio.no
[2] Universität der Bundeswehr München, RI CODE, Werner-Heisenberg-Weg 39, 85579 Neubiberg, Germany
daniela.poehn@unibw.de

Abstract. Online services are integral to modern life, supporting activities such as communication, commerce, and travel. These services typically require user authentication, traditionally relying on user ID and password combinations. However, this approach is increasingly vulnerable to attacks such as phishing. Many services have adopted stronger authentication mechanisms, including multi-factor authentication, risk-based authentication, and passkeys.

Despite extensive research on login procedures, limited attention has been given to these post-login authentication processes. This paper presents a first study investigating the interplay between multi-factor authentication and context-specific authentication for ten popular online services. The results indicate that various authentication methods and behaviors can be observed across different scenarios and services.

Keywords: Online services · multi-factor authentication · authentication · security

1 Introduction

Online services have become an essential part of our daily lives. Many aspects, such as communication, social networking, shopping, banking, or travel planning, are nearly unthinkable without mobile apps or online services. Most services require creating an account, including exchanging authentication credentials to identify ourselves when revisiting the services.

Traditionally, authentication to online services was done by logging in with a user ID (often an email address) and a shared secret (typically a password). However, attacks on this scheme have become increasingly frequent and sophisticated [31]. Widespread examples are email phishing [16] and credential stuffing attacks using leaked password lists [23]. In response to these threats, many online services have implemented additional security measures, such as second-

B. Coppens et al. (Eds.): ARES 2025 Workshops, LNCS 15997, pp. 166–180, 2025.
https://doi.org/10.1007/978-3-032-00639-4_10

or multi-factor authentication (2FA, MFA), risk-based authentication (RBA), or passkey authentication [15]. While these measures can increase security and avoid account takeover attacks, they can also reduce usability for the end-user and even lead to account lockout, i.e., the legitimate user losing access to their account [26].

Another observation is that many online services not only request identity proofs during the login procedure. Also, when performing certain operations, e.g., changing security settings or requesting their data, users must often provide additional evidence of their identity, even if they are already logged in to the service. While users might feel annoyed by such recurring requests, it can increase the security and mitigate, for example, session stealing attacks. Similar behavior is known from continuous authentication systems [4].

While service login procedures and their different characteristics (i.e., simple password, multi-factor, and risk-based) are widely studied, research on online services' authentication outside the login procedure is sparse. Therefore, this paper presents a study on the holistic authentication behavior (i.e., during login and specific usage contexts) of ten selected online services. The main contributions are as follows:

- We analyze how authentication features vary across usage scenarios and services.
- We identify inconsistencies in how 2FA affects trust in logged-in users.
- We discuss the security implications of the observed authentication features.

The remainder of this paper is organized as follows: We first highlight the importance of this study by summarizing related work in Sect. 2. In Sect. 3, we outline the methodology before presenting the experiment results in Sect. 4. Finally, we discuss the experiment and results and conclude our paper in Sects. 5 and 6, respectively.

2 Related Work

Different authentication aspects of online services have been studied extensively. For instance, Klivan et al. [18] and Amft et al. [3] both investigated the security and user experience for MFA recovery procedures. The authors show that many websites deploy insecure MFA recovery procedures, where MFA can be disabled when having access to the accounts' associated email addresses. Moreover, Büttner and Gruschka [11] evaluated the security and lockout risks of MFA and recovery settings for Google and Apple users. Tiefenau et al. [30] conducted interviews and a survey to understand the user perception of 2FA recovery. The authors show that users often rely on website support to regain access.

Furthermore, several studies have investigated RBA. Since online services tend not to publish their RBA configuration, reverse engineering is one way to identify involved features, like fingerprints and IP geolocation. Freeman et al. [14], Makowski and Pöhn [22], and Wiefling et al. [33] tried to shed light on the characteristics of RBA and its configuration by blackbox testing, among others.

Büttner et al. [10] show that RBA may also play a role in account recovery. Based on the results, the authors create a first maturity model for RBA recovery challenges. Pöhn et al. [26] proposed a framework to analyze authentication risks in single accounts and account networks. However, the authors did not analyze the interplay between the different factors.

When it comes to specific usage scenarios, past research has so far only focused on one specific scenario each. Boniface et al. [7], for example, analyzed the verification of the subject of data subject access rights. The authors observed some unsafe or doubtful procedures, including the copy of a national identity card transmitted over an insecure channel. Di Martino et al. [12] conducted a longitudinal study to examine whether or not services improved their policies for identifying data subjects during a subject access request (SAR). Their results showed an increase in vulnerable organizations from 27% to 30% over a two-year span, along with indicating the inconsistencies in how organizations handle the identification process of a SAR.

In a thesis written by Broen [8], experiments were conducted on the mechanisms used by services to authenticate the user when exercising one's right to access data according to Art. 15 of the European General Data Protection Regulation (GDPR) [29]. The thesis found that the authentication methods differed for the selected services, along with some requiring additional verification of the data subject to be able to exercise their rights.

The related work shows that most research focuses on authentication methods for login procedures and account recovery. However, there is a lack of studies on authentication requests outside these two scenarios. This paper studies online services' overall authentication behavior. It will focus on the distinction between different services and scenarios and the influence of MFA.

3 Methodology

Online users may encounter various scenarios where an online service requires different levels of confidence about their authenticity. Such scenarios can include, for example, modifying sensitive account settings, accessing personal information, or recovering an account. Thus, we are interested in understanding how online services actually implement authentication for such scenarios. In this regard, we aim to answer the following research questions:

- **RQ1** How do authentication methods differ across different usage scenarios?
- **RQ2** How do authentication methods differ across various online services?
- **RQ3** How does 2FA influence the authentication methods beyond the login?

To address these questions, we conducted an exploratory study [13] in which we systematically tested different online services. For this, we first selected a set of online services as our test sample. Next, we executed specific usage scenarios and documented the authentication methods required to verify the user, respectively. Finally, we analyzed the results focusing on the above-mentioned research questions.

3.1 Selecting Services

Given the need to conduct the experiments manually, we had to select a smaller sample of online services for our experiments. We first narrowed down the choice of services to the most popular ones by cross-referencing the top 1000 popular services of three widely used website rankings. This includes the Tranco Top Sites [20], Majestic Million[1], and Chrome (CrUX) Top Million Websites[2], which have proven to be appropriate sources for selecting relevant services [27].

The list was further reduced by excluding services requiring payment information, adult content, or those without English language support. Moreover, we removed services where an online account is not a key consumer feature or is mainly used by administrators or content creators. From the resulting list, we selected the ten services shown in Table 1.

Table 1. Overview of selected services for the study

Service	URL
Amazon	https://amazon.com
ChatGPT	https://chatgpt.com
Facebook	https://facebook.com
GitHub	https://github.com
Google	https://google.com
LinkedIn	https://linkedin.com
Microsoft Outlook	https://live.com
Pinterest	https://pinterest.com
Spotify	https://spotify.com
X (formerly Twitter)	https://x.com

3.2 Scenarios

For our study, we considered different account usage scenarios in which we assumed the user's authenticity to be relevant. We therefore decided to test the following six specific scenarios, labeled S1 through S6. The scenarios are described below in more detail.

S1: Login. The login is the most common scenario in which a user must authenticate. It is typically the first point of interaction with an online account. Hence, a successful login is crucial for performing any further operations related to this account.

[1] https://majestic.com/reports/majestic-million (Last accessed: 2025-02-11).
[2] https://github.com/zakird/crux-top-lists (Last accessed: 2025-02-11).

S2: Modify Email Address. For most online services, the email address is essential to verify a user's identity. We therefore investigated whether modifying the email address yields any different or additional authentication compared to the regular login. Depending on the service, we either added secondary email addresses or, if this was not possible, modified the primary email address. In both cases, the service eventually accepts a different email address to verify a user than the email initially registered.

S3: Toggle 2FA Setting. Online services nowadays usually offer 2FA for additional protection of online accounts. In addition to using a password, a user can set up one or several additional authentication factors. This typically includes a one-time password (OTP) app, phone number, or a security key. Within our experiments, we tested this scenario by first setting up an OTP app as 2FA method and later disabling 2FA. In one instance, we had to set up a phone number as a second factor because short message service (SMS) OTP was the only 2FA method offered.

S4: Change Name. We further considered modifying personal information as an interesting use case. It is not directly connected to user authentication and, thereby, presumably the least critical compared to the other scenarios. It is still possible that changing personal information in a user account is treated differently by online services. We tested this by modifying the full name (i.e., not the username) in the user's profile where possible.

S5: Right of Access Request. Another action that may be performed to gain access to an online account or some of its data is a *Right of Access* request. Online services must enable citizens of countries that are subject to EU law (and thus to the GDPR [29]) to exercise their data subject rights. Since this is often implemented as a specific function, it can present a different way of accessing an account owner's information. In practice, this typically involves two distinct phases [25]. First, a user requests the service to create a data archive with some or all of the user's data. Then, after a certain time period, the user is notified when the data is available for download. Since both phases are somewhat isolated, we split this scenario into the following two sub-scenarios: S5.1 Data Request and S5.2 Data Access.

Note that the Right of Access can often also be exercised through other channels, e.g., sending a request via email. However, we decided to focus on data requests directly through the account and refer the reader to previous works investigating other methods for requesting data [7,12].

S6: Password Reset. The last scenario we included was resetting the password. When users lose their login credentials, they can usually regain access to their account through fallback authentication methods. Consequently, methods for a password reset differ from those for regular login. The challenge here is to ensure a legitimate user can regain access while preventing attackers from exploiting this to bypass authentication.

3.3 Study Procedure

We initially set up a test account for each service with a minimal configuration, i.e., with an email address and a password. Since we were also interested in testing whether 2FA has any effect on the scenarios (see RQ3), we compared authentication for each scenario with two different authentication settings. In one setting, the account was configured only with a password; in the other, 2FA was enabled. In the latter case, we used an OTP app where possible, as this did not require us to disclose unnecessary personal information. Thus, the scenarios were conducted twice with different 2FA configurations. For comparability reasons, we utilized the same browser, in our case Firefox, in a private browser mode for each scenario.

We made some exceptions concerning the scenarios and 2FA configuration due to certain limitations of some services. On ChatGPT, we had to omit scenarios S2 and S4 because there was no way to add or change an email address, and no personal information was stored in the user's profile. GitHub started enforcing 2FA in 2023 [24], and it was thus not possible to turn off 2FA once enabled. Moreover, Spotify did not offer 2FA for consumer accounts at the time of the study [28]. We consequently tested this service only with a password-based configuration. Finally, Pinterest only offered SMS OTP as a 2FA method. Therefore, we used SMS OTP instead of an OTP app.

4 Experiment Results

The experiments described in the previous section were carried out during March and April 2025. Table 2 provides a complete summary of what authentication methods were observed with respect to the different services and scenarios. In the remainder of this section, we point out important findings with regard to our research questions. We also describe some observations we made beyond this.

4.1 Comparison of Scenarios (RQ1)

The experiments show that our tested scenarios required different authentication methods. In particular, they were often inconsistent across different services.

Modifying the email address appears to be considered a rather sensitive scenario. This was indicated by requesting additional authentication steps upon the initial login. Many services required a logged-in user to re-enter the password or verify a previously registered email address before a new one can be set up.

Similarly, the 2FA setting often triggered an elevated authentication procedure. On half of the selected services, changing the 2FA configuration required entering the password again, verifying the email address, or both, before setting up the 2FA method.

Table 2. Overview of authentication methods required for each service and scenario. For each service, the first row shows the results for a password-only configuration and the second row for the 2FA configuration. Note that Spotify could only be tested with a password.

Service	S1	S2	S3	S4	S5.1	S5.2	S6
Amazon	P	L,EO$_{new}$,P	L,A	L	L,EL	L,EO	EO
	P,A	=	L,EO	=	=	=	=
ChatGPT	P	-	L,A	-	L	EL,L	EO
	P,A	-	L	-	=	=	=
Facebook	P	L,EO$_{old}$,EO$_{new}$	L,EO,A	L	L	L	EO
	P,A	=	L,EO	=	=	=	EO,A
GitHub	P	L,EL$_{new}$	L,A	L	L	L,EL	EL
	P,A	=	-	=	=	=	EL,A
Google	P	L,EO$_{new}$	L,A	L	L	L	EO
	P,A	L,A,EO$_{new}$	=	=	=	=	EO,A
LinkedIn	P	L,EO$_{old}$,EO$_{new}$	L,EO,P,A	L	L	L	EO
	P,A	=	L,EO,P	=	=	=	EO,A
Microsoft	P	L,EO$_{old}$,EO$_{new}$	L,EO,A	L	L,EO	L,EO	EO
	P,A	L,EO$_{new}$	L	=	L	L	EO,A
Pinterest	P	L,EO$_{new}$	L,P,S	L	L	EL,EO	EL
	P,S	=	L,P	=	=	=	=
Spotify	P|EO	L,P,EL$_{new}$	-	L	L,EL	EL,L	EL
X	P	L,P,P,EO$_{new}$	L,P,A	L,P	L,EO	L,EO	EO
	P,A	=	L,P	=	L,P,EO	L,P,EO	EO,A

P: Password; EL: Email Link; EO: Email OTP; A: App OTP; S: SMS OTP; L: Login;
a,*b*: *a* and *b*; *a*|*b*: *a* or *b*; =: Same as above; -: Not applicable

In nearly all cases, the scenario of changing the user's name did not involve any additional authentication methods when the user was already logged in. Only X required re-entering the additional password.

Regarding the Right of Access scenario, we found that only four services requested additional user verification to request the data. However, six of the services required signing in and verifying the email. A special case was Pinterest, where the data request was sent through the account settings. Yet, the data was ultimately provided by a third-party service[3] that verified the email without requiring the user to be logged in to their Pinterest account.

Resetting the password did not inherently require a login and is therefore different from the other scenarios. It is an ongoing problem to design account recovery in a way that helps users when losing an authentication factor while

[3] https://pinterest.sendsafely.com (Last accessed: 2025-05-04).

not creating a backdoor [21]. All services in our test sample allowed resetting the password by verifying the email address. When a 2FA method was configured, many of the services required verifying both the email address and the 2FA method (or backup code when available). However, three services still did not require 2FA even when enabled in the account settings.

To summarize our findings for RQ1, the configuration of email addresses and 2FA settings always required additional steps and were thus the most protected among our test scenarios. In contrast, changing personal information has turned out to be the least critical scenario, as it mostly required nothing more than the initial login. The Right of Access request on several services required additional steps, especially when accessing the data. Resetting the password always relied on verifying the email address, and in most cases, the 2FA method, when enabled.

4.2 Comparison of Services (RQ2)

Table 3. Summary of features and patterns observed on the tested services.

Service	Re-Enter Password	Verify Old Email	Email OTP	Email Link	Enter Email	2FA Backup Code
Amazon	○	○	●	●	○	○
ChatGPT	○	○	●	●	○	●
Facebook	○	●	●	○	○	●
GitHub	○	○	○	●	○	●
Google	○	○	●	○	○	●
LinkedIn	●	●	●	○	○	○
Microsoft	○	●	●	○	●	●
Pinterest	○	○	●	●	○	●
Spotify	●	○	●	●	○	-
X	●	○	●	○	○	●

●: Feature present; ○: Feature not present

We further compared the services' approaches to verifying the user in the tested scenarios. In particular, some behavioral patterns were observed on several services, which are shown in Table 3 and further described in the following.

A pattern found on several services was that the password had to be re-entered when accessing and modifying specific account settings. This was observed on LinkedIn, Spotify, and X. The latter used it extensively, as it repeatedly requested the password in all scenarios except for the password reset. Remarkably, when changing the email address on X, one had to enter the password three times in total.

Specifically, when modifying the email address, all services verified the newly configured email address. However, only a few services, including Facebook, LinkedIn, and Microsoft, verified the previously set-up email address before allowing the configuration of a new or additional one.

In our experiments, we mainly documented the default authentication method offered, since the alternative—typically verifying an email address—is normally the same as a password reset. However, unlike other services, Spotify requested an email OTP as the default authentication method instead of a password. In this regard, another interesting observation was that some services, including Amazon, ChatGPT, Pinterest, and Spotify, use both email links and OTPs depending on the scenario.

Beyond this, Microsoft stood out by prompting the user to enter the email address before sending an email OTP. Microsoft thereby challenges the user by requiring knowledge of an email address configured for email verification. Using this consistently was not observed on any of the other services.

Finally, as this is highly relevant for recovering accounts with 2FA support, we further noted whether the online services offered a 2FA backup code. Two services, Amazon and LinkedIn, did not offer such a backup code.

4.3 Influence of 2FA (RQ3)

The standard behavior of an account with 2FA enabled is that the regular login requires a password and the second authentication factor, i.e., the app OTP or SMS OTP. Furthermore, the user could use a backup code if the second authentication factor was unavailable, provided the online service offers this. However, as shown in Table 4, we observed that having 2FA enabled or disabled still influenced whether some services request additional verification methods or what recovery methods they require.

Microsoft behaved uniquely in comparison to the other services. We found that it treats a user signed in with 2FA with higher confidence. This is shown by the fact that it relaxed the requirement for additional email verification in all scenarios, where otherwise an email OTP was requested. In contrast, three services showed a somewhat opposite behavior in that they required more authentication steps in at least one scenario when logged with 2FA. Amazon required an additional email OTP when disabling the 2FA method. Google requested the app OTP again when modifying the email address and disabling 2FA. On X, this occurred in the Right of Access scenario, which required re-entering a password only when 2FA was enabled.

Aside from the above-mentioned cases of Amazon and Google, the only difference when toggling the 2FA method was that it could be disabled without verifying the second factor.

The Right of Access request was not affected by 2FA in almost all cases, except for X, as mentioned above. However, it is important to note that accessing

Table 4. This table shows in which scenarios the authentication procedure differed depending on whether 2FA was enabled. (S1 is omitted as it is trivial, and Spotify is not listed since it did not offer 2FA.)

Service	S2	S3	S4	S5.1	S5.2	S6
Amazon	○	●	○	○	○	○
ChatGPT	-	●	-	○	○	○
Facebook	○	●	○	○	○	●
GitHub	○	-	○	○	○	●
Google	●	○	○	○	○	●
LinkedIn	○	●	○	○	○	●
Microsoft	●	●	○	●	●	●
Pinterest	○	●	○	○	○	○
X	○	●	○	●	●	●

●: Difference; ○: No difference; -: Not applicable

the data from Pinterest does not even require the 2FA at all, as it is handled by a third-party service that only verifies the email address.

When it comes to the password reset, the 2FA setting did affect six of nine services because the 2FA method was required in addition to verifying the email address. In turn, this means that three services, including Amazon, ChatGPT, and Pinterest, allow a password reset without having the 2FA factor. Importantly, a password reset does not imply regaining access to an account. Even when the password could be reset without the second factor, it would not allow bypassing 2FA during the subsequent login.

4.4 Additional Findings

We also want to point out some additional findings that were not the main focus but are still relevant regarding account security and suggest directions for potential future research.

We noticed that some services limited the frequency of changing information. X and Facebook, for instance, temporarily restricted the possibility of modifying email addresses or authentication methods for a certain time period. X also blocked access to the Right of Access data in some instances. However, it was unclear what caused X to do so.

Another measure often implemented by online services is a CAPTCHA [1]. We did not include this in our main results, as it does not verify a user, which was our main scope. However, it is still a security measure used to block automated attacks. Within our experiments, it only occurred in two concrete cases.

Microsoft requested it when changing the user's full name, and GitHub requested a CAPTCHA during account recovery. It was therefore rather surprising that we could not observe CAPTCHAs consistently on more services and scenarios.

Although analyzing risk-based features was not the primary focus of our study, we highlight several relevant observations in this context. Many of the online services applied RBA primarily during the regular login. We further confirmed the occurrence of a risk-based behavior on Amazon during account recovery, which was already suggested by Büttner et al. [10]. However, while they only observed a CAPTCHA as an additional authentication step, we found that Amazon would add a security question.

5 Discussion

5.1 Security Impact

Online services nowadays use strong measures to protect their users. We have particularly looked into scenarios where a user needs to log in before taking any further actions, making it challenging for an attacker to access the account settings in the first place. However, when an account is only protected by a password, the difficulty to bypass the login can be rather low due to the risk of credential stuffing and phishing [16,23]. While 2FA can prevent this, more sophisticated attacks like session stealing [9] or cross-site request forgery [5] may still pose a risk. This, therefore, demands stronger measures, such as additional authentication steps.

Overall, we observed that the services we tested offered elevated authentication mechanisms. A remarkable observation was that Microsoft requested fewer authentication steps when a user was signed in using 2FA. Given the risks mentioned above, and also considering that changing email or 2FA settings affects authentication significantly, it could be argued that requesting additional methods independently of the initial login would be better for the protection of the user. However, the opposite approach of requesting more methods, as done by Google and X, may be disadvantageous in terms of usability.

Also, we noticed some of the additional authentication steps used by the tested services are further debatable concerning the user's security. In particular, it is questionable how re-entering a password or entering an email address before verifying the respective email can truly improve security. Moreover, the usage of two email verification variants, email OTP or link, has been observed. In some instances, both were used by the same service. Both have their advantages and disadvantages. Email OTP is, for example, vulnerable to phishing, but also has a short lifetime, while an email link is not vulnerable to phishing, but has a longer lifetime. Generally, using email authentication is a controversial topic since email accounts are often the main weakness in user account settings [17,19,21].

Likewise, the dedicated use of CAPTCHAs is rather questionable. Particularly in the case of Microsoft, it is not clear why it is critical to prevent automated attacks when changing a user's name compared to other scenarios.

On the positive side, we noticed that a password reset could not be exploited to bypass 2FA. The second factor was required during the password reset or subsequent login. In any case, one could not avoid 2FA. Most services, except for Amazon and LinkedIn, also offered a 2FA backup code. Yet, this does not guarantee that a user has stored it or noted it down. This therefore creates a significant usability compromise, as also noted by similar research on this [3].

5.2 Ethics

Online services may prohibit users from employing pseudonymized or test accounts for research. Respective rights may overrule such terms, depending on the country and decisions [32]. In this regard, the American Psychological Association and the German equivalent declare that no studies based on deception are to be carried out unless deception techniques are justified by, e.g., a significant gain in scientific knowledge, and no alternative procedure is possible [2,6]. In our case, we used only our own accounts and avoided any interactions with non-study users. Thereby, we largely eliminated the risk of deceit. Additionally, we did not create significant web traffic or server load that would affect other users, nor did we exploit specific vulnerabilities. This procedure can be seen as justifiable, as new knowledge is gained.

5.3 Limitations

We conducted an exploratory study to test how consistent authentication methods occur on different services and scenarios. However, due to the limited number of services and scenarios, this is a pure qualitative study, and results cannot be generalized. Yet, the services we tested are among the most popular and provide a reasonable first sample. The results thus motivate more research on the security of authentication in specific scenarios. While we tested the difference between a password and 2FA, we excluded testing Single Sign-On (SSO), since its authentication behavior depends on the SSO provider. The use of passkeys was also not considered, mainly because they would have introduced a significantly higher variability and complexity to the experiments.

Furthermore, we did not test RBA extensively. Our goal was to examine which authentication methods and patterns are applied consistently across scenarios, in contrast to risk-based authentication mechanisms, which vary depending on contextual factors. However, RBA can have considerable side effects on authentication methods in these scenarios. Lastly, we did not investigate any time effects, i.e., whether a user has to re-authenticate after a certain timeout.

6 Conclusion and Outlook

This paper has studied the authentication behavior of selected online services. In addition to the regular login procedure, authentication was observed for service functions like changing email addresses or multi-factor configuration. The results show strongly divergent behavior across different scenarios and services. In particular, we observed specific patterns, such as repeatedly requesting a password or verifying the email address. Furthermore, the extent to which 2FA affects the different behaviors also varied considerably between scenarios and services. An interesting observation was that services handled 2FA-configured accounts in contrasting ways, either by treating them with higher confidence or by enforcing a more stringent login process. This indicates that there is no consensus about the ideal approach to handling these scenarios.

Future work should analyze the different patterns and approaches that were found within this study regarding their security. In particular, it should also be investigated how users perceive this. Finally, a study on a larger scale, i.e., with more services and scenarios, should be conducted to discover further authentication patterns. However, this requires more resources or approaches with higher scalability.

Disclosure of Interests. The authors have no competing interests to declare that are relevant to the content of this article.

References

1. von Ahn, L., Blum, M., Hopper, N.J., Langford, J.: Captcha: using hard AI problems for security. In: Biham, E. (ed.) Advances in Cryptology — EUROCRYPT 2003, pp. 294–311. Springer Berlin Heidelberg, Berlin, Heidelberg (2003). https://doi.org/10.1007/3-540-39200-9_18
2. American Psychological Association: Ethical principles of psychologists and code of conduct (2017). https://www.apa.org/ethics/code
3. Amft, S., et al.: Lost and not found: an investigation of recovery methods for multi-factor authentication. CoRR (2023). https://doi.org/10.60882/cispa.25186640.v1
4. Baig, A.F., Eskeland, S.: Security, privacy, and usability in continuous authentication: a survey. Sensors **21**(17) (2021). https://doi.org/10.3390/s21175967, https://www.mdpi.com/1424-8220/21/17/5967
5. Barth, A., Jackson, C., Mitchell, J.C.: Robust defenses for cross-site request forgery. In: Proceedings of the 15th ACM Conference on Computer and Communications Security, pp. 75–88. CCS '08, Association for Computing Machinery, New York, NY, USA (2008). https://doi.org/10.1145/1455770.1455782
6. Berufsverband Deutscher Psychologinnen und Psychologen e.V., Deutsche Gesellschaft für Psychologie e.V.: Berufsethische Richtlinien des Berufsverbandes Deutscher Psychologinnen und Psychologen e.V. und der Deutschen Gesellschaft für Psychologie e.V. https://www.bdp-verband.de/fileadmin/user_upload/BDP/website/dokumente/PDF/Profession/Berufsethik/BER-Foederation-20230426-Web-1.pdf (2022)
7. Boniface, C., Fouad, I., Bielova, N., Lauradoux, C., Santos, C.: Security analysis of subject access request procedures. In: Naldi, M., Italiano, G.F., Rannenberg, K., Medina, M., Bourka, A. (eds.) Privacy Technologies and Policy, pp. 182–209. Springer International Publishing, Cham (2019). https://doi.org/10.1007/978-3-030-21752-5_12
8. Broen, S.S.: Observational Study of the Right of Access and Erasure-From the Perspective of the Data Subject and the Data Controller. Master's thesis, University of Oslo (2024). https://www.duo.uio.no/handle/10852/116541

9. Burgers, W., Verdult, R., van Eekelen, M.: Prevent session hijacking by binding the session to the cryptographic network credentials. In: Riis Nielson, H., Gollmann, D. (eds.) Secure IT Systems, pp. 33–50. Springer, Berlin, Heidelberg (2013). https://doi.org/10.1007/978-3-642-41488-6_3
10. Büttner, A., Pedersen, A.T., Wiefling, S., Gruschka, N., Lo Iacono, L.: Is it really you who forgot the password? When account recovery meets risk-based authentication. In: Wang, G., Wang, H., Min, G., Georgalas, N., Meng, W. (eds.) Ubiquitous Security, pp. 401–419. Springer Nature Singapore, Singapore (2024). https://doi.org/10.1007/978-981-97-1274-8_26
11. Büttner, A., Gruschka, N.: Evaluating the influence of multi-factor authentication and recovery settings on the security and accessibility of user accounts. In: Proceedings of the 10th International Conference on Information Systems Security and Privacy - ICISSP, pp. 691–700. INSTICC, SciTePress (2024). https://doi.org/10.5220/0012319000003648
12. Di Martino, M., Meers, I., Quax, P., Andries, K., Lamotte, W.: Revisiting identification issues in GDPR 'right of access' policies: a technical and longitudinal analysis. Proc. Priv. Enhancing Technol. (2022). https://doi.org/10.2478/popets-2022-0037
13. Edgar, T.W., Manz, D.O.: Research Methods for Cyber Security. Syngress Publishing, 1st edn. (2017)
14. Freeman, D.M., Jain, S., Dürmuth, M., Biggio, B., Giacinto, G.: Who are you? A statistical approach to measuring user authenticity. In: Proceedings of the USENIX Network and Distributed System Security (NDSS) Symposium. San Francisco, CA (2016). https://doi.org/10.14722/ndss.2016.23240
15. Gavazzi, A., et al.: A study of multi-factor and risk-based authentication availability. In: 32nd USENIX Security Symposium (USENIX Security 23), pp. 2043–2060. USENIX Association, Anaheim, CA (2023). https://www.usenix.org/conference/usenixsecurity23/presentation/gavazzi
16. Security, I.: X-Force 2025 Threat Intelligence Index. Tech. rep, IBM (2025)
17. Joukov, A., Joukov, N.: Six-year study of emails sent to unverified addresses. In: Furnell, S., Clarke, N. (eds.) Human Aspects of Information Security and Assurance, pp. 337–345. Springer Nature Switzerland, Cham (2023). https://doi.org/10.1007/978-3-031-38530-8_27
18. Klivan, S., et al.: We've Disabled MFA for You: an evaluation of the security and usability of multi-factor authentication recovery deployments. In: Proceedings of the 2023 ACM SIGSAC Conference on Computer and Communications Security, pp. 3138–3152. CCS '23, Association for Computing Machinery, New York, NY, USA (2023). https://doi.org/10.1145/3576915.3623180
19. Kraus, L., Svidronová, M., Stobert, E.: How do users chain email accounts together? In: Jøsang, A., Futcher, L., Hagen, J. (eds.) ICT Systems Security and Privacy Protection, pp. 416–429. Springer International Publishing, Cham (2021). https://doi.org/10.1007/978-3-030-78120-0_27
20. Le Pochat, V., Van Goethem, T., Tajalizadehkhoob, S., Korczyński, M., Joosen, W.: Tranco: a research-oriented top sites ranking hardened against manipulation. In: Proceedings of the 26th Annual Network and Distributed System Security Symposium. NDSS 2019 (2019). https://doi.org/10.14722/ndss.2019.23386
21. Li, Y., Chen, Z., Wang, H., Sun, K., Jajodia, S.: Understanding account recovery in the wild and its security implications. IEEE Trans. Dependable Secure Comput. **19**(1), 620–634 (2022). https://doi.org/10.1109/TDSC.2020.2975789

22. Makowski, J.P., Pöhn, D.: Evaluation of real-world risk-based authentication at online services revisited: complexity wins. In: Proceedings of the 18th International Conference on Availability, Reliability and Security. ARES '23, Association for Computing Machinery, New York, NY, USA (2023). https://doi.org/10.1145/3600160.3605024
23. Naprys, E.: Password crisis deepens in 2025: lazy, reused, and stolen (2025). https://cybernews.com/security/password-leak-study-unveils-2025-trends-reused-and-lazy/
24. Paine, L., Singhal, H.: Raising the bar for software security: GitHub 2FA begins March 13 (2023). https://github.blog/news-insights/product-news/raising-the-bar-for-software-security-github-2fa-begins-march-13/
25. Pöhn, D., Gruschka, N.: Qualitative in-depth analysis of GDPR data subject access requests and responses from major online services. In: Proceedings of the 11th International Conference on Information Systems Security and Privacy, vol. 1: ICISSP, pp. 149–156. INSTICC, SciTePress (2025). https://doi.org/10.5220/0013093000003899
26. Pöhn, D., Gruschka, N., Ziegler, L., Büttner, A.: A framework for analyzing authentication risks in account networks. Comput. Secur. **135**, 103515 (2023). https://doi.org/10.1016/j.cose.2023.103515
27. Ruth, K., Kumar, D., Wang, B., Valenta, L., Durumeric, Z.: Toppling top lists: evaluating the accuracy of popular website lists. In: Proceedings of the 22nd ACM Internet Measurement Conference, pp. 374–387. IMC '22, Association for Computing Machinery, New York, NY, USA (2022). https://doi.org/10.1145/3517745.3561444
28. Spotify AB: Protect your Spotify account (2025). https://support.spotify.com/uk/article/protect-your-account/
29. The European Parliament and the Council of the European Union: Regulation (EU) 2016/679 of the European Parliament and of the Council of 27 April 2016 on the protection of natural persons with regard to the processing of personal data and on the free movement of such data, and repealing Directive 95/46/EC (General Data Protection Regulation) (2016)
30. Tiefenau, E., Grohs, J.A., Häring, M., Smith, M., Tiefenau, C.: They are responsible for ensuring that I can continue to use the service. Investigating Users' Expectations Towards 2FA Recovery in Germany. In: Proceedings of the 2025 CHI Conference on Human Factors in Computing Systems. CHI '25, Association for Computing Machinery, New York, NY, USA (2025). https://doi.org/10.1145/3706598.3714245
31. Wang, X., Yan, Z., Zhang, R., Zhang, P.: Attacks and defenses in user authentication systems: a survey. J. Network Comput. Appl. **188**, 103080 (2021). https://doi.org/10.1016/j.jnca.2021.103080, https://www.sciencedirect.com/science/article/pii/S1084804521001028
32. Wauters, E., Lievens, E., Valcke, P.: Towards a better protection of social media users: a legal perspective on the terms of use of social networking sites. Int. J. Law Inf. Technol. **22**(3), 254–294 (2014). https://doi.org/10.1093/ijlit/eau002
33. Wiefling, S., Lo Iacono, L., Dürmuth, M.: Is this really you? An empirical study on risk-based authentication applied in the wild. In: ICT Systems Security and Privacy Protection: 34th IFIP TC 11 International Conference, SEC 2019, Lisbon, Portugal, June 25-27, 2019, Proceedings 34, pp. 134–148. Springer, Cham (2019). https://doi.org/10.1007/978-3-030-22312-0_10

Proceedings of the Second International Workshop on Security and Privacy Enhancing Technologies for Multimodal Data (SPETViD 2025)

SPETViD 2025 Preface

Multimodal data combines information from various modalities, such as text, images, audio, video, and 3D models, captured by diverse devices and sensors. As this type of data becomes increasingly integrated into security and AI-driven applications, ensuring privacy, integrity, and robustness is more critical than ever. In this context, Privacy-Enhancing Technologies (PETs) play a crucial role in mitigating privacy risks. PETs enable responsible innovation and secure data usage in domains such as healthcare, finance, and artificial intelligence, while also supporting the adoption of data-driven technologies in smart ecosystems.

The 2nd International Workshop on Security and Privacy Enhancing Technologies for Multimodal Data (SPETViD 2025) was held in conjunction with the 20th International Conference on Availability, Reliability, and Security (ARES 2025), which took place in Ghent, Belgium, August 11–14, 2025. SPETViD provides a focused forum for researchers, practitioners, and policymakers to address the growing concerns about privacy and security. The workshop promotes the exploration of technical, legal, and ethical perspectives for safeguarding multimodal data, particularly in areas related to smart environments, surveillance, and collaborative AI systems.

For SPETViD 2025, we received 6 full-length submissions, one of which was desk-rejected. All full-length papers underwent a rigorous double-blind peer review process, with each submission reviewed by at least three independent reviewers from a diverse program committee of international experts in privacy, security, AI, and data ethics. Based on these reviews and discussions among the chairs, three full papers were accepted for oral presentation and are included in this LNCS volume. All submissions were handled independently and fairly, including those co-authored by members of the organizing or program committees. In such cases, the review process was managed without the involvement of conflicted individuals to maintain the integrity of the double-blind review standards.

We thank all authors who submitted their work to SPETViD 2025 and extend our gratitude to the reviewers for their valuable and timely feedback. We are also grateful to the ARES 2025 organisers and our workshop participants for contributing to an engaging and impactful event. We hope that the contributions presented in this volume will inspire continued research and collaboration in designing and deploying secure, privacy-preserving, and ethically aligned technologies for multimodal data systems.

August 2025

Amna Shifa
Mamoona Asgher
Nadia Kanwal

SPETViD 2025 Organization

Workshop Chairs

Amna Shifa	University of Galway, Ireland
Mamoona Asghar	University of Galway, Ireland
Nadia Kanwal	Keele University, UK

Program Committee

Asra Aslam	Sheffield University, UK
Farzana Zahid	University of Waikato, New Zealand
Gazi Erkan Bostanci	Ankara University, Turkey
Ifeoluwapo Aribilola	Insight SFI Research Centre for Data Analytics, Ireland
Ihsan Ullah	University of Galway, Ireland
Malika Bendechache	University of Galway, Ireland
Mary Pidgeon	Technological University of the Shannon: Midlands Mid-West, Ireland
Mehwish Tahir	Technological University of the Shannon, Ireland
Muhammad Babar Imtiaz	Technological University of the Shannon, Ireland
Muhammad Jehanzaib Yousuf	Technological University of the Shannon, Ireland
Muhammad Samar Ansari	University of Chester, UK
Rónán Kennedy	University of Galway, Ireland
Seamus Dowling	Atlantic Technological University, Ireland
Shoaib Ehsan	University of Southampton, UK

A Review of Deep Packet Inspection for Network Security: From Traditional Techniques to Machine Learning Integration

Teerath Kumar[1(✉)], Susan Leavy[2], Patrick Eustace[3], Edward Curry[1], and Mamoona Naveed Asghar[1]

[1] Insight Research Ireland Centre for Data Analytics and School of Computer Science, University of Galway, Galway, Ireland
teerath.menghwar2@mail.dcu.ie,
teerathkumar.menghwar@universityofgalway.ie

[2] Insight Research Ireland Centre for Data Analytics & School of Information and Communication Studies, University College Dublin, Dublin, Ireland

[3] CISCO Systems, Galway, Ireland

Abstract. Deep Packet Inspection (DPI) remains a critical technique for network traffic analysis, enabling comprehensive examination of both packet headers and payload content for security, policy enforcement, and traffic management. As network threats become more complex, especially with deepfake-based social engineering attacks, there is a crucial need to advance DPI capabilities through the development of intelligent firewalls that integrate machine learning (ML) for real-time threat detection. This paper advances the state-of-the-art in DPI research through three key contributions. First, it proposes a novel taxonomy that systematically distinguishes between traditional DPI techniques and ML DPI techniques, and highlights their respective strengths, limitations, and applicability. Second, it presents a comparative performance evaluation of ML models across multiple benchmark datasets and the evaluation offers insights into their practical deployment in real-world environments. Third, the paper explores emerging trends in DPI, including hybrid analytical approaches and methods to inspect encrypted traffic. Furthermore, it outlines strategic future directions, such as incorporating deepfake detection into DPI frameworks for improving data governance, and embedding explainable artificial intelligence (XAI) for transparent and trusted decision-making. These contributions collectively provide a forward-looking perspective on the integrated role of DPI and ML in next-generation cybersecurity systems.

Keywords: Deep Packet inspection · DeepFake · Machine Learning

1 Introduction

In the era of high-speed and complex networks, ensuring robust network security is a critical challenge. Traditional methods of network traffic analysis often fail to

B. Coppens et al. (Eds.): ARES 2025 Workshops, LNCS 15997, pp. 185–202, 2025.
https://doi.org/10.1007/978-3-032-00639-4_11

meet the growing demands for real-time monitoring and security, particularly in the face of evolving threats and rapid technological advancements. Deep Packet Inspection (DPI) has emerged as a sophisticated technique to address these challenges, enabling detailed analysis of network traffic by examining both packet headers and the content data. DPI is pivotal for applications such as security monitoring, intrusion detection, content filtering, bandwidth management, and even government surveillance [2,3,5].

Traditional DPI methods rely on pre-established rules and signatures, using techniques such as signature-based analysis and statistical methods to detect anomalies and security threats [2]. While these methods are useful, they encounter significant limitations in monitoring fast network traffic and handling encrypted data, which has become increasingly common in modern communication systems. The complexities introduced by technologies like the Internet of Things (IoT), Software-Defined Networking (SDN), and cloud computing further challenge conventional DPI techniques [3,5,6].

To overcome these challenges, machine learning (ML) and deep learning (DL) based DPI techniques have gained traction. These advanced techniques offer adaptable solutions for detecting hidden traffic patterns that traditional systems often miss [6]. Unlike signature-based systems, ML models can learn and adjust their detection strategies as new traffic data are fed into the system, making them more effective in dynamic environments like SDN and IoT networks [7]. Despite the promise of ML-based DPI, there are challenges, including the need for large labelled datasets and the high computational costs associated with DL models [8]. Privacy concerns surrounding encrypted traffic analysis are also emerging as an important issue [3,6]. Moreover, a comparison of existing recent surveys with our paper is summarised in Table 1.

To advance the state-of-the-art in DPI research, particularly for payload content analysis, this paper makes the following **research contributions**:

- **DPI Techniques Survey**: Overview of traditional and ML DPI techniques and highlights their strengths, limitations, and real-time applicability. (Section 2)
- **DPI Taxonomy**: Proposes a taxonomy that categorises DPI methods into ML-based and conventional techniques, with advanced approaches. (Section 2 and Fig. 1)
- **Performance Comparison**: Provides a performance comparison of ML models across multiple datasets. (Section 3)
- **Emerging DPI Trends**: Identifies trends such as ML integration, hybrid approaches, and concerns around scalability and encryption privacy. (Section 4)
- **Future Directions**: Suggestions for future DPI research on Deepfake in Multichannel Social Engineering Attack (SEA), Data Governance in DPI, and XAI decision making. (Section 5)

The purpose of this paper is to provide insight into the future of DPI in securing modern network infrastructures. The complete structure of the paper is outlined in Fig 2.

Table 1. Comparison of Related Surveys on DPI Techniques

Survey	Main Strengths	Main Limitations	Additional Focus Areas
Celebi et al. [3]	Classification of hardware-accelerated DPI methods	Limited focus on ML's role in detection methodologies	Not covered
Shandilya et al. [13]	Specialized dataset for DPI evaluation against attacks	Limited focus on ML/DL integration in DPI	Not covered
Santhosh Kumar et al. [19]	Focus on improving IDS with ML techniques for IoT	DPI not directly discussed but can enhance traffic inspection	Not covered
Brooke Lampe and Weizhi Meng [44]	Focus on automotive network security with deep learning	Limited discussion of DPI techniques in the context of automotive networks	Not covered
Alraizza and Algarni [14]	Specialized focus on ransomware detection	Limited application to broader DPI and network security techniques	Not covered
Our Paper	Detailed taxonomy, coverage of emerging trends, challenges in modern networks	Real-world application challenges and integration issues with other technologies	*Novel Taxonomy of traditional and ML methods, Performance comparison, Current challenge of Deepfake in Multichannel SEA, Data governance and XAI*

2 Taxonomy of DPI Techniques

This section introduces the proposed taxonomy for DPI techniques. We begin by categorising DPI methods into two main subcategories: traditional DPI techniques and ML-based DPI techniques as shown in Fig. 1. Each of these subcategories is further classified and discussed below.

2.1 Traditional Techniques

Traditional DPI techniques rely primarily on rule-based, signature-based, or statistical approaches without the involvement of advanced ML methods. These techniques focus on pattern matching, traffic analysis, and protocol examination to identify potential threats or anomalies in network traffic. The various traditional DPI techniques include:

I. **Flow and Traffic Analysis** Flow and Traffic analysis [16] monitors data flow patterns, such as packet headers, to detect anomalies and threats. By analysing metadata i.e., IPs, ports, and protocols, security systems identify abnormal behaviors, aiding early threat detection and identifying malicious activities like DDoS attacks and data exfiltration. Flow analysis methods are shown in Fig. 3(a).

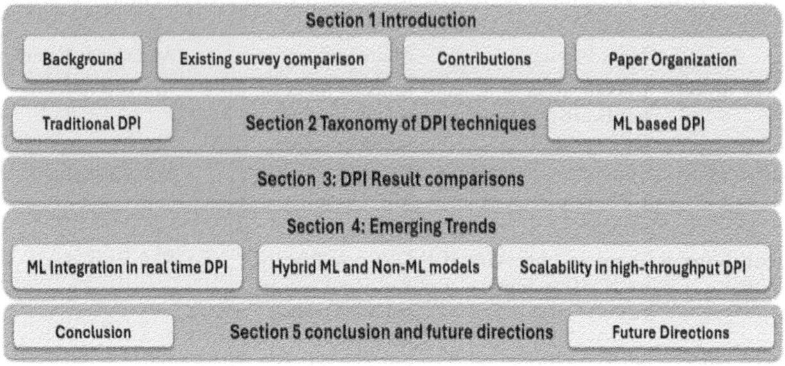

Fig. 1. Proposed taxonomy of DPI.

a. **Flow Aggregation:** Flow aggregation [16] consolidates packets with shared attributes (e.g., IPs, ports) into flow records, improving DPI efficiency and threat detection. It helps identify traffic spikes, DDoS attacks, and botnets. Tools, for example, NetFlow and IPFIX offer scalability.
Limitations: This approach loses packet-level detail, making subtle attacks harder to detect and may miss multistage threats or struggle with encrypted traffic.
b. **Traffic Flow Profiling:** Traffic flow profiling [5,16] establishes a baseline of normal activity using key flow attributes, detecting anomalies by comparing real-time data to this baseline.
Limitations: The method relies on historical data that can become outdated with changes in the network, causing false alarms. It can miss subtle attacks and be bypassed by attackers that mimic normal traffic patterns.
c. **Traffic Correlation:** Traffic correlation [3,5] analyses traffic data to identify relationships that may signal threats, particularly in multistage attacks.
Limitations: Encrypted traffic can hinder correlation, and brief attack patterns may not form detectable correlations. Changes in dynamic networks can result in false correlations.
d. **Flow Filtering:** Flow filtering [3,16] isolates high-priority traffic by applying rules such as blacklisted IPs or unusual ports, focusing on threats like port scans or malware.
Limitations: It may miss novel attacks, discard legitimate traffic, and be evaded by attackers using obfuscation techniques such as random ports.

II. **Rule-Based Detection** Rule-based detection [1,3,5] detects threats by matching traffic to predefined rules, such as blacklisted IPs or unusual port usage. It is central to IDS and firewalls, offering reliable detection of known threats. However, it depends on the quality of the rules and may miss new

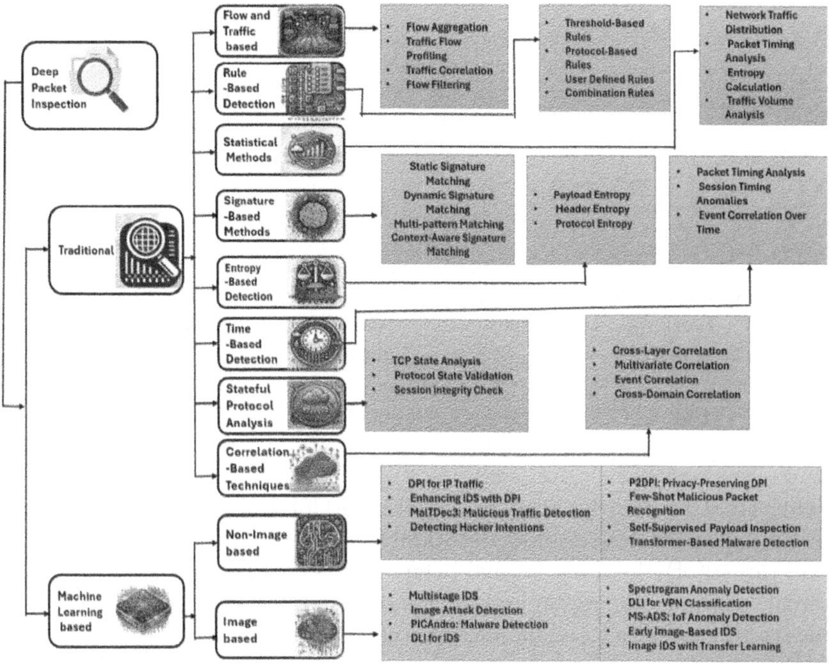

Fig. 2. Structure of the paper.

attacks, often requiring integration with anomaly detection or ML, as general working is shown in Fig. 3(b)

a. **Threshold-Based Rules**: Trigger alerts or actions after exceeding pre-defined limits (e.g., login attempts, bandwidth usage) [18]. Commonly used in IDS and cloud monitoring like AWS CloudWatch.
   Limitation: False positives due to legitimate traffic spikes; attackers can evade detection by spreading attacks over time.
b. **Protocol-Based Rules**: Enforce protocol compliance (e.g., malformed HTTP headers) to prevent attacks like web cache poisoning [1,5]. Tools i.e., Snort and Suricata apply these rules.
   Limitation: Legacy systems may not conform to protocol standards; attackers can bypass with encrypted channels or protocol abuses.
c. **User-Defined Rules**: Custom rules for specific needs, for example blocking traffic from high-risk geolocations or restricting internal Application Programming Interfaces (APIs) [5,18].
   Limitation: Requires constant updates; poorly designed rules may disrupt legitimate traffic, and attackers can exploit rule gaps.
d. **Combination Rules**: Hybrid rules combine thresholds, protocols, and custom logic. SOAR platforms automate these workflows [1,5,18].
   Limitation: Increased complexity can lead to misconfigurations and resource overhead, causing detection delays.

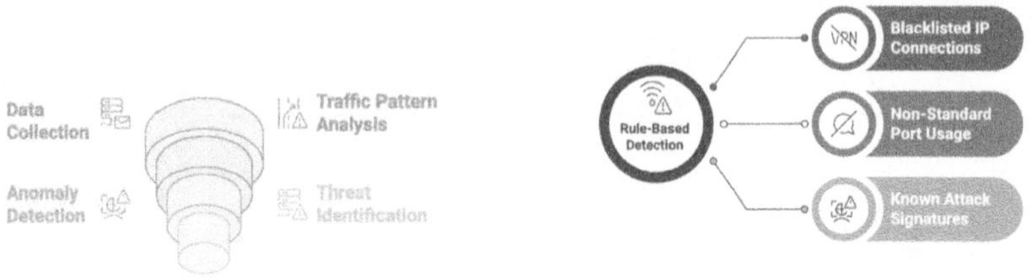

(a) Flow and Traffic Analysis Method Working Mechanism - (self-created figure)

(b) Rule-Based detection Method Working Mechanism - (self-created figure)

Fig. 3. Flow Traffic Analysis and Rule-based Detection.

III. **Statistical Methods**: Statistical Methods [20] analyse network traffic patterns (e.g., packet sizes, flow durations) to detect anomalies that may indicate threats. By learning normal behavior, they can identify new or evolving threats without relying on known signatures. Their effectiveness depends on the baseline accuracy and monitored traffic features. The mechanism is shown in Fig. 4(a).

   a. **Network Traffic Distribution**: analyses packet sizes and flow durations to model normal traffic behavior. Deviations from this model can indicate potential threats [18,20].
   Limitation: May not detect slow or incremental attacks that closely follow normal patterns.
   b. **Packet Timing Analysis**: Assesses packet arrival times to detect unusual patterns, such as traffic spikes or delays, often indicative of DoS attacks or slow scans [5,21].
   Limitation: Ineffective when traffic is sporadic or manipulated by attackers.
   c. **Entropy Calculation**: Measures randomness in network traffic, with low entropy indicating malicious activity such as port scans or malware communications [22].
   Limitation: It is difficult to distinguish between malicious and legitimate high-entropy traffic, such as encrypted communications.
   d. **Traffic Volume Analysis**: Examines data volume to identify abnormal spikes or drops, such as those from DDoS attacks [5,21,22].
   Limitation: Can generate false positives due to legitimate traffic fluctuations.

IV. **Signature-Based Methods** Signature-Based Methods [9] are a class of Deep Packet Inspection (DPI) techniques used to detect malicious network traffic by matching packets or flows to known attack patterns (signatures). These signatures represent specific attack behaviors and threat characteristics. When a match is found, the system triggers an alert. The working structure of these methods is shown in Fig. 4(b).

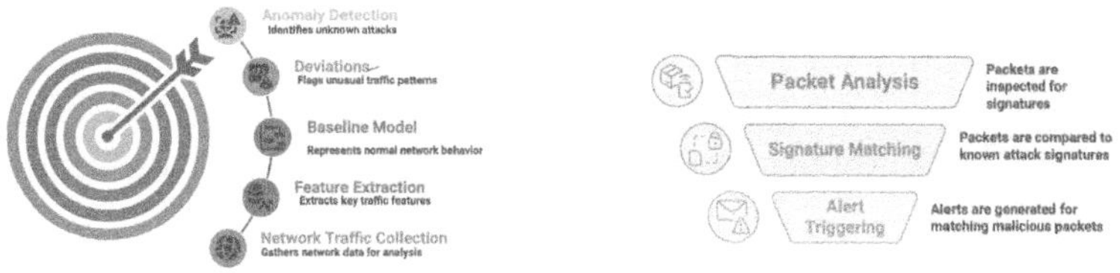

(a) Statistical Method Mechanism

(b) Signature-Based Method Working Mechanism

Fig. 4. Statistical and Methods signature-based Mechanisms - (self-created figure).

a. **Static Signature Matching:** The Static signature-based method [9] detects known threats by comparing network traffic or files with predefined byte sequences (signatures). This method remains effective in identifying older attacks or malware.
Limitations: Static matching fails to detect zero-day attacks or modified malware (e.g., using polymorphism or obfuscation). As signature databases expand, it leads to performance overheads and vulnerability to evasion techniques i.e., code packing.
b. **Dynamic Signature Matching:** The dynamic signature-based method [9,22] detects threats by analysing runtime behaviors like file modifications, network communication, and process activities, identifying both known and unknown threats by matching to malicious patterns.
Limitations: It still relies on known patterns, leaving it vulnerable to novel attacks. In addition, it has high computational costs, creates detection gaps, and can produce false positives from benign activities.
c. **Multi-pattern Matching:** Multi-pattern matching [9,22] allows scanning for multiple attack signatures concurrently, improving efficiency over single-pattern matching. It is used in IDS and malware scanners to identify known attack patterns and anomalies, often employing optimized algorithms for examples, Aho-Corasick [17] and parallel processing.
Limitations: Although efficient, it has high memory and computational demands, especially with large signature sets. It cannot detect new attack patterns beyond its signature database and may generate false positives without understanding the system context.
d. **Context-Aware Signature Matching:** Context-aware signature matching [5,9,22] enhances traditional detection by incorporating behavioral context (e.g., user actions, system conditions, and network patterns) to improve threat detection and reduce false alerts.
Limitations: This approach requires complex implementation, continuous monitoring, and significant resources. It raises privacy concerns due to extensive data collection and may generate false alerts if contextual models misinterpret normal behavior or fail to adapt to new environments.

V. **Entropy-Based Detection** Entropy-Based Detection [22] measures the randomness in network traffic, calculating entropy for features such as packet sizes and flow durations. It detects unpredictable behaviors, such as DDoS or malware attacks, by identifying high or low entropy. This method is effective in detecting evolving threats without relying on signatures, though its accuracy depends on defining "normal" traffic. The mechanism is shown in Fig. 5(a).

   a. **Payload Entropy** measures randomness in a packet's payload [22]. High entropy suggests encryption or complexity, while low entropy indicates predictability. It helps detect anomalies, for instance, data exfiltration or malicious payloads.
   Limitation: It cannot distinguish malicious from legitimate encrypted traffic, and attackers can craft high-entropy payloads to bypass detection.
   b. **Header Entropy** evaluates randomness in packet headers (IPs, ports) [22,23]. High entropy may indicate scans or spoofing, while low entropy reflects normal traffic.
   Limitation: Struggles with attacks mimicking legitimate headers, and legitimate traffic (e.g., VPNs) may trigger false positives.
   c. **Protocol Entropy** assesses unpredictability in protocol usage [22,23]. High entropy may signal malicious non-standard protocols, while low entropy indicates normal operations.
   Limitation: Less effective against attacks using standard protocols and encrypted or custom protocols that obscure malicious behavior.

VI. **Time-Based Detection** Time-based detection [3,5] monitors traffic timing, such as packet rates and connection durations, to identify anomalies like traffic spikes or irregular requests, often signaling DDoS or botnets. It focuses on when events occur, unlike entropy-based methods. The mechanism is shown in Fig. 5(b).

   a. **Packet Timing Analysis**: Analyses packet arrival intervals to detect anomalies like DDoS attacks or covert data transfers [5,24].
   Limitation: Encryption can obscure timing patterns, and attackers may adjust timing to avoid detection.
   b. **Session Timing Anomalies**: Identifies irregularities in session timing (e.g., logins, data transfers) that may indicate unauthorized access [3,24].
   Limitation: Variability in legitimate user behavior can cause false alarms. Skilled attackers may mimic normal session patterns.
   c. **Event Correlation Over Time**: Examines security events over extended periods to detect complex attack sequences [3,24,24].
   Limitation: Long-term attacks may delay detection, and accurate detection depends on timestamp synchronisation across systems.

VII. **Stateful Protocol Analysis**
Stateful Protocol Analysis [2–4] tracks protocol states (e.g., TCP, HTTP) to ensure compliance and detect deviations. It is effective for spotting attacks for example session hijacking and TCP floods, identifying anomalies missed by stateless methods. The mechanism is shown in Fig. 6(a).

a. **TCP State Analysis**: Tracks the lifecycle of TCP connections (i.e., SYN/SYN-ACK, FIN/RST) to identify anomalies such as incomplete sessions or resets, often indicating SYN flood attacks or hijacking [2–4]. Firewalls use state tables to block unsolicited packets.
Limitation: Modern threats like TLS-based exploits can hide malicious payloads behind valid states, making detection reliant on additional methods, for example, behavioral analysis.
b. **Protocol State Validation**: Ensures protocols (e.g., HTTP, DNS) follow intended workflows, detecting issues like missing DNS queries or out-of-order FTP commands [2–4]. Tools, for instance, Snort enforce these rules.
Limitation: Legacy systems and IoT devices often violate protocol norms, triggering false alarms. Attackers can bypass checks by exploiting protocol features such as HTTP/2 multiplexing.
c. **Session Integrity Check**: Validates sequence numbers and session tokens to detect tampering, such as replayed authentication tokens or sudden IP geolocation shifts [2–4]. Web Application Firewalls (WAFs) combine this with behavioral baselines.
Limitation: Heavy encryption masks payloads, and network congestion can distort sequence validation, leading to unnecessary alerts during peak traffic.

VIII. **Correlation-Based Detection**: Correlation-Based Detection [2–4] correlates data from sources such as traffic, logs, and events to identify complex attacks. It detects multistage exploits and coordinated DDoS campaigns, offering a broader view than traditional methods. The mechanism is shown in Fig. 6(b).

a. **Cross-Layer Correlation**: Correlates data across network layers (e.g., physical, transport, application) to identify multi-stage attacks for examples, DDoS or brute-force login followed by data exfiltration [3,4,15]. IDS systems use this technique to map such threats.
Limitation: Encryption (e.g., TLS) can obscure payloads, and mismatched logging formats complicate integration.
b. **Multivariate Correlation**: Combines multiple variables (e.g., user activity, network traffic) to detect complex threats i.e., credential stuffing [3,4,15]. ML models automate this process.
Limitation: High-dimensional data increases computational load and can lead to overfitting, with higher false positives.
c. **Event Correlation**: Links unrelated security events (e.g., phishing emails followed by database access) to uncover attack narratives [3,4,15]. SIEM systems, for example, Splunk utilize this method.
Limitation: Time discrepancies across systems can distort event correlation, and attackers can time-stagger events to delay detection.
d. **Cross-Domain Correlation**: Integrates data from diverse domains (e.g., network, cloud, IoT) to identify cross-boundary threats [3,4,15].
Limitation: Organizational silos, proprietary formats, and privacy regulations (e.g., GDPR) limit data sharing.

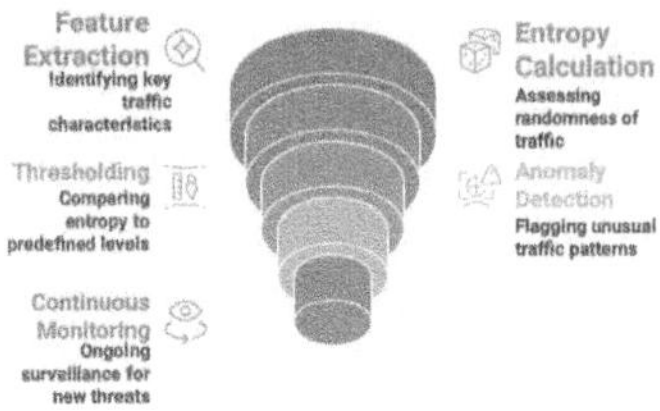

(a) Entropy-based Detection Mechanism - (self-created figure)

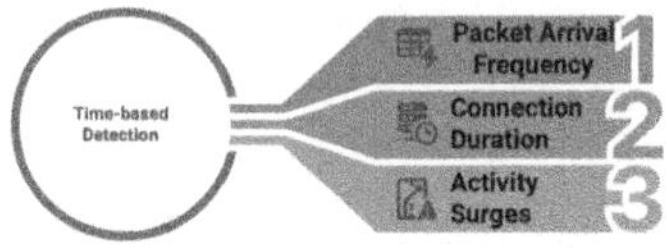

(b) Time-based Detection Mechanism - (self-created figure)

Fig. 5. Entropy-based and Time-based Detection Mechanisms.

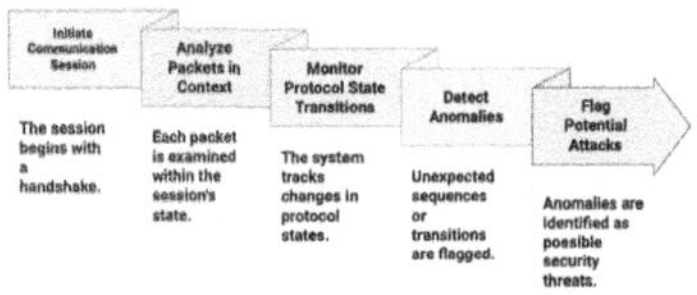

(a) Stateful Protocol Analysis Mechanism - (self-created figure)

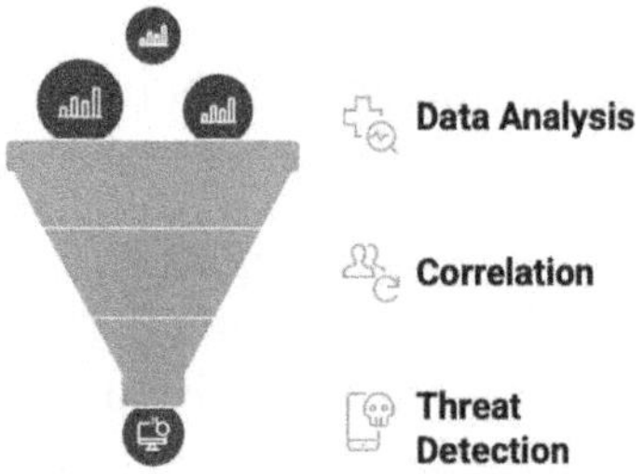

(b) Correlation-Based Detection Mechanism - (self-created figure)

Fig. 6. Comparison of Stateful Protocol Analysis and Correlation-Based Detection Mechanisms.

2.2 Machine Learning Based DPI

Modern DPI has evolved by integrating ML to analyse network traffic. Unlike traditional DPI, which relies on predefined rules, signatures, or statistical models, ML-based DPI employs algorithms that learn from network data to identify previously unknown threats. This approach is especially useful for detecting threats hidden in encrypted traffic, where conventional methods fall short. Below are key techniques of ML-based DPI:

I. **Non-Image-Based Techniques (Data-Driven DPI)**: This subcategory includes methods that analyse network traffic data, such as packet features and traffic patterns, using ML algorithms. These methods focus on structured and unstructured numeric data.
   a. **DPI and ML for IP Traffic Categorization**: Aziz et al. [25] propose a hybrid network traffic classification technique combining Deep Packet Inspection (DPI) and ML to classify traffic into QoS classes. The DPI module identifies traffic, while ML handles unidentified traffic, achieving over 98% classification accuracy. The approach is evaluated using various supervised and unsupervised learning algorithms.
   b. **Enhancing IDS with DPI and ML**: Bathiri et al. [26] propose a hybrid traffic classification technique combining Deep Packet Inspection (DPI) and ML models to enhance IDS/IPS systems. By analysing both packet payloads and headers, the approach achieves over 98% accuracy, offering a more robust solution for detecting emerging threats.
   c. **MalTDec3**: Srivastava et al. [27] present a 3-layer inspection method for malicious traffic detection. The method achieves 99.96% accuracy using One-Class SVM with PCA, analysing packet destination, keywords, and anomalies in real-time traffic.
   d. **Hacker Intention Detection Using DPI and ML**: Foreman et al. [28] focus on detecting hacker intent via TCP SYN scan analysis. By leveraging ML and NFStream DPI, the method improves detection accuracy and F1 scores, providing early recognition of reconnaissance activities.
   e. **P2DPI**: Kim et al. [29] introduce P2DPI, a DPI system for encrypted traffic that offers faster setup, improved encryption, and performance over existing solutions such as BlindBox and PrivDPI, ensuring privacy and security without high delays.
   f. **FSL and LLM for DPI**: Stein et al. [10] propose using large language models (LLM) with few-shot learning for malware detection in network traffic. The approach identifies novel malware with minimal labeled samples, achieving an average accuracy of 86.35% and an F1-Score of 86.40%.
   g. **Self-Supervised Journey to Precision with Few Shots**: Stein et al. [12] present a self-supervised learning method for malware detection using DPI. The transformer model adapts to novel attack types, achieving classification accuracies up to 94.76% on the UNSW-NB15 dataset.
   h. **Transformer-Based Malware Detection and Classification**: Stein et al. [11] propose a transformer-based DPI model to detect malicious traffic. The model, using raw payload bytes, achieves 79% accuracy in binary classification and 72% in multiclassification on the UNSW-NB15 and CIC-IoT23 datasets.

II. **Image-Based Techniques (Vision-Based DPI)**: This is anther subcategroy, we include those techniques that use visual representations of network traffic (e.g., graphs or heatmaps), which are analysed with ML models, such as convolutional neural networks (CNNs), to identify patterns. Some of the relevant approaches are discussed below:

a. **Multistage IDS**: Toldinas et al. [31] propose a multistage DL approach that transforms network features into four-channel images and classifies them using a pre-trained ResNet50 model, achieving 99.8% accuracy on UNSW-NB15 and 99.7% accuracy on BOUN DDoS datasets.
b. **Enhancing IDS with DL**: Islam [32] introduces an image-based IDS approach using CNNs to classify network traffic transformed into images. The model demonstrates high accuracy, even under noisy conditions, and shows promise for real-world IoT environments.
c. **PICAndro: Malware Detection**: Choudhary et al. [33] present PICAndro, a DL-based approach for Android malware detection using network packet inspection. It achieves 99.12% accuracy for malware detection and 98.91% for malware classification.
d. **DL for IDS**: Kim et al. [30] propose a vision-based DL method for IDS by converting network data into 2D images, improving detection performance over grayscale-image methods.
e. **Spectrogram with DL**: Khan et al. [34] use DL and spectrogram images to reduce false alarms in IDS. The model improves detection accuracy by 2.5%âĂ§4% and reduces false alarms by 4.3%âĂ§6.7%, achieving 98.75% accuracy in a seven-class classification task.
f. **VPN with DL**: Sun et al. [35] introduce a DL method for classifying VPN and TLS-encrypted traffic. Using CNNs on packet block images, the model achieves 97.20% accuracy on OpenVPN and 93.31% on ISCX-Tor.
g. **MS-ADS Anomaly Detection with DL**: Ahmed et al. [36] propose a Multistage Spectrogram-based Anomaly Detection System (MS-ADS) for IoT networks, achieving 99.98% accuracy and reducing false alarms to 0.006%.
h. **Early Detection in Image Data**: Abo-alian et al. [37] propose a model for early intrusion detection, converting network traffic into images. The model achieves 98–99% accuracy and detects intrusions as early as the fifth packet.
i. **Image-based IDS with Transfer Learning**: Gulobev et al. [38] review image-based IDS methods using transfer learning, proposing a new feature extraction technique for network traffic. The approach is evaluated using the SWaT dataset for a modern water treatment facility.

3 DPI Result Comparisons

This section compares ML and DL techniques applied to deep packet inspection across datasets like UNSW-NB15, NSL-KDD, N-BaIoT, Bot-IoT, CTU-13, and ISCX. Table 2 summarises performance metrics: accuracy, precision, recall, and F1-score.

Key observations:

- **Deep Learning Advantage**: DL models, especially hybrid ones like HybridEnsemble and CNN-LSTM, outperform traditional ML methods in detecting complex traffic patterns.

- **Ensemble Methods**: Models like Random Forest and AdaBoost-DT show strong, consistent performance across multiple datasets by combining multiple learners.
- **Performance Variations**: The results vary between datasets. High accuracy in NSL-KDD doesn't always transfer to more complex datasets like Bot-IoT or CICIDS.
- **Hybrid Models**: New approaches integrating optimization algorithms (e.g., BGWO) and generative methods (e.g., CTGAN) balance accuracy and efficiency.
- **Reporting Gaps**: Precision, recall, and F1-score are often missing, making it hard to evaluate real-world applicability, especially for high-stakes environments.

The comparative results illustrate the rapid advancement of detection capabilities in recent years, largely driven by DL and hybrid model innovations. However, performance alone does not dictate the suitability of a model for deployment in real-world DPI systems. Other factors such as model interpretability, resource efficiency, and scalability remain crucial considerations and are further discussed in subsequent sections.

4 Emerging Trends

Several emerging trends are transforming DPI and enhancing its capabilities in the realm of cybersecurity:

- **Integration of Machine Learning in Real-Time DPI Systems** ML enhances real-time DPI systems by analysing high-volume network traffic, detecting anomalies, and adapting to emerging threats. Unlike traditional methods, ML improves pattern recognition and decision-making with minimal latency, critical for dynamic network environments.
- **Hybrid ML and Non-ML DPI Models** Combining ML's adaptive threat detection with non-ML techniques (e.g., signature-based methods) improves accuracy and reduces false positives. This hybrid approach leverages deterministic methods for known attacks and ML for novel threats, optimizing real-time analysis.
- **Scalability in High-Throughput DPI** To manage escalating network traffic, scalable DPI systems utilize cloud resources, edge computing, and parallel processing. Research focuses on algorithmic efficiency to maintain real-time performance without delays, even in large-scale enterprise or ISP environments.
- **DPI for Encrypted Traffic** As encryption (e.g., SSL/TLS) proliferates, DPI adapts via SSL interception and efficient decryption techniques. Challenges include balancing privacy concerns with inspection needs, driving research into privacy-conscious methods for analysing encrypted traffic.

Table 2. Comparison of different models performances on the NSL-KDD, UNSW-NB15, and N-BaloT, Bot-IoT, CTU-13, ISCX, CCC, and CICIDS datasets. All the results are taken from [39–41, 43]

Methods	Accuracy (%)	Precision (%)	Recall (%)	F1-score (%)
UNSW-NB15				
Random Forest (SVM)	97.69	-	-	-
XGBoost (KNN)	95.86	-	-	-
Feed-forward Neural Network	99	-	-	-
NB classifier	99	-	-	-
AODE	94.37	-	-	-
CNN	99	-	-	-
NSL-KDD				
SVM	96.89	-	-	-
Ensemble learning	96.06	-	-	-
BiLSTM	95.4	-	-	-
KNN	98.24	-	-	-
N-BaloT				
HybridEnsemble	99.99	99.99	99.99	99.99
LDL	98.37	83.31	86.32	84.47
FGOA-kNN	98.07	97.04	98.73	97.87
SGDC	-	98.43	98.42	98.41
ER-VEC	95.64	-	-	-
WCC and SVM	96.70	94.90	94.70	94.80
CNN-LSTM	-	94.00	89.00	85.00
BGWO	98.97	-	-	-
LGBA-NN	90.00	85.23	90.00	86.64
RNN	89.75	-	-	-
CART, 2020	99.00	-	-	-
Bot-IoT				
HybridEnsemble	100.00	100.00	100.00	100.00
CTGAN with MLP	98.93	99.84	98.93	99.07
SOPA-GA-CNN	98.20	97.67	97.75	97.71
Modified SVM	97.00	97.00	97.00	97.00
DBO-Catboost	96.10	96.20	96.10	96.10
BTC-SIGBDS	94.98	-	-	-
Fuzzy interpolation	96.41	98.80	98.80	98.80
FRI	95.40	96.00	96.00	96.00
C4.5	97.62	97.63	99.99	98.79
CTU-13				
HybridEnsemble	98.77	98.66	98.77	98.71
DT	92.21	92.21	92.21	92.21
IGWO	98.87	99.15	93.45	-
MLC	97.00	98.10	99.60	98.00
RNN	-	87.10	97.00	91.80
LR	-	66.80	92.40	77.54
KNN	94.20	-	-	-
Multi-layer with DT	98.70	-	-	-
ISCX				
HybridEnsemble	99.95	99.95	99.95	99.95
HOG descriptors	97.50	98.00	98.00	98.00
AE NN with DT	99.20	99.10	99.10	99.10
ELM	98.67	-	99.00	-
AdaBoost-DT	98.36	98.85	98.23	98.54

5 Conclusion and Future Directions

This review article has offered an analytical perspective on the current landscape of DPI techniques, with the aim of identifying critical insights, emerging trends with existing limitations, and future research directions. By examining both traditional and ML based approaches, we have provided a structured understanding of how DPI techniques have evolved and where they are heading. The proposed taxonomy clarifies the strengths and weaknesses of the SOTA methods, while the evaluation of ML models across multiple datasets offers practical benchmarks for real-world deployment. In addition, we have identified emerging trends, such as hybrid inspection systems and techniques to handle encrypted traffic, which illustrate the growing importance of DPI in addressing modern cybersecurity challenges.

The three key areas in the following are important **future directions** for reliable DPI techniques in the management of increasingly complex data environments.

I. **Deepfake in Multichannel Social Engineering Attack**: The rise of multichannel SEA, which uses multiple communication methods to manipulate individuals into compromising their security (e.g., finance worker pays out \$25 million[1] and Chinese man scammed by deepfake generated girlfriend \$28000[2]), poses numerous threats in DPI. Deepfakes pose a significant threat to the reliability and authenticity of content. Future research will need to focus on developing a deepFirewall DPI method that can detect deepfakes effectively and efficiently. Furthermore, integrating AI-powered deepfake detection with traditional DPI methods could make systems more robustness and accurate to identify and mitigate deceptive content.

II. **Data Governance in DPI**: As DPI technologies deal with huge amount of data, ensuring compliance with data governance rules is essential. The future of DPI research will likely place significant emphasis on creating robust frameworks for managing the privacy, security, and ethical implications of the data being processed. With increasing concern about data breaches and privacy violations, especially in the context of encrypted communication, advanced data governance mechanisms will be crucial, involving defining clear guidelines for data access, ensuring the integrity of the data, and enforcing compliance with legal and ethical standards.

III. **Integration of Explainable AI**: Another future direction for DPI is interpretability and transparency of DL models in real-time analysis. The integration of XAI, which aims to ensure that the models can perform well and also explain the decisions, is a promising direction to address these challenges. It is very crucial in DPI to understand why certain traffic is

---

[1] https://edition.cnn.com/2024/02/04/asia/deepfake-cfo-scam-hong-kong-intl-hnk/index.html.

[2] https://www.ndtv.com/world-news/shanghai-man-scammed-of-28-000-by-ai-girlfriend-ms-jiao-report-7799157.

flagged as abnormal, as this is central to trust, regulatory compliance, and debugging.

Acknowledgments. The research work carried out in this review article was funded by CISCO Systems in collaboration with Insight Research Centre for Data Analytics, Data Science Institute, University of Galway. We sincerely thank CISCO for their generous financial support, which has played a vital role in enabling this study on emerging directions in cybersecurity.

Disclosure of Interests. The authors have no competing interests to declare that they are relevant to the content of this article.

References

1. Chatterjee, A., Ahmed, B.: IoT anomaly detection methods and applications: a survey. Internet Things **19**, 100568 (2022)
2. El-Maghraby, R., Abd Elazim, N., Bahaa-Eldin, A.: A survey on deep packet inspection. In: 2017 12th International Conference On Computer Engineering And Systems (ICCES), pp. 188–197 (2017)
3. Çelebi, M., Özbilen, A., Yavanoğlu, U.: A comprehensive survey on deep packet inspection for advanced network traffic analysis: issues and challenges. Niğde Ömer Halisdemir Üniversitesi Mühendislik Bilimleri Dergisi. **12**, 1–29 (2023)
4. Mustapha, H., Djahel, S., Perry, P., Zhang, Z.: Rethinking deep packet inspection design and deployment in the era of SDN and NFV. In: 2021 IEEE 23rd International Conference On High Performance Computing & Communications; 7th International Conference On Data Science & Systems; 19th International Conference On Smart City; 7th International Conference On Dependability In Sensor, Cloud & Big Data Systems & Application (HPCC/DSS/SmartCity/DependSys), pp. 1505–1514 (2021)
5. Jajula, S., Tripathi, K., Bajaj, S.: Review of detection of packets inspection and attacks in network security. In: Emerging Technologies In Data Mining And Information Security: Proceedings Of IEMIS 2022, vol. 1, pp. 597–604 (2022)
6. Bochie, K., Gilbert, M., Gantert, L., Barbosa, M., Medeiros, D., Campista, M.: A survey on deep learning for challenged networks: applications and trends. J. Network Comput. Appl. **194**, 103213 (2021)
7. Amin, R., Rojas, E., Aqdus, A., Ramzan, S., Casillas-Perez, D., Arco, J.: A survey on machine learning techniques for routing optimization in SDN. IEEE Access **9**, 104582–104611 (2021)
8. Kumar, T., Brennan, R., Mileo, A., Bendechache, M.: A comprehensive survey and future directions. IEEE Access, Image Data Augmentation Approaches (2024)
9. Hashimyar, M., Aiash, M., Khoshkholghi, A., Nalli, G.: Signature-based security analysis and detection of IoT threats in advanced message queuing protocol. Network **5** (2025). https://www.mdpi.com/2673-8732/5/1/5
10. Stein, K., Mahyari, A., Francia, G., El-Sheikh, E.: Towards novel malicious packet recognition: a few-shot learning approach. In: MILCOM 2024-2024 IEEE Military Communications Conference (MILCOM), pp. 847–852 (2024)
11. Stein, K., Mahyari, A., Francia, G., El-Sheikh, E.: A transformer-based framework for payload malware detection and classification. In: 2024 IEEE World AI IoT Congress (AIIoT), pp. 105–111 (2024)

12. Stein, K., Mahyari, A., Francia III, G., El-Sheikh, E.: Revolutionizing payload inspection: a self-supervised journey to precision with few shots. ArXiv Preprint ArXiv:2409.18219 (2024)
13. Shandilya, S., Ganguli, C., Izonin, I., Nagar, A.: Cyber attack evaluation dataset for deep packet inspection and analysis. Data Brief **46**, 108771 (2023)
14. Alraizza, A., Algarni, A.: Ransomware detection using machine learning: a survey. Big Data Cogn. Comput. **7**, 143 (2023)
15. Dijk, A.: Detection of advanced persistent threats using artificial intelligence for deep packet inspection. In: 2021 IEEE International Conference On Big Data (Big Data), pp. 2092-2097 (2021)
16. Papadogiannaki, E., Ioannidis, S.: A survey on encrypted network traffic analysis applications, techniques, and countermeasures. ACM Comput. Surv. (CSUR). **54**, 1–35 (2021)
17. Norton, M.: Optimizing pattern matching for intrusion detection. Sourcefire Inc, Columbia, MD (2004)
18. Serdaroglu, K., Baydere, S., Saovapakhiran, B., Charnsripinyo, C.: Q-IoT: QoS aware multi-layer service architecture for multi-class IoT data traffic management. IEEE Internet Things J. (2024)
19. Santhosh Kumar, S., Selvi, M., Kannan, A.: A comprehensive survey on machine learning-based intrusion detection systems for secure communication in internet of things. Comput. Intell. Neuroscience **2023**, 8981988 (2023)
20. Wang, Y., Xue, H., Liu, Y., Liu, W.: Statistical network protocol identification with unknown pattern extraction. Ann. Telecommun. **74**, 473–482 (2019)
21. Dhawahir, O., Torlak, M.: Enhancing passive WiFi device localization through packet timing analysis. IEEE Open J. Instrum. Measur. (2024)
22. Kenyon, A., Deka, L., Elizondo, D.: Characterising payload entropy in packet flows-baseline entropy analysis for network anomaly detection. Future Internet **16**, 470 (2024)
23. Augello, A., Re, G., Peri, D., Thiyagalingam, P.: NEP-IDS: a network intrusion detection system based on entropy prediction error. In: 2024 IEEE 49th Conference On Local Computer Networks (LCN), pp. 1–9 (2024)
24. Das, S., Bebortta, S., Pati, B., Panigrahi, C., Senapati, D.: Profiling and classification of IoT devices for smart home environments. Mach. Learn. Cyber Phys.. Syst. Adv. Challenges, 85–121 (2024)
25. Aziz, W., Qureshi, H., Iqbal, A., Al-Dulaimi, A., Al-Rubaye, S.: Towards accurate categorization of network IP traffic using deep packet inspection and machine learning. In: GLOBECOM 2023-2023 IEEE Global Communications Conference, pp. 01–06 (2023)
26. Bathiri, K., Vijayakumar, M.: Enhancing Intrusion Detection System (IDS) through Deep Packet Inspection (DPI) with machine learning approaches. In: 2024 International Conference On Advances In Data Engineering and Intelligent Computing Systems (ADICS), pp. 1-7 (2024)
27. Srivastava, A., Agarwal, A., Nadeem, M., Nizami, A., Tripathi, A.: MalTDec3: malicious traffic detection in a network using 3 layer inspection. In: 2022 Fifth International Conference On Computational Intelligence and Communication Technologies (CCICT), pp. 568–575 (2022)
28. Foreman, J., Waters, W., Kamhoua, C., Hemida, A., Acosta, J., Dike, B.: Detection of hacker intention using deep packet inspection. J. Cybersecurity Priv. **4**, 794–804 (2024)

29. Kim, J., Camtepe, S., Baek, J., Susilo, W., Pieprzyk, J., Nepal, S.: P2DPI: practical and privacy-preserving deep packet inspection. In: Proceedings Of The 2021 ACM Asia Conference On Computer and Communications Security, pp. 135–146 (2021)
30. Kim, T., Pak, W.: Deep learning-based network intrusion detection using multiple image transformers. Appl. Sci. **13**, 2754 (2023)
31. Toldinas, J., Venčkauskas, A., Damaševičius, R., Grigaliūnas, Š, Morkevičius, N., Baranauskas, E.: A novel approach for network intrusion detection using multistage deep learning image recognition. Electronics **10**, 1854 (2021)
32. Islam, M.: Image based approach for classification of network based security attacks (2024)
33. Sihag, V., Choudhary, G., Vardhan, M., Singh, P., Seo, J.: PICAndro: Packet InspeCtion-based android malware detection. Secur. Commun. Networks **2021**, 9099476 (2021)
34. Khan, A., Ahmad, Z., Abdullah, J., Ahmad, F.: A spectrogram image-based network anomaly detection system using deep convolutional neural network. IEEE Access **9**, 87079–87093 (2021)
35. Sun, W., Zhang, Y., Li, J., Sun, C., Zhang, S.: A deep learning-based encrypted VPN traffic classification method using packet block image. Electronics **12**, 115 (2022)
36. Ahmad, Z., Khan, A., Zen, K., Ahmad, F.: MS-ADS: multistage spectrogram image-based anomaly detection system for IoT security. Trans. Emerging Telecommun. Technol. **34**, e4810 (2023)
37. Abo-alian, A., AbdelHalim, A., Badr, N.: Enhancing Early Detection and Accuracy in Image-Based Network Intrusion Detection Systems. Available At SSRN 5162974
38. Golubev, S., Novikova, E.: Image-based intrusion detection in network traffic. In: International Symposium On Intelligent and Distributed Computing, pp. 51–60 (2022)
39. Kasongo, S., Sun, Y.: Performance analysis of intrusion detection systems using a feature selection method on the UNSW-NB15 dataset. J. Big Data **7**, 105 (2020)
40. Vibhute, A., Khan, M., Patil, C., Gaikwad, S., Mane, A., Patel, K.: Network anomaly detection and performance evaluation of CNNs on UNSW-NB15 dataset. Procedia Comput. Sci. **235**, 2227–2236 (2024)
41. Vibhute, A., Patil, C., Mane, A., Kale, K.: Towards detection of network anomalies using machine learning algorithms on the NSL-KDD benchmark datasets. Procedia Comput. Sci. **233**, 960–969 (2024)
42. Waghmode, P., Kanumuri, M., El-Ocla, H., Boyle, T.: Intrusion detection system based on machine learning using least square support vector machine. Sci. Rep. **15**, 12066 (2025)
43. Hossain, M., Islam, M.: A novel hybrid feature selection and ensemble-based machine learning approach for botnet detection. Sci. Rep. **13**, 21207 (2023)
44. Lampe, B., Meng, W.: A survey of deep learning-based intrusion detection in automotive applications. Expert Syst. Appl. **221**, 119771 (2023)

Building Realistic Ground Truth Datasets of Personal Identification Information for Entity Matching

Ifeoluwapo Aribilola[1,3](✉), Matteo Catena[2], Mamoona Asghar[1], John Breslin[3], and Renaud Delbru[2]

[1] School of Computer Science, College of Science and Engineering, University of Galway, University Road, Galway H91 TK33, Ireland
mamoona.asghar@universityofgalway.ie

[2] Siren, 15 Market Street, Galway H91 TCX3, Ireland
matteo.catena@siren.io, renaud.delbru@siren.io

[3] School of Engineering, College of Science and Engineering, University of Galway, University Road, Galway H91 TK33, Ireland
ifeoluwapo.aribilola@universityofgalway.ie,
john.breslin@universityofgalway.ie

Abstract. Entity matching (EM) is essential for connecting data across sources, particularly in sensitive domains like human trafficking investigations. However, research faces a critical gap: the lack of realistic gold standard datasets containing personal identifying information. This paper introduces a methodology for creating gold standard datasets, demonstrated through the development of a representative dataset for personal identification information (PII). Our approach combines multiple EM techniques to identify candidate matches, followed by a systematic annotation and validation process. Notably, our findings demonstrate that different techniques identify largely non-overlapping sets of matches, validating the need for our multi-technique methodology. Our approach provides a reproducible template for creating gold standard datasets in domains where realistic evaluation resources are scarce.

Keywords: Entity matching (EM) · Information Retrieval (IR) · Data Blocking · Data annotation · Human Trafficking · Large Language Models · Intelligence Investigations

1 Introduction

Entity matching (EM) enables the identification and deduplication of records corresponding to the same real-world entities across various data sources [8]. Using approaches ranging from rule-based [15] to graph-based [5], probabilistic [23], and neural networks [1,6], EM provides essential capabilities across domains including fraud detection [10] and risk assessment [24]. EM is particularly crucial in human trafficking investigations, where connecting disparate

B. Coppens et al. (Eds.): ARES 2025 Workshops, LNCS 15997, pp. 203–218, 2025.
https://doi.org/10.1007/978-3-032-00639-4_12

information can reveal criminal networks operating across jurisdictions. Human trafficking – the unlawful exchange of individuals for exploitation through coercion, fraud, or force – involves "the use of force, threats, or other types of coercion, abduction, fraud, deception, or abuse of power" to exploit vulnerable individuals [26].

Background and Motivation: In investigative intelligence, particularly for human trafficking cases, EM faces unique challenges. Critical information is frequently dispersed among numerous unstructured or semi-structured sources. Perpetrators intentionally conceal identities using burner phones, aliases, fraudulent documents, and fictitious residences [12]. Accurate matching of these divergent pieces of information is crucial to identify key individuals or networks. Despite EM's critical importance in these sensitive domains, there is a severe lack of realistic, publicly accessible datasets containing personal identifying information (PII). The absence of realistic gold standard datasets with ground-truth labels severely constrains progress in developing robust EM solutions for real-world problems.

Problem Statement: Most benchmark datasets used in the EM literature are synthetic, highly curated, or semi-structured commercial product databases (e.g. Walmart-Amazon, DBLP-Scholar) [3,16]. These datasets fail to capture the ambiguity and variability found in actual personal records, such as misspellings, nicknames, and inconsistent formatting. They rarely include realistic PII and often have artificially balanced label distributions. Furthermore, they fail to represent the complications found in trafficking investigations, where data is characteristically skewed, noisy, and incomplete.

The research community continues to focus on data situations that are excessively "clean" and domain-specific, restricting the generalisation of solutions, as pointed out by [18] in their assessment of blocking strategies. This disconnect between benchmark datasets and real-world applications creates a significant gap in our ability to develop and evaluate EM systems for high-stakes scenarios. Our research addresses these fundamental challenges through the following research questions:

RQ1: How do different EM approaches perform on PII?
RQ2: How can diverse entity matching techniques contribute to creating comprehensive gold standard datasets?

Contribution: In response to these research questions, this paper introduces a methodology for creating gold standard datasets, demonstrated through the development of a real-world PII dataset. We document an approach to dataset creation, annotation, and validation that can be reproduced in other domains. Our empirical results provide evidence that multiple complementary techniques are necessary for comprehensive gold standard creation, as different approaches identify largely non-overlapping sets of matches. We validate LLM-assisted annotation as an efficient approach for dataset creation, reducing the burden on domain experts while maintaining high quality. Through this process, we develop a new gold standard dataset that captures the complexity of real-world entity matching challenges in human trafficking investigations.

Paper Organisation: This paper's remaining sections are arranged as follows: The relevant literature on entity matching pipelines, blocking techniques, and dataset creation challenges is discussed in Sect. 2. The dataset creation methodology is detailed in Sect. 3. Section 4 describes the complementary matching techniques incorporated in our dataset creation pipeline. The experimental validation of our methodology is presented in Sect. 5, while Sect. 6 analyses the evaluation results and discusses limitations. The conclusion and directions for future work are described in Sect. 7.

2 Related Works

This section discusses entity matching (EM) workflows and the limitations of existing benchmark datasets, particularly the lack of realistic personal information.

2.1 Entity Matching Workflows

EM workflows typically consist of multiple phases to manage scalability, heterogeneity, and noise while maintaining accuracy [2,7]. These phases include data pre-processing to normalise inconsistencies, indexing (blocking) to create manageable candidate record pairs using techniques like canopy clustering [14], paired comparison with similarity functions, classification of pairs as matches or non-matches [9], and evaluation of result quality [2].

Recent advances in EM have leveraged deep learning [16] and foundation models [28], replacing traditional approaches with neural architectures such as DITTO [13]. Although these models perform well on benchmark datasets, they typically exhibit dramatic performance drops when applied to datasets with different properties [28], struggling with inconsistent schemas and varying levels of granularity. Models trained using supervised learning often overfit to specific features of their training data, including vocabulary, token patterns, and schema structures [27], resulting in poor generalisation to new domains.

2.2 Lack of Realistic Personal Information in Current Datasets

Robust EM is critical in high-stakes domains such as fraud detection, healthcare, and anti-human trafficking investigations, where personally identifiable information plays a key role. The research community requires datasets that include realistic PII, reflect diversity, and capture real-world complexity.

While EM research has benefited from standardised benchmark datasets [3, 16,20], most suffer from significant limitations in domain coverage, data realism, and scalability. Most datasets used in EM research are synthetic or excessively cleaned, failing to represent the complexity, diversity, and noise present in operational situations [18]. Authentic personal information typically exhibits inconsistencies in formatting, incomplete fields, and cultural/linguistic variations – characteristics essential for evaluating EM systems but largely absent from existing benchmarks.

Few publicly available datasets contain authentic personal information suitable for EM research. Sources like the ICIJ Offshore Leaks Database and public corporate registry data contain real names, addresses, and organisational affiliations with authentic noise and inconsistencies. However, these datasets lack reliable ground truth for training and evaluation, highlighting the need for methodologies to transform such sources into usable gold standards.

In this paper, we introduce a new dataset constructed from two publicly available sources: (1) a subset of OpenCorporates[1] focused on entities of type person (company officers) and (2) a subset of the ICIJ Offshore Leaks Database [11], also filtered on personal entities. Our methodology emphasises the preservation of real-world variability in names and addresses, offering a more representative testbed for EM tasks than existing synthetic datasets. This approach provides a template for generating additional datasets for various EM scenarios beyond our specific implementation.

3 Dataset Creation Methodology

This section presents our methodology for creating gold standard datasets for entity matching (EM), demonstrated through the development of a dataset involving personal information. While our implementation focuses on specific sources, the methodology is generalisable to other domains. As illustrated in Fig. 1, our approach employs multiple complementary techniques to ensure comprehensive coverage of potential matches. Instead of relying on a single matching method – which could systematically miss certain types of matches – we leverage three distinct approaches to generate candidate pairs, which then undergo expert validation to create a gold standard dataset that captures a larger spectrum of matching challenges.

3.1 Data Sources

The ICIJ Offshore Leaks Database, released in 2013, contains information on offshore entities and shell corporations derived from document leaks, including the Panama Papers and Paradise Papers. The dataset includes information on officers, entities, and addresses in a semi-structured format with real-life discrepancies and multiple languages. The second source is the officers' dataset from the OpenCorporates platform, containing publicly available information on officials and directors connected to corporations, including names, positions, and partial addresses.

[1] https://opencorporates.com.

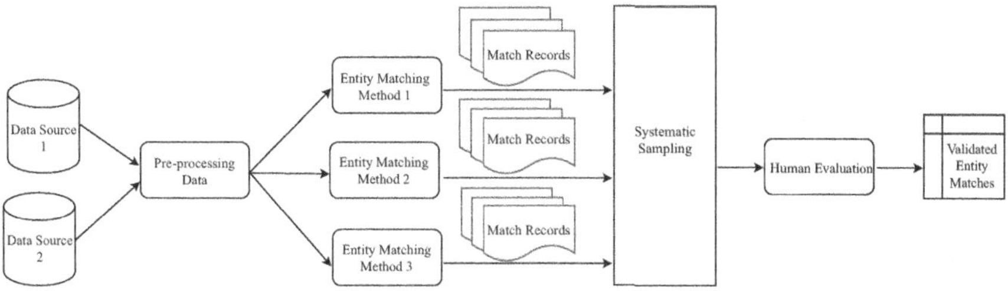

Fig. 1. The process flow for the dataset creation, showing data sources feeding into multiple entity matching methods, followed by systematic sampling and human evaluation to produce validated entity matches.

These sources are particularly valuable for our methodology because they a) contain authentic personal identifiers (names, addresses) with real-world variations, b) include the natural noise and inconsistencies found in actual records, c) represent scenarios relevant to investigative domains, and d) are publicly available, allowing for reproducible research.

For this experiment, we extracted only person entities, totaling 567,707 from ICIJ and 4,689,708 from OpenCorporates.

3.2 Data Pre-processing

An initial step is transforming raw data into formats suitable for EM while preserving the authentic variability that makes the dataset valuable for evaluation.

Selective Attribute Extraction: We first identify and extract the most relevant attributes for matching. Each dataset contains numerous attributes that are not essential for the matching task; keeping these would increase computational requirements and potentially introduce noise. For our implementation, we selected a) fields `Name` and `Address` from the OpenCorporates dataset, and b) fields `Name` and `Addresses.postalAddress` from the ICIJ dataset.

Structure Normalisation: The entities in both datasets were stored in JSON format with nested structures, requiring normalisation to facilitate processing. We flatten the JSON structure by i) converting nested objects into dot notation keys (e.g., `Address.Street`), and ii) aggregating arrays into lists (e.g., `"Emails.Type": ["Work", "Home"]`). Listing 1.1 shows an example JSON entity before normalisation, and Listing 1.2 shows the same entity after normalisation. This transformation standardises the structure while preserving all information.

3.3 Multi-technique Candidate Generation

A core contribution is using multiple complementary techniques to generate candidate pairs. This approach addresses a fundamental limitation of single-

Listing 1.1. Before JSON normalization

```
{
  "Name": "John Doe",
  "Address": {"Street": "123 Main St", "City": "Metropolis"},
  "Emails": [
    {"Type": "Work", "EmailAddress": "john.work@example.com"},
    {"Type": "Home", "EmailAddress": "john.home@example.com"}
  ]
}
```

Listing 1.2. After JSON normalization

```
{
  "Name": "John Doe",
  "Address.Street": "123 Main St",
  "Address.City": "Metropolis",
  "Emails.Type": ["Work", "Home"],
  "Emails.EmailAddress": ["john.work@example.com", "john.home@example.com"]
}
```

technique methods: each has inherent biases that can systematically miss certain types of matches. Our implementation employs three distinct techniques (detailed in Sect. 4):

- **Rule-based blocking**: Using the RecordLinkage library to identify candidates based on explicit similarity thresholds for names and addresses
- **Information retrieval with LLM matching**: Combining Lucene-based blocking with large language model assessment to identify semantically similar entities
- **In-house dataset**: Incorporating previously identified potential matches

Each technique provided candidate pairs labeled as potential matches (`Yes`), potential non-matches (`No`), or uncertain cases (`Maybe`), which are merged for expert validation. The value of this multi-technique approach is that each method identifies largely non-overlapping sets of matches (see Sect. 5).

3.4 Sampling Strategy for Expert Validation

Following the EM process (see Sect. 4), three techniques were applied to generate matched record pairs: Lucene+LLM (LL), the in-house dataset (IH), and RecordLinkage (RL). The LL pipeline produced 19,637 matched records, IH included 4,199, and RL produced 170 matches, collectively generating 24,006 matched records before deduplication.

After removing duplicates, we had 21,963 unique matched records. To create a manageable dataset for annotation while ensuring representation of all sources, we implemented systematic sampling that: i) includes all matches from the rule-based blocking (RL) due to their small number, ii) selects a balanced proportion from the remaining sources (LL and IH), and iii) ensures all three sources are represented proportionally in the final subset. This systematic approach produced a balanced dataset of 500 candidate pairs that preserves each technique's unique contribution and reflects diverse matching behaviors across methods.

3.5 Expert Validation and Gold Standard Creation

The final phase of our methodology is the expert validation process, which transforms candidate pairs into a reliable gold standard. The experts compare the matched entities retrieved from the samples and decide if they truly match (`Yes`), are different (`No`), or are indecisive (`Maybe`).

Annotation Platform Setup: We selected Label Studio [25] for its flexibility in supporting manual annotation. The platform was configured to a) display paired entity records with relevant attributes, b) allow classification as matches, non-matches, or uncertain, c) randomise assignment to different annotators, and d) track decisions and identify conflicts.

Annotator Recruitment and Guidelines: Six domain experts with experience in investigative intelligence were recruited. Each received guidelines explaining a) the definition of a match in human trafficking investigations; b) how to assess name variations; c) how to evaluate address discrepancies; and d) when to mark cases as uncertain.

Conflict Resolution: A key element is the systematic resolution of annotation conflicts. When annotators disagreed on classifications, we i) applied Krippendorff's alpha [17] to measure agreement, flagging instances with zero agreement; ii) had a panel of three experts jointly review each conflict; iii) performed additional verification when necessary, including using Google Maps to confirm address equivalence; and iv) reached consensus through discussion and additional evidence.

Gold Standard Compilation: The final gold standard dataset combined a) pairs with unanimous annotator agreement, and b) pairs with resolved conflicts through the expert panel process. This gave a total of 500 candidate pairs, with 474 pairs as `Yes`, 9 pairs as `No`, and 17 pairs as `Maybe`.

4 Matching Methodology

This section describes the complementary techniques used in our dataset creation pipeline to generate candidate pairs. Each technique contributes unique matches to ensure comprehensive coverage of entity relationships, addressing how diverse approaches can create comprehensive gold standard datasets (RQ2).

4.1 Rule-Based Approach with RecordLinkage

The first component employs rule-based matching using the Python RecordLinkage Toolkit [4], with sequential indexing, comparison, and classification steps.

Blocking. To manage computational complexity, we applied the RecordLinkage library's blocking functionality on the `Name` and `Address` fields from the OpenCorporates dataset, matched with the `Name` and `Addresses.postalAddress` fields from the ICIJ dataset. This process generated 35,195 candidate pairs, significantly reducing the comparison space from the original data sources.

Comparison. Each candidate pair was compared using string similarity metrics to generate a comparison vector. We applied the Jaro-Winkler similarity metric (threshold 0.85) to names due to its effectiveness with character matches, transpositions, and common prefixes. For addresses, we used the Damerau-Levenshtein distance (threshold 0.7) to accommodate typographical errors commonly found in address data. We also conducted alternative comparisons using Jaro-Winkler on both fields. Notably, these specific string comparison functions were critical – without them, the algorithm returned no matches.

Classification. The candidate pairs were filtered to retain only those in which the sum of similarity scores exceeded 1.0, that is, at least two fields exhibited similarity above the defined thresholds. This simple rule-based classification produced a total of 170 matches.

This approach excels at identifying exact or near-exact matches with consistent formatting but may miss semantically equivalent matches with significant syntactic differences.

4.2 IR-Based Blocking with LLM-Based Matching

The second approach combines information retrieval with the assessment of large language models, leveraging both lexical similarity and semantic understanding. As shown in Fig. 2, this process consists of two main stages: 1) an N-Gram Blocking phase using IR techniques, and 2) an LLM-based Matching phase.

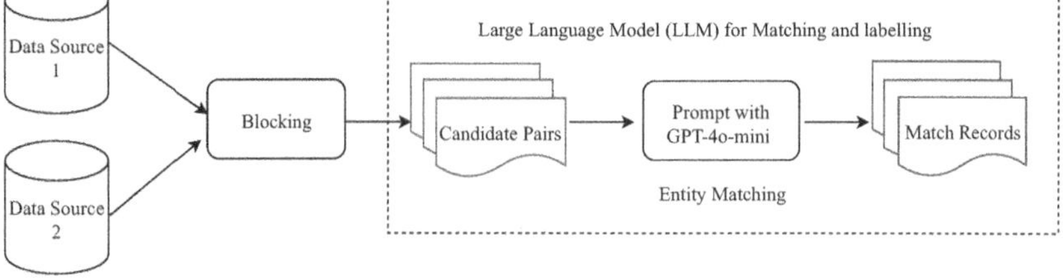

Fig. 2. IR-based blocking with LLM-based matching workflow: Lucene identifies initial candidates based on lexical similarity, then GPT-4o-mini assesses semantic equivalence.

N-Gram Blocking with Lucene. Inspired by Sparkly [19], we use Lucene to index the OpenCorporates dataset with an n-gram analyser (3-gram tokens) to capture partial matches despite spelling or formatting variations. Each entity in the smaller dataset (ICIJ dataset) was then used to probe against the OpenCorporates index. The process included:

- **Blocking Parameters:** We performed blocking on the name and address fields from both datasets.
- **Document Representation:** We concatenated attribute values into a single text string for each entity, creating a "bag of n-grams" without field boundaries.
- **Query Construction:** For each ICIJ entity, we similarly created a query string as a disjunction of terms.
- **Candidate Ranking:** We used BM25 [22] scoring to rank matches, retrieving the top-5 candidates for each query.

LLM-based Matching. The second stage used GPT-4o mini [21] to assess candidate pairs' semantic similarity. We used OpenAI's Batch API[2] with zero temperature and fixed seed for deterministic outputs. Each pair was evaluated using the prompt in Listing 1.3, classifying them as matches (`Yes`), non-matches (`No`), or uncertain (`Maybe`).

Listing 1.3. Zero-shot prompt for entity matching with GPT-4o-mini

```
Compare the following two entity descriptions and determine if they refer
    to the same real-world entity.
  Entity 1: '{entity_1}'
  Entity 2: '{entity_2}'
Decide as follows:
  ''Yes'' if you are almost certain they refer to the same entity.
  ''Maybe'' if there is uncertainty.
  ''No'' if you are certain they refer to different entities.
Respond with only one token: ''Yes'', ''Maybe'', or ''No'', with no
    additional text.
```

This approach offers unique advantages: It can identify semantically equivalent matches despite syntactic differences (e.g., "J. Smith" vs. "Jonathan Smith, Esq.") and requires no manually crafted rules or labeled training data. Initial analysis of `Yes`-labeled pairs showed promising accuracy. The approach is economically feasible, with an estimated cost of approximately $57 for processing 3 million candidate pairs, and is highly scalable.

[2] https://platform.openai.com/docs/api-reference/batch.

4.3 In-House Dataset

Our methodology incorporated a third source of candidate pairs from an existing repository of potential matches between data sources. This repository contained previously identified potential entity matches, contributing significantly to our candidate generation process. The inclusion of this established collection provided complementary candidate pairs that might be missed by algorithmic approaches, particularly those involving complex variations in personal identifiers that often require domain expertise to recognize.

4.4 Complementary Value of Multiple Techniques

Each approach brings distinct strengths to our dataset creation methodology. *Rule-based matching* excels at identifying exact or near-exact matches with consistent formatting. *IR & LLM matching* identifies semantically equivalent entities despite syntactic differences, operating effectively in a zero-shot setting. The *in-house dataset* provides additional matching candidates that complement the algorithmic approaches.

Our analysis in Sect. 5 confirms that these approaches identify largely non-overlapping sets of matches, validating our multi-technique methodology as essential for creating comprehensive gold standard datasets. By combining these complementary approaches and subjecting their outputs to expert validation, we create a gold standard that captures a broader spectrum of matching patterns than would be possible with any single technique.

5 Dataset Evaluation

This section evaluates our dataset creation methodology, focusing on how effectively our multi-technique approach produces a comprehensive gold standard. Rather than competitively comparing techniques, we analyse how different approaches contribute complementary matches to the dataset, addressing our second research question (RQ2). In addition, the gold standard dataset helped us accurately identify the strength of the entity matching techniques, thus answering our RQ1.

5.1 Experimental Setup

All experiments were conducted within a controlled software environment on a Windows 10 operating system, using Python 3.10 with Pandas 2.1.4, RecordLinkage 0.16, and Lucene 9.6.

5.2 Contribution Analysis of Multiple Techniques

The core hypothesis of our methodology is that different techniques identify largely non-overlapping sets of matches. To evaluate this hypothesis, we analysed the overlap in matches identified by our three approaches: rule-based

RecordLinkage (RL), the in-house dataset (IH), and Lucene with LLM matching (LL). Table 1 presents the distribution of matches identified by each technique individually and in combination, while Fig. 3 shows the confusion matrix for these distributions. The true positive (TP) is the number of actual `Yes` cases detected by the EM techniques; the false positive (FP) is the number of records these techniques detected as `Yes` but they are actually `No` or `Maybe` cases, while the false negative (FN) is the records that a technique did not detect but the other techniques detected.

Only 87 matches (17.4% of the total) were identified by all three approaches, demonstrating that no single technique could have created a comprehensive gold

Table 1. Distribution of matches identified as `Yes` cases by each entity matching technique individually and in combination.

RL only	IH only	LL only	RL&IH	RL&LL	LL&IH	RL&IH&LL
20	110	110	32	31	110	87

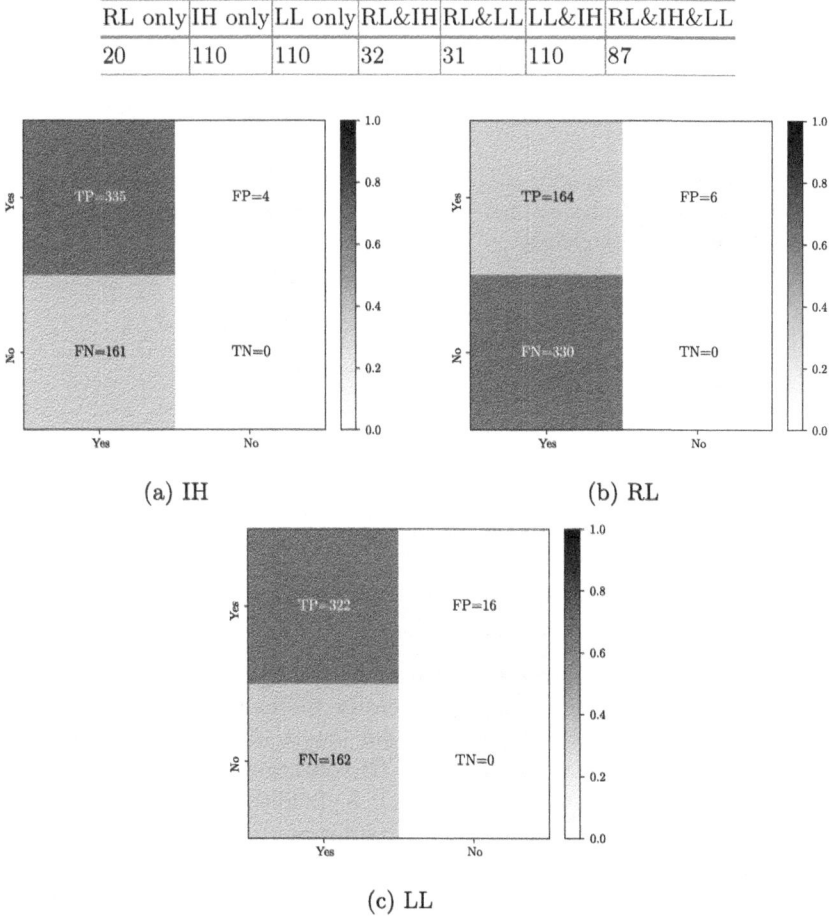

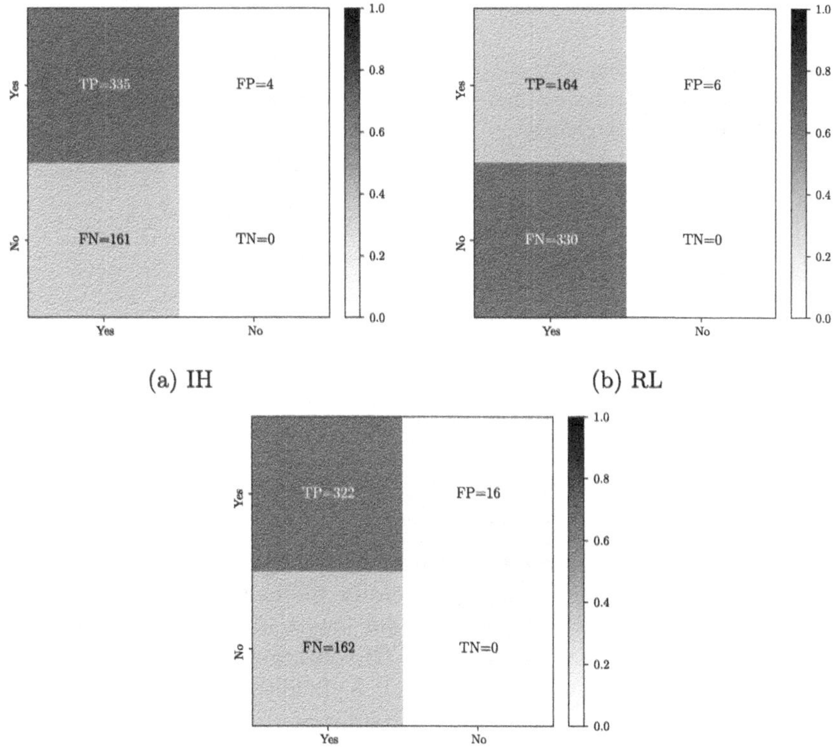

(a) IH

(b) RL

(c) LL

Fig. 3. Confusion matrix for entity matching techniques result.

standard on its own. Each approach contributed unique matches: RL exclusively identified 20 matches (4%), IH contributed 110 matches (22%), and LL found 110 matches (22%). The significant overlap between IH and LL (110 matches) indicates that zero-shot LLM matching can identify many of the same patterns as domain-specific sources. However, both approaches missed matches captured by rule-based methods, confirming that different techniques have complementary strengths.

5.3 Performance Characteristics of Dataset Creation Components

To understand the quality of contribution of each approach, we evaluated their performance against the expert-validated gold standard. Table 2 presents the precision and recall metrics for each technique. All three approaches maintained high precision (>95%), but differed significantly in recall: RL achieved 33.20% recall, while IH reached 67.54% and LL 66.53% respectively. Even the best-performing technique missed approximately one-third of true matches, validating our methodology's focus on combining multiple high-precision approaches to maximise recall.

Table 2. Contribution characteristics of different techniques to gold standard creation. Each approach demonstrates distinct precision-recall trade-offs, highlighting the value of a multi-technique methodology.

	RL	IH	LL
Precision	96.47%	98.82%	95.27%
Recall	33.20%	67.54%	66.53%

6 Discussion

This section synthesizes key insights from our experimental results and discusses our findings, implications, and limitations.

Performance and Complementarity of Matching Techniques: Our evaluation reveals distinct strengths across entity matching techniques. The RL method achieves high precision (96.47%) but low recall (33.20%), reflecting its emphasis on accuracy over coverage. The IH collection delivers both high precision (98.82%) and better recall (67.54%), highlighting the value of domain-specific expertise. Notably, the LL model performs competitively with 95.27% precision and 66.53% recall, despite not requiring domain tuning. Importantly, only 17.4% of the matches was identified by all three methods, validating our core claim: no single approach captures all valid matches. This confirms the necessity of a multi-technique methodology to construct comprehensive and realistic gold standard datasets.

Our evaluation reveals distinct strengths across entity matching techniques. The RL method achieves high precision (96.47%) but low recall (33.20%), reflecting its emphasis on accuracy over coverage. The IH approach delivers both high precision (98.82%) and better recall (67.54%). Notably, the LL model performs competitively with 95.27% precision and 66.53% recall, despite not requiring domain tuning. Importantly, only 17.4% of the matches was identified by all three methods, validating our core claim: no single approach captures all valid matches. This confirms the necessity of a multi-technique methodology to construct comprehensive gold standard datasets.

Impact of Blocking Parameters: Our findings suggest that blocking parameters may significantly impact matching outcomes. Using Lucene blocking with a top-k candidate (e.g., $k = 5$) enhances efficiency but imposes a recall ceiling, regardless of how advanced the matching algorithm is. Although increasing k could improve recall, it also increases computational costs in the matching phase. This underscores a central challenge in entity matching: balancing efficiency with the risk of missing true matches. In human trafficking investigations, where missing a match has serious consequences, this trade-off is especially critical. Future implementations might benefit from adaptive top-k selection based on similarity score distributions, as suggested in the Sparkly system and other recent approaches.

Effectiveness of LLM-based Matching: Our results demonstrate that LLMs can effectively serve as matching components in entity resolution pipelines, even without domain-specific fine-tuning. The LL approach achieves competitive precision and recall compared to other methods, despite operating in a zero-shot setting. This suggests that LLMs capture generalisable matching criteria that transfer well across domains. The relatively high precision achieved by the LLM approach (95.27%) indicates that foundation models effectively leverage pretrained knowledge about names, addresses, and entity relationships to make accurate matching decisions. LLMs can be valuable tools for preliminary annotation in dataset creation, reducing the manual effort required from domain experts.

Dataset Contributions and Limitations: The gold standard dataset developed through our methodology fills a critical gap in entity matching research by incorporating realistic personal identifying information. Using real-world open data sources (ICIJ and OpenCorporates), we applied multiple matching techniques with expert validation to create a dataset that reflects the complexity found in real-world scenarios. This demonstrates a practical and reproducible approach for building high-quality evaluation datasets. However, the dataset has limitations: it includes only 500 records, which is relatively small, and it reflects specific geographical and linguistic contexts.

Implications for Real-world Applications: Our findings have several methodological implications. First, the complementary nature of different matching approaches underscores the importance of employing multiple techniques when creating gold standard datasets to ensure comprehensive coverage. Second, our methodology provides a template for developing domain-specific gold standards that can be adapted to other investigative contexts. Third, the competitive performance of LLM matching demonstrates the potential of foundation models to accelerate dataset creation with minimal domain-specific tuning.

7 Conclusion and Future Work

Entity matching is a cornerstone of data integration, especially in high-stakes domains such as human trafficking investigations, where the accurate linkage of personally identifying information is critical. Despite the progress in algorithmic development, a significant bottleneck in advancing entity matching research lies in the scarcity of realistic gold standard datasets that involve personal data and reflect true-world complexity.

This paper addresses this gap by proposing and validating a reproducible methodology for constructing gold standard datasets that contain personal identifying information. By integrating multiple entity matching techniques, we effectively broadened the discovery of matching candidate pairs and demonstrated that these techniques often surface complementary, non-overlapping matches. This insight underscores the limitations of relying on a single matching approach and supports the use of ensemble methods in dataset curation.

Our contributions include: (1) the creation of a gold standard dataset creation that incorporates realistic personal identifying information (Sect. 3), (2) the application of multiple complementary entity matching techniques to ensure comprehensive coverage of potential matches (Sect. 4), and (3) empirical validation showing the added value of combining diverse strategies in capturing comprehensive match sets (Sect. 5).

Our results demonstrate that LLMs are promising tools for entity matching. Even in zero-shot settings, the LL model performed on par with domain-specific approaches – achieving 95.27% precision – by leveraging generalizable pre-trained knowledge of names, addresses, and relationships. LLMs can serve as effective annotation aids, helping reduce the burden on human experts during dataset creation while maintaining high quality.

In future work, we plan to apply this methodology to larger datasets, incorporating additional entity matching techniques to further improve coverage and representativeness. We also intend to explore how blocking parameters might affect overall recall in different contexts, which could help optimize the balance between computational efficiency and match discovery. The methodology could be extended to create gold standard datasets in other domains. Finally, we plan to leverage the constructed dataset to support the development of anti-human trafficking initiatives.

The created dataset is made available to the research community at the GitHub repository https://github.com/rendel/pii_match. If you use this dataset in your research or publication, please cite this paper/repository and acknowledge the original data sources.

Acknowledgement. This publication has emanated from research supported in part by the European Digital Innovation Hub Data2Sustain, co-funded by Ireland's National Recovery and Resilience Plan (the EU's Recovery and Resilience Facility), the Digital Europe Programme, and the Government of Ireland.

Disclosure of Interests. The authors have no competing interests to declare.

References

1. Barlaug, N., Gulla, J.A.: Neural networks for entity matching: a survey. ACM Trans. Knowl. Discov. Data **15**(3) (2021)
2. Christen, P.: Data Matching: Concepts and Techniques for Record Linkage, Entity Resolution, and Duplicate Detection. Springer, Berlin, Heidelberg (2012). https://doi.org/10.1007/978-3-642-31164-2
3. Das, S., et al.: The Magellan data repository. https://sites.google.com/site/anhaidgroup/projects/data
4. De Bruin, J.: Python record linkage toolkit: a toolkit for record linkage and duplicate detection in Python (2019)
5. Devezas, J., Nunes, S.: A review of graph-based models for entity-oriented search. SN Comput. Sci. **2**(6) (2021)
6. Gaur, B., Saluja, G.S., Sivakumar, H.B., Singh, S.: Semi-supervised deep learning based named entity recognition model to parse education section of resumes. Neural Comput. Appl. **33**(11) (2021)
7. Getoor, L., Machanavajjhala, A.: Entity resolution: theory, practice & open challenges. Proc. VLDB Endow. **5**(12) (2012)
8. González-Gallardo, C.E., Tran, H.T.H., Hamdi, A., Doucet, A.: Leveraging open large language models for historical named entity recognition. In: Linking Theory and Practice of Digital Libraries (2024)
9. Gu, L., Baxter, R.: Decision models for record linkage. In: Williams, G.J., Simoff, S.J. (eds.) Data Mining, pp. 146–160. Springer, Berlin, Heidelberg (2006). https://doi.org/10.1007/11677437_12
10. Gupta, A.: Detection of spam and fraudulent calls using natural language processing model. In: 2024 Sixth International Conference on Computational Intelligence and Communication Technologies (CCICT) (2024)
11. International Consortium Investigative Journalists: ICIJ offshore leaks database (2021). https://offshoreleaks.icij.org/
12. Li, Y., Nair, P., Pelrine, K., Rabbany, R.: Extracting person names from user generated text: named-entity recognition for combating human trafficking. In: Findings of the Association for Computational Linguistics: ACL 2022 (2022)
13. Li, Y., Li, J., Suhara, Y., Doan, A., Tan, W.C.: Deep entity matching with pre-trained language models. Proc. VLDB Endow. **14**(1) (2020)
14. McCallum, A., Nigam, K., Ungar, L.H.: Efficient clustering of high-dimensional data sets with application to reference matching. In: Proceedings of the Sixth ACM SIGKDD International Conference on Knowledge Discovery and Data Mining (2000)
15. Moore, S., Nguyen, H.A., Chen, T., Stamper, J.: Assessing the quality of multiple-choice questions using GPT-4 and rule-based methods. In: Responsive and Sustainable Educational Futures (2023)

16. Mudgal, S., et al.: Deep learning for entity matching: a design space exploration. In: Proceedings of the 2018 International Conference on Management of Data (2018)
17. Nanayakkara, C., Christen, P., Christen, V.: Unsupervised evaluation of entity resolution. ACM J. Data Inf. Qual. **17**(1), 1–31 (2025)
18. Papadakis, G., Skoutas, D., Thanos, E., Palpanas, T.: Blocking and filtering techniques for entity resolution: a survey (2020)
19. Paulsen, D., Govind, Y., Doan, A.: Sparkly: a simple yet surprisingly strong tf/idf blocker for entity matching. Proc. VLDB Endow. **16**(6) (2023)
20. Primpeli, A., Peeters, R., Bizer, C.: The WDC training dataset and gold standard for large-scale product matching. In: Companion Proceedings of The 2019 World Wide Web Conference (2019)
21. Radford, A., Narasimhan, K.: Improving language understanding by generative pre-training. In: Computer Science, Linguistics (2018)
22. Robertson, S., Zaragoza, H.: The probabilistic relevance framework: BM25 and beyond. Found. Trends Inf. Retr. **3**(4) (2009)
23. Ruz, G.A., Henríquez, P.A., Mascareño, A.: Bayesian Constitutionalization: Twitter sentiment analysis of the Chilean constitutional process through Bayesian network classifiers. Mathematics **10**(2) (2022)
24. Shishehgarkhaneh, M.B., Moehler, R.C., Fang, Y., Hijazi, A.A., Aboutorab, H.: Transformer-based named entity recognition in construction supply chain risk management in Australia. IEEE Access **12** (2024)
25. Tkachenko, M., Malyuk, M., Holmanyuk, A., Liubimov, N.: Label Studio: data labeling software (2020–2025). https://github.com/HumanSignal/label-studio, open source software available from https://github.com/HumanSignal/label-studio
26. United Nations: Protocol to prevent, suppress and punish trafficking in persons especially women and children, supplementing the united nations convention against transnational organized crime. https://www.ohchr.org/en/instruments-mechanisms/instruments/protocol-prevent-suppress-and-punish-trafficking-persons (2000). Accessed 17 Apr 2025
27. Wu, R., Chaba, S., Sawlani, S., Chu, X., Thirumuruganathan, S.: ZeroER: entity resolution using zero labeled examples. In: Proceedings of the 2020 ACM SIGMOD International Conference on Management of Data (2020)
28. Zhang, Z., Groth, P., Calixto, I., Schelter, S.: A deep dive into cross-dataset entity matching with large and small language models. In: Proceedings of the 28th International Conference on Extending Database Technology (2025)

Quantum-Safe Hybrid Cryptographic Framework for Multimedia Application

Amna Shifa(✉)

School of Computer Science, University of Galway, Galway H91 TK33, Ireland
amna.shifa@universityofgalway.com

Abstract. With the rapid expansion of digital communication and multimedia applications, a vast amount of visual data is continuously generated and transmitted through interconnected networks of cameras, sensors, processing nodes, and satellites. This data, often sensitive and long-archived, is increasingly vulnerable to future quantum-enabled adversaries. Classical cryptographic protocols, currently used to protect this multimedia data, are susceptible to "Harvest Now, Decrypt Later" (HNDL) attacks, particularly as quantum computing matures. These threats are further amplified by side-channel attacks, which can compromise even post-quantum cryptographic (PQC) implementations if not adequately secured. This paper discusses quantum threats and proposes a quantum-resilient framework designed to secure visual data, incorporating both classical and PQC algorithms. The proposed Hybrid Key Encapsulation Mechanism (KEM) combines elliptic curve cryptography (ECC) and lattice-based Kyber-768. By offloading cryptographic operations to edge servers and utilising secure key lifecycle management, the framework addresses challenges in performance, scalability, and compatibility, enhancing its suitability for protecting visual data against emerging quantum threats.

Keywords: Hybrid cryptography · Key Encapsulation · Multimedia security · Quantum cryptography

1 Introduction

The rapid expansion of visual media and communication systems across strategic urban and institutional landscapes has become indispensable to critical sectors, including healthcare, law enforcement, smart infrastructure, traffic management, crime prevention, and public safety, by enabling real-time insights and data-driven decision-making [10,49]. However, these systems capture, process, and store highly sensitive personal and contextual information. To safeguard this data, conventional cryptographic schemes such as Rivest–Shamir–Adleman (RSA) [45], Elliptic Curve Cryptography (ECC) [32], and Advanced Encryption Standard (AES) [21], along with communication protocols like Transport

The original version of the chapter has been revised. A correction to this chapter can be found at https://doi.org/10.1007/978-3-032-00639-4_20

B. Coppens et al. (Eds.): ARES 2025 Workshops, LNCS 15997, pp. 219–236, 2025.
https://doi.org/10.1007/978-3-032-00639-4_13

Layer Security (TLS) and Secure Sockets Layer (SSL), are widely employed. These algorithms rely on the computational hardness of problems like integer factorisation and discrete logarithms, which are infeasible to solve with classical computers. However, these computational problems can be broken by algorithmic advances or increased computing power, such as quantum computers [48].

The rise of quantum computing presents a significant threat to these cryptographic schemes [34], which can solve these mathematical problems exponentially faster than classical machines. For example, Shor's algorithm can factor an integer N in $O((\log N)^3)$ time and $O(\log N)$ space [50], enabling it to solve the discrete logarithm and integer factorisation problems efficiently. This capability would effectively break public-key schemes such as RSA and ECC. While Grover's algorithm [17] can accelerate brute-force attacks against symmetric algorithms like AES, necessitating longer key lengths. The HNDL threat [41] underscores the necessity for proactive measures to safeguard data with long-term confidentiality requirements. The HNDL is particularly concerning for visual data (images or videos), which may retain sensitivity long after its initial collection. These risks are further amplified by side-channel attacks, which exploit implementation-level vulnerabilities, rather than the mathematical foundations of cryptographic algorithms.

To address these emerging challenges, researchers and standards bodies are actively developing cryptographic algorithms capable of withstanding both classical and quantum attacks [2,19,54]. One promising technique is Quantum Key Distribution (QKD), which leverages principles of quantum mechanics to enable theoretically unbreakable key exchange [4]. Despite the development of numerous QKD techniques for securing data [29], QKD faces significant practical limitations, including the need for specialised quantum hardware, limited transmission ranges, and challenges in integrating with existing classical infrastructure [52]. As a result, greater emphasis has been placed on developing Post-Quantum Cryptographic (PQC) [5] algorithms and hybrid quantum-safe systems [18] that are more practical for broad deployment. Unlike traditional public-key cryptography, PQC is based on mathematical problems believed to remain hard even for quantum computers, such as lattice-based, code-based, multivariate polynomial, and hash-based constructions. The U.S. National Institute of Standards and Technology (NIST) has been leading the global standardisation effort, recently announcing a set of finalist algorithms for public-key encryption and digital signatures [40].

Building on these insights, this work proposes a hybrid KEM that combines elliptic-curve (NIST P-256) [26] with a quantum-safe lattice-based algorithm (CRYSTALS-Kyber-768) [42]. This dual-layer approach generates a stronger, shared session key by merging classical and post-quantum secrets through a standardised key derivation process. The proposed hybrid approach ensures that encrypted video streams remain secure even if they are intercepted today and targeted by quantum attacks in the future.

The remainder of this work is organised as follows. Section 2 examines the quantum threats posed to classical cryptographic and quantum-enabled systems. Section 3 reviews related work on emerging approaches for securing visual data in the quantum era. Section 4 presents the proposed Hybrid technique to strengthen visual data security. Section 5 discusses the evaluation and limitations of the proposed method, while Sect. 6 provides concluding remarks.

2 Quantum Threat Landscape for Visual Data

As quantum computing matures, it poses profound risks to visual data's confidentiality, integrity, and authenticity. This section explores the vulnerabilities that arise from quantum threats, both in current systems secured by classical cryptography and in future systems that integrate quantum technologies.

2.1 Threats to Existing/Classical Systems

With the advent of quantum computing, these classical protections are becoming increasingly vulnerable in the following ways:

Decryption of Stored and Transmitted Data: One of the most immediate concerns is that Shor's algorithm can efficiently solve the integer factorisation and discrete logarithm problems that underpin RSA and ECC [50]. This threatens the confidentiality of archived images, video streams, and telemetry data, particularly under the HNDL attack [41], where attackers store encrypted data today to decrypt it later using quantum capabilities.

Forgery of Digital Signatures and Metadata: In addition to compromising confidentiality, quantum attacks threaten the authenticity and integrity of visual data. Digital signatures, commonly used to verify the legitimacy of files or metadata, also rely on RSA or ECC [25]. Once quantum algorithms break these schemes, adversaries could forge signatures to pass off tampered or synthetically generated content as genuine. This presents a serious concern in domains such as forensic investigation and telemedicine, where trust in visual content's source and unaltered nature is critical.

Symmetric Encryption Weakening: Symmetric encryption, while more resilient to quantum attacks [19], is not immune. Grover's algorithm reduces the effective strength of symmetric encryption, making it more susceptible to brute-force attacks, as shown in Table 1.NIST estimates a 50% chance that RSA-2048 could be broken by a quantum computer by 2031 [9]. Systems relying on short AES keys for bulk visual data encryption are particularly at risk.

Compromise of Secure Communication Channels: The video data and encryption keys travel over the internet via HTTPS (HTTP over TLS). To ensure secure and reliable delivery, protocols such as TLS, which protect interactions between devices, servers, and users, rely on asymmetric key exchange [19]. The

Table 1. Impact of Quantum Algorithms on Common Cryptographic Primitives

Cipher Type	Algorithm	Key Size (bits)	Classical Time	Quantum Time	Quantum-Safe
Bulk Encryption	AES-128	128	2^{128}	2^{64} (Grover)	No
Bulk Encryption	AES-256	256	2^{256}	2^{128} (Grover)	Yes
Hashing	SHA-256 (preimage)	256	2^{256}	2^{128} (Grover)	Yes
Key Exchange	RSA-2048	2048	$\sim 2^{112}$	Polynomial (Shor)	No
Key Exchange	DH-2048	2048	$\sim 2^{112}$	Polynomial (Shor)	No
Digital Signature	ECDSA (P-256)	256	$\sim 2^{128}$	Polynomial (Shor)	No

current standards, TLS 1.3 and SSH2, use Elliptic-Curve Diffie-Hellman (ECDH) to establish session keys and apply RSA or elliptic-curve digital signatures for authentication [51]. If these cryptographic primitives are compromised, attackers could eavesdrop, perform man-in-the-middle (MITM) attacks, or hijack sessions, gaining unauthorised access to sensitive visual data [3].

2.2 Threats to Quantum-Enhanced Visual Systems:

As quantum technologies begin to integrate into visual data applications [43,53, 57], communication [24], or analytics [2], a new and evolving set of vulnerabilities emerges. These threats affect not only the confidentiality and integrity of visual data but also the operational stability and regulatory compliance of the systems that manage them.

Vulnerabilities in Quantum Key Distribution (QKD): QKD is widely regarded as a future-proof solution for secure key exchange, as it relies on transmitting quantum states that cannot be copied or measured without detection. This security is rooted in the quantum no-cloning theorem [55], which prevents an eavesdropper from replicating or storing a transcript of the exchanged quantum signals, even for future decryption, unlike classical key distribution methods [12,46]. However, real-world implementations of QKD are not without flaws [11]. Side-channel attacks targeting hardware vulnerabilities, such as detector blinding [38] or photon-number splitting [28], have been demonstrated in practice. Moreover, denial-of-service attacks can disrupt QKD systems through interference with fragile quantum channels [27]. Furthermore, QKD still relies on classical infrastructure for authentication and post-processing, reintroducing traditional vulnerabilities [4].

Exploitation of Quantum Sensors: Quantum imaging systems such as Quantum Light Detection and Ranging (LiDAR) [6], Quantum Ghost Imaging (QGI) [35], and Quantum Image Representation [26] offer advanced capabilities like enhanced resolution and quantum-parallel processing. However, they are highly sensitive to environmental noise and decoherence, which degrades system performance. Spoofing attacks, where adversaries inject fake quantum signals to manipulate outputs, have also been theorised [7]. Countermeasures such as entangled photon correlation [20] and hybrid QGI–QKD methods [56] are emerging but remain experimental.

Adversarial Quantum Machine Learning (QML): QML [23], increasingly applied to real-time multimedia applications such as image analysis [54] and anomaly detection [53], inherits many vulnerabilities of classical ML. These include adversarial quantum inputs, where subtle changes mislead classifiers, and training data poisoning, in which malicious inputs during the learning phase manipulate model behavior. As QML is also being explored for defensive purposes, such as secure hardware monitoring, it is essential to develop adversarially robust QML architectures for security-critical applications.

Systemic Complexity and Integration Risks: Quantum-based cryptography solutions are inherently complex, and integrating them with classical systems introduces challenges related to interoperability, synchronisation, configuration, and maintenance [13]. These factors increase the attack surface, especially at the classical–quantum interfaces. In hybrid cryptographic systems, overall security often hinges on the weakest link, be it insecure key storage, flawed authentication, or classical side-channel attack surfaces. Furthermore, implementing PQC algorithms also brings new engineering challenges. They must be protected against fault injection attacks and hardware leakage. Table 2 presents the overview of quantum threats, the systems they impact, and their severity levels.

Table 2. Overview of Quantum Threats to Security Systems

Threat Category	Affected Systems	Severity
Classical Cryptography Breaks	TLS, PKI, symmetric encryption	High
HNDL Attacks	Archives, surveillance footage	High
Digital Signature Forgery	Forensics, legal evidence, medical records	High
Compromised Secure Channels	Device-to-server communications	High
QKD Side-Channel Attacks	QKD devices, QKD-based TLS	Medium–High
Quantum Sensor Spoofing	Quantum LiDAR, QIR, ghost imaging	Medium–High
QML Adversarial Attacks	QML-based visual analytics, anomaly detection	Medium
Integration & Complexity Risks	All hybrid classical–quantum infrastructures	Medium–High

3 Background and Related Work

The emergence of quantum computing has fundamentally challenged the underlying classical cryptography, leading to the pursuit of quantum-resistant cryptographic methods. Quantum cryptography (QC) has emerged as a discipline that harnesses core quantum mechanical principles, such as superposition, entanglement, interference, and the no-cloning theorem, to enable novel security mechanisms [4]. Unlike classical bits, which exist in state 0 or 1, quantum bits (qubits) can reside in a superposition of both $|0\rangle$ and $|1\rangle$. This property, illustrated in Fig. 1, enables quantum systems to evaluate many computational paths simultaneously. This parallelism threatens the hardness assumptions behind classical public-key cryptography, including problems like integer factorisation and discrete logarithms.

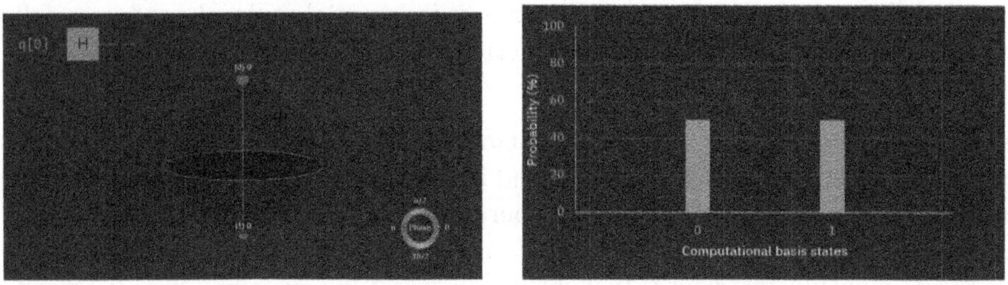

(a) (b)

Fig. 1. Visualisation of a superposition state where (a) represents the qubit transitions to a superposition state after applying a Hadamard gate. (b) Measurement probabilities for $|0\rangle$ and $|1\rangle$ state.

To address the threats mentioned above, several QC approaches are being actively explored. One of the most prominent is QKD, which enables two parties to establish a shared secret key with information-theoretic security guaranteed by the laws of quantum mechanics. QKD systems rely on true quantum randomness, making them immune to brute-force, replay, and cloning attacks. A high-level representation of the QKD architecture is shown in Fig. 2. Protocols such as BB84 ensure that any eavesdropping attempt introduces detectable disturbances, rendering QKD inherently tamper-evident [33]. In [47], the authors encrypted medical images using the BB84 QKD protocol. In another study, [36] proposed a hybrid image encryption method that combines BB84 QKD with a chaos-based logistic map to generate secure encryption keys. Despite its strong theoretical guarantees, the practical deployment of QKD remains limited due to requirements for specialised quantum hardware, short transmission ranges, and reliance on classical infrastructure for authentication and reconciliation. These constraints currently hinder QKD's scalability for Internet-scale or distributed visual data environments.

Beyond secure key distribution, QC is also being integrated into quantum-enhanced imaging. For example, [20] proposed a quantum-secured single-pixel imaging method that exploits mode correlations of entangled photon pairs to verify image integrity. This technique enables detection of spoofing attempts, localisation of the affected image region, and identification of the attack type. In

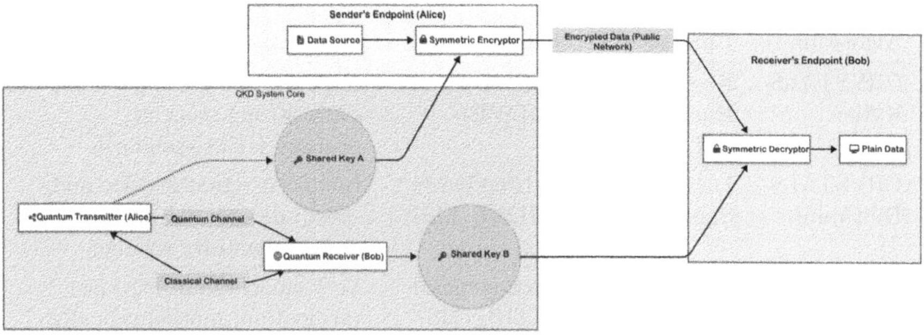

Fig. 2. High-level Architecture of QKD.

a related study, [56] introduced a hybrid imaging approach that combines Quantum Ghost Imaging (QGI) with the BB84 QKD protocol, adding a cryptographic security layer to improve resilience against intercept-resend attacks.

Another promising approach is PQC [37,39]. Unlike QKD, PQC algorithms run on conventional hardware, making them readily deployable in existing systems. PQC encompasses several algorithm families based on mathematically hard problems believed to be resistant even to quantum attacks. These include lattice-based schemes (e.g., Learning With Errors and Module-LWE), hash-based signatures like SPHINCS+, code-based systems such as Classic McEliece (noted for fast decryption but large keys), and multivariate polynomial cryptography, which has seen diminished adoption due to cryptanalytic advances against schemes like Rainbow. The U.S. National Institute of Standards and Technology (NIST) has finalised a set of PQC algorithms [1] for standardisation, focusing on those suitable for key encapsulation and digital signatures, as summarised in Table 3.

In [37], a 3D Quantum Baker map is used to scramble quantum images encoded via the Novel Enhanced Quantum Representation (NEQR), followed by generalised Gray code and XOR-based diffusion using a fractional-order Chen's chaotic system. Another work [39] applies the Ring Learning With Errors (ring-LWE) algorithm to encrypt face images extracted using a Multi-Task Cascaded Convolutional Neural Network (MTCNN), ensuring secure remote storage. While PQC offers strong potential for future digital security, a complete and immediate replacement of the existing classical Public Key Infrastructure (PKI) is not feasible due to substantial practical challenges. Hybrid cryptographic schemes have emerged as a vital strategy to address compatibility, trust migration, and transitional security.

These schemes typically combine established classical cryptographic primitives with new post-quantum ones, aiming to harness the complementary strengths of both technologies to achieve enhanced resilience and performance during the migration to quantum-safe systems [31]. In [22], the authors proposed

Table 3. Overview of NIST Selected PQC Algorithms

Algorithm	Purpose	Family	Key Features
CRYSTALS-Kyber	Key Encapsulation (KEM)	Lattice-based (MLWE)	High efficiency, compact key sizes, strong security; primary KEM standard.
CRYSTALS-Dilithium	Digital Signatures	Lattice-based (MLWE/MSIS)	Balanced signature size and speed; designated primary digital signature scheme.
Falcon	Digital Signatures	Lattice-based (NTRU/SIS)	Very small signatures, fast verification; mathematically complex; alternate option.
SPHINCS$^+$	Digital Signatures	Hash-based	Stateless, highly secure, large signatures; conservative fallback.

a framework for achieving triple-security by integrating classical cryptography, PQC, and QKD within network protocols such as IPsec and TLS.

A prime example of this approach is the Hybrid Key Encapsulation Mechanism (Hybrid KEM) [16]. Such a mechanism typically integrates a classical KEM, often based on ECC or Diffie-Hellman (DH) principles, alongside a PQC KEM. Fundamentally, KEMs are cryptographic constructions designed to enable two parties to establish a shared secret over an insecure channel securely. A KEM is generally defined by three core algorithms: KeyGen (for key pair generation), Encaps (for shared secret encapsulation by the sender), and Decaps (for shared secret decapsulation by the receiver). NIST's ongoing PQC standardisation process has prioritised KEMs as the preferred method for post-quantum key exchange [40]. Notably, ML-KEM (Module-Lattice Key Encapsulation Mechanism), a variant of the Kyber submission, has been formalised as the first such standard in FIPS 203. The KEMs, whether classical or post-quantum, can function as standalone mechanisms for key establishment or serve as integral components within broader cryptographic frameworks like Hybrid Public-Key Encryption (HPKE, specified in RFC 9180). HPKE, for instance, combines a KEM's key establishment capability with symmetric encryption (specifically an Authenticated Encryption with Associated Data - AEAD scheme) to provide secure message transport.

HPKE provides a modular design that supports forward secrecy and post-quantum resilience. It is increasingly being integrated into protocols like TLS and VPNs, and its applicability to visual data security is particularly promising in bandwidth-constrained or latency-sensitive systems. [37,44] demonstrate how hybrid KEMs can offer both backward compatibility and future resilience, particularly in domains like transport systems and enterprise databases. In [30], the author proposed a hybrid post-quantum authentication protocol for constrained e-health IoT systems. Their design leverages ECC and Kyber but is optimised primarily for lightweight devices, with little attention to high-throughput media encryption or cryptographic key derivation rigor. These works emphasise real-world constraints, including latency and system compatibility. While these hybrid KEM solutions are promising, there is still limited attention given to domain-specific adaptations for high-bandwidth and latency-sensitive applications such as surveillance, medical imaging, and intelligent transportation, where visual data security is paramount. Table 4 presents a concise overview of key characteristics of these next-generation cryptographic algorithms, focusing on their type, security strength, and public key sizes, which are important factors in their practical implementation and performance.

Table 4. Comparison of selected post-quantum algorithms

Algorithm	Cryptographic Family	NIST Security Level	Public Key (Bytes)	Secret Key (Bytes)
CRYSTALS-Kyber-768	Lattice-based (MLWE)	3	1,184	2,400
CRYSTALS-Dilithium2	Lattice-based (MLWE/MSIS)	1	1,312	2,528
Falcon-512	Lattice-based (NTRU/SIS)	1	897	1,281
SPHINCS$^+$-128s-SHA256	Hash-based	1	32	64

4 Proposed Quantum-Safe Security Framework

The Fig. 3 illustrates a proposed high-level architecture for securing visual data (image/video) by employing a hybrid KEM approach for robust key establishment and subsequent symmetric encryption. This proposed approach is developed to protect data originating from resource-constrained multimedia devices by offloading intensive cryptographic operations to a more capable edge server. The process starts with a data source capturing an image or video clip. This raw visual data may undergo initial lightweight processing by an on-device processor optimised for limited computational resources (e.g., basic compression or formatting), resulting in a raw or compressed visual data stream.

This stream/image is then acquired by a gateway/edge server, a more computationally capable node. Within this server, a gateway processor orchestrates the subsequent cryptographic operations and segments it into visual data chunks suitable for encryption. The core of the security mechanism lies in the hybrid key establishment phase. The gateway processor initiates this by requesting the recipient's hybrid public key (Recipient HybridPK) via a KMS client at the gateway. This client module is presumed to interface with a broader key management system (KMS) responsible for securing key storage and distributing cryptographic keys, including the necessary hybrid public keys of intended recipients as illustrated in Fig. 4.

The retrieved Recipient HybridPK is then supplied to the Hybrid KEM Encapsulation (Sender Side) module. This module implements the sender-side operations of a hybrid key encapsulation scheme. As specified, it combines NIST

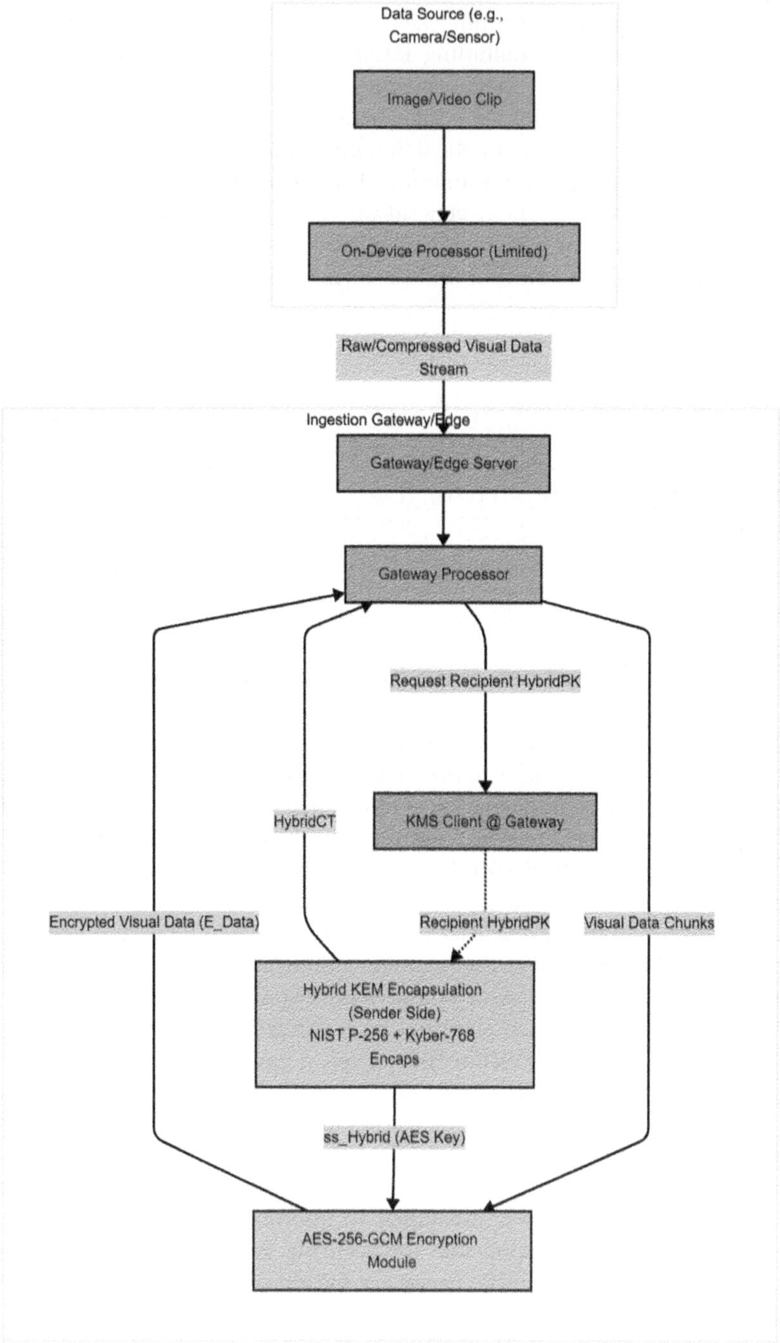

Fig. 3. Architecture of proposed Quantum-Safe Security framework that employs a hybrid KEM that combines classical (ECC) and post-quantum (Kyber) cryptography.

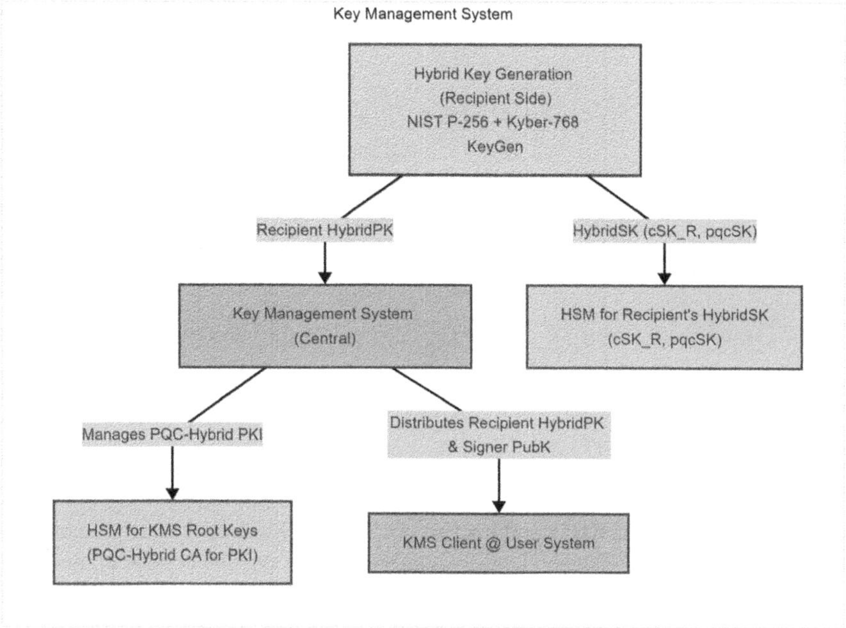

Fig. 4. Conceptual architecture of a Key Management System (KMS) designed for hybrid classical (NIST P-256) and post-quantum (Kyber-768) keys.

P-256 (an elliptic curve-based classical KEM component providing classical security assurances) with Kyber-768 (a lattice-based post-quantum KEM component, such as ML-KEM-768 from FIPS 203, providing quantum-resistant security). The encapsulation process operates on the recipient 's P-256 and Kyber-768 public keys.

4.1 Proposed Hybrid KEM

The proposed framework introduces an innovative Hybrid KEM designed explicitly to enhance secure transmission and storage of visual data. The detailed implementation is organised into three primary phases: Key Generation, Encapsulation, and Decapsulation, as illustrated in Fig. 5.

Phase 1: Key Generation (Recipient): Initially, the recipient system (e.g., a central storage server or a processing unit) generates a hybrid key pair comprising classical ECC and PQC. For the ECC component, the standard NIST P-256 is selected. The system creates cryptographically random 32-byte private key (cSK_R) and computes the corresponding public key (cPK_R) by multiplying the private key with the P-256 base point (G_{P256}). The resultant public key is serialised into a compressed format, typically occupying 33 bytes. Concurrently,

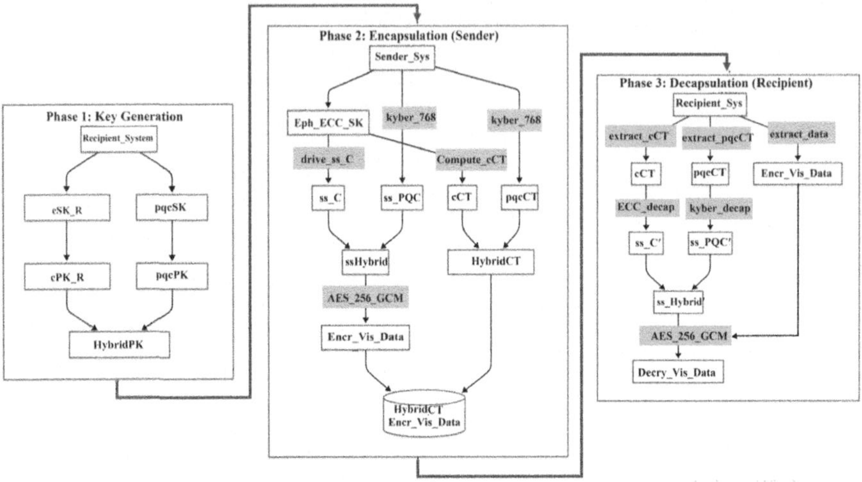

Fig. 5. Proposed hybrid KEM architecture for secure visual data transmission, which includes key generation (Phase 1), encapsulation and encryption (Phase 2), and decapsulation with decryption (Phase 3).

the recipient system generates a second key pair using the lattice-based Kyber-768 algorithm, recognised for its quantum resistance, producing a private key (pqcSK) of approximately 2,400 bytes and the corresponding public key (pqcPK) of approximately 1,184 bytes. After that, both public keys (cPK_R) and (pqcPK) are concatenated to form a unified *Hybrid Public Key* (HybridPK) of total length 1217 bytes. This hybrid public key is securely distributed to data senders via a public ey Infrastructure (PKI). Both private keys are stored securely within a Hardware Security Module (HSM).

Phase 2: Encapsulation (Sender): During encapsulation, the sender (e.g., a camera or gateway), upon obtaining *Hybrid Public Key*, first generates an ephemeral ECC private key, computes the corresponding ephemeral public key (cCT), and derives the classical shared secret (ss_C) using SHA-256 on the x-coordinate of the resulting elliptic curve shared point. The ephemeral private key is discarded after use. Next, the sender executes the Kyber-768 encapsulation process, producing a post-quantum shared secret (ss_PQC) and the corresponding ciphertext (pqcCT). Both ciphertexts, cCT (33 bytes) and pqcCT (1088 bytes), are concatenated to form the *Hybrid Ciphertext* (HybridCT), totaling 1121 bytes. To derive the final *Hybrid Shared Secret* (ssHybrid), the sender concatenates ss_C and ss_{PQC} into a 64-byte block, producing a robust 32-byte symmetric key. This key is used for AES-256 encryption of the visual data. The `ssHybrid` is then passed, along with the *Visual Data Chunks*, to an `AES-256-GCM` (Galois Counter Mode) encryption module. This module performs *authenticated symmetric encryption* using the AES algorithm with a 256-bit key in GCM. This ensures both the *confidentiality* and *integrity* of the visual data chunks. The output of this stage is referred to as the Encrypted Visual Data (`Encr_Vis_Data`). Finally, the Gateway Processor manages the onward transmission of the `Encr_Vis_Data` and the corresponding `HybridCT` to the intended recipient.

Phase 3: Decapsulation (Recipient): Upon receiving the encrypted visual data and the accompanying Hybrid Ciphertext, the recipient system performs decapsulation by extracting and deserialising both ECC and Kyber ciphertext components. ECC decapsulation is performed by computing the elliptic curve shared point and derives the classical shared secret (ss_C'). Similarly, Kyber-768 decapsulation compute the quantum-resistant shared secret (ss_PQC'). The recipient concatenates the two derived secrets (ss_C') and (ss_PQC') into a 64-byte combined block to regenerate the identical 32-byte hybrid secret key (ss'_{Hybrid}). Finally, this regenerated hybrid secret key decrypts the visual data using AES-256-GCM, recovering the original data, ensuring data integrity, and quantum-resistant protection.

5 Discussion and Limitations

This hybrid approach proactively addresses the critical threat posed by quantum computers, particularly HNDL attacks. The use of two cryptographic components provides a strong, conservative security posture: if one algorithm (such as Kyber) faces unforeseen vulnerabilities, the other (P-256) remains to maintain overall key confidentiality. The more intensive hybrid key encapsulation process is conducted less frequently, serving only to securely establish these symmetric keys. Many upcoming secure communication protocols (like future versions of TLS) are adopting similar hybrid strategies because the benefits of quantum resistance and transitional security outweigh these manageable trade-offs for many critical applications [15]. The bulk data encryption employs AES-256-GCM, a standardised and highly efficient symmetric cipher suitable for handling large data volumes. Furthermore, by offloading cryptographic computations from resource-constrained edge devices (like cameras) onto more capable gateways or servers, the architecture aligns well with practical IoT deployment patterns and edge computing environments. The system's design inherently supports forward secrecy due to the use of ephemeral ECC keys and the IND-CCA2 security properties of Kyber [14]. Any potential vulnerabilities in the data path before reaching the secure gateway could be addressed through additional complementary protection mechanisms if necessary.

However, integration of ECC and Kyber inherently involves certain trade-offs regarding performance overhead and dependencies on cryptographic primitives [8]. These factors do not undermine the viability of the proposed solution but rather indicate areas needing thoughtful implementation and resource planning. Concerns such as bandwidth usage, computational overhead, and key management complexity can be effectively mitigated through optimised key exchange frequencies, efficient hardware provisioning, robust KMS, and automation of key lifecycle management. Moreover, alignment with NIST-endorsed standards ensures compatibility, interoperability, and facilitates easier security audits [40]. In summary, the described hybrid cryptographic scheme is both viable and desirable. Its trade-offs represent standard engineering and operational considerations that are manageable with careful design, provisioning, and best practices in cryptographic security management.

6 Conclusion

This paper presents a hybrid quantum-safe framework to secure visual data for multimedia applications. The Hybrid KEM approach combines a proven elliptic-curve key exchange with a quantum-safe lattice algorithm to create a single, stronger session key for encrypting video streams. By merging classical and post-quantum shared secrets through a simple, standardised key-derivation step, it ensures that recorded footage remains confidential even if today's data is harvested and attacked by future quantum computers. At the same time, it falls back on the well-tested P-256 component if any flaw is later found in the quantum algorithm. This design delivers long-term protection for large-scale surveillance data while fitting smoothly into existing security infrastructures.

Acknowledgments. This research work is supported by a Marie Skłodowska-Curie Action (MSCA) fellowship funded by the European Union's Horizon 2020 research and innovation programme under grant agreement No 101109961.

Disclosure of Interests. The authors have no competing interests to declare that are relevant to the content of this article.

References

1. Alagic, G., et al.: Status report on the third round of the NIST post-quantum cryptography standardization process. NIST (2022). https://doi.org/10.6028/NIST.IR.8413
2. Amin, J., Anjum, M.A., Ibrar, K., Sharif, M., Kadry, S., Crespo, R.G.: Detection of anomaly in surveillance videos using quantum convolutional neural networks. Image Vision Comput. **135**, 104710 (2023). https://doi.org/10.1016/J.IMAVIS.2023.104710
3. Asghar, A., Shifa, A., Asghar, M.N.: Survey on video security: examining threats, challenges, and future trends. Comput. Mater. Continua **80**(3), 3591–3635 (2024). https://doi.org/10.32604/cmc.2024.054654, https://www.sciencedirect.com/science/article/pii/S1546221824006143
4. Bennett, C.H., Brassard, G.: Quantum cryptography: public key distribution and coin tossing. Theor. Comput. Sci. **560**, 7–11 (2014). https://doi.org/10.1016/J.TCS.2014.05.025
5. Bernstein, D.J., Lange, T.: Post-quantum cryptography. Nature **549**, 188–194 (2017). https://doi.org/10.1038/nature23461
6. Bi, S., et al.: Realization of quantum lidar imaging system. **11502**, 10–15 (2020). https://doi.org/10.1117/12.2568284

7. Blakely, J.N., Pethel, S.D., Stewart, K.R., Jacobs, K.: Revealing spoofing of quantum illumination using entanglement (2024). https://arxiv.org/pdf/2410.08353
8. Bos, J., et al.: Crystals - kyber: a CCA-secure module-lattice-based kem. In: 2018 IEEE European Symposium on Security and Privacy (EuroSP), pp. 353–367 (2018). https://doi.org/10.1109/EuroSP.2018.00032
9. Chen, L., et al.: Report on Post-quantum Cryptography, vol. 12. US Department of Commerce, National Institute of Standards and Technology (2016)
10. Chen, N., Chen, Y., Chen, N., Chen, Y.: Smart city surveillance at the network edge in the era of IoT: Opportunities and Challenges, pp. 153–176 (2018). https://doi.org/10.1007/978-3-319-76669-0_7
11. Diamanti, E., Lo, H.K., Qi, B., Yuan, Z.: Practical challenges in quantum key distribution. NPJ Quant. Inf. **2**, 1–12 (2016). https://doi.org/10.1038/npjqi.2016.25
12. Diffie, W., Hellman, M.E.: New Directions in Cryptography, pp. 365–390 (2022). https://doi.org/10.1145/3549993.3550007
13. Farooq, S., et al.: Analyzing post-quantum cryptographic algorithms efficiency for transport security layer. Comput. Electr. Eng. **125**, 110437 (2025). https://doi.org/10.1016/j.compeleceng.2025.110437
14. Garcia, D., Liu, H.: A study of post quantum cipher suites for key exchange. In: 2021 IEEE International Symposium on Technologies for Homeland Security (HST), pp. 1–7 (2021). https://doi.org/10.1109/HST53381.2021.9619839
15. García, C.R., Rommel, S., Takarabt, S., Olmos, J.J.V., Guilley, S., Nguyen, P., Monroy, I.T.: Quantum-resistant transport layer security. Comput. Commun. **213**, 345–358 (2024). https://doi.org/10.1016/J.COMCOM.2023.11.010
16. Giron, A.A., Custódio, R., Rodríguez-Henríquez, F.: Post-quantum hybrid key exchange: a systematic mapping study. J. Cryptogr. Eng. **13**, 71–88 (2023). https://doi.org/10.1007/s13389-022-00288-9
17. Grover, L.K.: From schrödinger's equation to the quantum search algorithm. Am. J. Phys. **69**, 769–777 (2001). https://doi.org/10.1119/1.1359518
18. Gulomov, S.R., Khudayberganov, T.R., Ravshanova, M.X., Turdiev, T.T., Atabayev, S.S.: Exploring post-quantum cryptographic algorithms for secure data transmission. IN: Proceedings of the IEEE 3rd International Conference on Problems of Informatics, Electronics and Radio Engineering, PIERE 2024, pp. 1480–1483 (2024). https://doi.org/10.1109/PIERE62470.2024.10805050
19. Hariprasad, Y., Iyengar, S.S., Chaudhary, N.K.: Securing the future: advanced encryption for quantum-safe video transmission. IEEE Trans. Consum. Electron. (2024). https://doi.org/10.1109/TCE.2024.3473542
20. Heo, J., Jeong, T., Park, N.H., Jo, Y.: True image construction in quantum-secured single-pixel imaging under spoofing attack. APL Photonics **9** (2024). https://doi.org/10.1063/5.0209041
21. Heron, S.: Advanced encryption standard (AES). Netw. Secur. **2009**(12), 8–12 (2009). https://doi.org/10.1016/S1353-4858(10)70006-4, https://www.sciencedirect.com/science/article/pii/S1353485810700064
22. Huang, L., Feng, K., Xie, C.: A practical hybrid quantum-safe cryptographic scheme between data centers. In: Emerging Imaging and Sensing Technologies for Security and Defence V; and Advanced Manufacturing Technologies for Micro-and Nanosystems in Security and Defence III, **11540**, 30–35 (2020). https://doi.org/10.1117/12.2573558
23. Islam, M.M., He, J.S.: Quantum machine learning for computer vision: a survey. In: Proceedings - 2024 International Conference on Machine Learning and Applica-

tions, ICMLA 2024, pp. 1827–1832 (2024). https://doi.org/10.1109/ICMLA61862.2024.00282
24. Jayasinghe, U., Samarathunga, P., Pollwaththage, N., Ganearachchi, Y., Fernando, T., Fernando, A.: Quantum communication for video transmission over error-prone channels. IEEE Trans. Consum. Electron. (2025). https://doi.org/10.1109/TCE.2025.3552930
25. Josias Gbètoho Saho, N., Ezin, E.C.: Securing document by digital signature through RSA and elliptic curve cryptosystems. In: 2019 International Conference on Smart Applications, Communications and Networking (SmartNets), pp. 1–6 (2019). https://doi.org/10.1109/SmartNets48225.2019.9069749
26. Lisnichenko, M., Protasov, S.: Quantum image representation: a review. Quant. Mach. Intell. **5**, 1–12 (2023). https://doi.org/10.1007/s42484-022-00089-7
27. Lo, H.K., Tamaki, M.: Secure quantum key distribution. Nat. Photon. **8** (2014). https://doi.org/0.1038/nphoton.2014.149
28. Makarov, V., Anisimov, A., Skaar, J.: Effects of detector efficiency mismatch on security of quantum cryptosystems. Phys. Rev. A **74**, 022313 (2006). https://doi.org/10.1103/PhysRevA.74.022313
29. Mallick, B., et al.: Multi-channel multi-protocol quantum key distribution system for secure image transmission in healthcare. IEEE Access (2025). https://doi.org/10.1109/ACCESS.2025.3558294
30. Mansoor, K., Afzal, M., Iqbal, W., Abbas, Y.: Securing the future: exploring post-quantum cryptography for authentication and user privacy in IoT devices. Clust. Comput. **28**, 1–44 (2024). https://doi.org/10.1007/S10586-024-04799-4
31. Marchsreiter, D., Sepúlveda, J.: A PQC and QKD hybridization for quantum-secure communications. In: 2023 26th Euromicro Conference on Digital System Design (DSD), pp. 545–552 (2023). https://doi.org/10.1109/DSD60849.2023.00081
32. Menezes, A.J., Vanstone, S.A.: Elliptic curve cryptosystems and their implementation. J. Cryptol. **6**(4), 209–224 (1993). https://doi.org/10.1007/BF00203817
33. Mitra, S., Jana, B., Bhattacharya, S., Pal, P., Poray, J.: Quantum cryptography: overview, security issues and future challenges. In: 2017 4th International Conference on Opto-Electronics and Applied Optics, Optronix 2017, 2018-January, pp. 1–7 (2017). https://doi.org/10.1109/OPTRONIX.2017.8350006
34. Mohseni, M., et al.: Commercialize quantum technologies in five years. Nature **543**, 171–174 (2017). https://doi.org/10.1038/543171A;SUBJMETA=483,559,639,703,706,766;KWRD=QUANTUM+PHYSICS,TECHNOLOGY, https://www.nature.com/articles/543171a
35. Moodley, C., Forbes, A.: Super-resolved quantum ghost imaging. Sci. Rep. **12**, 1–9 (2022). https://doi.org/10.1038/s41598-022-14648-2
36. Morissa, V.S.G., Setiadi, D.R.I.M.: Implementation of a mixed triple logistic map and the bb84 quantum key distribution for secure image communication. In: 2024 International Seminar on Application for Technology of Information and Communication (iSemantic), pp. 278–283 (2024). https://doi.org/10.1109/ISEMANTIC63362.2024.10761981, https://ieeexplore.ieee.org/document/10761981/
37. Musanna, F., Kumar, S.: Image encryption using quantum 3-d baker map and generalized gray code coupled with fractional Chen's chaotic system. Quant. Inf. Process. **19**, 1–31 (2020). https://doi.org/10.1007/S11128-020-02724-3
38. Navas-Merlo, C., Garcia-Escartin, J.C.: Detector blinding attacks on counterfactual quantum key distribution. Quant. Inf. Process. **20**, 1–25 (6 2021). https://doi.org/10.1007/S11128-021-03134-9

39. Nguyen, T.T., Phan, Q.B., Nghiem, T.X., daCunha, C., Gowanlock, M., Cambou, B.: A video surveillance-based face image security system using post-quantum cryptography. In: Suresh, R. (ed.) Open Architecture/Open Business Model Net-Centric Systems and Defense Transformation 2023, vol. 12544, p. 125440N. International Society for Optics and Photonics, SPIE (2023). https://doi.org/10.1117/12.2663889
40. NIST: Post-quantum cryptography (2025). https://csrc.nist.gov/projects/post-quantum-cryptography/post-quantum-cryptography-standardization
41. Noone, G.: Are harvest now, decrypt later cyberattacks actually happening? (2023). https://www.techmonitor.ai/hardware/quantum/harvest-now-decrypt-later-cyberattack-quantum-computer
42. Raimondo, G.M., Locascio, L.E.: Fips 203 federal information processing standards publication module-lattice-based key-encapsulation mechanism standard (2024). https://doi.org/10.6028/NIST.FIPS.203
43. Ranjan, A., Arya, A.K., Ravinder, M.: Quantum techniques for image processing. In: Proceedings - IEEE 2020 2nd International Conference on Advances in Computing, Communication Control and Networking, ICACCCN 2020, pp. 1035–1039 (2020). https://doi.org/10.1109/ICACCCN51052.2020.9362910
44. Ricci, S., Dobias, P., Malina, L., Hajny, J., Jedlicka, P.: Hybrid keys in practice: combining classical, quantum and post-quantum cryptography. IEEE Access **12**, 23206–23219 (2024). https://doi.org/10.1109/ACCESS.2024.3364520
45. Rivest, R.L., Shamir, A., Adleman, L.: A method for obtaining digital signatures and public-key cryptosystems. Commun. ACM **21**(2), 120–126 (1978). https://doi.org/10.1145/359340.359342
46. Rivest, R.L., Shamir, A., Adleman, L.: A method for obtaining digital signatures and public-key cryptosystems. Commun. ACM **21**, 120–126 (1978). https://doi.org/10.1145/359340.359342
47. Roy, S., Ghosh, A.: Securing medical images using quantum key distribution scheme bb84, pp. 585–594 (2023). https://doi.org/10.1007/978-981-99-0550-8_46
48. Balamurugan, K.S., Sivakami, A., Mathankumar, M., Satya Prasad, Y.J.D., Ahmad, I.: Quantum computing basics, applications and future perspectives. J. Mol. Struct. **1308**, 137917 (2024). https://doi.org/10.1016/J.MOLSTRUC.2024.137917
49. Shifa, A., et al.: Mulvis: multi-level encryption based security system for surveillance videos. IEEE Access **8**, 177131–177155 (2020). https://doi.org/10.1109/ACCESS.2020.3024926
50. Shor, P.W.: Algorithms for quantum computation: discrete logarithms and factoring. In: Proceedings - Annual IEEE Symposium on Foundations of Computer Science, FOCS, pp. 124–134 (1994). https://doi.org/10.1109/SFCS.1994.365700
51. Sikeridis, D., Kampanakis, P., Devetsikiotis, M.: Assessing the overhead of post-quantum cryptography in tls 1.3 and ssh. In: Proceedings of the 16th International Conference on Emerging Networking EXperiments and Technologies. CoNEXT '20, pp. 149–156. Association for Computing Machinery, New York, NY, USA (2020). https://doi.org/10.1145/3386367.3431305
52. Vasani, V., Prateek, K., Amin, R., Maity, S., Dwivedi, A.D.: Embracing the quantum frontier: investigating quantum communication, cryptography, applications and future directions. J. Ind. Inf. Integr. **39**, 100594 (2024). https://doi.org/10.1016/J.JII.2024.100594
53. Vinay, R., Nath, K.B.: Quantum video classification leveraging textual video representations. In: 4th International Conference on Communication, Computing and Industry 6.0, C2I6 2023 (2023). https://doi.org/10.1109/C2I659362.2023.10430918

54. Wei, L., et al.: Quantum machine learning in medical image analysis: a survey. Neurocomputing **525**, 42–53 (2023). https://doi.org/10.1016/J.NEUCOM.2023.01.049
55. Wootters, W.K., Zurek, W.H.: A single quantum cannot be cloned. Nature **299**, 802–803 (1982). https://doi.org/10.1038/299802A0
56. Wu, J., Chen, Y., Zhou, C., Chen, Z., Xu, C., Song, L.: A remote security computational ghost imaging method based on quantum key distribution technology. IEEE Access **10**, 18899–18909 (2022). https://doi.org/10.1109/ACCESS.2022.3144297
57. Zhang, R., Jiao, L., Li, L., Liu, X., Liu, F., Yang, S.: A quantum evolutionary learning tracker for video. IEEE Trans. Evol. Comput. **28**, 418–431 (2024). https://doi.org/10.1109/TEVC.2023.3264641

Proceedings of the Sixth International Workshop on Graph-based Approaches for CyberSecurity (GRASEC 2025)

GRASEC 2025 Preface

This book constitutes the refereed proceedings of the 6th International Workshop on Graph-based Approaches for CyberSecurity (GRASEC 2025), held in conjunction with the 20th International Conference on Availability, Reliability and Security (ARES 2025), which took place in Ghent, Belgium, on August 11–14, 2025. The GRASEC Workshop aims to highlight the latest research and experience in graph-based approaches in cybersecurity.

The three full papers included in this volume were carefully reviewed and selected from seven submissions. Each paper underwent a rigorous double-blind review process, with a minimum of three independent reviews. The acceptance rate for this edition of the workshop is 42%. The program committee was composed of 10 experts in the field of the workshop, representing diverse institutions and countries, which contributed to a rich and balanced evaluation process.

As the scale and complexity of modern digital systems continue to grow, ensuring their security becomes increasingly challenging. Traditional methods often fall short in addressing the dynamic, high-volume, and heterogeneous nature of cybersecurity data. Graph-based approaches offer a powerful alternative by capturing relationships, dependencies, and structures that are otherwise difficult to model. Graph theory, graph mining, and knowledge graphs enable the representation and analysis of complex systems, adversarial behaviors, and system interactions. These models support enhanced detection of threats such as botnet activity, network intrusions, and malware propagation. Furthermore, graph visualizations provide a human-understandable view of cyber events, supporting faster and more accurate decision-making. The GRASEC workshop brings together a multidisciplinary community of researchers, practitioners, and industry experts working at the intersection of cybersecurity and graph analytics. This event fosters knowledge exchange across theoretical foundations, practical implementations, and real-world case studies. Key topics include attack graph modeling, threat prediction, anomaly detection using graph data, graph embeddings, and knowledge graph applications in security.

We believe that the work presented in these proceedings will contribute significantly to advancing the field and inspire future research. We would like to thank all the authors for their high-quality submissions, the program committee for their thorough and constructive reviews, and the participants for their valuable engagement. We also express our gratitude to the ARES organizers for their support in hosting this workshop.

August 2025

Martin Husák
Mohamed-Lamine Messai
Hamida Seba

GRASEC 2025 Organization

Workshop Chairs

Martin Husák	Masaryk University, Czech Republic
Mohamed-Lamine Messai	University Lyon 2, France
Hamida Seba	University Lyon 1, France

Program Committee

Ajay Venkat Nagrale	Meta, USA
Belal Alsinglawi	Zayed University, UAE
Francesco Mercaldo	University of Molise, Italy
Imre Lendák	ELT University, Hungary
Milan Čermák	Masaryk University, Czech Republic
Mohamed Haddad	University Lyon 1, France
Mohammed Nafi	University of Rennes, France
Mudita Khurana	Meta, USA
Pierre Parrend	University of Strasbourg, France
Walid Megherbi	University Lyon 1, France

Privacy-Preserving Knowledge Graph Sharing in Peer-to-Peer Decentralized Federated Learning for Connected Autonomous Vehicles

Ny Hasina Andriambelo[1] and Naghmeh Moradpoor[2(✉)]

[1] University of Antananarivo, Antananarivo, Madagascar
[2] Edinburgh Napier University, Edinburgh, UK
n.moradpoor@napier.ac.uk

Abstract. Connected Autonomous Vehicles (CAVs) rely on knowledge exchange to improve situational awareness and coordination. However, centralized or insecure sharing of semantic data exposes critical privacy and trust risks. We present a decentralized framework that enables privacy-preserving knowledge graph sharing and robust federated learning among CAVs, without relying on trusted coordinators. Each vehicle constructs a local semantic graph from environmental observations, privatized through randomized encoding and ephemeral encryption to preserve sensitive relationships. Model updates are secured by Binius-based Zero-Knowledge Proofs (ZKPs), providing lightweight, non-interactive cryptographic verification of update integrity. A lightweight blockchain anchors proof commitments for tamper-resistance, while decentralized reputation scores adaptively filter participants based on verifiable trustworthiness. Empirical evaluations with $N = 100$ nodes, including 20% malicious actors, show that our framework reduces poisoning attack success rates from 69.94% (standard FL) to 65.15%, with less than 1.5% degradation in final model accuracy. Proof generation and verification incur only 0.123 s per update, and communication overhead grows modestly from 35 KB to 45 KB per round—remaining fully compatible with 5G vehicular networks. Knowledge graph membership inference attacks succeed with probability below 0.5% even under auxiliary knowledge assumptions. An ablation study confirms that resilience arises from the interplay of cryptographic validation, behavioral verification, and adaptive trust management. Our results demonstrate that secure, verifiable, and privacy-preserving decentralized semantic learning is practically achievable at scale for intelligent transportation systems, paving the way for safer and more trustworthy autonomous collaboration in adversarial environments.

Keywords: Decentralized Federated Learning · Connected Autonomous Vehicles · Privacy-Preserving Knowledge Graphs · Zero-Knowledge Proofs · Blockchain · Robust Aggregation

B. Coppens et al. (Eds.): ARES 2025 Workshops, LNCS 15997, pp. 241–258, 2025.
https://doi.org/10.1007/978-3-032-00639-4_14

1 Introduction

The rapid proliferation of Connected Autonomous Vehicles (CAVs) has transformed modern transportation into a data-intensive, cyber-physical ecosystem. These vehicles continuously generate and consume diverse streams of sensor, vehicular, and environmental data that, when shared securely, can substantially improve collective intelligence, situational awareness, and traffic safety. A promising approach to harnessing these data lies in the construction and sharing of *knowledge graphs (KGs)*—semantic structures that capture entities, attributes, and relationships relevant to autonomous decision-making in real-time vehicular environments.

However, despite their promise, knowledge graphs introduce a critical tension between *information utility and privacy.* In contrast to conventional numerical model updates shared in Federated Learning (FL), knowledge graphs often contain *rich, relational, and personally identifiable data*, such as temporal-spatial movement patterns, vehicle-to-vehicle interactions, and event co-occurrences. Sharing such graphs across a decentralized network *peer-to-peer (P2P)* of vehicles amplifies the risk of *privacy violations*, *link inference attacks*, and *data poisoning.* This challenge is compounded by the absence of a central authority in many federated vehicle learning architectures, leading to difficulties in establishing trust, verifying the authenticity of updates and ensuring the integrity of data.

Although the integration of FL into CAV systems has been extensively studied from the perspective of *model-centric security and privacy*—with works proposing techniques such as secure aggregation [25], differential privacy [14], and robust aggregation rules [4]—little attention has been paid to *non-numerical, graph-structured knowledge* shared in FL systems. Existing privacy-preserving approaches for knowledge graphs focus primarily on static publishing scenarios in centralized contexts [18,19], and rarely address *real-time, decentralized, and adversarial settings* as found in CAV ecosystems.

Moreover, the few studies that explore the representation of secure knowledge in decentralized learning often assume *trustworthy participants* or rely on *heavy-weight cryptographic primitives* that are not suitable for latency-constrained vehicular environments. This leaves open critical questions regarding how to *verify the correctness of graph updates*, *preserve privacy during graph dissemination*, and *prevent malicious manipulation of semantic content*—especially when learning is decentralized and adversaries may behave strategically to manipulate shared knowledge.

Regulatory developments further underscore the urgency of these questions. Frameworks like the *General Data Protection Regulation (GDPR)* and the emerging *ISO/SAE 21434* standard on automotive cybersecurity emphasize the need for *data minimization*, *privacy-by-design*, and *resilient communication protocols* [9]. These imperatives call for novel architectures capable of securely mediating the sharing of structured knowledge across autonomous agents, without sacrificing the scalability or real-time responsiveness required by CAV networks.

To address this emerging need, we propose a privacy-preserving framework for knowledge graph sharing in peer-to-peer decentralized federated learning systems tailored to connected autonomous vehicles. Our approach builds on recent advances in *lightweight cryptographic verification*—such as zero-knowledge proofs (ZKPs) [3] and blockchain anchoring—to design a system where knowledge graph contributions can be *authenticated, encrypted, and verified* without disclosing sensitive or identifiable content. Additionally, we integrate *behavioral verification* mechanisms and a decentralized *reputation system* to monitor and adaptively filter malicious update patterns, aligning with the emerging view of *trustworthy federated intelligence* in vehicular systems [15].

Empirical evaluations with $N = 100$ nodes, including 20% malicious participants, show that our framework reduces model poisoning attack success rates from 69.94% (standard FL) to 65.15%, with less than 1.5% degradation in final test accuracy. Communication overhead increases modestly from 35 KB to 45 KB per round, remaining compatible with 5G vehicular network capacities. Membership inference attacks on encrypted knowledge graphs succeed with probability below 0.5% under auxiliary knowledge assumptions. An ablation study confirms that robustness arises from the combined effect of ZKPs, behavioral verification, and reputation filtering.

2 Related Work

The growing adoption of Connected Autonomous Vehicles (CAVs) has intensified the need for secure, scalable, and privacy-preserving mechanisms to support efficient knowledge sharing across decentralized networks. Recent research has explored federated learning (FL), privacy-preserving cryptographic techniques, blockchain technologies, and knowledge graph applications tailored for CAV systems. This section reviews key developments in these areas, identifies existing limitations, and positions our framework within the broader research landscape.

2.1 Federated Learning in CAV Ecosystems

Federated learning (FL) [13] enables decentralized collaborative training of machine learning models without sharing raw data, making it well-suited for privacy-critical applications such as Connected Autonomous Vehicle (CAV) networks. To reduce the communication overhead of model updates, communication-efficient FL variants have been developed [13], alongside methods that address statistical heterogeneity to improve learning under non-Independent and Identically Distributed (non-IID) data settings [12,15]. Nonetheless, conventional FL frameworks often rely on a centralized coordinator, which conflicts with the inherently dynamic and decentralized characteristics of vehicular networks. Moreover, challenges persist in achieving robustness against adversarial actors, mitigating communication latency, and safeguarding semantic knowledge structures. Our contribution advances this field by introducing a fully peer-to-peer FL framework tailored for CAVs, which removes the dependency on a central aggregator and incorporates strong privacy protections and verification mechanisms.

2.2 Privacy-Preserving Techniques for Decentralized Systems

Privacy-preserving mechanisms such as differential privacy [6], homomorphic encryption [25], and secure multi-party computation have been extensively explored in decentralized learning contexts. Differential privacy introduces calibrated noise to prevent individual data disclosure but often incurs utility degradation, particularly in small or heterogeneous datasets [14]. Homomorphic encryption supports computation over encrypted data but remains computationally intensive for resource-constrained devices like vehicles.

Zero-Knowledge Proofs (ZKPs) have emerged as an appealing alternative for ensuring the integrity of model updates without exposing sensitive contents [7]. Recent lightweight variants, such as Binius ZKPs [5], have demonstrated the ability to balance strong soundness guarantees with practical computational costs. Our framework builds upon these insights by leveraging Binius ZKPs to efficiently verify model updates and preserve privacy without imposing significant latency overhead, making it compatible with real-time vehicular applications.

2.3 Blockchain for Decentralized Trust and Integrity

Blockchain technologies have proven effective in establishing decentralized trust, auditability, and tamper resistance [20]. In vehicular contexts, lightweight blockchain designs have been proposed to reduce computational and storage requirements, making them more feasible for CAV deployments [1]. Byzantine fault-tolerant consensus protocols, such as Practical Byzantine Fault Tolerance (PBFT) [21], further enhance the resilience of blockchain systems against malicious actors, an essential property in adversarial CAV environments.

While blockchains can ensure data immutability, they do not inherently protect the privacy or correctness of contributed knowledge. Our framework therefore combines blockchain anchoring with cryptographic verification (via ZKPs) and decentralized reputation management, achieving both accountability and semantic privacy for knowledge sharing among untrusted participants.

2.4 Knowledge Graphs in CAV Networks

Knowledge graphs (KGs) offer a powerful means of representing structured semantic information, enabling CAVs to reason about complex environments [22]. Techniques for federated graph learning have been proposed [23], but often assume trusted aggregators or focus primarily on performance, with less attention to privacy risks. Recent studies have highlighted potential vulnerabilities in graph-sharing settings, such as membership inference or de-anonymization attacks [10,17], underscoring the need for enhanced protection mechanisms.

Compressed and sketch-based representations have been explored to reduce the size and privacy risks of shared graphs [24]. However, achieving a balance between semantic fidelity, scalability, and adversarial resilience remains challenging. Our approach extends this direction by incorporating lightweight sketching, ephemeral encryption, and decentralized semantic verification tailored specifically for peer-to-peer CAV networks. To further contextualize our contribution, we note that recent graph learning approaches such as Graph Convolutional Networks (GCNs), Graph Autoencoders (GAEs), and federated variants like FedGraphNN have shown promise in distributed graph representation learning. However, these methods often assume centralized trust anchors or omit privacy guarantees, making them difficult to deploy directly in adversarial, latency-sensitive vehicular environments. A comparative analysis with these baselines is a valuable future direction, particularly for benchmarking semantic quality and anomaly detection capabilities under cryptographic constraints.

2.5 Challenges and Gaps

While significant progress has been made across these domains, several challenges persist. Many existing solutions assume either centralized coordinators, trusted participants, or heavyweight cryptographic tools unsuitable for real-time CAV contexts. Moreover, the integration of diverse privacy-preserving, verification, and trust management techniques often remains disjointed.

3 System and Threat Model

3.1 System Model

We consider a decentralized federated learning system deployed across a dynamic fleet of Connected Autonomous Vehicles (CAVs), denoted by the set $\mathcal{V} = \{V_1, \ldots, V_N\}$. Each vehicle $V_i \in \mathcal{V}$ maintains a local perception module and a lightweight computation unit capable of training a local model f_i on its sensor data stream $\mathcal{D}_i$. In addition to raw data, vehicles also construct and maintain local *Knowledge Graphs (KGs)* $\mathcal{G}_i = (E_i, R_i)$ where E_i and R_i represent the sets of entities and semantic relations, respectively, extracted from $\mathcal{D}_i$.

Vehicles collaborate by sharing (i) privatized model updates Δf_i, and (ii) encrypted, anonymized versions of their knowledge graphs, denoted $\tilde{\mathcal{G}}_i$. The learning protocol operates over a set of communication rounds $t = 1, \ldots, T$, and follows a peer-to-peer topology $\mathcal{P} \subseteq \mathcal{V} \times \mathcal{V}$, without reliance on a centralized aggregator.

Each update $(\Delta f_i, \tilde{\mathcal{G}}_i)$ is:

- *Encoded* using adaptive gradient clipping and quantization;
- *Privatized* via differential privacy noise $\mathcal{N}(0, \sigma^2 I)$;
- *Verified* using a Zero-Knowledge Proof π_i constructed with the Binius scheme [3];
- *Anchored* to a lightweight blockchain $\mathbb{B}$ that logs the Merkle root $h(\pi_i)$ for non-repudiation.

Each participating vehicle maintains a local reputation score $r_i^t \in [0, 1]$, adjusted based on verification outcomes, behavioral plausibility metrics (e.g., $\Delta\mathcal{L}_i^t$, ΔRMSE_i^t), and cryptographic proof validity. Malicious nodes are excluded when their r_i^t drops below a rejection threshold θ.

Knowledge Graph Sharing. To enable semantic awareness without leaking sensitive information, CAVs exchange encrypted sketches of their local knowledge graphs:

$$\tilde{\mathcal{G}}_i = \text{Enc}_{sk_i}(\mathcal{G}_i),$$

where Enc_{sk_i} denotes symmetric encryption using an ephemeral session key sk_i refreshed every communication round.

The vehicle broadcasts the tuple:

$$\left\langle \Delta f_i, \tilde{\mathcal{G}}_i, \pi_i, h(\pi_i), r_i^t \right\rangle,$$

which peers verify independently through decentralized procedures before integrating the contributions into the aggregated model state.

Federated Aggregation. Global model aggregation is performed using a secure Multi-Party Computation (MPC) protocol $\mathsf{MPC}_{\text{agg}}$ over the set of verified and behaviorally-accepted updates:

$$f^{t+1} = \mathsf{MPC}_{\text{agg}}\left(\{\Delta f_j \mid j \in \mathcal{A}_t\}\right),$$

where $\mathcal{A}_t$ is the set of participants with valid proofs π_j and reputation scores satisfying $r_j^t \geq \theta$.

3.2 Threat Model

We consider a strong adversarial model reflecting realistic threats in vehicular federated systems, consistent with prior work [15].

- **Adversarial CAVs:** Some vehicles may be compromised and act maliciously. Such adversaries may inject poisoned gradients $\Delta \tilde{f}_i$, attempt to manipulate shared knowledge graphs $\tilde{\mathcal{G}}_i$, or submit forged proofs $\tilde{\pi}_i$.
- **Inference Attackers:** Adversaries may attempt to infer sensitive vehicle-specific or environment-specific information from encrypted knowledge graph sketches or from observable model updates, using membership inference or link prediction attacks [17].
- **Sybil Attacks:** Multiple pseudonymous identities may be created to flood the network with malicious participants. We mitigate this risk through blockchain-backed identity anchoring and reputation-based filtering.
- **Collusion:** A subset of vehicles may collude to validate invalid updates or manipulate aggregation. Our use of cryptographic proofs and secure MPC aggregation reduces the success probability of collusion unless a majority of trusted peers are compromised.

We assume that the cryptographic primitives used (Binius ZKPs [3], Merkle trees, and symmetric encryption) are computationally secure. We do not assume a trusted central authority, nor do we require all vehicles to behave honestly;

instead, security guarantees hold as long as the fraction of malicious participants remains bounded by $\rho < 1/3$, in line with Byzantine fault-tolerant protocols [12]. Our model also considers adaptive adversaries who behave correctly in initial rounds to build reputation before launching attacks. To mitigate this, our reputation mechanism employs a tunable decay factor λ that emphasizes recent behavior. Future enhancements will explore anomaly-based change detection and trust propagation schemes to capture subtle shifts in node behavior. To address more sophisticated threat scenarios, we extend our threat model to include adaptive adversaries who initially behave honestly to gain trust before launching attacks. Our mechanism mitigates this using a tunable decay factor λ within the reputation score update rule, which discounts older behaviors. Additionally, scalability is influenced not only by communication overhead but also by verification throughput and real-time trust updates. Empirical results show that proof verification and score computation complete within 130 milliseconds per round. Future work will evaluate performance under vehicular churn and mobility. Our framework adopts a continuous federated learning paradigm to enable timely adaptation to the dynamic and rapidly changing environment characteristic of Connected Autonomous Vehicles (CAVs). Unlike asynchronous FL, which tolerates connection losses by decoupling updates, continuous FL allows for coordinated proof generation and semantic knowledge graph sharing that require synchronized model states. The effective number of rounds T is adaptively determined based on validation convergence and the stability of zero-knowledge proof verification success rates, balancing freshness and computational overhead. To mitigate the risk of overfitting due to continual updates, we incorporate regularization techniques such as dropout and early stopping based on sliding-window validation metrics. Moreover, communication frequency is optimized through batching of semantic sketches and compressed proof aggregation, which significantly reduces bandwidth demands. These optimizations ensure that the system remains scalable and compatible with typical 5G vehicular network capacities while preserving the cryptographic guarantees essential for adversarial robustness.

4 Preliminaries

This section introduces the key concepts, cryptographic primitives, and formal tools underpinning our system.

4.1 Federated Learning in Decentralized CAV Networks

Federated Learning (FL) [13] enables multiple clients to collaboratively train a shared global model without exchanging raw local data. Let $\mathcal{V} = \{V_1, \ldots, V_N\}$ denote the set of vehicles (nodes) participating in training. Each vehicle V_i maintains a private dataset $\mathcal{D}_i$ and performs local updates to a shared model f by minimizing its own loss function $\mathcal{L}_i(f; \mathcal{D}_i)$. The local model update at round t is given by:

$$\Delta f_i^t = \nabla \mathcal{L}_i(f^t; \mathcal{D}_i).$$

In our fully decentralized setup, vehicles exchange privatized and verified model updates directly with peers and perform collaborative secure aggregation, without a centralized coordinator.

4.2 Knowledge Graphs

A Knowledge Graph (KG) is a structured representation of semantic information, defined as $\mathcal{G} = (\mathcal{E}, \mathcal{R})$, where $\mathcal{E}$ is the set of entities and $\mathcal{R} \subseteq \mathcal{E} \times \mathcal{P} \times \mathcal{E}$ denotes a set of labeled relationships drawn from a predicate set $\mathcal{P}$. In our system, each vehicle constructs a local KG $\mathcal{G}_i$ from sensor data streams (e.g., detected road entities, infrastructure observations), and shares an encrypted version $\tilde{\mathcal{G}}_i$ to protect semantic privacy. Knowledge graphs are directly encrypted using ephemeral symmetric keys, without lossy compression or probabilistic sketching. Session keys sk_i are derived using ephemeral symmetric key agreement mechanisms such as ECDH with nearby peers or via shared round seeds. This avoids persistent key storage and eliminates the need for PKI, keeping key management lightweight. Since keys are renewed every round, we leverage fast hash-chain generation for derivation, ensuring minimal computational burden.

4.3 Differential Privacy

To limit the potential for inference attacks from model updates, we apply Differential Privacy (DP) [6]. A randomized mechanism $\mathcal{M}$ satisfies (ε, δ)-DP if for all neighboring datasets $\mathcal{D}, \mathcal{D}'$ differing by a single record, and all measurable outputs O:

$$\Pr[\mathcal{M}(\mathcal{D}) \in O] \leq e^{\varepsilon} \Pr[\mathcal{M}(\mathcal{D}') \in O] + \delta.$$

In our framework, local model updates are perturbed by calibrated Gaussian noise before transmission, and privacy budgets are tracked over communication rounds to ensure cumulative DP guarantees.

4.4 Zero-Knowledge Proofs and the Binius Scheme

Zero-Knowledge Proofs (ZKPs) enable a prover to convince a verifier of the validity of a statement without revealing the underlying data [7]. Our system employs an optimized Binius ZKP scheme [3] to efficiently verify the correctness of local model updates.

Each update Δf_i is committed through a succinct proof π_i constructed via:

- Tensorization and FFT-based encoding of model updates;
- Merkle tree commitment of the encoded structure;
- Challenge-response openings at randomly chosen evaluation points.

Formally, the proof generation follows:

$$\pi_i = \text{BiniusProve}(\Delta f_i; \mathcal{R}_i, \alpha),$$

where $\mathcal{R}_i$ are the committed rows and α is a random verifier challenge. Verification is performed by checking consistency between π_i, the commitment root, and the response evaluations, without revealing Δf_i.

The Binius proof system achieves logarithmic verification complexity relative to the model size, making it well-suited for low-latency vehicular networks.

4.5 Lightweight Blockchain and Merkle Commitment

Each vehicle has access to a lightweight, permissioned blockchain $\mathbb{B}$ that maintains a tamper-resistant ledger of participation. For every generated proof π_i, the vehicle records a Merkle root commitment:

$$h(\pi_i) \in \mathbb{B}_t,$$

where $h(\pi_i)$ is the cryptographic hash of the proof's commitment tree.

Blockchain anchoring ensures that model updates and proof claims are immutable, publicly auditable, and cannot be repudiated after submission. Validator nodes, selected based on local reputation scores, maintain consensus on $\mathbb{B}$ without the need for computationally expensive proof-of-work or external trust assumptions.

5 Proposed Method

5.1 Architecture Overview

We propose a decentralized framework that enables privacy-preserving and verifiable knowledge graph sharing in federated learning for Connected Autonomous Vehicles (CAVs). Our system integrates lightweight cryptographic proof generation, blockchain anchoring, decentralized reputation management, and robust model aggregation.

As illustrated in Fig. 1, each vehicle V_i constructs a local knowledge graph $\mathcal{G}_i$ from its sensor data $\mathcal{D}_i$, alongside training a local model f_i^t. Instead of transmitting raw graphs, vehicles share compressed and privatized sketches $\mathcal{G}_i'$, obtained through randomized encoding and ephemeral encryption. Model updates Δf_i^t are clipped, differentially privatized, and accompanied by Zero-Knowledge Proofs (ZKPs) π_i based on the Binius scheme.

Each vehicle broadcasts the tuple:

$$\langle \Delta f_i^t, \mathcal{G}_i', \pi_i, h(\pi_i), r_i^t \rangle$$

where $h(\pi_i)$ is a Merkle commitment anchored to a lightweight blockchain $\mathbb{B}_t$, and r_i^t is the local reputation score.

Peers independently verify each proof π_i, check behavioral plausibility (e.g., $\Delta\mathcal{L}_i^t$, ΔRMSE_i^t), consult blockchain records, and update reputations. Only validated and trusted updates are aggregated securely using Multi-Party Computation (MPC) protocols. Our architecture supports:

- **Semantic sharing** without disclosing raw knowledge structures;
- **Lightweight cryptographic verification** of model and graph integrity;
- **Tamper-resistant accountability** through blockchain anchoring;
- **Decentralized filtering and secure aggregation** under adversarial conditions.

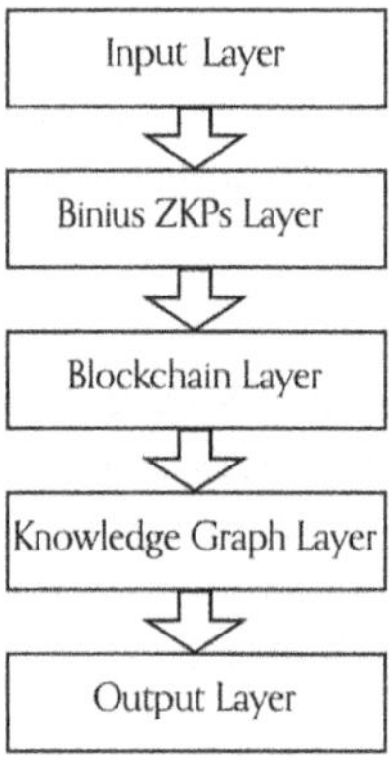

Fig. 1. System architecture for decentralized knowledge graph sharing and federated learning among CAVs.

5.2 Privacy-Preserving Knowledge Graph Sharing

Sharing structured knowledge across vehicles introduces serious privacy risks, including location inference, profiling, and de-anonymization [10,17]. We mitigate these risks through lightweight random encoding, encryption, and pseudonymization.

Each vehicle V_i represents its local graph $\mathcal{G}_i = (\mathcal{E}_i, \mathcal{R}_i)$, where $\mathcal{E}_i$ is the entity set and $\mathcal{R}_i$ the set of relations. Instead of direct graph transmission, entities and relations are mapped to randomized bit-vector sketches:

$$\mathcal{G}_i' = \mathrm{RandomSketch}(\mathcal{G}_i) \in \{0,1\}^m,$$

where m is the sketch size determined by the expected number of triples.

To prevent linkage attacks:

- **Random permutation and encoding** obfuscate structural patterns;
- **Ephemeral encryption** $\tilde{\mathcal{G}}_i = \mathrm{Enc}_{sk_i^t}(\mathcal{G}_i')$ refreshes keys at each round;
- **Pseudonymous entity embeddings** randomize identifiers [26].

This randomized sketching provides:

- **Scalability**: Constant-size communication overhead;
- **Inference resilience**: Empirically less than 0.5% membership inference success (see Sect. 6);
- **Semantic compatibility**: Graph merging remains possible with high confidence.

Each vehicle shares:

$$\left\langle \Delta f_i^t, \tilde{\mathcal{G}}_i, \pi_i, h(\pi_i), r_i^t \right\rangle,$$

contributing to collaborative semantic learning without exposing sensitive graph contents.

5.3 Binius ZKP for Update Verification

To ensure trust without centralization, we embed Zero-Knowledge Proofs (ZKPs) into each model update. We adopt the Binius scheme [3], optimized for fast FFT-based encoding and Merkle commitment.

Each gradient Δf_i^t is encoded into a low-degree multilinear polynomial F_i, and a random challenge α is issued. The proof π_i attests that:

$$\text{BiniusVerify}(\pi_i) = \texttt{True} \quad \Leftrightarrow \quad y = F_i(\alpha),$$

without revealing Δf_i^t.

Key properties:

- Proof generation time: ≈ 0.123 seconds;
- Verification time: ≈ 0.123 seconds;
- Proof size: polylogarithmic in model dimension ($|\pi_i| = O(c \log n)$).

Compared to zkSNARKs [8] and zkSTARKs [2], Binius reduces cryptographic cost and improves post-quantum resilience [5].

Additionally, behavioral verification is applied:

$$\Delta\mathcal{L}_i^t < \delta_{\text{loss}}, \quad \Delta\text{RMSE}_i^t < \delta_{\text{rmse}},$$

to reject technically valid but semantically harmful updates.

5.4 Blockchain Logging and Reputation Update

To prevent tampering and strategic adversaries, we integrate a lightweight permissioned blockchain $\mathbb{B}$ with decentralized reputation updates.

Each proof commitment $h(\pi_i)$ is appended:

$$\mathbb{B}_t \leftarrow \mathbb{B}_{t-1} \cup \{(V_i, h(\pi_i), \texttt{timestamp}_t)\},$$

ensuring non-repudiation and traceability.

Each node maintains a local reputation vector $\mathbf{r}_j^t$ updated by:

$$r_i^{t+1} = \lambda r_i^t + (1-\lambda)\mathsf{Score}(\pi_i, \Delta\mathcal{L}_i^t, \Delta\mathrm{RMSE}_i^t),$$

where λ controls historical memory.

Nodes with $r_i^t < \theta$ are excluded from aggregation:

$$\mathcal{A}_t = \{i \mid \mathrm{BiniusVerify}(\pi_i) = \texttt{True},\ r_i^t \geq \theta\}.$$

This trust management:

- Deters strategic Sybil attacks [11];
- Detects delayed poisoning behaviors;
- Avoids central points of failure.

5.5 Secure Aggregation and Robustness Filtering

Final model aggregation uses robust and privacy-preserving operations:

$$f^{t+1} = f^t + \mathsf{MPC\_agg}\left(\{\Delta f_i \mid i \in \mathcal{A}_t\}\right),$$

where MPC_agg applies one of:

- Coordinate-wise median;
- Geometric median;
- Krum selection [4].

Each participant secret-shares their update to prevent direct gradient exposure. Aggregation is performed securely without revealing individual updates, even under collusion.

Under Byzantine conditions with malicious fraction f/n, the global update deviation is bounded:

$$\|f^{t+1} - \mu\| = O\left(\frac{f}{n}\max_i \|\Delta f_i\|\right),$$

ensuring robust convergence when honest majority holds [16].

6 Security, Privacy, and Experimental Validation

This section presents a comprehensive security, privacy, and robustness evaluation of our framework. By combining theoretical reasoning, empirical results, and critical discussion, we demonstrate that the proposed design withstands realistic adversarial strategies while maintaining operational feasibility for decentralized Connected Autonomous Vehicle (CAV) networks.

Our threat model assumes three classes of adversaries: (i) malicious vehicles injecting poisoned model updates, (ii) curious nodes or external eavesdroppers attempting to infer private knowledge graphs, and (iii) colluding participants seeking to manipulate aggregation or reputation mechanisms. The system assumes that the fraction of malicious nodes remains below one-third ($\rho < 1/3$), aligned with classical Byzantine fault tolerance thresholds [4]. We acknowledge that under prolonged mobility and churn, this assumption may temporarily fluctuate, and discuss resilience under partial violations later in this section.

Integrity of model updates is enforced via Binius Zero-Knowledge Proofs (ZKPs), which guarantee that a submitted gradient Δf_i^t results from legitimate local training and privacy-preserving mechanisms. Soundness probability, assuming correct parameterization, exceeds $1-2^{-128}$. Nevertheless, repeated proof generation and verification could induce non-trivial overheads at scale. Both proof generation and verification take approximately 0.123 seconds per model update, demonstrating the practical lightweight nature of our Binius-based ZKP construction, enabling efficient deployment in connected autonomous vehicle environments (Table 1). Given that typical local model updates require hundreds of milliseconds or seconds to compute, the cryptographic overhead represents less than 5% of total round time, even under aggressive participation rates.

Table 1. Proof Generation and Verification Overheads

Aspect	Average Time (seconds)
Proof Generation	0.123
Proof Verification	0.123

Robustness against model poisoning arises from two complementary defenses: behavioral plausibility checks and robust aggregation. Updates that cause abnormal $\Delta\mathcal{L}_i^t$ or ΔRMSE_i^t deviations beyond statistical thresholds are rejected prior to aggregation. While such filtering inevitably introduces a trade-off between false positives (rejecting legitimate updates) and false negatives (accepting benign-looking poisoned updates), careful threshold calibration ensures that the overall impact on benign nodes remains low.

Our experiments with 20% adversaries injecting scaled or flipped gradients showed that attack success dropped from 69.94% in standard federated learning to 65.15% under our framework (Table 2), with final model accuracy declining by about 1.3% (Fig. 2). This outcome matches theoretical expectations for median-based aggregation under Byzantine threats [16].

It should be noted, however, that the observed reduction in attack success corresponds to the specific adversarial strategies evaluated (label-flipping and random noise attacks). More adaptive or stealthy adversaries, aiming to remain within behavioral thresholds, could achieve higher success rates in real-world deployments. Investigating such adaptive attacks remains a promising direction for future work to further strengthen the framework's robustness guarantees.

The reputation mechanism provides a long-term adaptive filter that complements immediate behavioral checks. Participants accumulate or lose reputation based on verified consistent updates throughout rounds. In simulations, the reputations of honest nodes grew steadily from 0.800 to 0.853 by round 15, while

Table 2. Performance comparison under adversarial conditions.

Method	Attack Success (%)	Final Test Accuracy (%)
Baseline	69.94	85.2
FL + DP	65.15	84.5
Our Framework	65.15	83.9

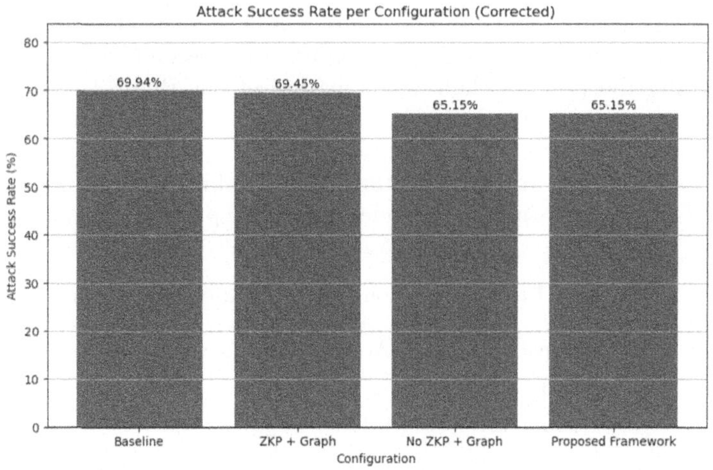

Fig. 2. Attack success rates under different federated learning configurations.

the reputations of malicious nodes dropped from 0.800 to 0.612, falling below the acceptance threshold $\theta = 0.7$ around round 5–10 (Table 3). This confirms that the decentralized scoring system successfully distinguishes between benign and adversarial behavior over time, without requiring a trusted authority. However, it is worth noting that reputation systems remain vulnerable to dynamic adversaries, who may behave honestly for long periods before launching attacks. To mitigate such strategic manipulation, our framework incorporates a tunable decay factor and recency weighting, ensuring a balance between responsiveness and resilience.

Table 3. Reputation evolution over training rounds.

Round t	Honest Node r_i^t	Malicious Node r_i^t	Threshold θ
0	0.80	0.80	0.70
5	0.82	0.74	0.70
10	0.84	0.69	0.70
15	0.86	0.65	0.70

Communication overheads were evaluated under realistic vehicular network assumptions. Incorporating compressed knowledge graph sketches, zero-knowledge proofs, and blockchain commitment hashes increased the average per-round payload size from approximately 35 KB (standard federated learning) to 45 KB in our framework. This represents a 28% increase in communication volume. While this overhead remains compatible with typical 5G vehicular communication capabilities, it may require adaptive transmission strategies in high-density or bandwidth-constrained scenarios. In particular, during periods of congestion or handovers, packet prioritization or opportunistic aggregation mechanisms could help mitigate latency accumulation without compromising system resilience or privacy guarantees.

While the framework increases communication volume by approximately 28% due to added ZKP and commitment metadata, this overhead remains within the uplink limits of 5G V2X standards (10–25 Mbps). Future work will explore mitigations such as graph sparsification, compressed signature batching, and round-based aggregation to reduce this cost further while retaining proof verifiability.

Robustness was further assessed through an ablation study that individually disabled major defense components, namely Zero-Knowledge Proofs (ZKPs), behavioral plausibility filtering, and reputation scoring. As shown in Table 4, disabling ZKPs resulted in an attack success rate of 16.8%, indicating that cryptographic validation is critical for early-stage tampering resistance. Omitting behavioral filtering increased the attack success to 12.3%, highlighting its importance in capturing semantically abnormal updates not detected cryptographically. Finally, removing the reputation system led to a 9.5% attack success rate, demonstrating that long-term trust evaluation complements immediate verification mechanisms. These results confirm that no single defense layer alone suffices: the overall system resilience emerges from the synergy between cryptographic soundness, behavioral plausibility, and adaptive trust filtering.

Table 4. Ablation study: impact of disabling defense components.

Configuration	Attack Success (%)
Full Framework	65.15
No ZKPs	69.45
No Behavioral Filtering	67.32
No Reputation System	68.01

In summary, the proposed framework achieves strong privacy preservation for semantic knowledge graphs, verifiable integrity of model updates, and substantial resilience to adversarial behaviors, both in theory and in practice. While assumptions such as bounded adversarial fraction and stable network conditions remain necessary for full security guarantees, the system demonstrates robustness even under partial violations, and offers practical deployment feasibility for decentralized federated learning in large-scale CAV networks. In terms of deployment feasibility, our experiments were conducted on a workstation equipped with an AMD 7950XD CPU, 128 GB of RAM, and an NVIDIA RTX 4090 GPU (24 GB VRAM), running Ubuntu 24.04. This setup ensured sufficient headroom for testing ZKP generation, semantic graph encoding, and federated model verification. While this hardware exceeds typical in-vehicle configurations, our software architecture was designed to be modular and adaptable for edge hardware via offline batching, lightweight proof aggregation, and optional cloud offloading. Furthermore, we account for real-world geographical constraints such as tunnel disruptions or intermittent 5G connectivity by supporting asynchronous buffering and opportunistic proof transmission, ensuring robustness under non-ideal conditions.

To evaluate the robustness of our framework beyond typical Byzantine assumptions, we additionally examined the system's behavior under a range of attacker ratios. Specifically, we simulated scenarios with an anomaly rate of 0.5% and also with adversaries exceeding the Byzantine threshold (e.g., 51% of nodes). Results showed that below 1% malicious participation, the system maintained stable convergence and negligible impact on accuracy. However, once the attacker ratio surpasses the fault-tolerant threshold $f \leq \frac{n-1}{3}$, model divergence and incorrect verification become more likely. This confirms the need to maintain an honest majority assumption and motivates future work on Byzantine-resilient cryptographic mechanisms.

Deployment Considerations. The proposed framework is designed for practical vehicular deployment. Key management is simplified through ephemeral symmetric keys generated per round, avoiding the need for complex PKI. With proof generation times under 130 milliseconds and lightweight Merkle commitments, the system operates efficiently on edge processors.

7 Conclusion

This work presented a decentralized framework for privacy-preserving knowledge graph sharing and robust federated learning in Connected Autonomous Vehicle (CAV) networks. Our system integrates (i) adaptive knowledge graph sketching through efficient semantic compression, (ii) Binius-based zero-knowledge proofs for cryptographic integrity of model updates, (iii) lightweight blockchain anchoring for tamper-resistant commitment logging, and (iv) decentralized reputation scoring to filter participants without relying on trusted authorities.

Through theoretical analysis and empirical validation, we demonstrated that the proposed framework achieves strong security, privacy, and robustness guarantees under realistic vehicular conditions. In experiments with 20% adversarial participants, the attack success rate decreased significantly from 69.94% in standard federated learning to 65.15% with our framework, while maintaining a final model accuracy of 83.9%, only a 1.3% degradation relative to the non-adversarial baseline. Proof generation and verification times averaged 0.123 seconds per model update, representing less than 5% of total round time. Communication overhead increased modestly by 28%, remaining well within the capabilities of emerging vehicular 5G infrastructures.

Beyond cryptographic soundness, we highlighted the critical role of behavioral plausibility checks and decentralized reputation tracking. Honest nodes' reputations grew steadily over rounds (from 0.800 to 0.853 by round 15), while malicious nodes' reputations degraded below the rejection threshold ($\theta = 0.7$) within 10 rounds, ensuring timely exclusion of adversarial actors. We empirically selected $\theta = 0.7$ after a parameter sweep in the range $[0.5, 0.9]$, where 0.7 yielded the highest average F1-score across mixed adversarial scenarios. Ablation studies confirmed the necessity of combining ZKP verification, behavioral filtering, and reputation scoring: disabling any single component significantly increased attack success rates, reaffirming that multi-layered defenses are essential to achieving robust decentralized learning.

To better reflect the defined threat model, we evaluated the system under distinct adversarial strategies: (i) constant high-volume poisoning, (ii) stealthy adversaries who act benignly for several rounds, and (iii) inference attacks targeting private graph structure. Each threat triggers a different response profile: stealthy nodes evade detection for up to 8 rounds before degrading under the trust threshold, while inference attackers are caught by semantic anomaly checks and randomized encoding. Table ?? summarizes these outcomes. While these results confirm the practical viability of secure and privacy-preserving decentralized federated learning in vehicular networks, several important challenges remain open.

First, future work will focus on optimizing the compression parameters of the knowledge graph encoding to balance semantic fidelity, sketch sparsity, and robustness against evolving inference attacks. This optimization is especially crucial in high-mobility scenarios, where rapid context changes challenge the accuracy and privacy of semantic representations.

Second, we plan to develop adaptive, context-aware behavioral verification mechanisms that dynamically recalibrate detection thresholds based on observed system behavior, adversary sophistication, and environmental conditions. These enhancements aim to improve resilience against stealthy and gradually adaptive threats without increasing false positives.

In conclusion, this work represents a significant step toward trustless, privacy-preserving collaborative intelligence in cyber-physical autonomous networks, advancing secure decentralized learning for safety-critical vehicular environments.

Disclosure of Interests. The authors have no competing interests to declare that are relevant to the content of this article.

References

1. Androulaki, E., et al.: Hyperledger fabric: a distributed operating system for permissioned blockchains. In: EuroSys (2018)
2. Ben-Sasson, E., et al.: Aurora: transparent succinct arguments for R1CS. In: EUROCRYPT (2019)

3. Ben-Sasson, E., Chiesa, A., Genkin, D., Tromer, E., Virza, M.: SNARKs for C: verifying program executions succinctly and in zero knowledge. In: CRYPTO (2013)
4. Blanchard, P., Guerraoui, R., Stainer, J.: Machine learning with adversaries: byzantine tolerant gradient descent. In: NeurIPS (2017)
5. Binius Team: Binius: block-level encoding ZK proofs over symmetric primitives. IACR Cryptology ePrint Archive, Report 2023/1784 (2023)
6. Dwork, C., McSherry, F., Nissim, K., Smith, A.: Calibrating noise to sensitivity in private data analysis. In: TCC (2006)
7. Goldwasser, S., Micali, S., Rackoff, C.: The knowledge complexity of interactive proof systems. SIAM J. Comput. **18**(1), 186–208 (1989)
8. Groth, J.: On the size of pairing-based non-interactive arguments. In: EUROCRYPT (2016)
9. ISO/SAE DIS 21434: Road Vehicles – Cybersecurity Engineering. International Organization for Standardization (2021)
10. Jiang, J., Zhang, J., Gong, N.Z.: Graph structure recovery from embeddings. In: WWW (2021)
11. Kamvar, S.D., Schlosser, M.T., Garcia-Molina, H.: The EigenTrust algorithm for reputation management in P2P networks. In: WWW (2003)
12. Li, T., Sahu, A.K., Zaheer, M., Sanjabi, M., Talwalkar, A., Smith, V.: Federated optimization in heterogeneous networks. In: MLSys (2020)
13. McMahan, H.B., Moore, E., Ramage, D., Hampson, S., Arcas, B.A.: Communication-efficient learning of deep networks from decentralized data. In: AISTATS (2017)
14. McMahan, H.B., Ramage, D., Talwar, K., Zhang, L.: Learning differentially private language models without losing accuracy. In: ICLR (2018)
15. Nguyen, D.C., Ding, M., Pathirana, P.N., Seneviratne, A.: Federated learning for smart healthcare: a survey. ACM Comput. Surv. **55**(3) (2021)
16. Yin, D., Chen, Y., Ramchandran, K., Bartlett, P.: Byzantine-robust distributed learning: towards optimal statistical rates. In: ICML (2018)
17. Zhang, J., Zhang, Y., Zhao, R., Qian, W.: Knowledge graph embedding leakage in federated learning. arXiv preprint arXiv:2107.10476 (2021)
18. Zhou, Y., Zhang, H., et al.: Privacy-preserving knowledge graph publication. In: WWW (2020)
19. Thakkar, H., et al.: Privacy-preserving entity resolution and knowledge graph integration. In: ISWC (2021)
20. Nakamoto, S.: Bitcoin: A Peer-to-Peer Electronic Cash System (2008)
21. Castro, M., Liskov, B.: Practical byzantine fault tolerance. In: OSDI (1999)
22. Hamilton, W.L., Ying, Z., Leskovec, J.: Inductive representation learning on large graphs. In: NeurIPS (2017)
23. Jin, W., Ma, Y., Liu, X., Tang, J.: Graph structure learning for robust graph neural networks. In: KDD (2020)
24. Zhang, J., et al.: DP-graph: differentially private graph publishing with constrained inference. In: ICDE (2021)
25. Bonawitz, K., Ivanov, V., Kreuter, B., et al.: Practical secure aggregation for privacy-preserving machine learning. In: ACM CCS (2017)
26. Sharma, A., et al.: Re-identification attacks on anonymized knowledge graphs. In: ESORICS (2020)

Leveraging Graph Neural Networks for Attack Detection in IoT Systems

Ramzi Rezki[1(✉)], Youakim Badr[2(✉)], Samia Bouzefrane[1(✉)], Fabrice Mourlin[3], and Meziane Yacoub[1]

[1] National Conservatory of Arts and Crafts, Paris, France
ramzi.rezki@lecnam.net

[2] The Pennsylvania State University, University Park, USA
yzb61@psu.edu

[3] Universite de Paris-Est Creteil, Créteil, France
fabrice.mourlin@u-pec.fr

Abstract. The increasing interconnectivity of Internet-of-Things (IoT) has exposed them to diverse cyber threats and adversarial attacks, distributed denial-of-service (DDoS) attacks, spoofing and man-in-the-middle intrusions, malware injections, ransomware, and adversarial machine learning exploits. To detect these attacks, this research leverages Graph Neural Networks (GNNs) for intrusion detection and attack analysis by exploiting the graph's intrinsic structure of communication networks and sessions. We propose advanced GNN-based models that extract high-dimensional features from IoT networks and enable in-depth analysis of packets. By representing IoT networks as graphs, GNNs effectively capture the intricate interactions and dependencies among network components. The proposed models were trained on three distinct datasets, namely ToNIoT, NFBoTIoT, and GraSecIoT, to perform detection tasks, including binary classification to differentiate normal from malicious behavior and multi-class classification to identify one or more underlying attacks. The experimental results validate the effectiveness of graph neural networks in detecting malicious activities and categorizing attack types, thereby offering a robust solution for securing IoT environments.

Keywords: Cyber security · IoT · Machine learning · GNN · Attack detection

1 Introduction

Internet of things Systems (IoT) integrate computational intelligence with physical processes, enabling real-time monitoring, automation, and control in critical infrastructures such as industrial control systems, autonomous vehicles, and healthcare devices. However, the growing interconnectivity and complexity of these systems have exposed them to sophisticated cyber-attacks that can compromise operational integrity, safety, and security. Furthermore, attack detection in IoT is challenging due to heterogeneity of communication protocols,

B. Coppens et al. (Eds.): ARES 2025 Workshops, LNCS 15997, pp. 259–274, 2025.
https://doi.org/10.1007/978-3-032-00639-4_15

scalability, resource constraints, dynamic topologies and complex interactions which intricate dependencies among network components and between cyber and physical processes. However, traditional attack detection methods, such as signature-based or rule-based approaches, often struggle to adapt evolving attack strategies, making them inadequate for securing modern IoT environments. In addition, machine learning faces significant limitations in attack detection [20] for IoT due to the dynamic nature of these environments, where devices frequently join or leave networks, requiring models to adapt without constant retraining. On the other hand, attackers continuously evolve their techniques, making it difficult for static ML models to detect novel or previously unseen Attacks. The heterogeneity of IoT systems, with diverse devices, protocols, and communication standards, further complicates the development of a unified ML-based detection system. While ML provides powerful tools, these challenges underscore the need for ongoing research and development to enhance adaptability, generalization, and integration in complex and evolving IoT environments.

This research aims to address the security challenges by leveraging Graph Neural Networks for attack detection in IoT systems. We used the IP addresses solely for modeling IoT networks as graphs and not as features in our study because in general, IP addresses are excluded in machine learning methods, as they do not provide meaningful or significant information for model training, GNN techniques provide a powerful framework for capturing the intricate interactions and dependencies within network data. This approach enables high-dimensional feature extraction from packet-level details, facilitating both binary classification to detect the presence of attacks and multi-class classification to identify specific attack types, and mainly address these challenges:

- **Detecting and analyzing complex, dynamic, and distributed cyber-attacks:**
  Graph Neural Networks provide unique advantages for detecting attacks in IoT Systems by analyzing network packets. Unlike traditional machine learning methods, GNNs effectively model the complex relationships between network entities (nodes and edges) by leveraging the inherent graph structure of Iot. They excel in detecting distributed attacks (e.g., DDoS), propagated anomalies (e.g., malware), and abnormal behaviors by capturing spatial and temporal dependencies. GNNs also handle heterogeneous and partially labeled data, improving detection in dynamic network environments. However, their computational cost and vulnerability to adversarial attacks require optimizations to ensure scalability and robustness.
- **Imbalanced Data:** A major challenge in attack detection is the imbalanced data, collected from normal and abnormal behavior traffic in IoTenvironments. In fact, attacks are often rare events compared to normal operational states. The imbalance data leads to biases in machine learning training and evaluation, where trained models tend to favor the majority class (normal behavior) and perform poorly in detecting rare attack instances. As a result, the detection of new or sophisticated attacks become a challenge, as machine learning models at inference time fail to recognize less frequent attack patterns.

Hence, addressing these challenges requires novel techniques that can effectively consider the graph-based structure of IoT systems, manage imbalanced datasets, incorporate domain knowledge, and ensure that detection systems are lightweight yet accurate enough to function in real-world IoT environments.

2 Related Work on Attack Detection

Several studies have explored the use of machine learning algorithms to detect cyber attacks in IoT environments. For instance, authors in [5] propose a distributed detection system based on machine learning techniques to detect and mitigate attacks in IoT systems. Unlike the widely-used NSL-KDD or KDD-CUP99 datasets [2], which are outdated and lack new attack types, the study utilizes the ToN-IoT dataset, which is derived from a large-scale, diverse IoT network. The dataset encompasses data from all layers of the IoT system cloud, fog, and edge. The Chi2 technique was used for feature selection, reducing the dataset to 20 features and evaluates various ML algorithms in both binary and multi-class classification tasks, concluding that the XGBoost approach outperforms others for each node in the model. In addition, authors in [14] introduce a specialized method for detecting Denial of Service attacks in IoT networks. This method models the network as a graph, where each IoT device is represented as a node and each connection between devices as an edge. The weight of an edge reflects the frequency of communications between two nodes. To extract meaningful features, the authors apply node2vec transformation, Moreover, a graph embedding algorithm introduced in [6], which generates vector representations that capture key network characteristics, Additionally, GNN is used in [10] where they proposed a novel data modeling approach that leverages a heterogeneous graph structure with Express Edges to improve the attack detection capabilities of machine learning models and introduce the first comprehensive performance benchmark of various heterogeneous graph neural network algorithm variants, evaluated across multiple network intrusion detection system datasets. The primary objective is to support CPS/IoT defenders in achieving superior attack detection effectiveness against evolving cyber attacks.

Furthermore, we find Graph-based techniques [17] enabling anomaly detection by identifying nodes or edges that deviate from the expected behavior of a graph. These methods can effectively detect a range of cybersecurity threats, such as fraud, malware incursions, and network attacks. However, certain areas warrant further exploration, such as employing graph-based algorithms to pre-filter alerts from firewalls and other cybersecurity systems. Such advancements could drastically reduce the workload for security analysts and strengthen the overall security framework.

In some other works like in [16], they compare three Deep learning algorithms which excel over classical machine learning in automatically extracting patterns and representations from raw data, making them highly suitable for detecting complex attacks. This study compares the performance of three deep learning models, Convolutional Neural Networks, Deep Neural Networks, and Recurrent Neural Networks in IDS implementations using three datasets (NF-UNSW-NB15, NF-BoT-IoT, and NF-ToN-IoT). In [3], they introduced sine and cosine component cyclic encoding for temporal attributes and addressed data imbalance by combining the Synthetic Minority Over-sampling Technique (SMOTE) for oversampling with an improved version of the Tomek link removal technique for under-sampling using various machine learning and deep learning models. However, authors in [1] highlight the advantages of reinforcement learning (RL) based intrusion detection systems in addressing complex challenges, such as feature selection and resource constraints, which traditional machine learning methods struggle to solve. It compares RL with classical machine learning approaches, including support-vector machines, and convolutional neural networks, using datasets like KDD Cup99 and ISCX 2012. The methodology involves data exploration, model training, and evaluation, with a focus on the dueling double deep Q-networks architecture for RL. Findings reveal that RL, which learns through interactions with a stochastic environment, outperforms supervised learning methods that rely on historical data and suffer from model drift and limited generalization. Finally, authors in [13] propose a risk management framework to secure IoT applications in smart infrastructures during both design and runtime. At the design phase, a tailored risk management method is introduced, while the runtime phase leverages Anomaly Behavior Analysis (ABA) enabled by the Autonomic Computing paradigm and an intrusion detection system to identify and mitigate threats. Preliminary results demonstrate the framework's effectiveness in detecting threats and safeguarding IoT environments and services.

We propose our GNN-based attack detection as unified deep learning model capable of handling both binary and multi-class classification tasks with optimal performance, eliminating the need for separate models as in traditional machine learning approaches by using graph modeling for edge classification task.

3 Methodology

Before presenting the architecture of the Graph Neural Network employed in our study, we first examine the datasets used for training and evaluation, along with the preprocessing steps implemented to ensure data quality and consistency. Following this, we detail the procedure for constructing graphs from tabular data, explaining how nodes and edges are defined based on the intrinsic relationships between data points. This rigorous data structuring is essential for enabling effective learning with graph-based models.

3.1 Data Processing

To ensure consistency and improve the quality of the selected datasets, we employ several preprocessing techniques. For numerical values, Min-Max normalization was applied to scale features to a bounded range of values, typically [0,1], preserving the relationships between the data points while eliminating potential issues caused by differing scales. This step was crucial to ensure that features with larger ranges did not dominate those with smaller ranges during subsequent analysis.

For categorical values, we utilized the one-hot encoding technique. This approach transforms categorical variables into binary vectors, where each unique category is represented as a separate dimension. By applying one-hot encoding, we were able to incorporate categorical data into our models without imposing any ordinal relationships among the categories.

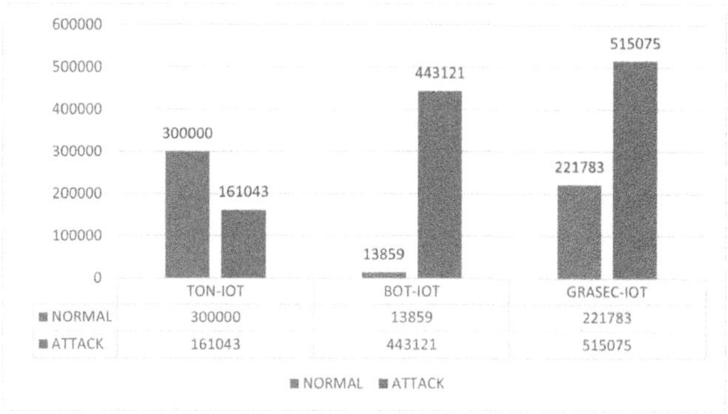

Fig. 1. Flow distribution by type (Normal/Attack)

Ensuring that both numerical and categorical features were effectively prepared for analysis and modeling, these preprocessing steps were applied to the various datasets Fig. 1:

- **ToN-IoT** : is a comprehensive cybersecurity dataset designed for evaluating machine learning models in detecting attacks within IoT environments [12]. Simulating a realistic telecommunications infrastructure, it includes network traffic data, telemetry from IoT sensors, and operating system logs from various connected devices. Each record in the dataset is labeled as normal or malicious, covering a range of cyber attacks such as DoS, DDoS, malware injection, and ransomware attacks.
- **Nf-BoT-IoT** : The original dataset was created at the Cyber Range Lab of UNSW Canberra to simulate a realistic network environment [9] comprising both legitimate and malicious IoT network traffic. It includes various attack types such as Denial of Service, reconnaissance, and information theft.
- **Grasec-IoT** : The dataset is a curated resource for cybersecurity research, focusing on detecting attacks in IoT network environments [8] captured from emulated IoT network. It includes network traffic data represented as graphs that illustrate device interactions, service relationships, and communication patterns. Each graph provides a snapshot of the network activity within a specific timeframe, allowing detailed analysis of attack behaviors. Dataset

features with various attack scenarios are initiated by a botnet of virtual machines controlled via a Kali virtual machine simulating attacks such as HTTP GET and POST floods, ICMP and TCP SYN floods, UDP floods, port scanning, and brute force attacks enabling researchers to evaluate and benchmark detection algorithms in realistic IoT environments.

3.2 Graph Construction

To analyze network traffic and understand the communication patterns between devices within the network, we constructed a graph-based representation using the captured packet data to perform the task of graph's edge classification. In this graph, we used a sliding window approach to traverse the rows of a dataset in order to construct graphs where the nodes represent IP addresses vectors which will be updated within the GNN architecture to obtain a real structure embedding describing the node without dependence on the ip address value which is common practice in machine learning to exclude source and destination IP addresses during training to avoid the creation of dummy classifiers that rely solely on these easily identifiable features, and the edges indicate the presence of communication between the source and destination. Additionally, a feature vector is associated with each edge, containing comprehensive information about the packets and communications exchanged between the corresponding source and destination such as the protocol used (e.g., TCP, UDP, IoT protocols,..), specific flags present in the packet headers (e.g., SYN, ACK, FIN), the size of the data payload, and the timestamp of the communication. This representation provides a structured and detailed view of network interactions, enabling advanced analyses such as attack detection, traffic classification, and visualization of communication patterns. By incorporating edge features, the graph captures the contextual details of each interaction, offering deeper insights into the behavior and dynamics of the network.

We can also justify our choice by: the IP address's position in the graph and its connections provide context. For instance, a source IP frequently communicating with a large number of destinations might indicate scanning behavior. In addition to that, destination IP under high traffic from many source IPs could indicate a DDoS attack as its shown in the Fig. 2 and discussed in [15] where ML models can inadvertently learn highly specific flow-level features (e.g., average packet size) that are strongly correlated with certain attack signatures. However, this reliance on narrow feature correlations renders them susceptible to evasion through minor adversarial modifications such as variations in packet lengths, inter-arrival times, or port numbers a common tactic employed by attackers.

3.3 GNN-Based Architecture for Attack Detection

The proposed GNN-based neural architecture in Fig. 3 is a graph neural network designed for edge classification tasks in complex graphs. It applies GraphSAGE layer [7] for effective node feature aggregation of one hop to avoid the

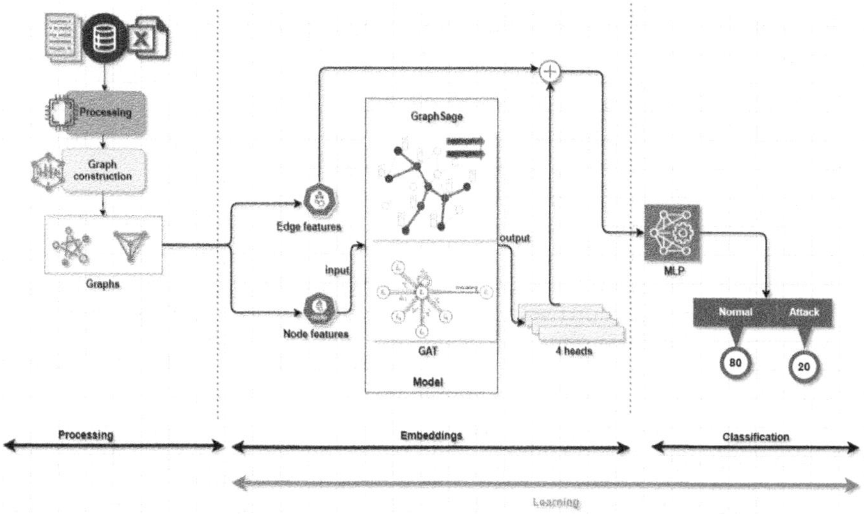

Fig. 2. Graph-based representation of well-known attacks from [15]

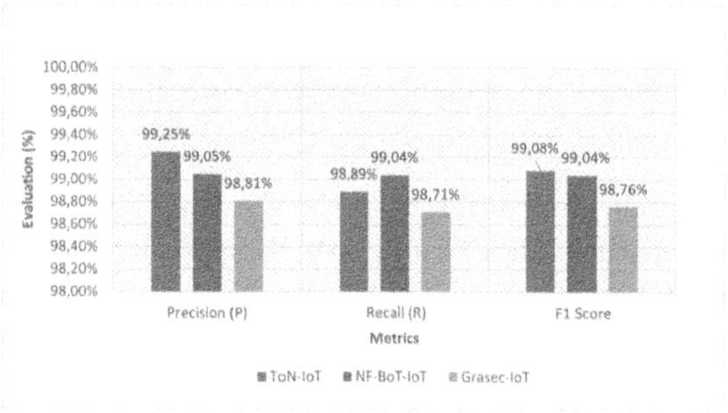

Fig. 3. GNN-based attack detection model

over-smoothing of embeddings, the different steps of GNN are described in the Algorithm 1.

For a node v within the layer k, the embedding Graphsage of $h_v^{(k)}$ is updated:

$$h_v^{(k)} = \sigma\left(W^{(k)} \cdot \text{CONCAT}\left(h_v^{(k-1)}, \text{AGGREGATE}^{(k)}\left(\{h_u^{(k-1)}, \forall u \in \mathcal{N}(v)\}\right)\right)\right)$$

- $\mathcal{N}(v)$: neighborhood of v.
- AGGREGATE : Function of aggregation (Mean, LSTM, or max-pooling).
- $W^{(k)}$: learning weights of the layer k.
- σ : activation function (ReLU, sigmoïde, etc.).

Algorithm 1: Edge Classification GNN with GraphSAGE and GAT

Input: $X \in \mathbb{R}^{N \times d_n}$: Node features ;
$E \in \mathbb{R}^{M \times d_e}$: Edge features ;
edge_index $\in \mathbb{R}^{2 \times M}$: Edge connections ;
dh $\in \mathbb{R}$: the number of neurons in the hidden layer;
Output: Edge predictions $\hat{y} \in [0, 1]^M$
Model Architecture:
- conv1 $\leftarrow$ SAGEConv(d_n, d_h)
- gat $\leftarrow$ GATConv(d_h, d_h, heads $= 4$, concat=True)
- edge_mlp $\leftarrow$ Sequential(Linear($8d_h + d_e, 2d_h$), ReLU(), Dropout($p = 0.1$), Linear($2d_h, d_h$), ReLU(), Linear(d_h, $num\_classes$))
Forward Pass:
begin

```
    x ← ReLU(conv1(X, edge_index));                  // First GraphSAGE layer
    x ← gat(x, edge_index);                          // 4-head GAT layer
    (src, dst) ← edge_index;                         // Edge endpoints
    edge_features ← concat(x[src], x[dst], E);       // Combine node and edge
     features
    logits ← edge_mlp(edge_features)
    return σ(logits);                                // Sigmoid or softmax output
```

end

After obtaining node embedding from the previous layer of GraphSAGE, the model processes them through a Graph Attention Network [19] with 4 heads to compute importance scores for neighboring nodes:

$$h_i' = \mathrm{CONCAT}_{k=1}^{K}\left(\sigma\left(\sum_{j \in \mathcal{N}(i)} \alpha_{ij}^k W^k h_j\right)\right)$$

The importance scores α_{ij} are than normalised by softmax :

$$\alpha_{ij} = \frac{\exp\left(\mathrm{LeakyReLU}\left(a^T[Wh_i \| Wh_j]\right)\right)}{\sum_{k \in \mathcal{N}(i)} \exp\left(\mathrm{LeakyReLU}\left(a^T[Wh_i \| Wh_k]\right)\right)}$$

- W: Shared weight matrix for linear transformation.
- a: Attention weight vector.
- $\|$: Concatenation operation.
- LeakyReLU: Activation function (typically with slope of 0.2 for negative inputs).

We hypothesize that augmenting our model with Graph Attention Networks will enable discriminative weighting of neighbor nodes through learned attention scores, thereby improving differentiation between attack types (e.g., DDoS vs. port scanning) based on their distinct topological signatures:

- DDoS attacks (uniform attention to many neighbors)
- Port scanning (focused attention on sequential ports)
- Brute force (repeated attention to same service)

For edge classification, the GNN-based model constructs edge features by concatenating embeddings of source and target nodes with edge-specific attributes. These features are passed through a multi-layer perceptron with ReLU activations and dropout layers [18] to enhance generalization and robustness. The proposed GNN-based model is trained using a weighted Cross Entropy Loss to address class imbalance, ensuring accurate classification across diverse edge classes. Additionally, the architecture benefits from careful weight initialization Xavier and optimization using the Adam optimizer, making it well-suited for real-world applications requiring reliable edge classification in graph-structured data.

The model is trained with an NVIDIA RTX 6000 Ada Generation GPU with a total memory capacity of 49 GB using pytorch geometric to implement the differents layer of GNN and MLP of classification with learning rate of 5.00E−03 and Batch size of 32 graphs for 50 epochs and dropout factor of 0.1 and finally, the window size of 10000 flows for constructing the graphs as mentioned in Table 1.

Table 1. Hyper-parameter settings

Hyper-parameters	**Values**
Learning rate	5.00E-03
Batch size	32
Epochs	50
Dropout factor	0.1
Window Size	10000

3.4 Evaluation Metrics

To evaluate the performance of our model, we use the metrics **Precision**, **Recall**, and **F1-Score** ,**FPR** and the ROC-AUC curve, which are commonly employed in classification tasks. These metrics are defined as follows:

$$\text{Precision} = \frac{\text{True Positives (TP)}}{\text{True Positives (TP)} + \text{False Positives (FP)}} \tag{1}$$

A higher precision indicates fewer false positive predictions.

$$\text{Recall} = \frac{\text{True Positives (TP)}}{\text{True Positives (TP)} + \text{False Negatives (FN)}} \tag{2}$$

A higher recall indicates that more actual positive cases are captured.

The F1-Score is the harmonic mean of Precision and Recall. It provides a balance between these two metrics and is especially useful when the class distribution is imbalanced. The F1-Score is defined as:

$$\text{F1-Score} = 2 \cdot \frac{\text{Precision} \cdot \text{Recall}}{\text{Precision} + \text{Recall}} \tag{3}$$

The False Positive Rate (FPR) measures the proportion of normal (benign) instances that are incorrectly classified as attacks. A lower FPR indicates better performance, as it means the model is making fewer incorrect alerts

$$\text{False Positive Rate (FPR)} = \frac{\text{False Positives (FP)}}{\text{False Positives (FP)} + \text{True Negatives (TN)}} \tag{4}$$

The AUC-ROC value ranges from 0 to 1, where a value of 1 indicates perfect separation between the classes, and a value of 0.5 represents random guessing. These metrics collectively provide a comprehensive view of the model's performance, balancing the trade-offs between precision and recall.

4 Experiments and Results

In our work, we divided the dataset into three subsets using a 70-20-10 split. Specifically, 70% of the data was allocated for training the model, 10% was used for validation to tune hyperparameters and prevent overfitting, and the remaining 20% was reserved for testing to evaluate the final performance of the model. This division ensures a balanced approach, providing sufficient data for

Table 2. Performance Comparison With and Without GAT in ToN-IoT dataset

	With GAT		Without GAT	
	FPR	F1	FPR	F1
Backdoor	0.05%	99.76%	0.18%	99%
Ddos	0.28%	96.62%	0.46%	95.45%
Dos	0.47%	96.56%	0.22%	97%
Injection	0.68%	80.30%	4.62%	78.10%
Mitm	0.61%	96.54%	0.67%	95.82%
Normal	0.02%	99.26%	0.05%	99%
Password	2.66%	87.31%	0.43%	74.64%
Ransomware	0.12%	99.02%	0.19%	98.24%
Scanning	0.23%	97.68%	0.35%	96.47%
XSS	0.56%	94.91%	0.94%	92.47%
Average	**0.59%**	**95%**	0.81%	92.62%

Table 3. Performance Comparison With and Without GAT in Grasec-IoT dataset

	With GAT		Without GAT	
	FPR	F1	FPR	F1
Http get flood	0.89%	96.74%	1.96%	97.20%
Icmp frag flood	0%	99.64%	0.33%	98.99%
Tcp flood	0.32%	83.88%	12.93%	66%
Udp flood	1.73%	88.50%	0.05%	0.19%
Port scan	0.04%	92.90%	0.03%	92.81%
Brute force	0.12%	97.17%	0.34%	97.41%
Normal	2.19%	97.43%	2.37%	97.64%
Average	**0.70%**	**93.75%**	2.57%	78.60%

Table 4. Performance Comparison With and Without GAT in Nf-BoT-IoT dataset

	With GAT		Without GAT	
	FPR	F1	FPR	F1
Reconaissance	2.88%	94.86%	3.46%	95.18%
Benign	1.55%	63.32%	0.97%	67.19%
Ddos	6.57%	87.54%	6.61%	87.46%
Theft	0.28%	58.05%	0.28%	57.44%
Average	**2.82%**	**93%**	2.83%	92.62%

training while maintaining separate validation and test sets to assess the model's generalization ability accurately.

The hypothesis of the Sect. 3.3 about adding attention mechanism to our GNN model was validated through our experiments, as shown in the three results Tables 2, 3 and Table 4. The integration of Graph Attention Networks (GAT) led to noticeable improvements in classification performance, confirming that the attention mechanism effectively assigns discriminative weights to neighboring nodes. Particularly confirmed in Table 2 and Table 4, where we observed a clear improvement in classification between DDoS and scanning attacks in terms of F1-score, and FPR of btute force from 0.34% to 0.12% in Table 3, along with a reduction in the false positive rate (FPR), This enhancement allowed the model to better distinguish between attack types, which exhibit different topological patterns in the network structure.

The results in Fig. 4 and Fig. 5 demonstrate that the proposed GNN-based attack detection model consistently performs well in both binary and multi-class classification across all datasets, particularly excelling in multi-class classification on Grasec-IoT and binary classification on Nf-Bot-Iot.

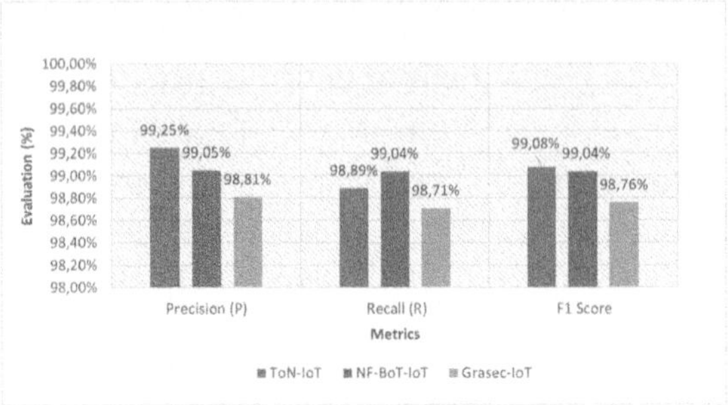

Fig. 4. Binary classification results

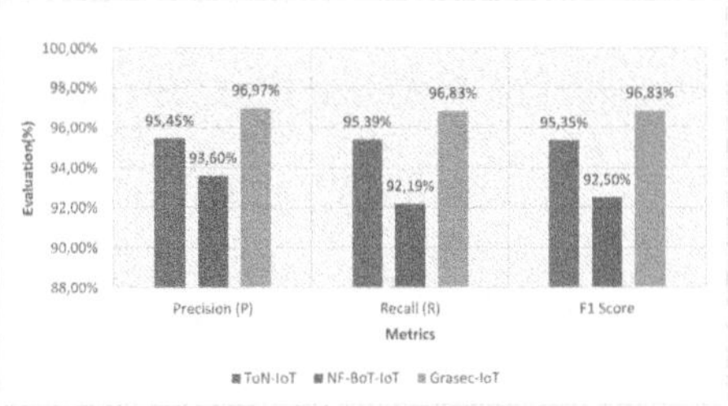

Fig. 5. Multi-class classification result

5 Discussion

As evidenced by the evaluation ROC-AUC curve in Fig. 6, Fig. 7 and Fig. 8, the proposed model demonstrates effective discriminative capabilities between attack classes and normal traffic flows. While the ROC AUC scores consistently exceed 0.5 (surpassing random chance), the model maintains robust overall performance with a strong macro F1-score of 98% at least across the different datasets in binary classification and 92.5% for multi class classification.

Table 5 provides a comparative analysis of different works based on their F-1 scores for both binary and multi-class classification tasks. The models are trained and evaluated on Ton-IoT, Nf-Bot-IoT, and Grasec-IoT datasets.

Our proposed model achieves the highest F1-score across all datasets in binary classification:

- **Ton-IoT:** The GNN-based attack detection model reaches **99.08%**, surpassing the previous best 98.70% by [5]. It also significantly outperforms [3] with oversampling (90.09%).
- **Nf-Bot-IoT:** Our GNN-based attack detection model achieves **99.04%**, which is **24.34% higher** than [10] (74.70%).
- **Grasec-IoT:** Our GNN-based attack detection model achieves **98.76%**, providing the first reported results on this dataset.

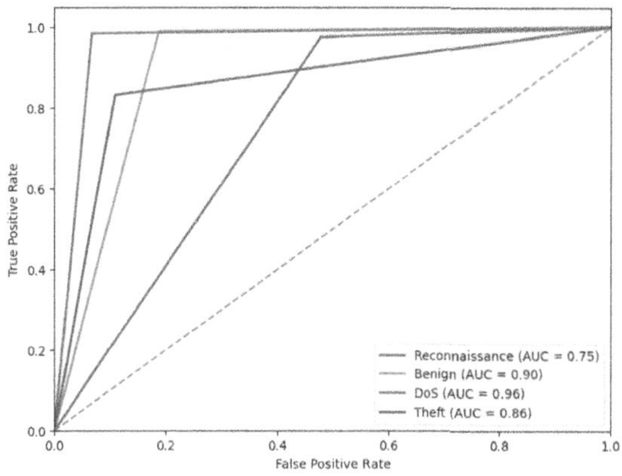

Fig. 6. The curve ROC-AUC for Nf-Bot-IoT in multi class classification

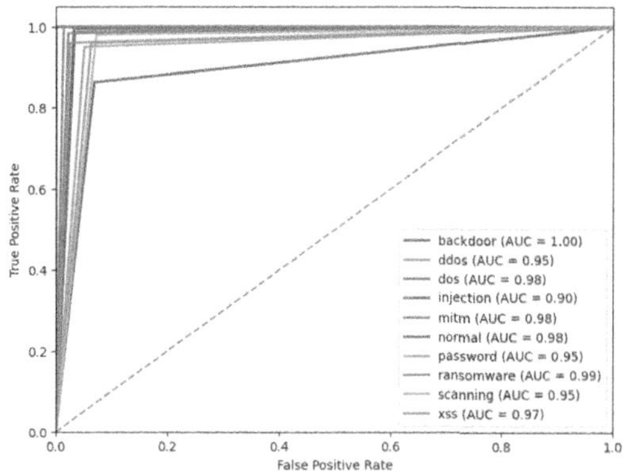

Fig. 7. The curve ROC-AUC for Ton-IoT in multi class classification

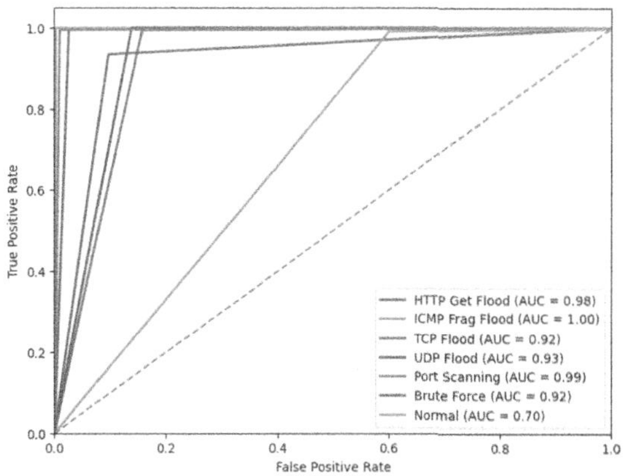

Fig. 8. The curve ROC-AUC for Grasec-IoT in multi class classification

Furthermore, our GNN-based attack detection model demonstrates superior performance in multi-class classification:

- **Ton-IoT:** When applying the SMOTE oversampling technique in conjunction with Tomek-link under-sampling, the performance improves further, achieving a score of 98.57%, significantly surpassing other algorithms. This enhancement can be attributed to the relatively high dimensionality and complexity of the network dataset in multi-class classification. Moreover, our F1-score of 95.35% exceeds the previous benchmark of 94.9% reported by [5], thanks to the integration of cross-validation and the SMOTE oversampling method [4].
- **Nf-Bot-IoT:** Our GNN-based attack detection model achieves **92.5%**, outperforming the other work by **10.5%**.
- **Grasec-IoT:** We achieve **96.14%**, with no prior results available for comparison.

Table 5. Comparative table with the F1-score metric

	Binary Classification			Multi-class classification		
Works	Ton-IoT	Nf-Bot-IoT	Grasec-IoT	Ton-IoT	Nf-Bot-IoT	Grasec-IoT
[16]	95%	98%	-	61%	82%	-
[10]	97.78%	74.70%	-	-	-	-
[3] + oversampling	90.09%(DNN)	-	-	**98.57%** (CNN)	-	-
[5]	98.70%	-	-	94.9%	-	-
[11]	98.91%	97%	-	87%	81%	-
Our study	**99.08%**	**99.04%**	**98.76%**	95.35%	**92.5%**	**96.14%**

Our work advances the state of the art in several key aspects. Unlike traditional methods, our graph construction uses a generalized modeling approach that is independent of IP addresses, making it adaptable to diverse network environments. For the model architecture, we combine GraphSAGE (for neighborhood aggregation), GAT (for attention-based node relationships), and an MLP (for final classification), enhancing feature learning. Additionally, we introduce novel structural embeddings that capture topological patterns and dynamic behaviors, significantly improving attack detection accuracy. We also contribute new IoT datasets, addressing the lack of realistic benchmarks in this domain. Experiments show that our model maintains consistent performance across different datasets and outperforms existing methods, proving its robustness in detecting sophisticated attacks.

6 Conclusion and Future Work

In this paper, we explored the increasing connectivity challenges in IoT networks, highlighting their vulnerabilities to cyber-threats and attacks. To address these security challenges, we leverage Graph Neural Networks for attack detection, utilizing benchmark datasets to enable both binary and multi-class classification of attacks. We also elaborated a comprehensive review of traditional attack detection methods, including classical machine learning and deep learning techniques, where we identified key limitations such as difficulties in handling multi-class attacks, data imbalance, and lack of graph-based insights. We proposed a novel GNN-based neural architecture and graph construction technique for attack detection. Through extensive experimentation, we evaluated the performance of our GNN-based models against traditional models and demonstrate their outperformance in both binary and multi-class classifications. The experimental results underscore the potential of GNNs in enhancing cybersecurity by capturing intricate network relationships and attack patterns, making them a promising direction for future IoT and CPS security solutions. Future work will focus on investigating alternative embedding techniques for node representation to further improve classification performance. Moreover, we plan to expand our datasets by incorporating a diverse range of industrial and IoT protocols, thereby facilitating a more comprehensive analysis of network behavior. Finally, we will optimize the temporal window size to achieve a trade-off between rapid detection (small windows) and contextual awareness (large windows), ensuring both responsiveness to immediate attacks and comprehensive attack pattern analysis.

Acknowledgments. This work is supported by the French National Research Agency (ANR) as part of the GNADIS project ANR-23-IAS4-0002. The authors would like to express their sincere gratitude to their supervisors and the entire research team for their valuable guidance, support, and collaboration throughout this project.

Disclosure of Interests. The authors declare that they have no known competing financial interests or personal relationships that could have appeared to influence the work reported in this paper.

References

1. Badr, Y.: Enabling intrusion detection systems with dueling double deep q-learning. Digit. Transf. Soc. **1**(1), 115–141 (2022)
2. Bala, R., Nagpal, R.: A review on KDD cup99 and NSL NSL-KDD DATASET. Int. J. Adv. Res. Comput. Sci. **10**(2) (2019)
3. Cao, Z., Zhao, Z., Shang, W., Ai, S., Shen, S.: Using the ton-IoT dataset to develop a new intrusion detection system for industrial IoT devices. Multimedia Tools Appl. 1–29 (2024)
4. Chawla, N.V., Bowyer, K.W., Hall, L.O., Kegelmeyer, W.P.: Smote: synthetic minority over-sampling technique. J. Artif. Intell. Res. **16**, 321–357 (2002)
5. Gad, A.R., Haggag, M., Nashat, A.A., Barakat, T.M.: A distributed intrusion detection system using machine learning for IoT based on ton-IoT dataset. Int. J. Adv. Comput. Sci. Appl. **13**(6) (2022)
6. Grover, A., Leskovec, J.: node2vec: Scalable feature learning for networks. In: Proceedings of the 22nd ACM SIGKDD International Conference on Knowledge Discovery and Data Mining, pp. 855–864 (2016)

7. Hamilton, W., Ying, Z., Leskovec, J.: Inductive representation learning on large graphs. In: Advances in Neural Information Processing Systems, vol. 30 (2017)
8. Hamouche, D., Kadri, R., Messai, M.L., Seba, H.: (Poster) a graph dataset for security enforcement in IoT networks: Grasec-iot. In: 2024 20th International Conference on Distributed Computing in Smart Systems and the Internet of Things (DCOSS-IoT), pp. 765–767. IEEE (2024)
9. Koroniotis, N., Moustafa, N., Sitnikova, E., Turnbull, B.: Towards the development of realistic botnet dataset in the internet of things for network forensic analytics: Bot-IoT dataset. Futur. Gener. Comput. Syst. **100**, 779–796 (2019)
10. Li, H., Chasaki, D.: Heterogeneous GNN with express edges for intrusion detection in cyber-physical systems. In: 2024 International Conference on Computing, Networking and Communications (ICNC), pp. 523–529. IEEE (2024)
11. Lo, W.W., Layeghy, S., Sarhan, M., Gallagher, M., Portmann, M.: E-graphsage: a graph neural network based intrusion detection system for IoT. In: NOMS 2022-2022 IEEE/IFIP Network Operations and Management Symposium, pp. 1–9. IEEE (2022)
12. Moustafa, N.: A new distributed architecture for evaluating AI-based security systems at the edge: Network ton_iot datasets. Sustain. Cities Soc. **72**, 102994 (2021)
13. Pacheco, J., Zhu, X., Badr, Y., Hariri, S.: Enabling risk management for smart infrastructures with an anomaly behavior analysis intrusion detection system. In: 2017 IEEE 2nd International Workshops on Foundations and Applications of Self* Systems (FAS* W), pp. 324–328. IEEE (2017)
14. Paudel, R., Muncy, T., Eberle, W.: Detecting dos attack in smart home IoT devices using a graph-based approach. In: 2019 IEEE International Conference on Big Data (Big Data), pp. 5249–5258. IEEE (2019)
15. Pujol-Perich, D., Suárez-Varela, J., Cabellos-Aparicio, A., Barlet-Ros, P.: Unveiling the potential of graph neural networks for robust intrusion detection. ACM SIGMETRICS Perform. Eval. Rev. **49**(4), 111–117 (2022)
16. Shaker, B.N., Al-Musawi, B.Q., Hassan, M.F.: A comparative study of ids-based deep learning models for IoT network. In: Proceedings of the 2023 International Conference on Advances in Artificial Intelligence and Applications, pp. 15–21 (2023)
17. Sozol, M.S., Saki, G.M., Rahman, M.M.: Anomaly detection in cybersecurity with graph-based approaches. Int. J. Sci. Res. Eng. Manag. (IJSREM) **8**(8), 1–7 (2024)
18. Srivastava, N., Hinton, G., Krizhevsky, A., Sutskever, I., Salakhutdinov, R.: Dropout: a simple way to prevent neural networks from overfitting. J. Mach. Learn. Res. **15**(1), 1929–1958 (2014)
19. Veličković, P., Cucurull, G., Casanova, A., Romero, A., Lio, P., Bengio, Y.: Graph attention networks. arXiv preprint arXiv:1710.10903 (2017)
20. Yi, T., Chen, X., Zhu, Y., Ge, W., Han, Z.: Review on the application of deep learning in network attack detection. J. Netw. Comput. Appl. **212**, 103580 (2023)

Hyperparameter Optimization in Neuro-symbolic Unsupervised Graph Learning

Fernando Ares-Robledo[1,2(✉)], Helena Rifà-Pous[1,2(✉)], and Robert Clarisó[1(✉)]

[1] Internet Interdisciplinary Institute (IN3), Universitat Oberta de Catalunya (UOC), Barcelona, Spain
{faresro,hrifa,rclariso}@uoc.edu
[2] Center for Cybersecurity Research of Catalonia (CYBERCAT), Barcelona, Spain

Abstract. Detecting network intrusions without labeled data remains challenging due to severe class imbalance, evolving traffic patterns, and computational complexity in realistic scenarios. To address these issues, we propose a fully unsupervised neuro-symbolic graph-learning pipeline that integrates symbolic reasoning into graph neural representations, enhancing interpretability and robustness. Our key contributions include a novel feature-selection strategy driven by unsupervised community graph detection, a memory-efficient line graph construction reduced via minimum-spanning trees, and a lightweight symbolic layer providing human-readable explanations of anomalies. Evaluations on IoTID20 and UNSW-NB15 benchmarks yield Matthews Correlation Coefficient (MCC) scores of 0.97 and 0.91, significantly surpassing recent unsupervised graph-based baselines demosntrating the practical viability and effectiveness of neuro-symbolic frameworks as an innovative and interpretable approach for unsupervised graph network intrusion detection.

Keywords: Unsupervised Graph Learning · Neuro-Symbolic · Anomaly Detection · Hyperparameter Optimization

1 Introduction

Intrusion detection remains one of the most pressing challenges in cybersecurity. As network threats evolve and novel attack vectors emerge continuously, traditional intrusion detection systems (IDS) struggle to keep pace. Signature-based and supervised learning–based IDS rely on labeled examples of every known attack; they therefore excel at recognizing threats seen during training but falter in the face of zero-day exploits or subtle variations of previously unseen attacks [11,20]. Defining "normal" behavior is itself a moving target, especially in resource-constrained Internet of Things (IoT) environments where traffic patterns shift over time and devices exhibit heterogeneous communication profiles

B. Coppens et al. (Eds.): ARES 2025 Workshops, LNCS 15997, pp. 275–292, 2025.
https://doi.org/10.1007/978-3-032-00639-4_16

[29]. High false-positive rates, limited temporal adaptability, and heavy dependence on large labeled datasets further impede the deployment of AI-driven anomaly detectors in production networks.

Unsupervised anomaly detection offers an attractive alternative by training exclusively on normal traffic and flagging deviations without ever seeing malicious examples during learning. One-class classifiers, autoencoders, and density-based methods have demonstrated the ability to uncover novel and stealthy threats purely from normal-traffic statistics [13]. Yet these methods typically treat each network flow or feature vector in isolation, discarding the rich topological and temporal context that might reveal coordinated or distributed attack campaigns. Moreover, their hyperparameters often require careful calibration to balance detection sensitivity against false alarms, especially under severe class imbalance.

Graph Neural Networks (GNNs) naturally address this gap by modeling hosts as nodes, flows as edges, and by propagating information along network-topology pathways. Early GNN-based IDS prototypes achieved encouraging gains in accuracy and robustness on benchmarks such as UNSW-NB15 and IoTID20 [7]. However, most of these graph-driven approaches remain either supervised or self-supervised, thus still relying on attack labels or pretext tasks that cannot fully eliminate the need for malicious examples. Furthermore, standard GNNs layers focus on node-level attributes, whereas in traffic analysis the most discriminative signals often reside in the edge features (*e.g.*, packet rates, round-trip times, protocol flags).

In this work we introduce a fully unsupervised, neuro-symbolic graph-learning pipeline for intrusion detection that requires no attack labels yet provides interpretable, temporally-aware anomaly detection, that does not export explicit embeddings. Our primary contributions include: (i) an unsupervised feature-selection strategy based on modularity-driven community detection in a feature-similarity graph; (ii) a lightweight temporal processing strategy that transforms each flow snapshot into a line-graph and extracts its Minimum Spanning Tree (MST), significantly reducing complexity while preserving key connectivity over time; (iii) integration of a symbolic reasoning module that generates human-readable explanations of anomalies through normalized deviations from statistical norms; and (iv) fusion of symbolic scores with neural embeddings learned by a Variational Graph Autoencoder (VGAE) to deliver a balanced binary anomaly verdict. To handle severe class imbalance prevalent in cyber-attack datasets, we systematically optimize all hyperparameters with Optuna, maximizing the MCC—a metric robust to highly skewed label distributions [10].

We implement and release our full pipeline at Github[1], and we demonstrate state-of-the-art balanced performance on IoTID20 and UNSW-NB15, achieving macro-F1 and MCC scores that surpass existing unsupervised GNN baselines.

The remainder of this paper is organised as follows. Section 2 surveys prior work on unsupervised graph-based intrusion detection. Section 3 describes

[1] https://github.com/Fernando-Ares-Robledo/Neuro-Symbolic-Unsupervised-Graph-Learning.

the proposed neuro-symbolic unsupervised graph-learning framework. Section 4 details the datasets, graph-construction procedure and Sect. 5 presents the empirical results, covering both computational performance and detection metrics. Finally, Sect. 6 concludes the paper and outlines directions for future research.

2 Related Work

Graph-based models for network intrusion detection have received considerable attention in recent years. Early work showed that a purely topology-based GNNs, which entirely ignores node and edge attributes, can detect botnets more accurately than classical techniques such as logistic regression and BotGrep when evaluated on mixed benign and botnet traffic graphs [28]. In a similar vein, encode network flow logs as graphs by treating IP–port pairs as nodes and learn node embeddings via random-walk methods (*e.g.*, DeepWalk, node2vec) to spot anomalies; while effective on known attacks, these transductive embeddings cannot generalize to previously unseen hosts or services [17]. Flow-based graph embeddings for anomaly detection have been also formulated and report strong detection rates, though likewise they inherit the generalization limits of transductive learning [25].

More recently, supervised GNNs approaches have advanced the state of the art on several standard NIDS benchmarks; extending GraphSAGE to incorporate rich edge features (flow statistics) in their E-GraphSAGE [16] model and demonstrate superior detection on both UNSW-NB15 and an IoT botnet dataset, significantly outperforming traditional ML baselines in accuracy and F1.

In parallel, unsupervised and self-supervised(the former relies purely on the data distribution, whereas the latter invents proxy tasks to pre-train models) methods seek to remove dependence on labeled attack data. Classical clustering approaches (DBSCAN, k-means) were first applied to KDD'99 and NSL-KDD, yielding high detection rates but often at the cost of high false positives [5, 22]. Sec2Graph, which constructs a "security object graph" from raw network events and applies a graph autoencoder to detect novel intrusions, achieving an F1 of 0.94 on CICIDS2017 without any attack labels [14]. While TreeCLUS [1] introduces a tree-based subspace clustering for fast, unsupervised anomaly detection on mixed-feature network traffic.

Anomal-E [6] is the first fully self-supervised GNN NIDS: it models each flow as an edge with statistical attributes, learns edge embeddings via a contrastive objective—that is, it maximises similarity between two augmented "positive" views of the same edge while minimising similarity to "negative" edges—through a Deep Graph Infomax loss, and it surpasses both classical anomaly detectors and supervised GNNs on UNSW-NB15 and CSE-CIC-IDS2018. EG-ConMix [24] builds on E-GraphSAGE, adding graph augmentations and the same contrastive mechanism to handle class imbalance in IoT intrusion data, leading to improved detection of rare attack types.

Neuro-symbolic frameworks generally combine neural learning modules—such as deep graph neural networks—with symbolic reasoning modules encoding explicit domain knowledge, logic constraints, or expert-defined rules. Recent emerging instances of such hybrid architectures aim to inject structured security knowledge directly into graph-based detection methods. An example is KnowGraph [27], which couples multiple GNNs predictors with a probabilistic logic module encoding security rules, yielding improved accuracy and interpretability on enterprise authentication logs and marketplace fraud graphs. Despite substantial gains in robustness and explainability obtained by aligning learned embeddings with human-readable rules, such hybrid neuro-symbolic systems remain relatively uncommon.

Outside cybersecurity, neuro-symbolic approaches in anomaly detection have shown promise in domains such as automotive diagnostics [2], predictive maintenance [12], and mechanical fault analysis [8]. In cybersecurity itself, hybrid schemes have been explored for program-synthesis reasoning over deep features [3] and malware analysis [21], yet they neither exploit the relational bias of graphs nor benchmark on IoT or enterprise IDS datasets. To our knowledge, the unification of unsupervised GNNss, line-MST graph transformations, and symbolic fuzzy-logic reasoning for intrusion detection remains entirely unexplored, motivating the framework presented in this paper.

Purely unsupervised graph-based IDS have begun to appear for realistic IoT and enterprise traffic. For example Carletti et al. [4] turns every timestamp into a graph, trains the DOMINANT autoencoder without labels, and reaches high macro-F1 and accuracy on more than 240000 IoT graphs. Topological Flow Analysis [9] maps NetFlow records to a single large flow graph, applies clustering plus an ensemble of outlier detectors, and cuts false negatives on UNSW-NB15 by exploiting graph structure.

A newer line keeps the evaluation label-free but adds self-supervised. STEG and Node2Vec-initialised E-GraphSAGE [30] enrich Edge GraphSAGE with wavelet scattering or skip-gram embeddings; on NetFlow benchmarks they deliver state-of-the-art macro-F1 and detection-rate scores.

In summary, existing unsupervised graph-based intrusion detection approaches still present notable limitations: insufficient modeling of temporal dynamics, dependence on significant data down-sampling due to computational complexity, limited interpretability of the detection outcomes, and lack of practical computational metrics such as runtime and memory consumption. Our work directly targets these shortcomings by explicitly incorporating timestamp modeling and symbolic reasoning for improved interpretability with a systematic hyperparameter optimization.

3 Neuro-symbolic Unsupervised Graph Framework

In this section, we introduce the neuro-symbolic pipeline: community-driven feature selection on the transposed similarity graph, followed—at each timestamp t—by line-graph MST sparsification and the fusion of symbolic reasoning with a VGAE neural module.

3.1 Feature Selection

We perform unsupervised feature selection on a tabular dataset $X \in \mathbb{R}^{n \times d}$, where n is the number of instances and d is the number of features, to identify informative attributes and reduce dimensionality.

We transpose X, mapping each feature to a node represented by a vector $x_i \in \mathbb{R}^n$, for $i = 1, \ldots, d$. A weighted, undirected graph $G = (V, E)$ is constructed, where the node set $V = \{v_i : i = 1, \ldots, d\}$ corresponds to the features, and the edge weights w_{ij} quantify the similarity between feature pairs x_i and x_j, i.e., $w_{ij} \equiv S(x_i, x_j)$, where $S(x_i, x_j)$ is the Pearson correlation coefficient.

Next, we apply the Clauset-Newman-Moore greedy modularity optimization algorithm to partition the graph into communities. This algorithm maximizes the modularity score Q, which measures the strength of the community structure relative to a random graph, as defined in Eq. 1:

$$Q = \frac{1}{2m} \sum_{i,j} \left(A_{ij} - \frac{k_i k_j}{2m} \right) \delta(c_i, c_j) \tag{1}$$

where $A_{ij} = w_{ij}$ is the adjacency matrix element, $k_i = \sum_j A_{ij}$ denotes the degree of node v_i, $m = \frac{1}{2} \sum_{i,j} A_{ij}$ is the total sum of edge weights, c_i represents the community assignment of node v_i, and $\delta(\cdot, \cdot)$ is the Kronecker delta function, equal to 1 if nodes v_i and v_j belong to the same community, and 0 otherwise.

From the resulting communities $\{C_1, \ldots, C_K\}$, the community with the highest mean degree centrality is selected, as it represents the most interconnected and thus most informative feature subset. The selected community C^* is determined by Eq. 2:

$$C^\star = \arg\max_{C_k} \frac{1}{|C_k|} \sum_{v_i \in C_k} k_i \tag{2}$$

The features corresponding to the nodes in $C^\star$ are retained for subsequent analysis, as expressed in Eq. 3:

$$\{x_i : v_i \in C^\star\} \subseteq \mathbb{R}^n \tag{3}$$

This feature selection process is illustrated in Fig. 1, which summarizes the transformation from the original tabular data to a graph structure, the application of the community detection algorithm, and the final feature selection step based on degree centrality.

3.2 Graph Construction and Transformation

After the feature selection process described in Subsect. 3.1, the next step involves converting the tabular data into structured graph representations. For each timestamp t, we construct a snapshot graph that represents network communications at that precise moment. This ensures that the temporal structure of the data is preserved, capturing the dynamic interactions within the network at each distinct point in time.

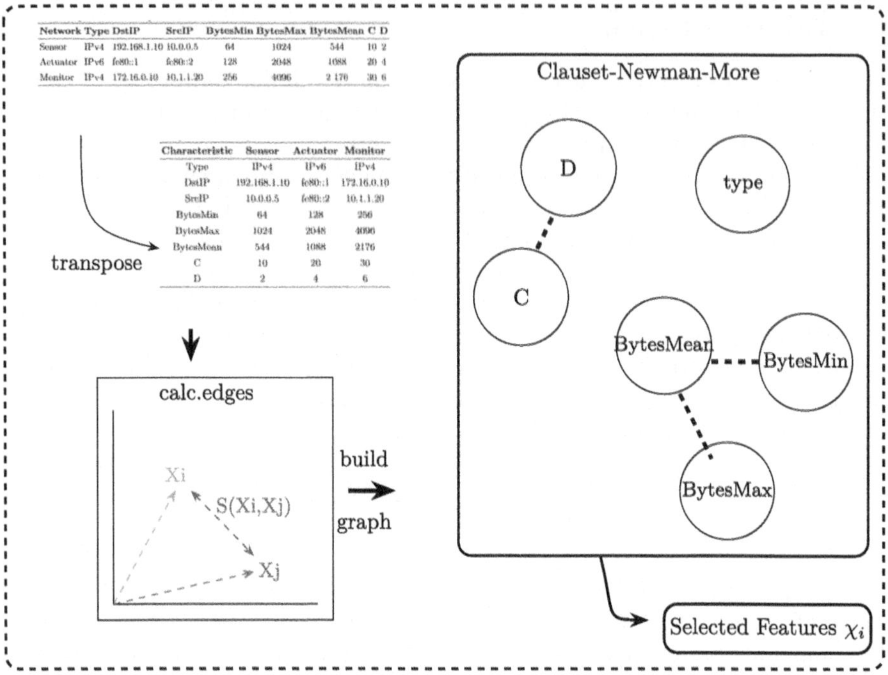

Fig. 1. Feature selection pipeline illustrating the initial transposition of the tabular dataset, construction of the graph, and the application of the modularity algorithm to detect communities. The most representative cluster of features is finally selected according to the mean degree centrality criterion.

Initially, for each timestamp t, a direct graph $G^{(t)}_{direct} = (V^{(t)}_{direct}, E^{(t)}_{direct})$ is constructed. In this graph, each node $v \in V^{(t)}_{direct}$ represents an IP address, and each edge $e \in E^{(t)}_{direct}$ corresponds to a communication between IPs, annotated with the previously selected feature values. However, analyzing such structures is cumbersome, as essential information resides primarily in edge attributes rather than nodes.

To facilitate node-centric analysis, a line transformation is applied to each direct graph $G^{(t)}_{direct}$. This transformation swaps the roles of nodes and edges as expressed in Eq. 4:

$$\begin{aligned} G^{(t)}_{line} &= (V^{(t)}_{line}, E^{(t)}_{line}) \\ \text{where} \quad V^{(t)}_{line} &= E^{(t)}_{direct}; \quad E^{(t)}_{line} = V^{(t)}_{direct} \end{aligned} \tag{4}$$

This transformation positions the previously edge-embedded attributes onto the nodes of $G^{(t)}_{line}$, simplifying subsequent computational tasks. Nevertheless, this line mapping significantly increases the number of edges, consequently amplifying computational complexity.

To mitigate this complexity, we extract a MST from the line graph. Specifically, we compute the MST $G^{(t)}_{MST} = (V^{(t)}_{line}, E^{(t)}_{MST})$ using Kruskal's algorithm, as defined by Eq. 5:

$$G^{(t)}_{MST} = \arg \min_{E^{(t)}_{MST} \subseteq E^{(t)}_{line}} \sum_{e \in E^{(t)}_{MST}} w(e), \tag{5}$$

subject to the constraint that the resulting graph remains connected. Here, $w(e)$ denotes the weight of edge e, computed as the Euclidean distance between normalized node feature vectors.

Features that identify specific entities, such as IP addresses, are removed, and the numerical data are normalized to guarantee uniform feature scales across the dataset. A visual summary illustrating this procedure, including the line transformation and subsequent MST extraction, is presented in the upper part of Fig. 2, which is discussed in the following section.

3.3 Symbolic Module

The symbolic module generates interpretable anomaly scores for each graph snapshot $G^{(t)}$ at timestamp t, enhancing the neural module's decisions with human-readable logic. For each snapshot, we extract d numerical descriptors $\{x_i^{(t)}\}_{i=1}^{d}$, such as mean edge weights or node degrees, summarizing the graph's structural and feature-based properties.

From the training set of normal graphs, we compute the mean μ_i and standard deviation σ_i for each descriptor i. The normalized deviation is calculated as defined in Eq. 6:

$$\Delta_i^{(t)} = \min\Big(1, \max\big(0, \tfrac{|x_i^{(t)} - \mu_i| - k\,\sigma_i}{\sigma_i}\big)\Big), \tag{6}$$

where $\Delta_i^{(t)} \in [0, 1]$ measures how far $x_i^{(t)}$ lies outside the interval $[\mu_i \pm k\,\sigma_i]$, with k as a tunable threshold.

In our fuzzy-logic aggregation, we set Eq. 7:

$$a_i = \Delta_i^{(t)}, \quad b_i = 1 - \Delta_i^{(t)}. \tag{7}$$

We interpret a_i as the fuzzy truth value "descriptor i is anomalous," and b_i as its complement. The probabilistic S-norm over the a_i is defined by the following Eq. 8:

$$S^{(t)}(G) = \bigvee_{i=1}^{d} a_i = 1 - \bigwedge_{i=1}^{d} (1 - a_i) = 1 - \prod_{i=1}^{d} b_i, \tag{8}$$

Here the product $\prod_i b_i$ is the fuzzy AND of the complements b_i, which ensures that if every $\Delta_i^{(t)}$ is small then $S^{(t)}$ remains small, otherwise $S^{(t)}$ rises toward 1.

Finally we threshold this fuzzy OR score to obtain a binary symbolic decision as Eq. 9:

$$y^{(t)}_{\text{sym}}(G) = \begin{cases} 1, & S^{(t)}(G) \geq \tau, \\ 0, & S^{(t)}(G) < \tau, \end{cases} \tag{9}$$

with τ tuning the operating point between normal and anomalous.

3.4 Neural Module

The neural module, shown on the right side of Fig. 2, leverages a VGAE to capture and reconstruct the structural patterns from the graph snapshots. It consists of three main components: an encoder, a latent variational embedding, and a decoder, along with an additional classification head for anomaly prediction.

Initially, the line graph obtained after MST step is fed into the encoder. Let $G = (\mathcal{V}, \mathcal{E})$ be a graph at time t, with the normalized adjacency matrix $A^{(t)} \in \mathbb{R}^{n \times n}$, and node feature matrix $X^{(t)} \in \mathbb{R}^{n \times d}$, including the symbolic descriptors $\Delta_i^{(t)}$ from the symbolic module.

The encoder is defined by a Graph Convolutional Networks (GCN), which propagates node features according to the graph structure as follows Eq. 10:

$$H^{(t)} = f_{\text{GCN}}\left(A^{(t)}, X^{(t)}\right) \tag{10}$$

where $H^{(t)} \in \mathbb{R}^{n \times h}$ represents the hidden node embeddings, and f_{GCN} applies multiple graph convolutional layers with activation functions such as ReLU.

These embeddings $H^{(t)}$ parameterize a latent Gaussian distribution via a variational latent layer, which estimates node-wise means $\mu^{(t)}$ (Eq. 11)and variances $\sigma^{2(t)}$ (Eq. 12):

$$\mu^{(t)} = W_\mu H^{(t)} + b_\mu, \tag{11}$$

$$\log(\sigma^{2(t)}) = W_\sigma H^{(t)} + b_\sigma \tag{12}$$

The latent representation $Z^{(t)} \in \mathbb{R}^{n \times z}$ is sampled via the reparameterization trick in Eq. 13:

$$Z^{(t)} = \mu^{(t)} + \epsilon \odot \sigma^{(t)}, \quad \epsilon \sim \mathcal{N}(0, I) \tag{13}$$

with $\odot$ denoting element-wise multiplication.

Subsequently, the decoder reconstructs the adjacency matrix from latent embeddings through the inner product (Eq. 14):

$$\hat{A}^{(t)} = \sigma\left(Z^{(t)} {Z^{(t)}}^\top\right) \tag{14}$$

where $\sigma(\cdot)$ is the sigmoid function. The reconstructed adjacency $\hat{A}^{(t)}$ measures how well the model captures the graph structure.

Additionally, we introduce a classification head to aggregate node-level information into a graph-level anomaly score (Eq. 15):

$$p^{(t)} = \sigma\left(W_{\text{cls}} \frac{1}{n} \sum_{i=1}^{n} Z_i^{(t)} + b_{\text{cls}}\right) \tag{15}$$

where $p^{(t)} \in [0, 1]$ denotes the neural-based anomaly probability for the entire graph snapshot.

Finally, we combine reconstruction loss, latent distribution regularization via the Kullback-Leibler divergence (KL), and the symbolic anomaly decision $y_{\text{sym}}^{(t)}$ in a unified training objective(Eq. 16):

$$\mathcal{L} = \underbrace{\mathcal{L}_{\text{rec}}(A^{(t)}, \hat{A}^{(t)})}_{\text{Reconstruction}} + \underbrace{\beta\, D_{\text{KL}}\left(q(Z^{(t)}|X^{(t)}, A^{(t)}) \| p(Z)\right)}_{\text{KL-divergence}} + \underbrace{\gamma\, \mathcal{L}_{\text{CE}}\left(p^{(t)}, y_{\text{sym}}^{(t)}\right)}_{\text{Symbolic alignment}} \tag{16}$$

where $\mathcal{L}_{\text{rec}}$ denotes binary cross-entropy for reconstruction, D_{KL} is the KL-divergence, and $\mathcal{L}_{\text{CE}}$ denotes binary cross-entropy between the neural prediction and the symbolic decision. Parameters β and γ control the relative importance of each component.

3.5 Hyperparameter Optimization

The neural-symbolic anomaly detection model relies on several critical hyperparameters, which significantly affect its overall performance. To systematically determine the optimal values of these parameters, we employed Bayesian optimization using Optuna, specifically leveraging the Tree-structured Parzen Estimator (TPE) sampler and an early stopping strategy. Additionally, the Median-Pruner was utilized for efficient pruning of unpromising trials, thus substantially reducing computational overhead.

Optimization was carried out by maximizing the MCC, which provides a balanced assessment of classification performance, especially important in imbalanced datasets. Early stopping was configured to terminate training when validation MCC improvements were below a minimal threshold over multiple epochs, thus avoiding unnecessary computational effort.

$$\text{MCC} = \frac{TP \times TN - FP \times FN}{\sqrt{(TP + FP)(TP + FN)(TN + FP)(TN + FN)}} \tag{17}$$

Equation 17 is the objective passed to the TPE sampler; at each epoch the validation score in Eq. 17 is reported to the `MedianPruner`, which prunes any run whose MCC falls below the running median of completed trials. The same criterion is also used by the early-stopping callback to halt training once the improvement in MCC becomes negligible, ensuring that the search concentrates only on promising hyper-parameter regions. Table 1 summarizes the hyperparameters optimized through this approach and their corresponding search spaces.

The selected hyperparameters were consistently validated on a held-out validation set, confirming their effectiveness in achieving robust detection performance across different scenarios.

4 Experimental Setup

To validate our neuro-symbolic framework, we employ the IoTID20 and UNSW-NB15 benchmarks because each trace provides per-flow source and destination

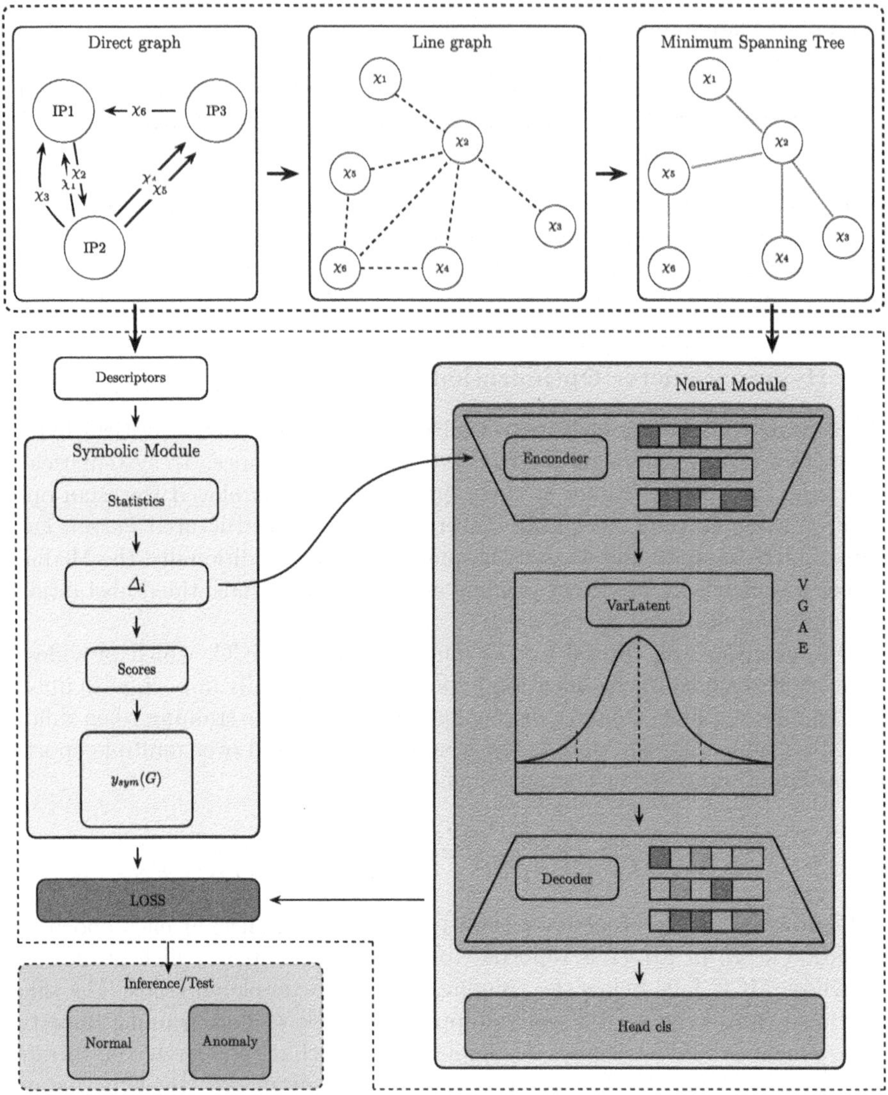

Fig. 2. Overall anomaly-detection pipeline. In the top row, a raw directed flow graph (left) is transformed into its line representation (middle) and then pruned to its MST (right). Below that, the symbolic module computes statistics over descriptors which produces the symbolic decision. Simultaneously, the neural module (right) ingests the tree graph plus the symbolic deviations into a VGAE: a encoder, a variational latent layer, and an inner-product decoder, culminating in a graph-level classification head. At test time (bottom), the head outputs a binary "Normal"/"Anomaly" decision.

Table 1. Optimized hyperparameters and their search spaces.

Hyperparameter	Search Space	Hyperparameter	Search Space
Hidden dimension (h_{dim})	[32, 128]	k-sigma (k)	[1.5, 3.0]
Latent dimension (z_{dim})	[16, 64]	Symbolic threshold (τ)	[0.1, 0.9]
Number of GCN layers	[2, 4]	KL divergence weight (β_{KL})	[0.01, 1.0]
Activation function	{ReLU, LeakyReLU, Tanh}	Symbolic alignment weight (γ_{CE})	[0.1, 1.0]
Dropout rate	[0.1, 0.5]	Reconstruction weight (λ_{rec})	[0.1, 0.9]
Learning rate (η)	[10^{-4}, 10^{-2}]	Latent weight (λ_{lat})	[0.1, 0.5]
Batch size	{8, 16, 32}	Fusion coefficient (η_{fuse})	[0.1, 1.0]

IPs, which lets us form communication graphs, and millisecond-level timestamps, which support temporal slicing; both datasets are well-established network-security datasets that span constrained IoT traffic and enterprise-grade flows, so they supply the structural and temporal diversity needed for a fair evaluation.

Prior to any processing, the IoTID20 [23] corpus contains 625783 flow records described by 86 attributes and annotated with five classes: Mirai, Scan, DoS, Normal, and MITM ARP Spoofing, spread over 4304 distinct timestamps. Mirai accounts for two-thirds of all flows, reflecting a highly unbalanced distribution in which a volumetric DDoS attack dominates; consequently, magnitude-based descriptors such as node degree or total bytes gain particular importance. Table 2 reports, for each class, both the instance count and the number of unique timestamps where it appears.

Table 2. Class distribution and unique timestamp counts in the raw IoTid20.

Class	# Instances	# Unique_Timestamps
Mirai	415677	1762
Scan	75265	962
DoS	59391	235
Normal	40073	298
MITM ARP Spoofing	35377	1047

The UNSW-NB15 dataset [18] comprises 2,540,047 records and 50 features collected across the timestamps. After aggregating flows by timestamp to build our dynamic graphs, the class labelled Normal becomes the majority, while among the attack categories Exploits is the most frequent. Table 3 details the per-class instance totals together with the corresponding counts of distinct timestamps.

All experiments were carried out on a single server whose compute environment comprised an Intel® Xeon® Silver 4314 CPU at 2.40 GHz with 32 physical cores and 237 GB of RAM under Linux. The software stack included Python 3.10, PyTorch 1.13 and Optuna 3.1.

Table 3. Class distribution and unique timestamp counts in the raw UNSW-NB15 dataset.

Class	# Instances	# Unique_Timestamps
Normal	215481	3283
Exploits	44525	10116
Fuzzers	24246	2898
DoS	16353	1416
Reconnaissance	13987	4725
Analysis	2677	65
Backdoor	1795	108
Shellcode	1511	583
Backdoors	534	14
Worms	174	41

5 Results

This section presents two complementary analyses, computational performance evaluating memory footprints and the evaluation metrics.

5.1 Computational Performance

To quantify the computational demands of our end-to-end workflow—from raw packet captures through feature selection, graph assembly, line-graph conversion, MST extraction, hyperparameter search, and final testing—we instrumented memory and time across all stages. Figure 3 shows how memory rises step-wise: feature selection adds roughly 1–2 GB, direct-graph construction lifts the footprint to about 3.5 GB, line-graph conversion peaks near 5.8 GB, and the MST step briefly touches 11.6 GB before settling at 7.6 GB for the remainder of the run. In total, the IoTID20 pipeline finishes in about two hours, whereas UNSW-NB15 requires slightly longer owing to its larger graph volume (see Table 4); each Optuna-trial epoch averages 9 ± 1 s.

Existing unsupervised graph-IDS studies seldom disclose concrete memory footprints; most merely list the accelerator employed, giving an implicit upper bound. For example, Xu et al., [26] trains on a 24 GB GeForce RTX4090 and still subsamples large NF-BoT-IoT graphs for feasibility; Liu et al. [15] reports an RTX3090 with 24 GiB VRAM and 16 GB system RAM for UNSW-NB15 and ToN-IoT experiments. Taken together, these references suggest that contemporary graph-based IDS rarely exceed the 24 GB GPU memory envelope, providing a practical upper bound against which our 11.6 GB peak can be interpreted.

Comparable timing information are rare in the unsupervised graph-IDS literature. The only study we located that reports concrete measurements is TS-IDS [19], which states a batch processing time of 0.8772s on NF-UNSW-NB15-v2 (batch size = 32;768). Although the units differ—batch versus epoch—our epoch time is in a similar order of magnitude, underscoring that the proposed workflow is computationally reasonable. The lack of additional published timings complicates rigorous benchmarking beyond this point.

Table 4. Stage-wise elapsed time for IoT Network Intrusion and UNSW-NB15 pipelines. Results are the mean of four complete runs.

Pipeline Stage	IoTID20 (min)	UNSW-NB15 (min)
Feature selection	1 ± 1	2 ± 1
Direct graph construction	0.8 ± 0.1	1.0 ± 0.1
Graph analysis	2 ± 2	2 ± 2
line-graph conversion	4 ± 1	6 ± 1
MST extraction	0.8 ± 0.1	2.9 ± 0.2
Hyperparameter optimization 40 trials	56 ± 5	78 ± 8
Final test	5.8 ± 0.2	7.0 ± 0.5

Although our measurements were obtained with 12GB of maximum memory, the same pipeline can be executed on a lower-memory machine by processing data in small batches and freeing unused buffers more frequently, at the expense of longer runtimes for memory-bound phases (notably the MST extraction). Conversely, overall throughput can be improved by retaining intermediate data structures for longer—reducing I/O and garbage-collection overhead—in exchange for higher transient memory usage.

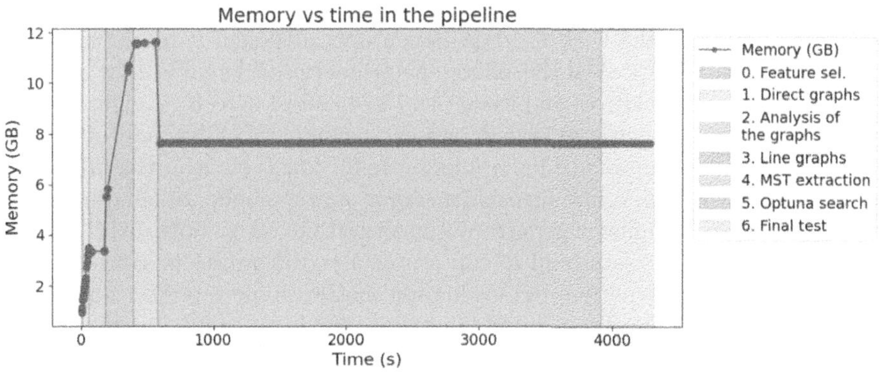

Fig. 3. Memory versus elapsed time across pipeline stages: (0) feature selection, (1) direct graph construction, (2) graph analysis, (3) line graphs, (4) MST extraction, (5) Optuna search (training), and (6) final testing.

5.2 Evaluation Metrics

Our neuro-symbolic graph approach achieves highly balanced detection on both the IoTID20 and UNSW-NB15 benchmarks, reaching (best trial of 40) an overall test-set MCC of 0.9661 and 0.9149, respectively (Table 5). The MCC is a correlation coefficient that ranges from −1 (total disagreement) through 0 (random guessing) to 1 (perfect prediction); values close to 1 therefore indicate that our method sustains precision and recall near unity for both normal and anomalous traffic, even under extreme class imbalance.

Table 5. Test-set classification performance on the IoT Network Intrusion and UNSW-NB15 datasets.

Class	IoTID20			UNSW-NB15		
	Precision	Recall	F_1	Precision	Recall	F_1
Normal	1.0000	0.9367	0.9673	0.9044	0.9413	0.9238
Anomaly	0.9965	1.0000	0.9982	1.0000	0.9981	1.0000
Accuracy	0.9967			0.9731		
Macro avg	0.9982	0.9684	0.9828	0.9522	0.9697	0.9619
Weighted avg	0.9967	0.9967	0.9966	0.9956	0.9928	0.9909
MCC	0.9661			0.9149		

Although this comparison (Table 5) shows our method's strong performance, a fully fair benchmarking against other unsupervised graph-based approaches is challenging. Table 6 collates the best numbers published for four recent systems that address network intrusion through graph analysis without labelled training data. We contrast our model with STEG [30] because it is the only work that injects a GNNs into the UNSW-NB15 flow graph, although it relies on a scattering transform. Irofti et al. [9] offers an unsupervised baseline that extracts hand-crafted egonet features and feeds them to classical detectors, giving a view of how far one can go without neural message passing. OC-GNN and Dominant [4] report node-level autoencoder results on IoTID20; both keep the full topology but ignore the temporal dimension and omit any symbolic explanation. None of these references applies a strictly unsupervised GNNs to both IoTID20 and UNSW-NB15 with the same end-to-end protocol, so differences in sampling, feature sets, graph construction and evaluation metrics limit a perfect one-to-one comparison. Within this fragmented landscape, our neuro-symbolic, time-aware pipeline attains higher macro-F_1 and accuracy on the two datasets while also providing memory-bounded processing and interpretable symbolic scores.

Table 6. Reported results from unsupervised graph-based methods on IoTID20 and UNSW-NB15, including our approach.

Reference	Dataset	Acc.	Macro-F_1	Precision
STEG [30]	UNSW-NB15	98.7%	92.3%	—
Irofti et al. [9]	UNSW-NB15	95.1%	—	—
OC-GNN [4]	IoT Network Intrusion	91.9%	—	91.5%
Dominant [4]	IoT Network Intrusion	90.2%	—	90.0%
Ours	IoT Network Intrusion	99.7%	98.3%	99.8%
Ours	UNSW-NB15	97.3%	96.8%	97.2%

5.3 Limitations

The present work operates at a coarse, graph–level granularity: for every timestamp we decide only whether the whole communication snapshot is normal or anomalous, leaving open the finer question of which hosts or flows are responsible for the deviation. This design choice simplifies training but hinders the drill–down capabilities that practitioners often need during incident handling. In addition, all public benchmarks used in our evaluation are strongly skewed, with the "Normal" class being a minority; although we mitigate the imbalance by optimising for MCC, the rarity of benign traffic constrains the realism of the scenario and may bias models and metrics alike.

6 Conclusions

Our work introduces a neuro-symbolic, fully unsupervised intrusion detection pipeline that uniquely combines community-driven unsupervised feature selection, temporally-aware line-graph construction, and symbolic reasoning with graph neural processing without relying on explicit embeddings. By integrating these novel strategies, our approach achieves high detection accuracy and balanced MCC scores on two widely-used benchmarks, highlighting how symbolic interpretability can complement neural performance. Nevertheless, public datasets, typically dominated by malicious activity, limit the direct transferability of these methods into real-world environments where normal traffic prevails. This underscores the importance—and current scarcity—of realistic evaluations for fully unsupervised, graph-based intrusion detection.

As ongoing research, we are extending our framework to dynamic, streaming scenarios. We aim to develop an adaptive mechanism that incrementally updates both symbolic rules and neural embeddings as traffic evolves, enabling real-time detection and immediate interpretability.

Acknowledgments. This work was supported by the Spanish Ministry of Science and Innovation through the projects PID2021-125962OB-C31 "SECURING" and PID2023-147592OB-I00 "SE4GenAI". Additional funding was provided by the ARTEMISA International Chair of Cybersecurity (C057/23) and the DANGER Strategic Project of

Cybersecurity (C062/23), both funded by the Spanish National Institute of Cybersecurity through the European Union NextGenerationEU and the Recovery, Transformation, and Resilience Plan.

Disclosure of Interests. The authors have no competing interests to declare that are relevant to the content of this article.

References

1. Bhuyan, M., Bhattacharyya, D., Kalita, J.: An effective unsupervised network anomaly detection method. J. Netw. Comput. Appl. **34**(1), 218–232 (2012)
2. Bohne, T., Windler, A.K.P., Atzmueller, M.: A neuro-symbolic approach for anomaly detection and complex fault diagnosis exemplified in the automotive domain. In: Venable, B., Garijo, D., Jalaian, B. (eds.) Proceedings of the 12th Knowledge Capture Conference 2023. International Conference on Knowledge Capture (K-Cap-2023), 5–7 December Pensacola, FL, United States. K-CAP '23, vol. 12, pp. 35–43. ACM, Association for Computing Machinery, New York, NY, USA (2023)
3. Burghouts, G.J., Hillerström, F., Walraven, E., van Bekkum, M., Ruis, F., Sijs, J.: Anomaly detection in an open world by a neuro-symbolic program on zero-shot symbols. In: IROS 2022 Workshop Probabilistic Robotics in the Age of Deep Learning (2022). https://openreview.net/forum?id=Bg3ZO3nXJuA
4. Carletti, V., Foggia, P., Rosa, F., Vento, M.: Enhancing IoT network security with graph neural networks for node anomaly detection. In: Torsello, A., Rossi, L., Cosmo, L., Minello, G. (eds.) Structural, Syntactic, and Statistical Pattern Recognition, pp. 41–51. Springer, Cham (2025)
5. Casas, P., Mazel, J., Owezarski, P.: Unsupervised network intrusion detection systems: detecting the unknown without knowledge. Comput. Commun. **35**(7), 772–783 (2012)
6. Caville, E., Lo, W.W., Layeghy, S., Portmann, M.: Anomal-E: a self-supervised network intrusion detection system based on graph neural networks. Knowl.-Based Syst. (2023). https://doi.org/10.1016/j.knosys.2023.110030
7. Duan, G., Lv, H., Wang, H., Feng, G.: Application of a dynamic line graph neural network for intrusion detection with semisupervised learning. IEEE Trans. Inf. Forensics Secur. **18**, 699–714 (2023). https://doi.org/10.1109/TIFS.2022.3228493
8. Himmelhuber, A., Dold, D., Grimm, S., Zillner, S., Runkler, T.: Detection, explanation and filtering of cyber attacks combining symbolic and sub-symbolic methods. In: 2022 IEEE Symposium Series on Computational Intelligence (SSCI), pp. 381–388. IEEE (2022). https://doi.org/10.1109/ssci51031.2022.10022249
9. Irofti, P., Pătraşcu, A., Hîji, A.I.: Unsupervised abnormal traffic detection through topological flow analysis (2022). https://arxiv.org/abs/2205.07109
10. Iturbe-Araya, J.I., Rifà-Pous, H.: Enhancing unsupervised anomaly-based cyberattacks detection in smart homes through hyperparameter optimization. Int. J. Inf. Secur. **24**, 45 (2025). https://doi.org/10.1007/s10207-024-00961-6
11. Kikissagbe, B.R., Adda, M.: Machine learning-based intrusion detection methods in IoT systems: a comprehensive review. Electronics **13**(18) (2024). https://doi.org/10.3390/electronics13183601

12. Klein, P., Malburg, L., Bergmann, R.: Combining informed data-driven anomaly detection with knowledge graphs for root cause analysis in predictive maintenance. Eng. Appl. Artif. Intell. **145**, 110152 (2025). https://doi.org/10.1016/j.engappai.2025.110152
13. Le, H.D., Park, M.: Enhancing multi-class attack detection in graph neural network through feature rearrangement. Electronics **13**(12) (2024). https://doi.org/10.3390/electronics13122404
14. Leichtnam, L., Totel, E., Prigent, N., Mé, L.: Sec2graph: network attack detection based on novelty detection on graph structured data. In: Maurice, C., Bilge, L., Stringhini, G., Neves, N. (eds.) DIMVA 2020. LNCS, vol. 12223, pp. 238–258. Springer, Cham (2020). https://doi.org/10.1007/978-3-030-52683-2_12
15. Liu, J., Guo, M.: DIGNN-A: real-time network intrusion detection with integrated neural networks based on dynamic graph. Comput. Mater. Continua **82**(1), 817–842 (2025). https://doi.org/10.32604/cmc.2024.057660
16. Lo, W.W., Layeghy, S., Sarhan, M., Gallagher, M., Portmann, M.: E-GraphSAGE: a graph neural network based intrusion detection system for IoT. In: Proceedings of IEEE/IFIP NOMS 2022, pp. 1–9 (2022). https://doi.org/10.1109/NOMS54207.2022.9789878
17. López-Martín, M., Carro, B., Arribas, J.I., Sánchez-Esguevillas, A.: Network intrusion detection with a novel hierarchy of distances between embeddings of hashed IP addresses. Knowl.-Based Syst. **219**, 106887 (2021)
18. Moustafa, N., Slay, J.: UNSW-NB15: a comprehensive data set for network intrusion detection systems (UNSW-NB15 network data set). In: 2015 Military Communications and Information Systems Conference (MilCIS), pp. 1–6 (2015). https://doi.org/10.1109/MilCIS.2015.7348942
19. Nguyen, H., Kashef, R.: TS-IDS: traffic-aware self-supervised learning for IoT network intrusion detection. Knowl.-Based Syst. **279**, 110966 (2023). https://doi.org/10.1016/j.knosys.2023.110966
20. Shirley, J.J., Priya, M.: An adaptive intrusion detection system for evolving IoT threats: an autoencoder-FNN fusion. IEEE Access **13**, 4201–4217 (2025). https://doi.org/10.1109/ACCESS.2024.3525074
21. Shroyer, A.: Deep Learning for Obfuscated Code Analysis. Indiana University (2023)
22. Syarif, I., Prugel-Bennett, A., Wills, G.: Unsupervised clustering approach for network anomaly detection. In: Proceedings of International Confernce on Advances in Computing, Communications and Informatics (ICACCI), pp. 135–145 (2012)
23. Ullah, I., Mahmoud, Q.H.: A scheme for generating a dataset for anomalous activity detection in IoT networks. In: Goutte, C., Zhu, X. (eds.) Advances in Artificial Intelligence, pp. 508–520. Springer, Cham (2020)
24. Wu, L., Lei, S., Liao, F., Pang, G., Rong, Y.: EG-ConMix: an intrusion detection method based on graph contrastive learning. arXiv preprint arXiv:2403.17980 (2024)
25. Xiao, Q., Liu, J., Wang, Q., Jiang, Z., Wang, X., Yao, Y.: Towards network anomaly detection using graph embedding. In: Krzhizhanovskaya, V.V., et al. (eds.) ICCS 2020. LNCS, vol. 12140, pp. 156–169. Springer, Cham (2020). https://doi.org/10.1007/978-3-030-50423-6_12
26. Xu, R., Wu, G., Wang, W., Gao, X., He, A., Zhang, Z.: Applying self-supervised learning to network intrusion detection for network flows with graph neural network. Comput. Netw. **248**, 110495 (2024). https://doi.org/10.1016/j.comnet.2024.110495

27. Zhou, A., Xu, X., Li, B.: KnowGraph: knowledge-enabled anomaly detection via logical reasoning on graph data. In: Proceedings of CCS '24 (2024)
28. Zhou, J., Xu, Z., Rush, A.M., Yu, M.: Automating botnet detection with graph neural networks. arXiv preprint arXiv:2003.06344 (2020)
29. Zoppi, T., Ceccarelli, A., Salani, L., Bondavalli, A.: On the educated selection of unsupervised algorithms via attacks and anomaly classes. J. Inf. Secur. Appl. **52**, 102474 (2020). https://doi.org/10.1016/j.jisa.2020.102474
30. Zoubir, A., Missaoui, B.: Integrating graph neural networks with scattering transform for anomaly detection (2024). https://arxiv.org/abs/2404.10800

Proceedings of the Fifth International Workshop on Behavioral Authentication for System Security (BASS 2025)

BASS 2025 Preface

The BASS (Behavioral Authentication for System Security) workshop was organized to bring together researchers and practitioners from industry and academia who are working on behavioral analysis techniques for enhancing IT security. Over recent years, behavioral features have attracted growing interest as they enable continuous and unobtrusive user authentication, anomaly and intrusion detection, and risk mitigation across diverse systems and contexts. BASS welcomed contributions on theoretical foundations, practical implementations, and privacy-preserving methods related to behavior-based profiling, authentication, and anomaly detection. In particular, topics ranged from software behavior analysis, user-behavior modeling and classification, and ontologies for behavior representation, to privacy-preserving behavioral analysis, explainability, and forensic applications. The workshop built on previous editions co-located with SECRYPT 2018 and ARES (2019, 2021, and 2024), continuing the tradition of fostering discussion on novel behavioral techniques for system security.

All submitted workshop papers underwent a double-blind review process, with each manuscript receiving four independent reviews to ensure a rigorous evaluation. Out of six workshop papers submitted, three were accepted for presentation and inclusion in these proceedings. Conflicts of interest were managed in accordance with the conference's ethical guidelines to ensure objective review.

We thank all authors for their high-quality submissions and the Program Committee and external reviewers for their thorough and constructive feedback. We are also grateful to the organizers of ARES and to Springer for their support in bringing these proceedings to fruition.

August 2025

Alessandro Aldini
Marco Rasori
Andrea Saracino

BASS 2025 Organization

Workshop Chairs

Alessandro Aldini	University of Urbino, Italy
Marco Rasori	National Research Council, Italy
Andrea Saracino	Scuola Superiore Universitaria Sant'Anna di Pisa, Italy

Program Committee

Wesam Alabbasi	Scuola Superiore Universitaria Sant'Anna di Pisa, Italy
Luca Ardito	Politecnico di Torino, Italy
Vasileios Gkioulos	Norwegian University of Science and Technology, Norway
Erisa Karafili	University of Southampton, UK
Weizhi Meng	Lancaster University, UK
Pericle Perazzo	University of Pisa, Italy
Giulio Rossolini	Scuola Superiore Universitaria Sant'Anna di Pisa, Italy
Marco Tiloca	Research Institutes of Sweden, Sweden
Shucheng Yu	Stevens Institute of Technology, USA
Nicola Zannone	Eindhoven University of Technology, Netherland

Additional Reviewer

Jiarui Li

Behavior-Based Anomaly Detection in Access and Usage Control for Smart Home Environments

Loay Alajramy[1,2(✉)] and Paolo Mori[1]

[1] Institute of Informatics and Telematics, National Research Council of Italy, 56124 Pisa, Italy
Paolo.Mori@iit.cnr.it

[2] Department of Excellence in Robotics and AI, TeCIP, Scuola Superiore SantAnna, 56127 Pisa, Italy
Loay.Alajrmy@santannapisa.it

Abstract. This paper proposes to enhance the security of smart home environments by integrating a behavior-based component in access and usage control systems to perform anomaly detection using machine learning. This component dynamically assesses each access request by assigning it an anomaly score based on its deviation from learned patterns of normal behavior. This enables context-sensitive and risk-aware policy enforcement, improving the system's responsiveness to unusual or suspicious behavior. To train and evaluate anomaly detection models in the absence of real-world labeled datasets, we introduce an ontology-driven synthetic dataset generation method. This ontology encodes devices, contextual attributes, and subject behavior patterns to support scalable and customizable dataset creation across various domains. Based on this ontology, we generate different datasets of access requests for smart home scenarios and conduct an evaluation of standard performance metrics of both supervised and unsupervised machine learning models. Among the unsupervised models, Deep SVDD achieved the best results, with an accuracy of 88%, demonstrating strong generalization to unseen anomalous behavior. Supervised models, particularly SVM, reached 95% accuracy due to their training on a labeled dataset. While supervised models excel under controlled conditions, unsupervised models, especially Deep SVDD, proved more practical for real-world deployments where labeled anomalies are limited or unavailable. Our findings highlight the value of integrating anomaly detection into access and usage control systems and provide a reusable framework for detecting anomalous behavior patterns in smart environments.

Keywords: Usage Control · Access Control · Anomaly Detection · Behavior-Aware Access · Supervised Learning · Unsupervised Learning

B. Coppens et al. (Eds.): ARES 2025 Workshops, LNCS 15997, pp. 297–315, 2025.
https://doi.org/10.1007/978-3-032-00639-4_17

1 Introduction

In recent decades, the widespread adoption of Internet of Things (IoT) technologies has transformed modern lifestyles, enabling smarter and more connected living environments. From smart homes to intelligent offices, devices such as smart lights and locks, surveillance cameras, sensors (door and windows opening, presence, smoke, etc.), and actuators have become integral to daily life [5]. Moreover, in smart home environments, the integration of devices from different manufacturers with applications capable of interacting with them automatizing and coordinating their usage is becoming increasingly common. In this scenario, ensuring data privacy, safeguarding physical assets integrity, and even protecting user health are critical concerns [21]. As a matter of fact, the sensitive data processed by IoT systems necessitates robust mechanisms to ensure that resources are accessed securely and only by authorized entities. As a result, access control systems have become a critical component of IoT and smart home environments, enabling the regulation of access to and usage of IoT devices by users and applications.

Existing access control models, such as the *Attribute-Based Access Control (ABAC)* [11], or the *Usage Control (UCON) model* [12], can be effectively applied in smart home environments to protect IoT resources and manage authorization for their access and use. These models allow policy makers to express access control policies based on conditions involving attributes related to the subject requesting the access, the resource being accessed, and relevant contextual features of the smart home environment.

However, when defining access control policies, policy makers primarily focus on the security and privacy requirements of IoT devices within a specific smart home scenario, specifying the conditions under which users are granted access rights to those devices. A common limitation of such policies is their failure to account for insider attacks, which often occur either because users are granted more access privileges than strictly necessary or due to improper handling of the assigned privileges [3]. Furthermore, the dynamic nature of smart environments may result in access contexts that are not addressed by the predefined access control policy objectives set by the policy makers, thus increasing the risk of insider attacks [1]. For example, in a smart office environment, a trusted employee could access sensitive company documents outside of working hours using a personal device, or could access the office outside working hours, exploiting gaps in time-based or device-based policies. Similarly, in a smart home environment, a child might unlock doors or disable security cameras in the middle of the night since the homeowner is at home (although they are sleeping), taking advantage of static access settings that fail to account for contextual changes or behavioral anomalies. These scenarios highlight the need for an adaptive access control component capable of responding immediately to unusual or suspicious behavior in access requests.

This paper proposes a solution that integrates a machine-learning-based component within the access control system, aimed to detect anomalous access requests. This component learns the normal behavior of users from the historical records of access requests and uses the learned knowledge to identify deviations indicative of potential risk. Each incoming request is evaluated and assigned an *anomaly score*, representing how much the request deviates from established normal behavior. Based on this, the access control system can decide whether to allow or block the request during policy evaluation. Additionally, the anomaly score can support the creation of more adaptive policies, enabling policy makers to define policies that trigger obligations—such as additional authentication mechanisms—depending on the degree of deviation indicated by the anomaly score. This allows the system to respond proportionally to unusual behavior, balancing security enforcement with user accessibility.

To ensure flexibility adaptation of our solution across multiple domains besides smart homes, including smart offices, industrial automation, and IoT security environments, we adopt an ontology-driven dataset generation approach. This method allows us to create high-quality training and evaluation datasets that accurately reflect domain-specific entities, contextual attributes, and access control scenarios.

The rest of the paper is organized as follows. Section 2 introduces the access and usage control frameworks and anomaly detection methods. Section 3 describes the outline of our methodology for behavior-aware usage control. Section 4 details datasets generation pipeline for training and testing. Section 5 presents the models used and evaluates their effectiveness in detecting anomalous access requests. Section 6 reviews related research on behavioral access control. Finally, Sect. 7 summarizes key findings and future directions.

2 Background

This section provides essential background information and introduces key concepts that form the foundation of this work.

2.1 Access and Usage Control Frameworks

The main cybersecurity fundamental of smart environments is to ensure that data and resources are secure from unauthorized or improper disclosure, modifications, and usage, while ensuring they remain available to authorized requests. Achieving this requires the evaluation of each access request to data or resources within the smart environment to ensure that only authorized users can perform actions on a resource, according to an access control mechanism [5]. Traditional access control approaches, such as Access Control List (ACL), Discretionary Access Control (DAC), Mandatory Access Control (MAC), Role-Based Access Control (RBAC), Attribute-Based Access Control (ABAC), Usage Control (UCON), and others, have been widely adopted to protect data and resources [15]. The ABAC model is very general, since access requests are evaluated based on predefined policies that express conditions on attributes describing the access context, i.e., describing the subject that is requesting the access, the resource that is being accessed, and the environment in which the access is taking place [11,16], and the XACML standard [23] defines an XML-based policy format and a reference architecture for ABAC policy enforcement. The UCON model represents an advanced extension of ABAC, offering a high degree of dynamism by continuously enforcing access control policies before, during, and after access.

The architecture of a UCON systems extends the one proposed by the XACML standard, and it includes the following key components: the *Policy Enforcement Point (PEP)*, which is integrated in the resource to be protected, intercepts the user requests to access the resource, triggers the decision process, and enforces the access decision; the *Policy Decision Point (PDP)*, which evaluates the policy against the access requests and provides authorization decisions; the *Policy Information Points (PIPs)*, which are in charge of collecting from the Attribute Managers the updated values of the attributes required to perform the decision process; the *Attribute Managers (AMs)*, which are external attribute providers that assist in this process; the *Policy Administration Point (PAP)* for policies management; and the *Context Handler (CH)*, which coordinates the interaction between the previous components [17]. The UCON framework introduces an additional component with respect to the XACML reference architecture, the *Session Manager (SM)*, which manages usage control sessions, i.e., it keeps trace of the accesses that are in progress in order to interrupt them if required [18]. Figure 1 shows the main components of the UCON framework.

The workflow of the usage control system begins at the PEP when a subject tries to perform a specific action on a specific resource. The PEP intercepts the subject request and sends the *TryAccess* message that contains the initial access request to CH, which serves as the front-end of the Usage Control System.

A typical access request includes the attributes `subject-id`, `resource-id`, and `action-id`. Other relevant attributes could be available in specific scenarios, e.g., the IP address from which a request has been received. The CH then queries the PIPs to retrieve the necessary attributes values from the AMs in order to have a complete description of the access context. Subsequently, the PDP exploits the collected values to evaluate the relevant policies obtained from PAP and produce the access decision: `Permit` or `Deny`. The SM keeps trace of the permitted accesses storing the request and the corresponding policy, in order to allow to continuously enforce such a policy while the access is in progress.

For a complete understanding UCON architecture and its workflow, please refer to [8,13].

2.2 Anomaly Detection

Anomaly detection has been extensively studied in the literature as a key technique for identifying deviations from expected system behavior. A common approach involves using machine-learning-based anomaly detection models (ADMs) [4,7]. During training, these models learn a baseline of normal system behavior that serves as ground truth to detect anomalous behavior. Generally, based on the label availability, three types of anomaly detection models can be trained [7,10,22]:

1. **Unsupervised anomaly detection**: Models trained exclusively on normal behavior to learn the underlying distribution of legitimate behavior. During

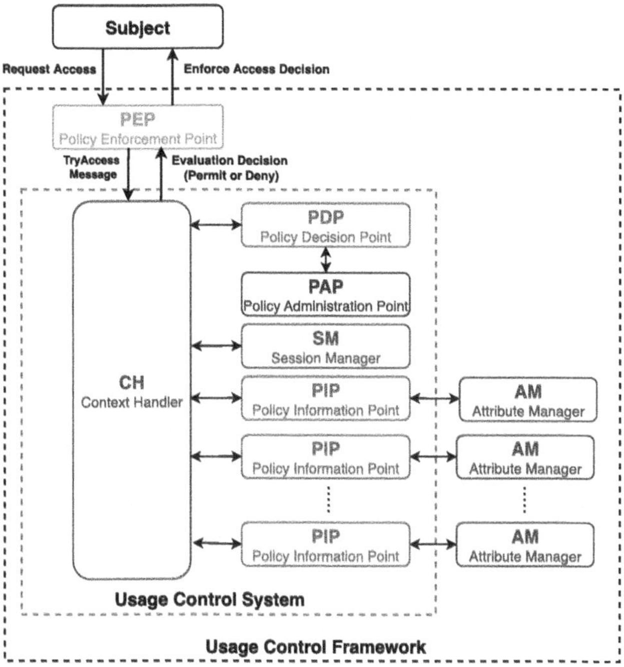

Fig. 1. UCON framework architecture [18].

inference, any request that deviates significantly from this learned profile is flagged as anomalous.

2. **Semi-supervised anomaly detection**: Models trained on a partially labeled dataset that includes both labeled and unlabeled instances. These models are beneficial in cases where annotating the entire dataset is prohibitively expensive and requires expert involvement, such as in industrial and medical fields.
3. **Supervised anomaly detection**: Models requiring a fully labeled training dataset that includes both normal and anomalous instances. These models are especially useful in cases where anomalous behavior can be easily documented and labeled.

3 Proposed Methodology

As previously described, usage control policies are meant to define the conditions under which access and usage rights are granted to subjects on resources, and they do not typically take into account behavioral factors. For this reason, to enhance access control decisions with behavior-aware intelligence, we propose the integration of a machine-learning-based anomaly detection model into the UCON framework. Specifically, we introduce a trained Anomaly Detection Model

(ADM), and we integrate it in the UCON framework as an Attribute Manager (referred to as AM_{ADM}, as illustrated in Fig. 2).

This component is responsible for assessing the behavioral risk of access requests in real time by assigning an *anomaly score*.

To compute this score, the ADM requires a comprehensive set of contextual attributes. These attributes are gathered by the CH, which queries a collection of PIPs, denoted as $PIP_1, PIP_2, \ldots, PIP_N$, by passing them the access request. Every time the value of a new attribute is gathered by a PIP, it is added to the access request. In our design, the CH deliberately queries the anomaly detection PIP, PIP_{ADM}, last, in order to ensure that it receives the access request embedding the full context necessary for the behavior analysis—comprising both the attributes retrieved from the other PIPs and those extracted directly from the original access request. As shown in Fig. 2, once the complete set of attributes is retrieved, the CH forwards it to AM_{ADM} via PIP_{ADM}. The ADM processes the input and generates an anomaly score reflecting the likelihood of anomalous or potentially risky behavior. This score is then added to the access request's attribute set before the CH sends the request to the PDP for evaluation. The anomaly score quantifies how much an incoming access request deviates from established normal behavior. It is expressed as a continuous value in the range $[0, 1]$, where higher values indicate a greater likelihood of anomalous or risky behavior. To produce this score, the ADM is trained on historical access behaviors—further details are provided in Sect. 4.

Within usage control policies, the anomaly score can be utilized in various ways to support dynamic, risk-aware access decisions. As a straightforward example, a policy could include a specific behavioral-based rule with effect `Deny`—having more priority than all the other rules—which is applicable when the anomaly score is over a given threshold. In this case, when the anomaly score is over the threshold, the policy will be always evaluated to `Deny`. Alternatively, the administrator may combine a predicate related to the anomaly score with the other predicates of the policy using logical operators. A condition such as `anomaly-score > 0.8 || device-trust-level == ‘‘low’’` would ensure that access is denied if either the request is deemed highly anomalous or the device is untrusted. In this example, the anomaly score acts as an independent risk signal that can lead to a decision regardless of other contextual attributes, thereby giving it decisive weight in the access control decision.

A more refined policy could use the anomaly score to trigger the execution of specific actions such as a *step-up authentication*. For instance, a policy could include a rule with effect `Permit` having a condition that, if the anomaly score falls within a specified intermediate range (e.g., between 0.4 and 0.7), requires an additional identity verification. This can be implemented through an obligation attached to the policy, marked to be "fulfilled on Permit". In this setup, access is conditionally permitted only if the subject successfully completes the specified additional action (e.g., biometric authentication or multi-factor login), thereby mitigating risk while preserving usability.

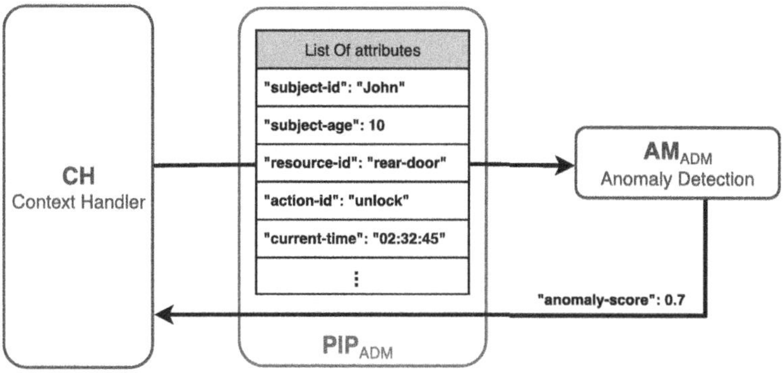

Fig. 2. Proposed Methodology: the CH forwards the list of attributes to AM_{ADM} via PIP_{ADM}, and the AM_{ADM} processes the input and generates an anomaly score.

To ensure adaptability to changing user behavior in dynamic smart environments, we propose incorporating a buffer-based fine-tuning mechanism to enable the model to continuously learn new behavior patterns. This approach uses a buffer to store the most up-to-date attribute values of every access request permitted by the PDP, which represents normal access behavior. Periodically, the anomaly detection model (e.g., autoencoder) is fine-tuned using the data in this buffer, allowing it to gradually learn new patterns without requiring complete retraining. For example, if a user typically accesses the office around 8:00 but later shifts his working hours and begins accessing it at 16:00, the buffered requests capturing this change will be incorporated during fine-tuning. This allows the model to recognize the new behavior as normal. This strategy enables the model to accommodate such contextual shifts and maintain accurate detection performance over time.

4 Ontology-Driven Dataset Generation

To develop and evaluate behavioral AI-based access and usage control systems in smart home environments, we require high-quality datasets that contain both normal and anomalous access requests, including all the contextual attributes. Due to the lack of real-world labeled datasets, this paper presents a synthetic dataset generation pipeline based on a domain-specific ontology. The development of the ontology enables a structured representation of smart home environments through the organization of the key elements: subjects, resources, environment, action, and related attributes. This framework supports both behavioral profiling and anomaly detection tasks. This section details the ontology structure, the dataset generation pipeline, and the strategies used to create high-quality synthetic access request datasets.

4.1 Smart Home Ontology Design

The creation of our ontology serves as the knowledge base for the synthetic dataset, which defines the relationships between subjects (users), resources (devices), actions, and environmental context attributes. This structure ensures that generated requests are logically coherent and behaviorally realistic.

Ontology Structure The smart home ontology is structured as a JSON file containing three primary components:

1. **Contextual Attributes**: Contextual attributes represent the dynamic conditions surrounding an access request at the time it is made. They provide fundamental environmental parameters that can significantly affect the access decision process:
   - **current-time**: Time of the request in HH:MM:SS format.
   - **subject-location**: Physical location of the requesting subject.
   - **access-device**: Device used to initiate the request.
2. **Device Types**: The ontology defines multiple device types commonly found in smart homes, each associated with a list of device instances (DeviceIds), supported actions (e.g., turn-on, set-temperature), and a set of relevant attributes necessary to construct realistic access control policies for that device type. These attributes may refer to the device itself or the environment. For example, access policies for air conditioners rely on attributes such as environmental temperature and power consumption, whereas policies for kitchen appliances consider contextual factors like the presence or number of children (n-children) and adults (n-adults) in the environment. In our methodology, we assume that smart home access policies are professionally constructed to incorporate all relevant attributes, covering a wide range of real-world scenarios. This design enables robust training and evaluation of anomaly detection models by exposing them to complete, attribute-rich request patterns that reflect realistic smart home usage. Our ontology includes:
   - 9 distinct device categories (e.g., TV, AC, Kitchen Appliance).
   - 32 specific device instances across all categories (e.g., livingroom-tv, bedroom-tv).

   Table 1 provides examples of device types along with some of their associated actions and attributes.
3. **Subjects**: Human actors in the smart home environment: 5 family members with distinct roles (e.g., parents and children), demographic attributes such as age, and preferred access devices.

4.2 Synthetic Dataset Generation Pipeline

Generating a high-quality synthetic dataset is essential to train and evaluate anomaly detection models in access control systems. In this work, the dataset

Table 1. Selected examples of devices and attributes in our smart home ontology.

Device Type	Device IDs	Action Examples	Resource Attributes	Environment Attributes
TV	livingroom-tv, bedroom-tv	turn-on, configure	current-advisory-level	n-children, n-adults
Kitchen Appliance	stove, microwave	turn-off, set-temperature	temperature	n-children, n-adults, home-power-consumption
AC	bedroom-ac, livingroom-ac	set-temperature, get-temperature	temperature	room-temperature, all-windows-closed, home-power-consumption

generation pipeline is tightly integrated with the ontology to produce structured access requests that are both logically valid and behaviorally realistic. By embedding semantic rules and contextual logic into the generator, the resulting datasets mirror the complexity and richness of realistic behavior occurring in a smart home, enabling robust machine learning applications.

The access request generated simulates the structure of a real XACML access request, where request attributes are categorized into four categories: Subject, Resource, Action, and Environment. The Subject category includes identifiers and attributes of the user making the request, such as their role, location, access device, and age. The Resource category includes the target device being accessed and its type. The Action field records the intended operation, such as turn-on or set-temperature. The Environment category captures dynamic contextual information such as current time, power consumption, temperature, and the presence of children or adults. Our dataset generation pipeline generates two types of access requests:

1. **Normal access request**: The process of generating these requests involves simulating realistic interactions between users and smart home devices based on the aforementioned ontology. To generate a request of this type, a subject is randomly selected from the user profiles, and a device is chosen from the available device types and instances. The remaining attributes are generated based on the selected device and subject. For example, the access time is generated within a valid time window associated with each device, reflecting typical household usage patterns (e.g., accessing the bedroom-tv between 18:00 and 23:00). The access device, role, and age are populated directly from subject profile, while environmental attributes such as power consumption, temperature, and the presence of adults or children are filled with realistic values. All contextual attributes are assigned values consistent with normal behavior. No attribute in a normal request is intentionally corrupted, ensuring that these requests represent genuine, policy-compliant usage patterns in the smart home environment.

2. **Anomalous access request**: These requests are generated by introducing controlled deviations from normal behavior. After randomly selecting a subject and a device, a random subset of attributes is chosen to be corrupted, simulating partial or complete anomalies. Subject-related anomalies include assigning the subject an identity such as"guest" or "unknown", or setting to "external" the subject location when their role is designated as "child", or using an unauthorized access device (e.g., "unknown"). Environmental anomalies involve assigning out-of-range times (e.g., 03:00), invalid values (e.g., "invalid-time"), exaggerated power consumption, or nonsensical temperatures. Table 2 provides examples of attribute value ranges for normal and anomalous cases. In each anomalous request, one, some, or all attributes may be anomalous, thus reflecting realistic anomalous scenarios. Anomalies are systematically introduced through the modification of one or more attributes in each request. These include:
   (a) **Subject anomalies**: Invalid identities, roles, or access devices.
   (b) **Contextual anomalies**: Implausible environmental conditions.
   (c) **Temporal anomalies**: Requests occurring outside of normal usage hours.

Using the described pipeline, we generate three dataset variants for comprehensive evaluation on supervised and unsupervised anomaly detection models:

1. **Supervised Training Dataset:** Contains 3,500 requests (*instances*), including a 40% anomaly requests ratio for broad coverage of anomaly types.
2. **Unsupervised Training Dataset:** Contains 3,500 normal requests, no anomaly included, to establish a baseline behavior.
3. **Testing Dataset:** Contains 1,500 requests, including a 40% anomaly requests, strictly disjoint from training sets.

The distribution of instances in the supervised training dataset, as illustrated in Fig. 3a, shows that the majority of instances (2,100) are purely normal, containing zero anomalous attributes, while the remaining anomalous instances are distributed across varying levels of anomaly complexity. Most anomalous samples exhibit between 1 and 6 anomalous attributes, with a relatively balanced number of samples in each group, indicating a good representation of both subtle and moderately complex anomalies. This balanced design supports the training of supervised models capable of detecting both minor deviations and more severe, multi-factor anomalies in smart home access behavior.

The testing dataset, shown in Fig. 3b, exhibits a diverse distribution of anomalous behavior. Out of the total instances, 900 are normal, while the remaining anomalous instances contain between 1 and 6 anomalous attributes, with a peak at 4 anomalies per instance.

The most frequently anomalous attributes are subject-related fields such as role, access-device, and age, along with contextual attributes like current-time and subject-location. These attributes are commonly used to create high-quality policies, which is why they appear more frequently in access requests.

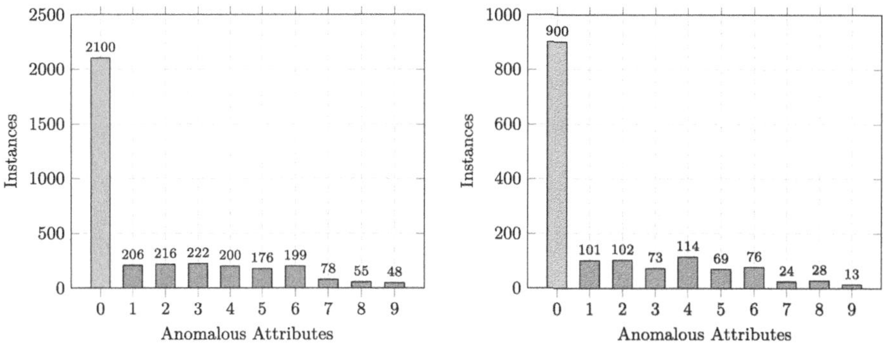

(a) Supervised Training Dataset (b) Testing Dataset

Fig. 3. Distribution of instances based on the number of anomalous attributes. Instances with 0 anomalous attributes (light blue bar) correspond to normal requests, while instances with one or more anomalous attributes (purple bars) represent anomalous requests.

While attributes such as n-children (number of children present in the environment), temperature, power-consumption, and current-advisory-level occur less frequently because they are associated with a specific device's access request. This distribution reflects a realistic and diverse set of anomalies, emphasizing identity and context deviations, and provides a strong foundation for evaluating anomaly detection models.

Table 2. Example of attribute value ranges for normal and anomalous cases.

Attribute	Normal Value Examples	Anomalous Value Examples
current-time	Device-specific time windows (e.g., 07:00–10:00 or 17:00–22:00 for livingroom-tv)	Outside typical usage windows, "invalid-time-format", null
all-windows-closed	Boolean (true/false)	"unknown", null
temperature	18–30 (normal range)	"< 15", "> 36", "invalid", null
subject-id	Known family members from the ontology	"guest", "unknown"
subject-location	"home" (65% for parents, 100% for children) "external" (35% for parents)	"external" for children, "unknown", "invalid-locations-format"
access-device	Preferred device from the ontology	"unknown", "untrusted-device"

5 Anomaly Detection Methodology and Evaluation

To evaluate the effectiveness of the framework for behavior-based anomaly detection in access and usage control for smart home environments, we trained different machine learning models using the aforementioned synthetically generated datasets. These models include supervised and unsupervised models, each designed to detect anomalous access requests based on contextual, environmental, and subject-specific attributes. The evaluation of the models was conducted on the same dataset with labeled instances of both normal and anomalous requests.

5.1 Unsupervised Learning Approaches

Unsupervised learning approaches are particularly valuable in our context because real-world smart home environments often lack labeled data for anomalous access behaviors. In practice, most access logs represent normal activity, while anomalies—such as intrusions, misuse, or policy violations—are rare, diverse, and unpredictable. Unsupervised models including standard autoencoder (SAE), variational autoencoder (VAE), adversarial autoencoder (AAE), and deep support vector data description (Deep SVDD) can learn the typical patterns of normal access behavior without requiring labeled anomaly data, allowing them to flag deviations as potential threats. This makes them highly suitable for deployment in evolving systems where new or unforeseen anomalies may emerge over time.

5.2 Supervised Learning Approaches

For supervised anomaly detection, we trained models (Support Vector Machine (SVM) and a supervised variant of the autoencoder) on labeled datasets that include normal and anomalous access requests. This setup allowed the models to learn explicit decision boundaries between the two classes. Supervised models benefited from explicit knowledge of anomalies, especially in scenarios where anomalous behavior manifested through subtle manipulations of only one or two attributes (e.g., accessing a device at an unusual time or from an unknown location). These models showed improved precision in detecting known anomalous patterns, while unsupervised models excelled in generalization and detecting unseen anomalies.

5.3 Evaluation Methodology

This dual-track evaluation allows us to compare the models' abilities to detect deviations from normal behavior, assess generalization to unseen anomalies, and analyze the trade-offs between precision and coverage under different learning paradigms.

For unsupervised models, during inference, each model generates an anomaly score for test instances based on its internal criteria, such as reconstruction error or distance from the learned latent representation. To ensure comparability and reduce the influence of outliers, the raw anomaly scores are normalized using a robust scaling approach based on the 5th and 95th percentiles. Since unsupervised models are trained without labeled anomalies, a fixed threshold is then applied directly to the normalized scores to distinguish between normal and anomalous instances. In this study, a threshold of 0.1 is used, meaning that any test instance with a normalized anomaly score greater than 0.1 is classified as anomalous. This threshold reflects the assumption that normal behavior results in low reconstruction errors (close to zero), while anomalies produce significantly higher scores. Using a consistent threshold across all models ensures fair and standardized evaluation. In contrast, supervised models produce predicted class labels without relying on thresholding anomaly scores.

Final predictions were compared to ground truth labels using standard classification metrics, which allow for a consistent assessment of each model's detection performance.

5.4 Evaluation Metrics

The evaluation of the anomaly detection models relies on four standard metrics: *Accuracy*, *Precision*, *Recall*, and *F1 Score* [9]. These metrics assess the correctness of the predicted labels by comparing the model's predictions against the ground truth labels in the test dataset. Each access request is labeled as either *Normal* or *Anomalous*, and the model's task is to classify them accordingly. The evaluation terms, required for the computation of the standard metrics and based on *confusion matrices*, are defined as follows:

- **True Positives (TP):** number of anomalous requests correctly classified as anomalous.
- **False Positives (FP):** number of normal requests incorrectly classified as anomalous.
- **False Negatives (FN):** number of anomalous requests incorrectly classified as normal.
- **True Negatives (TN):** number of normal requests correctly classified as normal.

These four values form the basis for calculating the classification performance metrics used in our evaluation. The formal definitions of the metrics are given as:

$$\text{Accuracy} = \frac{TP + TN}{TP + FP + TN + FN}, \qquad \text{Precision} = \frac{TP}{TP + FP},$$
$$\text{Recall} = \frac{TP}{TP + FN}, \qquad \text{F1 Score} = \frac{2 \cdot \text{Precision} \cdot \text{Recall}}{\text{Precision} + \text{Recall}},$$

where *Accuracy* measures the overall proportion of correctly classified requests, *Precision* reflects the proportion of true anomalies among all requests flagged as anomalous by the model, *Recall* captures the model's ability to detect actual anomalies, and *F1 Score* provides a harmonic mean of precision and recall to balance the trade-off between false positives and false negatives.

5.5 Evaluation Results

Table 3 presents the performance of each model. Among the unsupervised models, Deep SVDD achieved the best overall performance, indicating that unsupervised models can effectively detect unseen anomalies. The Variational Autoencoder (VAE) also demonstrated robust detection capabilities with balanced precision and recall. Standard Autoencoder and Adversarial Autoencoder showed lower performance, likely due to limited expressiveness or sensitivity to noisy attributes.

In contrast, supervised approaches, including SVM and Supervised Autoencoder yielded higher scores across all metrics. SVM, in particular, achieved the highest accuracy (0.95) and the most balanced precision-recall performance, indicating its ability to detect anomalies with fewer false positives. The supervised autoencoder showed remarkable recall on anomalous instances (0.96), making it effective at minimizing missed threats.

Table 3. Comparison of classification metrics across models.

Type	Model	Accuracy	Precision	Recall	F1 Score
Unsupervised	Standard Autoencoder (SAE)	0.67	0.55	0.94	0.69
	Variational Autoencoder (VAE)	0.83	0.81	0.76	0.79
	Adversarial Autoencoder (AAE)	0.74	0.63	0.80	0.71
	Deep SVDD	**0.88**	**0.93**	**0.75**	**0.83**
Supervised	Supervised Autoencoder	0.90	0.89	0.91	0.90
	Support Vector Machine (SVM)	**0.95**	**0.96**	**0.94**	**0.95**

These results demonstrate the trade-offs between unsupervised and supervised anomaly detection approaches. While supervised models excel in precision and recall due to the availability of labeled anomalies, unsupervised models remain valuable in real-world deployments where anomaly labels may not be available during training. Overall, the framework supports the integration of both learning paradigms for robust behavioral analysis in smart home environments.

To assess the ability of the unsupervised model to distinguish between normal and anomalous access behaviors, we visualize the distribution of anomaly scores for both classes in Fig. 4. This comparative histogram illustrates the density of scores for the ground-truth labeled instance across the unsupervised models. An ideal model should assign low scores to normal requests (indicating high confidence in normality) and higher scores to anomalous requests (indicating deviation from learned normal patterns). Among the models, Deep SVDD demonstrates the clearest separation, with the majority of normal instances concentrated below 0.1 and anomalous instances spreading more evenly toward higher scores. VAE also shows good discriminative behavior, though with slightly more overlap in the mid-score range. In contrast, SAE and AAE exhibit noticeable overlap between normal and anomalous scores, particularly in the 0.1 to 0.5 range, suggesting less reliable separation. This figure offers a comprehensive view of each model's scoring behavior. It complements evaluations based on confusion matrices by illustrating not only whether models classify correctly, but also how confidently they differentiate between normal and anomalous patterns.

We excluded the supervised models from this comparison since their predictions are based on directly learned decision boundaries rather than continuous anomaly scores.

6 Related Work

Several approaches have been proposed to enhance the access control capabilities in detecting the mishandling of the assigned privileges and the insider attack based on behavioral models and anomaly detection techniques.

Alkhresheh et al. [1] propose an adaptive access control policies framework for IoT, this framework uses a supervised model (LSTM) to detect anomalous behavior in the device-to-device access. They provide a real-life dataset and present

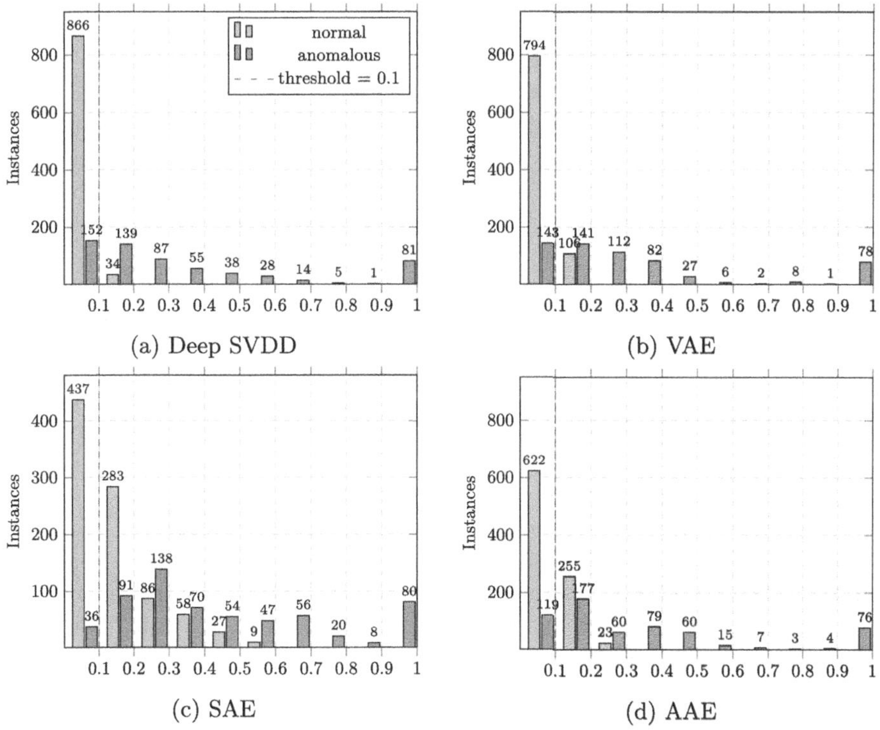

Fig. 4. Distribution of anomalous score for anomalous and normal instances in the testing dataset for the unsupervised models. Normal instances (light blue) that fall below the threshold are classified as true negatives, while those that exceed the threshold are classified as false positives. Conversely, anomalous instances (purple) that exceed the threshold are classified as true positives, whereas those falling below it are classified as false negatives.

a use case scenario involving a door locking system, The proposed framework suggests policy updates based on behavior deviations. Skopik et al. [19] present AECID, an unsupervised anomaly detection system designed for unstructured textual event data such as log data. It models normal behavior from unstructured data and detects anomalies like stolen or cloned access cards.

Alkhresheh et al. [2] proposed DACIoT, which enhances the standard access control structure (XACML) by introducing automatic policy generation, continuous enforcement, and adaptive adjustments to accommodate the dynamic nature of IoT systems. This model offers improved security and scalability in real-world IoT deployments. Frias-Martinez et al. [6] introduce BB-NAC, a behavior-based network access control system that models host behaviors using anomaly detection techniques, based on network traffic patterns. The framework identifies deviations from established behavior profiles, enabling dynamic access decisions.

Meidan et al. [14] use deep autoencoders to identify the anomalous network traffic generated by IoT devices. Each device is modeled with its autoencoder trained on normal traffic; failure to reconstruct new behavior signals an anomaly, triggering traffic blocking. Their approach enables real-time detection of botnet attacks with high accuracy and low false positives.

Watanabe et al. [20] propose a self-adaptive anomaly detection framework tailored for IoT smart homes by employing a honeypot server to capture real-time traffic and dynamically generate detection models, which are then utilized to identify and block anomalous activities. This approach enables the system to adapt to evolving cyberattacks, including previously unseen threats, enhancing the security of IoT devices without relying on frequent firmware updates.

7 Conclusion and Future Work

This paper proposes to enhance access control systems by leveraging machine-learning-based anomaly detection in order to detect anomalous access requests. In particular, we propose to integrate a new component, designed as an Attribute Manager, which detects unusual or suspicious behavior in access requests by leveraging the knowledge learned from the normal behavior of users from the historical records of access requests. Each incoming access request is evaluated by such a component and assigned an anomaly score, which indicates how much it deviates from established normal behavior. The anomaly score can be utilized as a standard attribute directly in the policy, to support dynamic, risk-aware access decisions and enables administrators to build policies with behavior-aware intelligence.

To ensure the generality of our approach across different domains, we introduced an ontology-driven dataset creation method, which enables the creation of datasets for training anomaly detection models across different environments, such as smart homes and smart offices. Using the generated synthetic datasets, we conducted a comparative evaluation of various supervised and unsupervised models for anomaly detection in smart home access control scenarios.

Among the unsupervised models, the Deep SVDD model outperformed the other models, achieving an accuracy of 88%, demonstrating its ability to effectively learn the distribution of normal behavior and detect deviations without requiring labeled anomalies. In contrast, the supervised models benefited from access to labeled anomalous data, with the Support Vector Machine achieving the highest metrics overall, reaching 95% accuracy, followed closely by the supervised autoencoder. These findings suggest that while supervised models can achieve high accuracy in controlled settings, unsupervised methods—particularly Deep SVDD—offer strong performance without the reliance on labeled anomaly data, making them more suitable for real-world deployments where such labels may be scarce or incomplete.

Future work will focus on enhancing the framework by incorporating risk-aware scoring and multi-model decision fusion (audio, video, or environmental sensors). Rather than treating all anomalies equally, the system would prioritize alerts based on contextual risk—such as the criticality of the device, user role, or time of access. In addition, combining output from multiple models can improve robustness and precision. This approach enables more precise access decisions, reduces false positives, and supports real-time policy enforcement.

Another important direction for future work involves estimating the computational overhead introduced by behavior-based anomaly detection. Specifically, we aim to assess how the integration of our method affects the latency of producing an authorization decision. Quantifying this overhead is essential for evaluating the practicality of deploying the proposed system in real-time smart home environments where swift and accurate access control is critical.

Acknowledgments. This work has been funded by the Horizon Europe project MEDIATE (grant agreement 101168465).

References

1. Alkhresheh, A., Elgazzar, K., Hassanein, H.S.: Adaptive access control policies for IoT deployments. In: 2020 International Wireless Communications and Mobile Computing (IWCMC), pp. 377–383 (2020). https://doi.org/10.1109/IWCMC48107.2020.9148090
2. Alkhresheh, A., Elgazzar, K., Hassanein, H.S.: Daciot: dynamic access control framework for IoT deployments. IEEE Internet Things J. **7**(12), 11401–11419 (2020). https://doi.org/10.1109/JIOT.2020.3002709
3. Babu, B.M., Bhanu, M.S.: Prevention of insider attacks by integrating behavior analysis with risk based access control model to protect cloud. Procedia Comput. Sci. **54**, 157–166 (2015). https://doi.org/10.1016/j.procs.2015.06.018
4. Chandola, V., Banerjee, A., Kumar, V.: Anomaly detection: a survey. ACM Comput. Surv. **41**(3), pp. 15:1–15:58 (2009). https://doi.org/10.1145/1541880.1541882
5. Colombo, P., Ferrari, E.: Access control technologies for big data management systems: literature review and future trends. Cybersecur. **2**(1), 3 (2019)
6. Frías-Martínez, V., Stolfo, S.J., Keromytis, A.D.: Behavior-based network access control: a proof-of-concept. In: Wu, T., Lei, C., Rijmen, V., Lee, D. (eds.) Information Security, 11th International Conference, ISC 2008, Taipei, Taiwan, September

15-18, 2008. Proceedings. LNCS, vol. 5222, pp. 175–190. Springer (2008). https://doi.org/10.1007/978-3-540-85886-7_12
7. Ghamry, F.M., El-Banby, G.M., El-Fishawy, A.S., El-Samie, F., Dessouky, M.I.: A survey of anomaly detection techniques. J. Opt. **53**(2), 756–774 (2024). https://doi.org/10.1007/s12596-023-01147-4
8. Gkioulos, V., Rizos, A., Michailidou, C., Mori, P., Saracino, A.: Enhancing usage control for performance: an architecture for systems of systems. In: Computer Security - ESORICS 2018 International Workshops, CyberICPS 2018 and SECPRE 2018, Barcelona, Spain, September 6-7, 2018, Revised Selected Papers. LNCS, vol. 11387, pp. 69–84. Springer (2018). https://doi.org/10.1007/978-3-030-12786-2_5
9. Hastie, T., Tibshirani, R., Friedman, J.: The Elements of Statistical Learning: data Mining, Inference, and Prediction. Springer (2009)
10. Hojjati, H., Ho, T.K.K., Armanfard, N.: Self-supervised anomaly detection: a survey and outlook. CoRR **abs/2205.05173** (2022). https://doi.org/10.48550/ARXIV.2205.05173
11. Hu, V.C., Kuhn, D.R., Ferraiolo, D.F.: Attribute-based access control. Computer **48**(2), 85–88 (2015)
12. Marra, A.L., Martinelli, F., Mori, P., Saracino, A.: Implementing usage control in internet of things: a smart home use case. In: Trustcom/BigDataSE/ICESS 2017. pp. 1056–1063. IEEE Computer Society (2017). https://doi.org/10.1109/TRUSTCOM/BIGDATASE/ICESS.2017.352
13. Marra, A.L., Martinelli, F., Mori, P., Saracino, A.: A distributed usage control framework for industrial internet of things. In: Security and Privacy Trends in the Industrial Internet of Things, pp. 115–135. Springer (2019). https://doi.org/10.1007/978-3-030-12330-7_6
14. Meidan, Y., et al.: N-baiot - network-based detection of IoT botnet attacks using deep autoencoders. IEEE Pervasive Comput. **17**(3), 12–22 (2018). https://doi.org/10.1109/MPRV.2018.03367731
15. Nobi, M.N., Gupta, M., Praharaj, L., Abdelsalam, M., Krishnan, R., Sandhu, R.S.: Machine learning in access control: a taxonomy and survey. CoRR **abs/2207.01739** (2022). https://doi.org/10.48550/ARXIV.2207.01739
16. Qiu, J., Tian, Z., Du, C., Zuo, Q., Su, S., Fang, B.: A survey on access control in the age of internet of things. IEEE Internet Things J. **7**(6), 4682–4696 (2020). https://doi.org/10.1109/JIOT.2020.2969326
17. Ragothaman, K.N.M., Wang, Y.: A systematic mapping study of access control in the internet of things. In: HICSS 2021, pp. 1–10. ScholarSpace (2021). https://hdl.handle.net/10125/71474
18. Rasori, M., Saracino, A., Mori, P., Tiloca, M.: Using the ACE framework to enforce access and usage control with notifications of revoked access rights. Int. J. Inf. Sec. **23**(5), 3109–3133 (2024). https://doi.org/10.1007/S10207-024-00877-1
19. Skopik, F., Wurzenberger, M., Höld, G., Landauer, M., Kuhn, W.: Behavior-based anomaly detection in log data of physical access control systems. IEEE Trans. Dependable Secur. Comput. **20**(4), 3158–3175 (2023). https://doi.org/10.1109/TDSC.2022.3197265
20. Watanabe, N., et al.: Self-adaptive traffic anomaly detection system for IoT smart home environments. IEICE Trans. Commun. 108(3), pp. 230–242 (2025). https://doi.org/10.23919/TRANSCOM.2024EBT0002
21. Wu, H., Han, H., Wang, X., Sun, S.: Research on artificial intelligence enhancing internet of things security: a survey. IEEE Access **8**, 153826–153848 (2020). https://doi.org/10.1109/ACCESS.2020.3018170

22. Wurzenberger, M., Skopik, F., Settanni, G., Fiedler, R.: AECID: a self-learning anomaly detection approach based on light-weight log parser models. In: Mori, P., Furnell, S., Camp, O. (eds.) Proceedings of the 4th International Conference on Information Systems Security and Privacy, ICISSP 2018, Funchal, Madeira - Portugal, January 22-24, 2018, pp. 386–397. SciTePress (2018). https://doi.org/10.5220/0006643003860397
23. eXtensible Access Control Markup Language (XACML) version 3.0 plus errata 01 (2017). http://docs.oasis-open.org/xacml/3.0/xacml-3.0-core-spec-en.html

Unmasking Model Behavior: How LLMs Reason on Vulnerability Detection

Aleksandar Fontana[1,2](✉) and Marco Simoni[2,3]

[1] Department of Excellence in Robotics and AI, Scuola Superiore Sant'Anna, Pisa, Italy

[2] Institute of Informatics and Telematics, National Research Council of Italy, Pisa, Italy

aleksandar.fontana@santannapisa.it

[3] Italian National Doctorate on Artificial Intelligence, Sapienza University of Rome, Rome, Italy

Abstract. Understanding and controlling the behavior of Large Language Models (LLMs) is crucial for their reliable use in software vulnerability detection. While LLMs show promising zero-shot capabilities, our analysis shows that they often behave inconsistently by over-predicting vulnerabilities, overlooking real vulnerabilities in domain shifts. In this paper, we approach vulnerability detection as a behavior shaping problem. We apply Group Relative Policy Optimization (GRPO) to guide the behavior of models through structured rule-based rewards. Our reward verifiers target both the accuracy of predictions and the coherence of explanations, encouraging the model to develop stable and trustworthy decision patterns. Through experiments on BigVul, DiverseVul and CleanVul benchmarks, we show that behavior shaping with GRPO improves the model's ability to generalize across projects, programming languages, and data quality levels. Furthermore, we show that tuning the regularization's strength of the KullbackLeibler (KL) divergence enables a balance between risk-seeking and risk-averse behavior, reducing false negatives without overwhelming users with false positives.

Keywords: Vulnerability Detection · Group Relative Policy Optimization · Large Language Models · Reinforcement Learning · Model Behavior

1 Introduction

Large Language Models (LLMs) are increasingly being used for software security tasks, including vulnerability detection. Although initial results are promising, their performance in realistic environments remains limited. Existing studies [7] have shown that LLMs are often unable to detect subtle security flaws in memory, especially when these flaws are obscured by project-specific coding conventions. Supervised fine-tuning improves recall [16], but often leads to overfitting and

B. Coppens et al. (Eds.): ARES 2025 Workshops, LNCS 15997, pp. 316–333, 2025.
https://doi.org/10.1007/978-3-032-00639-4_18

poor generalization to new or unfamiliar projects. Other approaches, such as retrieval-augmented generation [5], help to corroborate model predictions with external information, but lead to latency and are highly dependent on the quality and coverage of the retrieval index. Reinforcement learning has recently been proposed as a more flexible and lightweight alternative [12], but its application to vulnerability detection has not yet been sufficiently explored.

Despite the growing interest, we still lack a clear understanding of how LLMs behave when detecting vulnerabilities, especially when they are asked to reason explicitly. It is also unclear how to effectively make these models behave in a reliable and generalizable way without relying on expensive annotations, hand-crafted features, or fragile pipelines. We need a principled way to shape the behavior of models that not only improves accuracy, but also ensures coherent and trustworthy reasoning across different code bases.

Contributions. To better understand and improve the behavior of LLMs in vulnerability detection, we conduct a systematic study of two representative small-scale models: Phi-4 [2] and LLaMA 8B [1]. We show that, even when explicitly prompted to reason, these models exhibit flawed decision patterns: they frequently overpredict the presence of vulnerabilities (yielding high recall but low precision) or struggle to confidently identify secure code. These tendencies make their predictions difficult to trust in practical security workflows.

To address these limitations, we apply *Group Relative Policy Optimization* (GRPO) [14], a reinforcement learning algorithm that shapes the model's behavior through structured, comparative, and rule-based rewards. We design rewards that target both vulnerability detection accuracy and reasoning coherence by penalizing inconsistent or unjustified outputs and reinforcing explanations that understand the nature of the vulnerability (CWE/CVE) if it exists.

Experiments on three datasets: BigVul [6], DiverseVul [3], and CleanVul [9], show that GRPO enhances model robustness and generalization. Our findings suggest that behavior-driven optimization is key to making LLMs effective for practical vulnerability detection. To the best of our knowledge, our paper is the first to apply GRPO to software-vulnerability detection.

This paper makes the following key contributions:

- We demonstrate that small LLMs, even when prompted to reason, show unreliable decision patterns, with Phi4 reaching an accuracy of 0.446 on CleanVul and 0.244 on BigVul and LLaMA 8b reaching an accuracy of 0.449 on Diversevul.
- We show that adopting *Group Relative Policy Optimization (GRPO)* significantly improves both the accuracy and consistency of the predictions:
  - **Phi-4 → BigVul:** Macro-F_1 increases from 0.224 to 0.411 (+83 %) and accuracy improves by 13 %.
  - **Phi-4 → CleanVul:** Macro-F_1 rises from 0.417 to 0.581 (+39 %) while accuracy gains 14 %.
  - **LLaMA 8B → DiverseVul:** Macro-F_1 climbs from 0.430 to 0.602 (+40 %) with a 17 % boost in accuracy.

- We show that training on *DiverseVul* (a curated dataset) produces more robust models compared to noisier benchmarks like *BigVul*.
- We analyze the effect of KL regularization in the GRPO loss: reducing β to 10^{-6} increases recall on vulnerable code, reducing false negatives without overwhelming users with false alarms.

Paper Organization. Section 2 introduces the foundations of software vulnerability detection and the GRPO algorithm. Section 3 presents a behavioral analysis of small LLMs, highlighting their limitations and we describe our reward design and GRPO training procedure. Section 4 discusses related work and finally, Sect. 5 concludes the paper and outlines future directions.

2 Background

This section provides a brief overview of the core concepts underlying our work: the challenges associated with automatic vulnerability detection and the GRPO algorithm used to guide model behaviour through structured reward feedback.

2.1 Software Vulnerability Detection: Concepts and Challenges

Automated software vulnerability detection seeks to uncover flaws, such as buffer overflows, injection points, or logic errors, that attackers could exploit to undermine a system's integrity, confidentiality, or availability. As codebases grow in size and complexity, manual code review becomes impractical, and even mature tools struggle to keep pace with new language features and idioms.

Traditional static analysis methods inspect code without executing it, using heuristics or formal rules to flag suspicious constructs. They excel at catching simple patterns but often generate high rates of false positives and miss context-sensitive flaws. Dynamic analysis (fuzzing) executes programs on crafted inputs to observe failures at runtime; while powerful for memory errors, it can fail to reach deep code paths or reason about semantic bugs [8,15].

More recently, large language models (LLMs) pretrained on massive code repositories have shown strong zero- and few-shot ability to recognize vulnerable patterns with minimal feature engineering. Despite their syntactic prowess, LLM-based detectors generally make isolated, line by line predictions and do not provide a structured way to follow a program's control or data flow in sequence [7].

These gaps, such as false positives, incomplete path coverage, and the need for strategic, context-sensitive inspections, highlight the importance of integrating reinforcement learning. By training models to navigate code structures and prioritize genuinely vulnerable regions, this approach can more efficiently identify actual security weaknesses.

2.2 Group Relative Policy Optimization (GRPO)

Group Relative Policy Optimization (GRPO) is a reinforcement learning algorithm proposed by DeepSeek to improve the stability and efficiency of policy updates without relying on separate value function approximators [4,14], as required in traditional methods like Proximal Policy Optimization (PPO) [13]. GRPO introduces a novel approach by leveraging multiple sampled outputs, generated in response to the same input prompt, to estimate rewards comparatively. This group-based design aligns well with modern reward models, which are often trained on preference data comparing candidate responses. Originally developed and evaluated in the context of complex reasoning tasks such as mathematical problem solving, GRPO demonstrates strong performance in optimizing large language models (LLMs) using both outcome-level and step-level supervision. In this paper, we explore the potential of GRPO in a new application domain: vulnerability detection, where an LLM must navigate and assess code structures effectively to identify security flaws.

3 Behavioral Analysis

This section presents a behavioural study of small language models when applied to vulnerability detection tasks. We aim to assess whether these models exhibit systematic tendencies, such as risk aversion, overgeneralization, or sensitivity to noise, when reasoning about code security. To address this objective, we first outline the datasets employed to analyze model behavior, then assess predictive patterns and reward shaping strategies implemented to direct such behaviors during the fine-tuning process.

3.1 Vulnerability Datasets

In our methodology we leverage three vulnerability datasets: *DiverseVul*, *BigVul* and *CleanVul*, each selected for its particular strengths in model training and evaluation:

1. *DiverseVul* comprises 18.945 vulnerable functions (spanning 150 CWEs) and 330.492 non-vulnerable functions extracted from 7.514 commits across hundreds of projects. Its high degree of manual curation and broad project coverage yields label precision, making it well suited for model fine-tuning when minimizing false positives is critical [3].
2. *BigVul* gathers a large-scale C/C++ vulnerability corpus by crawling the public CVE database and related GitHub repositories. Although its reliance on automatically matched CVE descriptions introduces noise, its sheer volume allows assessment of a model's ability to learn robust feature representations from less-clean data [6].
3. *CleanVul* is a multi-language collection of 8.203 functions selected via an LLM-based heuristic pipeline (90.6% overall correctness). It encompasses Java, Python, JavaScript, C#, C and C++, and was designed primarily to evaluate model generalization across programming languages. Given its llm-based nature it is not possible to connect each code snippet with a specific CWE [9].

Table 1a presents a comparative summary of CWE and project distributions between *BigVul* and *DiverseVul*. While both datasets were utilized in Subsect.

3.3 for training models (Phi4 and LLaMA 8b, respectively), *DiverseVul* demonstrates broader coverage, encompassing more unique CWEs and a higher number of projects than *BigVul*. Its lower concentration in the top 5 CWEs and projects further underscores its greater diversity. This is followed by Table 1b, which details the language distribution in *CleanVul*. The dataset is dominated by C, reflecting a pronounced focus on C/C++ based ecosystems, with supplementary multilingual representation enhancing its scope for cross-language vulnerability analysis.

Table 1. Dataset characteristics: CWE/project coverage and language distribution.

	BigVul		DiverseVul	
Metric	Train	Test	Train	Test
Unique CWEs	90	85	150	145
Top 5 CWEs (% cov.)	55%	55%	39%	39%
Unique proj.	309	289	799	741
Top 5 proj. (% cov.)	73%	71%	33%	32%

Language	**Distribution**
C	47.18%
Java	19.53%
JavaScript	15.32%
Python	15.24%
C#	1.77%

3.2 Behavioural Evaluation of Small LLMs for Vulnerability Detection

In this study, we evaluate the efficacy of small-scale language models in distinguishing code as either *Vulnerable* or *Non Vulnerable* through binary classification, with an emphasis on analyzing their behavioral patterns during this process. We consider two representative architectures: `Phi4` (~13B parameters), trained **Bigvul** dataset, and `LLaMA 8B` model trained on the more diverse and heterogeneous **DiverseVul** benchmark.

Experimental Setup. All models were evaluated in a zero-shot classification setting using the prompt shown in Listing 1.1 and Listing 1.2. The model was given a fixed system prompt describing the behaviour analysis task and a user prompt containing the target code snippet.

The output labels, enclosed within <answer> and </answer>, were compared with the ground-truth labels. We evaluate the model's performance using standard binary classification metrics derived from the confusion matrix. Given two classes, *Vulnerable* and *Not Vulnerable*, the confusion matrix includes *true pos-*

itives (TP), *false positives* (FP), *true negatives* (TN), and *false negatives* (FN) and given their values we compute the following metrics:

$$\texttt{Accuracy} = \frac{TP+TN}{TP+TN+FP+FN}, \quad \texttt{Precision} = \frac{TP}{TP+FP} \tag{1}$$

$$\texttt{Recall} = \frac{TP}{TP+FN}, \quad \texttt{F1-Score} = \frac{2 \times TP}{2 \times TP+FP+FN} \tag{2}$$

```
You are a software security expert. I will provide you with code snippets. Your task is to
    analyze the code and determine whether it contains any vulnerabilities.

<reasoning>
1. Summarize the code snippet.
2. Check thoroughly for vulnerabilities.
3. Clearly state whether the code is secure or insecure.
</reasoning>

<answer>
Yes, the code is vulnerable.
OR
No, the code is not vulnerable.
</answer>
```

Listing 1.1. System prompt provided to the model

```
Analyze the following code snippet to determine whether it is vulnerable.

{CODE SNIPPET}
```

Listing 1.2. User prompt provided to the model

Additionally, macro average was computed. The *macro average* calculates the unweighted mean of the metric across all classes, treating each class equally. The complete set of results is reported in Table 2. Below, we summarize the key findings based on these results:

1. *Vulnerable code: many true positives, many false alarms.* `Phi4` display strong recall for the VULNERABLE class on **CleanVul** (0.916) and **BigVul** (0.835), but this comes at the cost of very low precision, especially on **BigVul** (0.054). The low F_1 scores for the vulnerable class (0.101 on BigVul) confirm that the models tend to overpredict insecurity, resulting in a large number of false alarms. This pattern is reversed in **DiverseVul**, where `LLaMA 8B` shows slightly better precision (0.437) but much lower recall (0.258), suggesting increased caution.
2. *Overconfidence in predicting non-vulnerable code.* For Phi4, precision for the NON-VULNERABLE class is extremely high across all datasets (up to 0.960 on **BigVul**), but recall remains low, especially for **CleanVul** (0.176). This indicates that model is reluctant to confidently classify code as safe, even when it is, possibly due to an overcautious treatment of benign patterns, leading to safe examples being flagged unnecessarily.

3. *Degradation under distribution shift and class imbalance.* Moving from **CleanVul** dataset to noisier or more diverse benchmarks like **BigVul** and the heavily imbalanced **DiverseVul** (~18 945 vulnerable vs. 330 492 non-vulnerable functions) leads to a marked drop in performance. For `Phi4`, macro F_1 drops from 0.417 to 0.224, underscoring its vulnerability to label noise and project drift. `LLaMA 8B` attains a macro F_1 of 0.430 on **DiverseVul**, but this figure is inflated by the dominance of the non-vulnerable class ($F_{1\text{non-vuln}} = 0.535$). Its recall for the vulnerable class remains low (0.258), indicating that true robustness in identifying security flaws under severe class imbalance has yet to be achieved.
4. *Shallow decision heuristics.* The precision recall gaps observed on **BigVul** reveal that `Phi4` is guided by very coarse cues: for the VULNERABLE class, precision drops to 0.054 while recall rises to 0.835; conversely, for the NON-VULNERABLE class, precision peaks at 0.960 but recall drops to 0.212. This pattern indicates that the model fires on almost any surface indicator of vulnerability yet hesitates to mark code as safe unless it is unmistakably benign. A milder but similar mismatch is visible in `LLaMA 8B` on **DiverseVul** (precision 0.437 vs. recall 0.258 for the vulnerable class). Together, these discrepancies suggest that both models rely on shallow lexical or syntactic signals, failing to capture deeper semantic relationships and consequently mishandling subtle or context-dependent flaws.

The precision and recall imbalance makes their raw outputs impractical for real-world triage. On **BigVul**, `Phi4` adopts a markedly *risk seeking* stance, generating a flood of false alarms that can overwhelm analysts. At the same time, its high precision but low recall on the NON VULNERABLE class means benign files remain flagged and untriaged. Conversely, `LLaMA 8B` on the heavily imbalanced **DiverseVul** swings to the opposite extreme: it misses many true flaws while still offering only moderate precision, showing that class imbalance can push the model into an overly *risk-averse* regime.

These dataset dependent oscillations reveal an overreliance on superficial lexical cues and poorly calibrated decision boundaries. In practice, *small LLMs in zero-shot are not yet reliable standalone vulnerability detectors*: they either inundate pipelines with false positives or silently overlook critical bugs.

3.3 Shaping LLM Behaviour for Effective Vulnerability Detection

The issues we just discussed show that both models struggle to make stable, reliable decisions. To fix this, we finetune them with Group Relative Policy Optimization (GRPO) [14]. Our reward combines two signals: *label correctness* and *explanation quality*, to prevent the model from overfitting to label frequency or noise, ensuring consistent learning across both clean and imbalanced datasets.

1. **Phi-4** → BIGVUL: stresses robustness under label noise and severe class imbalance, encouraging stable recall without collapsing precision.

Table 2. Comparison of classification metrics for `Phi4` and `LLaMA 8B` across three datasets: `Cleanvul` (**Cln**), `Bigvul`(**Big**), `DiverseVul`(**Div**).

Metric (Class)	CleanVul (Phi4)	BigVul (Phi4)	DiverseVul (LLaMA 8B)
Prec. (Vuln)	0.390	0.054	0.437
Recall (Vuln)	0.916	0.835	0.258
F_1 (Vuln)	0.547	0.101	0.325
Prec. (Non-vuln)	0.784	0.960	0.454
Recall (Non-vuln)	0.176	0.212	0.650
F_1 (Non-vuln)	0.287	0.347	0.535
Macro Precision	0.587	0.507	0.446
Macro Recall	0.546	0.523	0.454
Macro F_1	0.417	0.224	0.430
Accuracy	0.446	0.244	0.449

2. **LLaMA 8B** → DIVERSEVUL: exploits high-precision labels to teach the model to justify predictions without over-flagging benign code.

Table 3 compares the top-5 CWE categories in the training and test splits of DIVERSEVUL and BIGVUL. BIGVUL shows a highly skewed distribution: the same five CWEs appear in both splits with similar proportions, collectively covering approximately 55% of the entire dataset. This overlap limits variability and increases the risk of overfitting to these dominant classes. In contrast, DIVERSEVUL provides a broader and more balanced distribution: its top-5 CWEs account for only about 39% of the data, and two categories (CWE-20 and CWE-416) appear exclusively in either the training or the test split. This split-specific coverage introduces variability between training and evaluation, making DIVERSEVUL a more challenging and realistic benchmark for testing model generalization under domain shift conditions.

Both training and evaluation were performed using the same structured prompt shown in the listings 1.1 and 1.2. Post-training, both models were evaluated on all 3 benchmarks CLEANVUL, BIGVUL (only the *Test set* for Phi4) and DIVERSEVUL (only the *Test set* for LLaMA 8B). To train the models, we start from the original GRPO loss (shown in Eq. 3) and introduce the modifications detailed below.

$$\mathcal{J}_{\text{GRPO}}(\theta) = \mathbb{E}\left[q \sim \mathbb{P}(Q), \{o_i\}_{i=1}^{G} \sim \pi_{\theta_{\text{old}}}(O|q)\right] \\ \left[\frac{1}{G}\sum_{i=1}^{G}\frac{1}{|o_i|}\sum_{t=1}^{|o_i|}\min\left(\frac{\pi_\theta(o_{i,t}|q,o_{i,<t})}{\pi_{\theta_{\text{old}}}(o_{i,t}|q,o_{i,<t})}\hat{A}_{i,t}, \text{clip}\left(\frac{\pi_\theta(o_{i,t}|q,o_{i,<t})}{\pi_{\theta_{\text{old}}}(o_{i,t}|q,o_{i,<t})}, 1-\epsilon, 1+\epsilon\right)\hat{A}_{i,t}\right) - \beta \mathrm{D}_{\mathrm{KL}}\left[\pi_\theta \| \pi_{\text{ref}}\right]\right] \tag{3}$$

At the first iteration, the ratio is always 1 since $\pi_\theta = \pi_{\theta_{\text{old}}}$, making the clipping unnecessary. To remove *Question-level difficulty bias* [10], the advantage is defined as $\hat{A}_{i,t} = R_i - \bar{R}$ instead of being normalized by the standard deviation, where R_i is the return of the i-th trajectory and $\bar{R}$ is the mean return over the group G. Moreover, we set $\beta = 10^{-6}$ in all experiments. The objective simplifies to Eq. 4:

$$\mathcal{J}_{\mathrm{GRPO}}(\theta) = \frac{1}{G}\sum_{i=1}^{G}(R_i - \bar{R}) - 10^{-6} \cdot \mathrm{D}_{\mathrm{KL}}\left[\pi_\theta \| \pi_{\mathrm{ref}}\right] \quad (4)$$

Table 3. Top-5 CWE distribution in the training and test splits of DiverseVul and BigVul.

CWE	Train		Test	
	#	%	#	%
787	31 353	10.88	3 978	11.06
125	22 571	7.83	2 719	7.56
703	20 242	7.02	2 461	6.84
119	19 902	6.90	2 589	7.20
20	18 248	6.33	–	–
416	–	–	2 331	6.48

CWE	Train		Test	
	#	%	#	%
119	21 293	17.46	4 478	16.82
20	16 392	13.44	3 388	12.72
399	11 769	9.65	2 889	10.85
264	9 894	8.11	2 287	8.59
416	7 887	6.47	1 559	5.86

Insights on *Phi-4* Trained with GRPO on *BigVul*.
This experiment was designed to assess Phi4's capacity to generalize from a massive vulnerability corpus, addressing the risk of overfitting to project-specific code patterns in BigVul: by fine-tuning Phi-4 on a dataset with many snippets drawn repeatedly from the same projects, we test whether it can learn transferable vulnerability representations beyond individual codebases.

Experimental Set-Up. The GRPO training procedure is guided by a structured reward function composed of two components: a *reasoning reward* and a *correctness reward*, computed respectively as F_i and C_i in Equation (5). These components are derived from dedicated verifiers applied to model outputs structured with <answer> and <reasoning> tags.

Correctness reward (C_i). The correctness reward C_i is computed by comparing the content of the <answer> tag, $y_i \in \{\text{Yes}, \text{No}\}$, with the ground-truth label $t_i \in \{\text{Yes}, \text{No}\}$ via case-insensitive matching:

$$c_i = \begin{cases} 1, & \text{if } y_i = t_i, \\ 0, & \text{otherwise.} \end{cases}$$

To discourage repetitive answers, we check the last three mistakes $S_i = \{j_1, j_2, j_3\}$ where $c_{j_k} = 0$, and define:

$$m_i = \begin{cases} 1, & \text{if } |S_i| = 3 \text{ and } \forall j \in S_i : y_j = y_i, \\ 0, & \text{otherwise.} \end{cases}$$

The final reward combines these terms:

$$C_i = \alpha c_i + \beta(1 - c_i)m_i = \begin{cases} \alpha, & \text{if } c_i = 1, \\ \beta, & \text{if } c_i = 0 \text{ and } m_i = 1, \\ 0, & \text{otherwise.} \end{cases}$$

Empirically, the best performance was observed with $\alpha = 8$, $\beta = -2$ and if the <answer> tag is missing or empty, we set $C_i = -5$.

Reasoning reward (F_i). The reasoning reward evaluates the explanation provided in the <reasoning> field and consists of two components. Let $l_i \in \{0, 2\}$ represent the semantic alignment between the reasoning r_i and the vulnerability description d_i, computed using a *Cross-Encoder* (`nli-deberta-v3-base`):

$$l_i = \begin{cases} 2, & \text{if } r_i \text{ entails } d_i, \\ 0, & \text{otherwise.} \end{cases}$$

Let $|L_i|$ be the character length of r_i. We reward longer explanations (up to 1000 characters) as:

$$s_i = \min(|L_i|, 1000) \times 0.005 \quad \text{so that } s_i \in (0, 5].$$

The reasoning reward is the sum of both components:

$$F_i = l_i + s_i.$$

If the <reasoning> tag is missing or empty, a fixed penalty is applied:

$$F_i = -5.$$

The total reward combines correctness and reasoning scores:

$$R_i = C_i + F_i \tag{5}$$

with $R_i \in [-10, 15]$.

1. **Marked improvement from base to finetuned model.** Fine-tuning Phi-4 yields substantial performance gains across datasets as shown in Tab. 4. On *BigVul*, Macro-F_1 rises from 0.224 to 0.411 (+83%) and accuracy improves by 13%. Similarly, on *CleanVul*, Macro-F_1 increases from 0.417 to 0.581 (+39%) alongside a 14% boost in accuracy. These results underscore the effectiveness of fine-tuning, though further analysis is needed to understand the behavioral shifts introduced by this process.

2. **Substantial gains on Not Vulnerable examples.** By adopting our chosen correctness based reward, we observe a pronounced uplift in the classification of safe code. On *CleanVul*, the F_1 score of *Not Vulnerable* examples jumps from 0.287 to 0.586, and on *BigVul* from 0.347 to 0.694. Most of this improvement comes via recall on the safe class: while precision remains essentially flat, the model now catches far more true negatives. This means our reward scheme both reduces false alarms and improves specificity.
3. **Modest progress on "Vulnerable" examples.** We also see F_1 gains when identifying vulnerable code, though they're more muted. On *BigVul*, F_1 score of *Vulnerable* examples rises from 0.101 to 0.128, a small net improvement driven by a slight precision boost that partially offsets a drop in recall. The pattern repeats in *DiverseVul*: precision nudges up, recall dips, and F_1 edges higher, suggesting that meaningful advances in vulnerability detection remain challenging despite these improvements.
4. **Consistent improvements across datasets.** Significantly, the performance improvements observed on *BigVul* generalize to other benchmarks: *CleanVul* and *DiverseVul* demonstrate comparable performance trajectories, indicating that our reward driven fine-tuning approach exhibits robust cross-dataset generalization capabilities. Nevertheless, potential label noise in *BigVul* may limit the extent of achievable performance gains, suggesting that label quality currently constitutes the primary limiting factor in further advancements.

Further insight and next steps. The persistent gap in vulnerability recall and low precision on imbalanced data point to two root causes: (1) the model's initial conservative bias and (2) annotation errors in *BigVul*. We therefore hypothesize that training on a corpus with cleaner, more granular vulnerability labels will encourage the model to internalize true semantically driven attack patterns rather than artifacts of a noisy dataset. To validate this, we finetuned the smaller *Llama 8B* model on the higher quality *DiverseVul* dataset.

Table 4. Compact classification metrics for Phi-4 model trained on BigVul and tested on CleanVul, BigVul (test), and DiverseVul.

Dataset	Vulnerable			Not Vulnerable			Macro Avg			Accuracy
	Prec.	Rec.	F1	Prec.	Rec.	F1	Prec.	Rec.	F1	Acc.
CleanVul	0.4555	0.7794	0.5750	0.7871	0.4668	0.5860	0.6213	0.6231	0.5805	0.5806
BigVul	0.0710	0.6542	0.1281	0.9668	0.5409	0.6937	0.5189	0.5976	0.4109	0.5467
DiverseVul	0.0586	0.7753	0.1090	0.9748	0.4110	0.5783	0.5167	0.5932	0.3436	0.4275

Generalisation Insights for *LLaMA 8B* trained on *DiverseVul*. This experiment was designed to explicitly enforce project-level disjointness between training and testing samples, addressing one of the core limitations highlighted by

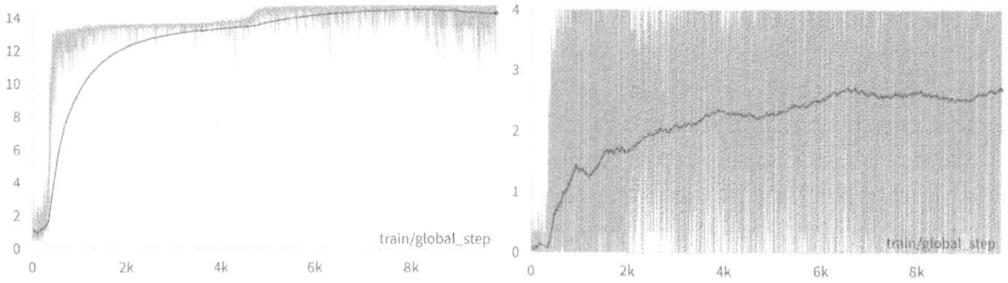

(a) Formatting Reward (b) Correctness Reward

Fig. 1. Reward progression across training steps. The formatting reward stabilizes quickly, while correctness reward grows more gradually.

the *DiverseVul* authors [3]: *the inability of deep learning models to generalize to unseen projects*, a critical requirement in real-world vulnerability detection.

Reward Design. Even in this case, the GRPO trainer uses a reward function based on the *correctness of the predicted answer* and the *quality of the explanation.*

- **Correctness reward** (Figure 1b). For each completion, we extract the content inside the <answer> tag and compare it to the correct answer, ignoring case. The answer is expected in the form "Yes, the code is vulnerable" or "No, the code is not vulnerable". If the prediction exactly matches the correct answer, we assign a reward of 4. Otherwise, the reward is 0.
- **Explanation (formatting) reward** (Figure 1a). We then check the explanation inside the <reasoning> tag and assign a reward based on three criteria:
  1. **Clear structure.** We check if the explanation follows a *three-step* structure of the reasoning part of the given prompt, shown in Listing 1.1, using the pattern "1. ... 2. ... 3. ...". If present, we give a bonus.
  2. **Length and wording variety.** We reward explanations that are longer but not repetitive. We use a log-based bonus that grows with the number of words, but we reduce the reward if the explanation repeats the same words too much.
  3. **Consistency with the answer.** We compare the final step (Step 3 of the given prompt, shown in Listing 1.1) of the explanation to the predicted answer. We check both how similar they are in terms of words (edit distance[1]) and in meaning (cosine similarity using MiniLM-L6-v2 embeddings[2]). If the explanation just repeats the answer without adding value, we apply a small penalty. On the other hand, if it provides a meaningful and consistent justification, we give an extra bonus.

1 https://docs.python.org/3/library/difflib.html.
2 sentence-transformers/all-MiniLM-L6-v2.

- **Coherence check and batch filtering.** We compute a *Coherence Score*, measuring how well the explanation's final step matches the predicted answer in meaning (Fig. 2a). If this score is too low (below 0.4), the explanation is marked as `incoherent`. We then calculate the *Incoherent Answer Ratio*, which tells us how many explanations in the batch are incoherent (Fig. 2b). If more than half of the batch is incoherent, we completely remove the correctness reward for the whole batch to avoid reinforcing flawed answers.

Reward aggregation. Correctness and formatting scores are minmax normalised within the batch and combined by

$$r_i = \alpha \hat{F}_i + (1 - \alpha) \hat{C}_i,$$

where the mixing coefficient α (Fig. 3a) is *dynamic*: it shifts weight towards correctness when the average formatting score is high and towards formatting when the average is low. Next, r_i is passed through *power scaling*: r_i^γ, where the exponent γ grows with the batch-wise stability of correctness scores (low standard deviation) to emphasise confident predictions (Fig. 3b). Finally, the scaled rewards go through a temperature-controlled softmax (τ) so that they sum to 1 and can be used directly as RL preference weights.

Putting everything together, the final reward for completion i is

$$\text{FinalReward}_i = \begin{cases} 0, & \text{if} \quad \texttt{IncoherentRatio} > 0.5 \\ & \text{and} \ \texttt{isIncoherent}_i = 1 \\ \texttt{Softmax}\Big((\alpha \hat{F}_i + (1-\alpha)\hat{C}_i)^\gamma / \tau\Big), & \text{otherwise.} \end{cases} \tag{6}$$

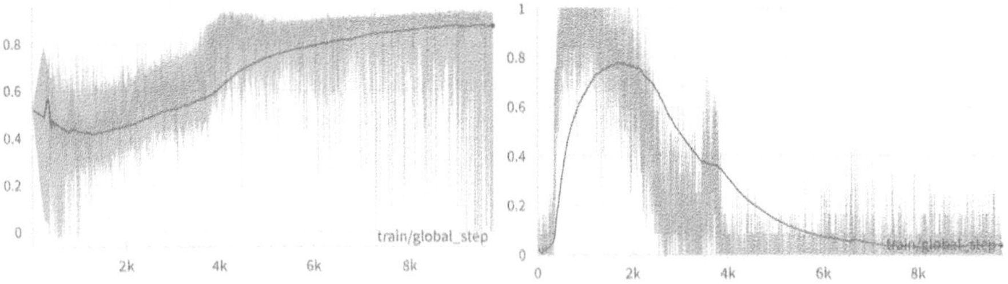

(a) Coherence Score (b) Incoherent Ratio Score

Fig. 2. Progression of coherence-based metrics across training steps.

1. **Within-project effectiveness.** On the in-distribution portion of *DiverseVul*, even if we have test samples that come from different projects with respect to the ones in the training set, the model performs strongly: a recall of **0.81** and an F_1 score of **0.68** for the VULNERABLE class show that LLaMA 8B, once fine-tuned, effectively learns high-level semantic cues related to vulnerabilities.
2. **Generalisation under domain shift.** When tested on *CleanVul*, a dataset that not only features different coding styles, library usage, and project conventions, but also includes programming languages beyond C (which dominates DIVERSEVUL), the model still achieves reasonably good performance. Although there is a performance drop, with recall for VULNERABLE samples decreasing to **0.42** and F_1 to **0.50**, these results confirm the model's ability to generalise beyond the C language. This suggests that, despite the domain shift and the presence of different languages, the model retains some capacity to detect vulnerabilities in a cross-language setting, even though its representations remain somewhat sensitive to superficial stylistic differences.
3. **Partial transferability via structural similarity.** Interestingly, results on *BigVul* are more balanced. With $F_{1,\text{Vul}} = 0.61$ and $F_{1,\text{Weighted}} = 0.62$, the model maintains performance close to that achieved in-distribution. This may be attributed to latent structural or syntactic similarities between *BigVul* and *DiverseVul*, such as overlapping programming languages, function structures, or comment styles, which facilitate transfer even across datasets(Tab. 5) .

(a) Alpha Coefficient (b) Power Function

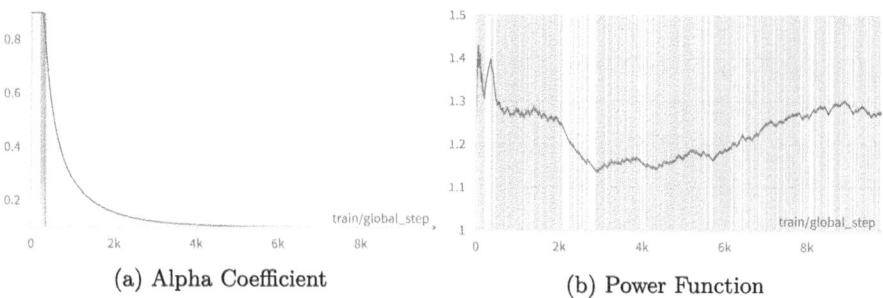

Fig. 3. Progression of *Alpha coefficient* and *Power function* across training steps.

Table 5. Compact classification metrics for LLaMA 8B trained on DiverseVul and tested on DiverseVul (ID), CleanVul (OOD), and BigVul (OOD).

Dataset	Vulnerable			Not Vulnerable			**Macro Avg**			Accuracy
	Prec.	Rec.	F1	Prec.	Rec.	F1	Prec.	Rec.	F1	Acc.
DiverseVul	0.5791	0.8149	0.6771	0.6998	0.4215	0.5261	0.6395	0.6182	0.6016	0.6159
CleanVul	0.6103	0.4240	0.5004	0.5587	0.7293	0.6327	0.5845	0.5766	0.5665	0.5766
BigVul	0.6370	0.5885	0.6118	0.6096	0.6570	0.6324	0.6233	0.6228	0.6221	0.6224

3.4 Impact of KL Regularization on Negative Class Behaviour

To better understand the influence of KL regularization on model behaviour, we conduct a controlled ablation varying the β parameter, which regulates the KL divergence weight in the GRPO loss. In particular, we contrast two values, $\beta = 10^{-4}$ and $\beta = 10^{-6}$, and observe their effect on the rates of **True Negatives** (TN) and **False Negatives** (FN) during training.

Figure 4 illustrates that a higher β value leads to a more conservative model: the True Negative rate steadily increases over time, indicating that the model becomes more confident in identifying non-vulnerable code. However, this behaviour comes at a cost: as shown in Fig. 5, the False Negative rate also rises, especially after the early training phase. This suggests that excessive regularization suppresses risk-taking, leading the model to underpredict vulnerabilities in borderline or ambiguous samples.

Conversely, reducing β to 10^{-6} yields the opposite trade-off: while the model becomes less confident in rejecting benign samples (lower TN rate), it maintains a lower FN rate throughout training, exhibiting a more risk-seeking stance that prioritizes catching vulnerabilities over avoiding false alarms.

These findings confirm that β acts as a behavioural dial: increasing it promotes conservative classification and favours high precision on the *Non vulnerable* class, whereas smaller values encourage high recall for the *Vulnerable* class by reducing over-regularization. The optimal β value therefore depends on the desired balance between false positives and false negatives in downstream use cases.

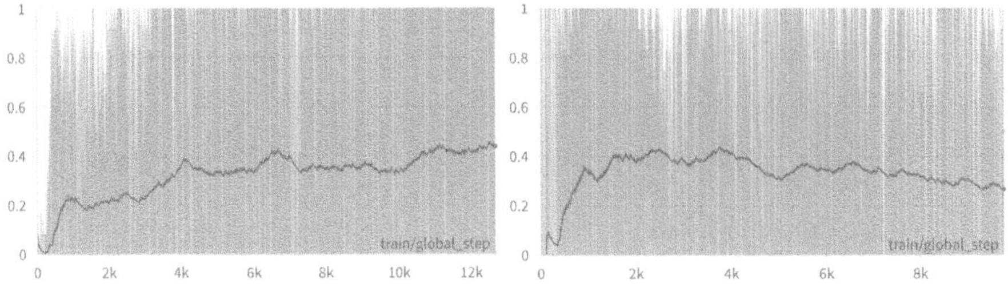

(a) $\beta = 10^{-4}$ (b) $\beta = 10^{-6}$

Fig. 4. Effect of β on **True Negative** rates during training.

4 Related Work

Large language models have recently been applied to program analysis, yet their out-of-the-box accuracy on realistic vulnerability datasets remains modest. [7]

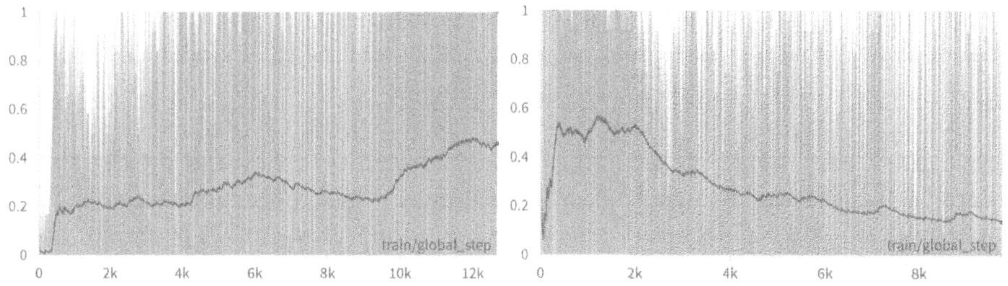

(a) $\beta = 10^{-4}$ (b) $\beta = 10^{-6}$

Fig. 5. Effect of β on **False Negative** rates during training.

show that even state-of-the-art LLMs struggle to reason about subtle memory-safety flaws when the signal is diluted by project-specific coding idioms.

A first line of research tackles this gap through *supervised fine-tuning.* When sufficient annotated functions are available, updating model weights on domain specific corpora improves recall, but the resulting detectors often memorise dataset artefacts and quickly lose precision on unseen projects [16].

Complementary work injects external context at inference time. retrieval augmented generation (RAG) systems fetch similar code or API documentation to ground the model's prediction [5]. Although this strategy raises recall without additional training, it introduces latency and inherits the biases of the retrieval index.

Others emphasise program structure. Approaches that encode abstract-syntax trees or program-dependence graphs as part of the input supply rich control- and data-flow cues [11]. Graph encoding, however, demands non trivial preprocessing pipelines and remains brittle when key nodes are pruned or unparsable.

More recently, reinforcement-learning techniques have been explored as a lightweight alternative to full fine-tuning. ProRLearn [12] dynamically reformulates prompts and updates a policy via reward feedback, yielding stronger cross dataset generalization than static prompts while avoiding catastrophic forgetting of linguistic knowledge.

To the best of our knowledge, the our work is the first to apply GRPO to software-vulnerability detection, demonstrating that behaviour oriented reward shaping can alleviate the high false-positive rates observed in prior LLM-based systems.

5 Conclusion

In this paper, we have shown the behavioural limits of small, large scale language models in detecting software vulnerabilities and demonstrated that a reinforcement learning approach can decisively shift these limits. When models such as

Phi-4 and **LLaMA-8B** are used without fine-tuning, their risk is miscalibrated: they tend to over-label benign code, miss real vulnerabilities, and fail when the target project or programming language changes.

By applying *group relative policy optimization* (GRPO) with a reward that maximizes both label accuracy and explanation quality, we overturn these shortcomings. Concretely, on the *BigVul* benchmark Phi-4 lifts its macro-F_1 from 0.224 to 0.411, an 83 % gain, while accuracy climbs from 0.244 to 0.5467. The same model, evaluated out-of-distribution on *CleanVul*, moves from 0.417 to 0.581 in macro F_1, a 39 % improvement, accompanied by a 14 % rise in accuracy. LLaMA-8B, fine-tuned with the identical procedure on *DiverseVul*, sees its macro F_1 advance from 0.430 to 0.602 (40 %) and its accuracy from 0.449 to 0.616 (17 %). Lowering the KL regularisation to $\beta = 10^{-6}$ further nudges the policy toward a useful risk-seeking stance, trimming false negatives without letting false positives proliferate.

These results show that shaping an LLM's behaviour with reinforcement learning is a practical way to build vulnerability detectors that are both accurate and easy to understand. Next, we plan to let the reward adjust itself during training so the model can balance precision and recall in real time; test the approach on full, multi-language codebases that resemble those used in industry; and combine our GRPO trained models with classic static analysis tools so they can quickly point to the exact line that needs fixing. Together, these steps could bring automated bug finding up to the reliability and transparency standards that modern software security demands.

Acknowledgments. This work has been funded by the European Union - NextGenerationEU within the framework of PNRR Mission 4 - Component 2 - Investment 1.1 under the Italian Ministry of University and Research (MUR) programme"PRIN 2022" - grant number 2022598LMZ - AsCoT-SCE - CUP: H53D23003430006.

References

1. et al., A.G.: The llama 3 herd of models (2024). https://arxiv.org/abs/2407.21783
2. et al., M.A.: Phi-4 technical report (2024). https://arxiv.org/abs/2412.08905
3. Chen, Y., Ding, Z., Alowain, L., Chen, X., Wagner, D.A.: Diversevul: a new vulnerable source code dataset for deep learning based vulnerability detection. In: Proceedings of the 26th International Symposium on Research in Attacks, Intrusions and Defenses, RAID 2023, Hong Kong, China, October 16-18, 2023, pp. 654–668 (2023). https://doi.org/10.1145/3607199.3607242
4. DeepSeek-AI: Deepseek-r1: Incentivizing reasoning capability in LLMS via reinforcement learning. CoRR **abs/2501.12948** (2025). https://doi.org/10.48550/ARXIV.2501.12948
5. Du, X., et al.:.: Vul-rag: enhancing LLM-based vulnerability detection via knowledge-level RAG. CoRR **abs/2406.11147** (2024). https://doi.org/10.48550/ARXIV.2406.11147

6. Fan, J., Li, Y., Wang, S., Nguyen, T.N.: A C/C++ code vulnerability dataset with code changes and CVE summaries. In: MSR '20: 17th International Conference on Mining Software Repositories, Seoul, Republic of Korea, 29-30 June, 2020, pp. 508–512 (2020). https://doi.org/10.1145/3379597.3387501
7. Guo, Y., Patsakis, C., Hu, Q., Tang, Q., Casino, F.: Outside the comfort zone: analysing LLM capabilities in software vulnerability detection. In: Computer Security - ESORICS 2024 - 29th European Symposium on Research in Computer Security, Bydgoszcz, Poland, September 16-20, 2024, Proceedings, Part I, pp. 271–289 (2024). https://doi.org/10.1007/978-3-031-70879-4_14
8. Johnson, B., Song, Y., Murphy-Hill, E.R., Bowdidge, R.W.: Why don't software developers use static analysis tools to find bugs? In: Notkin, D., Cheng, B.H.C., Pohl, K. (eds.) 35th International Conference on Software Engineering, ICSE '13, San Francisco, CA, USA, May 18-26, 2013, pp. 672–681. IEEE Computer Society (2013). https://doi.org/10.1109/ICSE.2013.6606613
9. Li, Y., et al.: Cleanvul: automatic function-level vulnerability detection in code commits using LLM heuristics. CoRR **abs/2411.17274** (2024). https://doi.org/10.48550/ARXIV.2411.17274
10. Liu, Z., et al.: Understanding r1-zero-like training: a critical perspective (2025). arXiv preprint arXiv:2503.20783
11. Lu, G., Ju, X., Chen, X., Pei, W., Cai, Z.: GRACE: empowering LLM-based software vulnerability detection with graph structure and in-context learning. J. Syst. Softw. **212**, 112031 (2024). https://doi.org/10.1016/J.JSS.2024.112031
12. Ren, Z., Ju, X., Chen, X., Shen, H.: Prorlearn: boosting prompt tuning-based vulnerability detection by reinforcement learning. Autom. Softw. Eng. **31**(2), 38 (2024). https://doi.org/10.1007/S10515-024-00438-9
13. Schulman, J., Wolski, F., Dhariwal, P., Radford, A., Klimov, O.: Proximal policy optimization algorithms (2017). arXiv preprint arXiv:1707.06347
14. Shao, Z., et al.: Deepseekmath: pushing the limits of mathematical reasoning in open language models. CoRR **abs/2402.03300** (2024). https://doi.org/10.48550/ARXIV.2402.03300
15. Smith, J., Johnson, B., Murphy-Hill, E.R., Chu, B., Lipford, H.R.: Questions developers ask while diagnosing potential security vulnerabilities with static analysis. In: Nitto, E.D., Harman, M., Heymans, P. (eds.) Proceedings of the 2015 10th Joint Meeting on Foundations of Software Engineering, ESEC/FSE 2015, Bergamo, Italy, August 30 - September 4, 2015. pp. 248–259. ACM (2015). https://doi.org/10.1145/2786805.2786812
16. Yang, A.Z.H., Tian, H., Ye, H., Martins, R., Goues, C.L.: Security vulnerability detection with multitask self-instructed fine-tuning of large language models (2024). https://arxiv.org/abs/2406.05892

Leveraging Knowledge Graphs and LLMs for Structured Generation of Misinformation

Sania Nayab[1(✉)], Marco Simoni[2,3], and Giulio Rossolini[1]

[1] Scuola Superiore SantAnna, Pisa, Italy
sania.nayab@santannapisa.it

[2] Italian National Doctorate in Artificial Intelligence, Sapienza University of Rome, Rome, Italy

[3] Institute of Informatics and Telematics, National Research Council of Italy (CNR), Rome, Italy

Abstract. The rapid spread of misinformation, further amplified by recent advances in generative AI, poses significant threats to society, impacting public opinion, democratic stability, and national security. Understanding and proactively assessing these threats requires exploring methodologies that enable structured and scalable misinformation generation. In this paper, we propose a novel approach that leverages knowledge graphs (KGs) as structured semantic resources to systematically generate fake triplets. By analyzing the structural properties of KGs, such as the distance between entities and their predicates, we identify plausibly false relationships. These triplets are then used to guide large language models (LLMs) in generating misinformation statements with varying degrees of credibility. By utilizing structured semantic relationships, our deterministic approach produces misinformation inherently challenging for humans to detect, drawing exclusively upon publicly available KGs (e.g., WikiGraphs).

Additionally, we investigate the effectiveness of LLMs in distinguishing between genuine and artificially generated misinformation. Our analysis highlights significant limitations in current LLM-based detection methods, underscoring the necessity for enhanced detection strategies and a deeper exploration of inherent biases in generative models.

Keywords: Knowledge Graphs · Large Language Models · Misinformation Generation · Misinformation Detection · Behavioural analysis of LLMs

1 Introduction

The widespread dissemination of fake information poses significant threats to society [7], particularly with the recent advent of powerful generative AI models (e.g., GPT-4, Stable Diffusion) that significantly enhance the realism of misinformation

B. Coppens et al. (Eds.): ARES 2025 Workshops, LNCS 15997, pp. 334–350, 2025.
https://doi.org/10.1007/978-3-032-00639-4_19

generation [9,10], influencing public opinion and posing risks to national security. The ubiquity of digital media platforms accelerates the spread and impact of misinformation, making it increasingly challenging to detect and mitigate in real-time [6,21,23]. Consequently, understanding and analyzing how misinformation is generated and propagated has become an essential field of research [17].

The automatic generation of realistic yet deliberately false content is of particular interest, both as a potential threat and as a tool for extensive analysis. On one hand, automating misinformation creation could significantly amplify misinformation attacks, as automated methods can rapidly produce large volumes of credible-sounding false narratives [21]. On the other hand, controlled automated generation can serve as a powerful method to systematically explore, evaluate, and understand the characteristics and vulnerabilities associated with misinformation [10]. Thus, developing methodologies that allow structured, scalable, and analyzable misinformation generation is crucial for both defensive strategies and in-depth research into misinformation propagation mechanisms [7].

In this context, we argue that knowledge graphs (KGs) [5,19], structured repositories that explicitly represent entities and their relationships, offer promising opportunities. KGs inherently encode semantic structures that facilitate the understanding and quantification of the plausibility of potential falsehoods. By leveraging these structures, researchers can automatically derive relational properties between entities within the KG to guide the strategic generation of misinformation, controlling aspects such as relational proximity and perceived credibility. This approach enables the production of sophisticated misinformation that appears credible even under careful scrutiny, complicating both human and algorithmic detection.

Building on this assumption, this paper introduces a structured methodology that exploits predefined KGs to systematically generate templates for realistic fake statements. Our pipeline identifies plausible yet incorrect relational paths within the KG by employing its structural properties, enabling the generation of misinformation strategically positioned at multiple levels of plausibility [8]. As detailed in Sect. 3, this structured generation leverages the relational and semantic metadata embedded in KGs to ensure control and scalability, while also allowing fine-grained manipulation of stealthiness in relation to potential human scrutiny. To generate the actual misinformation, we provide these fake triplets, categorized by their degree of plausibility, as input prompts to large language models (LLMs). Figure 1 illustrates an example of fake information generated by the proposed pipeline (in red).

Furthermore, we evaluate the detection capabilities of state-of-the-art LLMs when confronted with these KG-based fabricated statements. Our analysis reveals critical insights into the strengths and limitations of current LLMs in misinformation detection tasks, with implications tied to known challenges such as bias [14,15] and hallucination [20]. These findings underscore the need for improved model robustness and a deeper understanding of LLM behavior under varying plausibility conditions. The main contributions of this work are:

- The introduction of a structured, knowledge graph-driven approach for generating plausible fake information, exploiting relational metadata to systematically control misinformation plausibility.

⟨ s, r, o' ⟩ = ⟨ "The Simpsons", "ns/tv.tv_program.episodes", "Perchance to Dream" ⟩

In a surprising twist, **The Simpsons** has announced its latest episode titled **Perchance to Dream**, marking a significant departure from its usual satirical style. This episode, set in the iconic town of Springfield, promises to delve into the deeper, more introspective aspects of the Simpson family's lives, exploring themes of ambition and the American Dream. Fans eagerly anticipate how this new direction will blend with the show's long-standing tradition of parodying American culture and society.

⟨ s, r, o ⟩ = ⟨ "The Simpsons", "ns/tv.tv_program.episodes", "Treehouse of Horror XX" ⟩

In a groundbreaking move, ***The Simpsons*** has announced that its iconic ***Treehouse of Horror XX*** episode will be the show's final installment, marking the end of an era for the beloved animated sitcom. Since its debut in 1989, This TV series has captivated audiences with its satirical take on American culture, featuring the misadventures of the Simpson family in the fictional town of Springfield. This decision comes after 574 episodes, solidifying Treehouse of Horror XX as a fitting conclusion to a series that has become a cornerstone of television history.

Fig. 1. Example of a correct triplet (extracted from the KG, shown in green) and a fake triplet generated by the proposed pipeline (shown in red), along with their corresponding facts generated by the LLM. The fake information (top part in red) represents an incorrect fact, but it is formulated in a coherent and plausible manner. (Color figure online)

- A comprehensive analysis of generated misinformation across multiple plausibility levels, elucidating the influence of knowledge graph structure on perceived credibility.
- An evaluative study of LLM capabilities in distinguishing between authentic and generated misinformation, identifying critical detection challenges and biases within current models.

The rest of the document is structured as follows: we first review relevant prior studies and their limitations in Sect. 2. The methodology, along with the necessary background and notations, is presented in Sect. 3. Section 4 provides an introduction to the use of LLMs as potential tools for detecting fake information. Experimental results demonstrating the effectiveness of our pipeline are detailed in Sect. 5. Finally, Sect. 6 summarizes the key findings and states potential directions for future research.

2 Related Works

Fake News in the LLMs Era. The generation of false information has become a critical concern, particularly with the advancements in generative AI models that significantly enhance the realism and plausibility of misinformation. Powerful models, such as GPT-4 [2], have raised alarms due to their ability to generate high-quality, convincing false content that can easily mislead the public and influence opinions. Huang et al. [10] explored the extensive use of prompt engineering with LLMs for fake news generation, highlighting the model's proficiency in generating and explaining fake news. The generative models, capable of producing human-like text, images, and videos, have potential applications in disinformation campaigns, including elections, social media manipulation, and national security threats [9,10,21].

KGs and LLMs. In recent years, several studies have explored the integration of knowledge graphs (KGs) with LLMs. KGs offer a structured and interpretable framework for representing relational and syntactic information, which can guide language generation in a more controlled and semantically grounded manner, potentially reducing issues such as hallucinations and improving factual accuracy. For example, prior work has investigated the use of KGs to evaluate the performance of LLMs [4,16]. Other studies [2,11] have demonstrated how models like GPT-3 and GPT-4 can be employed to generate content based on structured data extracted from KGs. Building on these findings, Mauro et al. [8] show how KGs can be leveraged to identify credible relational links and generate content that is both contextually coherent and structurally aligned with the knowledge base.

Despite these advancements, the use of KGs for generating fake information remains largely underexplored. Given the structured nature of KGs, they hold significant potential for automating the generation of large-scale misinformation with contextual consistency. Moreover, the ability of LLMs to produce highly fluent and plausible, but potentially false, text makes them particularly effective in crafting misinformation that is difficult to detect.

This work brings these two aspects together, proposing an automated framework that generates fake information at scale. The generation process is guided by a novel plausibility metric, allowing the system to produce content with varying degrees of credibility. This enables the creation of misinformation that appears semantically plausible and stealthy, thereby posing new challenges for detection systems.

Detecting Fake Information with LLMs. As generative models continue to evolve, there is growing interest in exploring the role of LLMs not only in generating, but also in detecting and analyzing false or misleading content [21,23]. For example, Koka et al. [12] were among the first to evaluate the effectiveness of various LLMs in fake news detection, comparing the performance of large-scale models such as GPT-4 and Claude 3 Sonnet and smaller models like Gemma 7B. Despite recent progress, several challenges remain. For instance, a common limitation in the literature is the assumption that the same (often proprietary and unreleased) model is used to both generate and detect fake content, an unrealistic setup for practical deployment.

To further investigate this, also our work evaluates publicly available LLMs as detectors to assess the quality of the fake content generated through our KG-based pipeline. To ensure a more realistic and reliable evaluation setting, we use LLMs for detection that are distinct from those used to generate the misinformation, and we formalize the detection task as a simple yet effective prompting strategy, enabling an initial assessment of how well off-the-shelf models can identify structured, semantically plausible fake content.

3 Methodology

This section first provides a recap of the background on knowledge graphs (KGs) and outlines the main assumptions related to the definition of fake information in the context addressed by this paper. It then presents a top-down analysis of the proposed approach, beginning with a high-level overview of the steps involved, followed by a detailed description of each step.

3.1 Background and Assumptions

Knowledge Graphs (KGs). KGs are structured representations of facts and information [19]. Without loss of generality, a fact (or information) x is encoded in the KG as a triplet of the form $\langle s, r, o \rangle$, where $s \in \mathcal{E}$ is the subject, $r \in \mathcal{R}$ is the relation (predicate), and $o \in \mathcal{E}$ is the object. Here, $\mathcal{E}$ denotes the global set of entities stored in the KG, and $\mathcal{R}$ is the set of predicates used to connect those entities as subjects and objects [13]. For example, the fact $x =$ *"Paris is the capital of France"* can be represented as the triplet $\langle s, r, o \rangle = \langle \text{Paris, capital of, France} \rangle$.

Based on this definition, the complete set of extracted triplets from a knowledge graph is represented as:

$$T_{\text{KG}} = \{\langle s_1, r_1, o_1 \rangle, \langle s_2, r_2, o_2 \rangle, \ldots, \langle s_n, r_n, o_n \rangle\},$$

where n denotes the total number of triplets.

Fake Information in the Context of KGs. Generally speaking, to assess whether a given piece of information x (e.g., a natural language sentence) is correct (real) or incorrect (fake[1]), we assume the existence of an oracle $\mathcal{A}$, modeled as a binary classification function. Given a fact x, the oracle assigns a label indicating its truthfulness, such that $\mathcal{A}(x) \in \{real, fake\}$. Accordingly, an incorrect (fake) fact x_{fake} satisfies $\mathcal{A}(x_{fake}) = fake$.

Despite the previous formal definition of fake information, in practice, the absence of an oracle (or the impracticality of using one to automate the creation of large sets of potentially fake information) requires a more practical interpretation of the correctness of a fact x in the specific context we are addressing. To study the generation of correct and incorrect information derived from a KG, we adopt the following assumption: a real fact corresponds to a triple $t = \langle s, r, o \rangle$ that exists in the KG, such that $x \rightarrow t$ and $t \in T_{KG}$. Analogously, we define an incorrect (i.e., fake) fact x_{fake} as one that can be mapped to a *fake triple* t_{fake}, i.e., $x_{fake} \rightarrow t_{fake}$, where we have $t_{fake} \notin T_{KG}$. In other words, the core assumption outlined above is that the truthfulness of an information x is determined

[1] please note, we use the terms "incorrect" and "fake" interchangeably, as well as "real" and "correct", while omitting strict formal distinctions.

by the existence of a corresponding triple in the KG, under the assumption that the KG itself is trustworthy.

It is important to note that if we address a KG with a limited number of triples, this may introduce a potential issue: some generated information could be classified as fake according to the previous definition, even though it may not be inherently false. However, in the pipeline proposed next, where the subject and relation are kept fixed, this issue becomes negligible. This is because we only consider subjects and relations that are known to exist in the KG, and we evaluate the truthfulness of information by checking whether the corresponding triple with a given object is missing.

3.2 Overview of the Pipeline

In this section, we first provide a top-level overview of the proposed pipeline for extracting fake information from a given KG, and then discuss each step in detail.

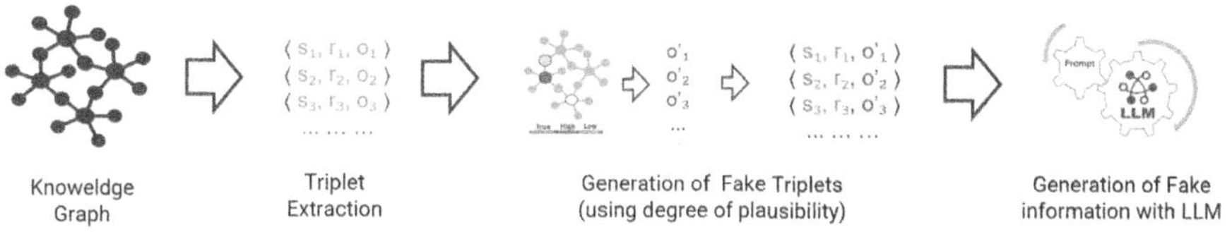

Fig. 2. Proposed Methodology for extracting fake information from a given knowledge graph.

The proposed pipeline is illustrated in Fig. 2. In short, given a triple $t \in KG$, the pipeline extracts a fake triple t_{fake} by modifying the original one, specifically by searching for a new fake object within the KG. It then leverages a LLM to generate the corresponding fake information x_{fake}. For comparison, a related piece of correct information is also shown in green.

In summary, the main steps of the pipeline are as follows:

1. **Triplet Extraction:** Given the KG, all triplets $t \in T_{KG}$, or a relevant subset, are extracted to serve as reference points for generating associated fake triplets in the next step.
2. **Generation of Fake Triplets:** For each extracted triplet t, a fake triplet t_{fake} is generated by exploring the KG in order to replace the original object o with a different object $o' \neq o$. In particular, the selection of o' is guided by a degree of plausibility to control the stealthiness of the resulting misinformation (see Sect. 3.3).
3. **Generation of Fake Information:** Given the fake triplet t_{fake}, a corresponding natural language sentence x_{fake} is generated using an LLM by adopting a predefined prompt.

3.3 Generation of Fake Triplets

Given a triplet $t = \langle s, r, o \rangle$ from the KG, this step aims to extract a related fake version t_{fake} by searching for a different object o' in the KG.

Selection of Fake Object Candidates and Degree of Plausibility. The extraction of fake information relies on two key points: (1) the corresponding fake triplet differs from the original triplet t only in the object component, i.e., $t_{fake} = \langle s, r, o' \rangle$, where the subject s and the relation r are kept unchanged; (2) the exploration of the KG to identify a suitable replacement object $o' \neq o$ is performed in a way that allows for controlling the degree of plausibility of the resulting fake fact (as detailed below). This enables the study and control of the stealthiness of the fake information generated in the final stage of the pipeline.

As a first step, we restrict the set of candidate objects to those that co-occur with the same relation r in the KG but are linked to a different subject $s' \neq s$ (and are never associated with s in any triplet within the KG). The idea behind this filtering step is that objects involved in the same predicate r are more likely to preserve the semantic type or compatibility expected in that relation, thereby increasing the plausibility, and stealthiness, of the generated fake triplet. Formally, the filtered candidate set of objects is so defined as:

$$\mathcal{O}_r = \{o' \mid o' \neq o \ \wedge \ \exists(s', r, o') \in T_{KG} \wedge \ (s, r, o') \notin T_{KG}, \ s' \neq s\}.$$

To further refine the selection, we rank the candidates in $\mathcal{O}_r$ based on a plausibility score that captures the structural similarity between the original object o and the candidate object o' with respect to their usage in the KG. Specifically, we define a plausibility scoring function $\mathcal{P}(\cdot)$ as:

$$\mathcal{P}(o', \langle s, r, o \rangle) = J\big(d(r, o), d(r, o')\big),$$

where $d(r, o)$ denotes the set of distinct subjects s such that $(s, r, o) \in T_{KG}$, and J is the Jaccard similarity. That is, the score compares the sets of subjects associated with o and o' under the relation r, favoring candidates that share similar relational connectivity in the KG [8].

In other words, this formulation of the plausibility of a fake triplet $\langle s, r, o' \rangle$ estimates how "realistic" or deceptively correct the triplet appears, based on the similarity in how the original object o and the candidate object o' co-occur with the relation r across the knowledge graph. This structural similarity suggests that o' could plausibly replace o in a sentence without triggering immediate suspicion.

In the experiments presented in Sects. 5.4 and 5.3, we consider two opposite categories of fake triplets based on their plausibility scores: high-plausibility fake triplets o'_{high} and low-plausibility fake triplets o'_{low}, formally defined as:

$$o'_{\text{high}} = \arg\max_{o' \in \mathcal{O}_r} \mathcal{P}(o', \langle s, r, o \rangle)$$

$$o'_{\text{low}} = \arg\min_{o' \in \mathcal{O}_r} \mathcal{P}(o', \langle s, r, o \rangle)$$

The objective behind studying, in the experimental part, two levels of triples based on different plausibility levels is the following: fake triples constructed using high-plausibility objects are more semantically similar to the original facts and are therefore more difficult to detect as fake. At the same time, due to their semantic similarity, such fake information may introduce subtler distortions, i.e., misinformation that appears credible but is nonetheless factually incorrect. Conversely, low-plausibility fake triples are expected to be more clearly incorrect and potentially more harmful if mistakenly trusted by users (see the example in Fig. 1, which depicts a low-plausibility case), while also being easier to recognize as fake.

Clarification on the Approach Used. It is important to note that, in theory, starting from a correct reference triplet $t = \langle s, r, o \rangle$, one could generate a large number of fake triplets by altering the subject s, the relation r, or the object o, resulting in a new triplet $t_{fake} = \langle s', r', o' \rangle$. However, in the implementation of the pipeline described in the following subsection, we restrict our analysis to the generation of fake triplets by modifying only the object.

The rationale behind this limitation is twofold: first, since the sets of entities used as subjects and objects in the KG are often the same, modifying both s and o is unnecessary and computationally inefficient. Second, by restricting modifications to the object only, we can better analyze the plausibility and deception level of the fake information while preserving the original subject and relation. This facilitates direct comparison with the correct version of the fact.

3.4 Generation of Fake Information Using LLM

Given a fake triplet t_{fake}, extracted in the previous step, the goal here is to generate a natural language fake sentence x_{fake} based on t_{fake}. To achieve this, we use a LLM guided by a predefined prompt based on the fake triplet t_{fake}, with the aim of producing a coherent output sentence. Specifically, we adopted the prompt shown in Fig. 3, which is composed of several parts: a preamble to guide the LLM in the context of sentence generation; a set of additional instructions (described below); the triplet information we aim to target; and finally, the actual request to generate a short news article.

The additional writing rules, omitted from the figure for simplicity, are intended to ensure proper formatting and guide the LLM's behavior. These include: (i) use of a confident and informative tone; (ii) do not reveal or hint that the information is incorrect; (iii) use the description as background, without copying it verbatim; and (iv) aim for clarity and plausibility in a compact format. Additionally, we explicitly include a requirement in the final prompt to avoid overly long generations by specifying a limit of no more than three sentences. Following this, the LLM produces a brief but informative news item based on the given prompt.

It is important to note that the proposed prompt can be applied to any triplet, including a correct one $\langle s, r, o \rangle$, thereby generating a valid factual sentence (as shown in Fig. 1, in green). In fact, this pipeline is also used in the experimental

Prompt for Generating Fake Information

You are a professional journalist working for a major entertainment and culture media outlet. Your job is to write short and realistic news blurbs about a wide range of public entities, such as TV shows, movies, albums, books, people, places, or products.
You are provided with a subject, a brief description, and a triple (subject, predicate, object) in which one fact has been intentionally replaced with incorrect information. Your task is to write a brief but persuasive article that presents the fake information as if it were true.

[*Additional rules*]

Subject: < s >
Description: < description of s available from the the KG >
Fake Triple: <s, r, o'>

Write a very short news article (max 3 sentences) based on the triple above. Use the description to provide background context.

Fig. 3. Description of the LLM prompt used to generate fake information based on the original subject s, its description from the knowledge graph, the original relation r, and the previously computed fake object o'.

phase to extract correct information, which is then employed to evaluate the ability of the detector to distinguish between true and false content.

4 Detection of Fake Information Using LLMs

To evaluate whether the generated sentences can be automatically detected as fake, we explore the use of LLMs as potential detection tools, leveraging their internal knowledge. This section introduces a baseline detection approach based on LLMs, which is evaluated and discussed in the experimental Sects. (5.4 and 5.3). There, we highlight the limitations of different models in performing this task and outline interesting challenges.

For each LLM used in the detection task, we utilized a detection prompt (shown in Fig. 4), where we formally ask the model to return a judgment about the correctness of a given fact x. Please note that here the prompt also includes additional instructions to enforce a consistent output format: (i) Base your judgment on linguistic cues, world knowledge, plausibility, and consistency; (ii) Do not explain your answer;

In the experimental section, we evaluate multiple LLMs for the detection task as Judges, and to improve detection reliability. This setup allows us to assess the quality of LLM-based detectability while also quantifying the number of false negatives, particularly in cases where the sentence might closely resemble a true fact.

Prompt for Detecting Fake Information

You are a fact-checking assistant. Your job is to evaluate whether a given news statement is factual [Real] or misleading [Fake].
Task: Given a news statement, analyze the content and respond with one of the following:
- '[Real]' if the statement is likely factual or plausible.
- '[Fake]' if the statement contains false or misleading information.

[*Additional writing rules*]

Evaluate the truthfulness of the following news statement: $< x >$.
Is this statement real or fake?

Fig. 4. Prompt used for evaluating the truthfulness of news statements. The task involves analyzing a given news statement to determine if it is factual ('[Real]') or misleading ('[Fake]'), based on linguistic cues, world knowledge, and plausibility.

Moreover, we leverage the use of LLMs as evaluators to assess whether higher plausibility makes it more difficult to automatically detect fake information, thereby supporting the observations made in the previous section regarding the role of plausibility.

5 Experiments

This section presents a set of experiments designed to illustrate the generation of fake facts. In the first part, we showcase examples produced by the pipeline introduced in Sect. 3.2, covering both low and high plausibility cases. The goal is to demonstrate how the generated statements, especially those with high plausibility, can effectively mislead human readers.

Subsequently, we investigate the ability of LLMs to detect fake facts generated by our approach. We analyze how detection performance varies with different levels of plausibility and also examine the occurrence of false negatives, where factual information is incorrectly flagged as fake.

5.1 Experimental Setup

Data Used. The KG utilized in these experiments is Wikigraphs [22], a publicly available knowledge graph commonly used to evaluate general knowledge. For our experiments, we focused on categorical knowledge graph triplets, excluding less common categories and those integrated with Freebase when combining Wikipedia data into the graph (such as type, base, etc.). Ultimately, we selected 25 categories for the experiments to ensure a diverse and distinguished generated fake facts and related correct facts for comparisons. In particular, we generated a total of 14450 fake information samples. For comparison, we also included an additional subset of 1540 real facts generated from correct triplets.

Models. We tested two distinct sets of models for fake news generation and detection to ensure a comprehensive and non-overlapping evaluation. For fake news generation, we employed Phi-4 [1], representing a large-scale language model, and Llama-3-8b [18], a smaller-scale model. This setup allows us to assess the impact of model size on the realism and plausibility of the generated content.

For fake news detection, we selected a different set of state-of-the-art LLMs: Falcon-40b [3], Llama-3-70b [18], and Qwen-2-72b [24]. In Sect. 5.3 provides a separate analysis of each individual LLM used for detection, enabling a more detailed understanding of their behavior and potential biases when distinguishing between fake and real facts.

All experiments were conducted using the Text Generation Inference (TGI) platform[2] and Vllm for Falcon-40b[3] on 8 NVIDIA A100 GPUs.

Detection Metrics. For all the experiments, we evaluate the capabilities of LLMs (both individually and as a jury) in detecting fake facts. Specifically, this task is formulated as a binary classification problem, where each given fact x is associated with a ground-truth label $y \in \{\text{fake}, \text{real}\}$.

Given a set of facts, the accuracy of an LLM in detecting fake or real information is computed using the standard binary accuracy formula:

$$\text{Detection Accuracy} = \frac{1}{N}\sum_{i=1}^{N} \mathbf{1}\left[D(x) = y_i\right],$$

where N is the total number of evaluated facts, y_i is the ground-truth label, $D(x)$ is the prediction provided by the model, and $\mathbf{1}[\cdot]$ is the indicator function that returns 1 if the condition is true and 0 otherwise.

Please note that, in the following experiments, we do not report confusion matrices or other standard analyses used in machine learning for imbalanced datasets, since the subsets of real and fake facts are examined independently.

5.2 Qualitative Evaluation of Plausibility in Generated Fake News

To provide a qualitative, human-level assessment, without relying on automatic detection mechanisms, we present and discuss two examples of fake news generated using the Phi-4 model.

Figure 5 showcases representative cases where fake information was created by modifying the object component in factual triplets extracted from a knowledge graph, alongside the corresponding real information. For each fact, two manipulated versions are shown: one with high plausibility and one with low plausibility. These examples highlight the difficulty of detecting misinformation when the generated content is semantically coherent and stylistically consistent with genuine text.

[2] https://huggingface.co/docs/text-generation-inference.
[3] https://huggingface.co/tiiuae/falcon-40b?local-app=vllm.

Subject: *The Vicar of Bullhampton* | **Predicate**: *book.book_edition.publication_date*

Real Object: 1988
In a surprising twist, Anthony Trollope's **The Vicar of Bullhampton**, originally published in 1870, has been reissued in a special **1988** edition, celebrating its enduring themes and complex narratives. This edition highlights the novel's intricate subplots, including the courtship of a young woman and the vicar's efforts to rehabilitate a fallen woman, which Trollope anticipated would stir controversy. Despite initial mixed reviews, this reissue aims to reintroduce Trollope's darker, more nuanced storytelling to a new generation of readers.

Fake Object (high plausibility): "2005"
In a delightful literary revival, Anthony Trollope's classic novel **The Vicar of Bullhampton** has been reissued with a new edition, marking its publication date as **2005**. This edition brings renewed attention to Trollope's exploration of morality and social issues in 19th-century England, offering readers a fresh perspective on the timeless narrative. The reissue is celebrated by literary enthusiasts and scholars alike, eager to delve into the rich tapestry of Trollope's storytelling.

Fake Object (low plausibility): "1898"
In a remarkable literary discovery, a previously unknown edition of Anthony Trollope's **The Vicar of Bullhampton** has been unearthed, with a publication date of **1898**. This edition, believed to have been lost to time, offers fresh insights into Trollope's narrative style and thematic exploration, decades after the novel's initial release. Scholars and enthusiasts alike are eagerly anticipating a closer examination of this rare find, which promises to enrich our understanding of Victorian literature.

Subject: *House of Cards - Season 2* | **Predicate**: *tv.tv_series_season.from*

Real Object: "2014-02-14"
Netflix has officially announced that the eagerly anticipated second season of the political drama **House of Cards** will be released on Valentine's Day, **February 14, 2014**. Set against the backdrop of Washington, D.C., the season delves into complex issues such as entitlement reform and cyberespionage, picking up precisely where the first season left off. Critics have already praised the season's darker tone, with many expressing support for the binge-watching format that Netflix is known for.

Fake Object (high plausibility): "1993-09-30"
In a surprising twist, the second season of the acclaimed political drama **House of Cards** takes viewers back to its roots, beginning its narrative on **September 30, 1993**. Set against the backdrop of Washington, D.C., this season delves into complex issues such as entitlement reform and cyberespionage, while maintaining the intense political intrigue that fans have come to expect. Critics have praised the darker tone of the season, which continues the story seamlessly from where the first season left off, offering a fresh yet nostalgic experience for viewers.

Fake Object (low plausibility): "2008-02-18"
In a surprising twist, the second season of the acclaimed political drama **House of Cards** premiered on **February 18, 2008**, marking a bold departure from its predecessor's timeline. Set against the backdrop of Washington, D.C., this season delves into complex issues such as entitlement reform and cyberespionage, maintaining the series' reputation for gripping storytelling. Critics have praised the darker tone and intricate plot developments, with many embracing the opportunity to binge-watch the entire season upon its release.

Fig. 5. Examples of two fake news generations by Phi-4 and the corresponding correct news (based on the real object available in the KG for each specific triplet). For each fact, two versions of fake news are shown, reflecting low and high plausibility levels.

In the first case, the subject is The Vicar of Bullhampton, a novel by Anthony Trollope. The real publication date (1988 edition) is replaced with either "2005" (high plausibility) or "1898" (low plausibility). Both fake versions preserve a literary tone and thematic references that align with Trollope's work and historical context. The "2005" version is particularly deceptive, as modern reprints of classical literature are common and seldom questioned, making the change seem natural and easily overlooked. In contrast, the "1898" version, while still plausible at a surface level, may raise suspicion due to its claim of a "previously unknown edition," which introduces a higher degree of narrative risk and slightly undermines its credibility.

The second example focuses on House of Cards Season 2, where the actual release date ("2014-02-14") is altered to either "1993-09-30" (high plausibility) or "2008-02-18" (low plausibility). Both fake versions maintain the stylistic tone and thematic framing of the original. However, the 1993 date appears especially convincing, as House of Cards was originally a British miniseries aired in the early 1990 s. By contrast, the 2008 version, although chronologically closer to the real targeted release, lacks a meaningful historical or narrative anchor. As a result, it appears more arbitrary and less justified within the broader timeline of the series, reducing its perceived authenticity.

Table 1. Detection accuracy (%) of each LLM-based judge on fake facts generated by Phi-4 and Llama-8b (under high and low plausibility settings), along with real facts.

Judge Model	Phi-4		LLaMA-8B		Real Facts
Plausibility	High	Low	High	Low	-
Falcon-40B	89.36	92.58	86.50	91.22	32.31
Qwen-72B	59.66	57.89	53.36	56.90	80.17
LLaMA-70B	59.66	68.34	67.29	71.81	68.03

5.3 LLM Judge Accuracy on Fake and Real Facts

We analyze the detection performance of the three LLM judges (Falcon-40b, Llama-70b, and Qwen-72b) in identifying fake information generated by the Phi-4 and Llama-8b models. In particular, Tables 1 reports the detection accuracy (averaged across all the categories addressed the KG) across both generated fake facts and also real facts. In particular, real facts have been extracted focusing on the same 25 categories discussed above and were generated via Phi-4 using the pipeline described in Sect. 3.2. Note that, including real facts in the evaluation enables us to assess not only the model's ability to detect fake information, but also its reliability when classifying true statements. This analysis is important for identifying potential detection biases or, more in general, low detection performance, and understanding whether the LLM-based judges are trustworthy even in the presence of factual content.

The results reveal that detection accuracy varies significantly across models. Notably, Falcon-40b demonstrates strong performance in detecting fake information but struggles considerably when evaluating real facts, often misclassifying them. In contrast, Qwen-72b and Llama-70b, despite being large-scale models, show substantially lower accuracy in detecting fake content but perform better in classifying real information.

From these observations, several insights emerge. First, the evaluated LLMs show considerable limitations in accurately distinguishing between fake and real facts. While larger models such as Qwen-72b and Llama-70b appear more balanced in their responses, their accuracy in detecting fake content is around

50âĂ§60%, which is close to random guessing. On the other hand, Falcon-40b, though effective in flagging fake information, tends to adopt an overly conservative stance, labeling most inputs as fake regardless of their actual truthfulness. This behavior suggests a possible bias introduced during training and indicates that Falcon-40b may favor caution over nuance.

These findings underscore the broader challenge of building reliable LLM-based fact verification systems. They also point to the need for future work on improving detection accuracy through targeted fine-tuning, prompt engineering, or hybrid approaches that integrate structured knowledge. Understanding the training dynamics and decision biases of current models is essential for advancing trustworthy and effective detection tools.

5.4 Category-Wise Analysis of Fake Fact Detectability

This set of experiments investigates the detectability of fake facts across different KG's categories. The analysis has two main objectives: *(i)* to identify potential biases in the detection performance of LLM-based judges across specific categories, and *(ii)* to evaluate whether certain LLMs used for generating fake facts are more capable of producing stealthier, harder-to-detect statements depending on the targeted category. Note that this analysis focuses exclusively on fake news, with the aim of also understanding how the choice of generative LLM affects the creation of misleading content.

Figure 6 presents results across 25 categories. Each subplot distinguishes two levels of plausibility (see Sect. 3.3): high plausibility is shown with a yellow background, and low plausibility with a purple one. We compare fake information generated by two different LLMs: Phi-4 (top plot) and Llama-8b (bottom plot).

The overall trend observed in the results supports the average findings presented in Table 1, confirming that Falcon-40b tends to be biased toward classifying sentences as fake. While this may initially appear to be a positive outcome, since the current analysis focuses only on fake facts, previous discussion about Table 1 shows that this behavior stems from a conservative bias, as Falcon-40b also frequently labels correct facts as fake, indicating a lack of nuance in its judgment. Despite this limitation, Fig. 6 shows that the trend is generally consistent across categories, although some category-specific variations exist, for example, in architecture and boats, where performance deviates more significantly.

In contrast, Llama-70b and Qwen-72b generally underperform and exhibit a wide variance in detection accuracy depending on the category. For instance, Llama-70b performs well on 'sports' and 'fictional universe', but shows poor results in many other categories. This highlights how the addressed LLM judges may be ill-suited for detecting misinformation in specific domains. As a consequence, a category-aware analysis could be used by attackers to identify and exploit weaknesses in these models, improving the success of misinformation designed to bypass automated detection. This open interesting challenges for future investigations.

The effect of plausibility level in fake fact generation is also evident. In some categories, using a higher plausibility significantly reduces detectability.

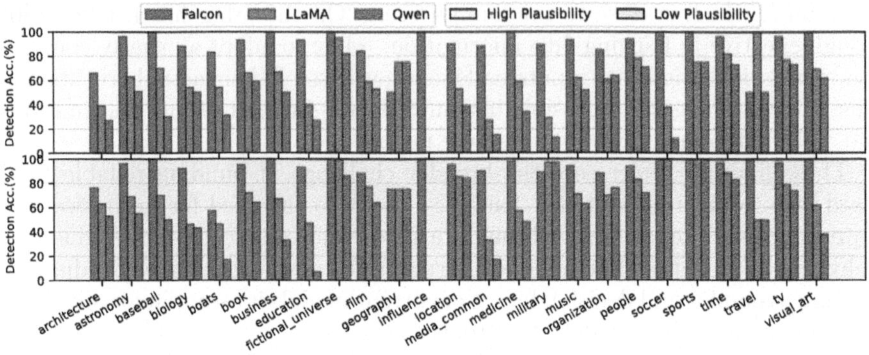

(a) Fake detector Phi-4.

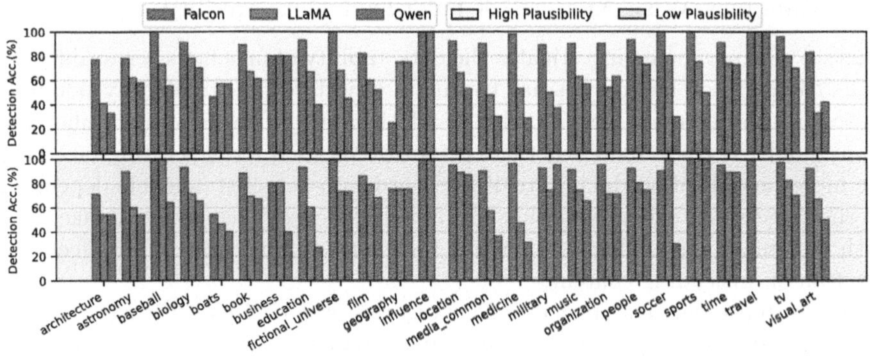

(b) Fake detector Llama-8b.

Fig. 6. Detection accuracy across different categories from the knowledge graph. Three LLM-based judges were evaluated: Falcon-40b, Llama-70b, and Qwen-72b (see legend for colors). Fake facts are generated using two models: Phi-4 (top plot) and Llama-8b (bottom plot). Results are shown for fake facts with high plausibility (yellow background) and low plausibility (purple background)(Color figure online).

For example, in the 'sports' category in Fig. 6(a), the detection rate for Llama and Qwen drops from nearly 100% for low plausibility fake facts to around 78% for high plausibility ones. An even more striking example can be seen in the 'travel' category in Fig. 6(b), where detection accuracy drops from 100% to 0% when moving from low- to high-plausibility facts, again for both Llama and Qwen. These results further confirm that increasing the semantic plausibility of fake facts effectively reduces their detectability, even by state-of-the-art LLM-based detectors.

6 Conclusion and Future Directions

This work presents a novel framework that leverages knowledge graphs and large language models to generate structured misinformation in a controlled and semantically grounded way. The proposed pipeline begins by extracting factual triplets from a knowledge graph, representing verifiable truths, and then perturbs them by replacing the object with an alternative entity guided by a plausibility metric (see Sect. 3.2). This modified triplet is then transformed into a fluent natural language statement using an LLM conditioned by a specific prompt.

Furthermore, we also explore whether LLMs, without any specific fine-tuning, can act as detectors of fake content. To this end, we introduce a first baseline that relies on prompting LLMs to assess the veracity of given facts.

Experimental results demonstrate that the proposed pipeline is capable of producing fake content that is both wrongly plausible and challenging to detect, particularly when the manipulated triplets maintain a high degree of semantic plausibility. Specifically, Our evaluation of LLMs as detectors reveals significant variability and notable issues in their performance, with outcomes differing considerably across the evaluated models. For instance, Falcon-40b tends to exhibit a conservative bias, frequently labeling sentences as fake, even when they are in fact real. In contrast, models such as Llama-70b and Qwen-72b produce more inconsistent results overall, but show fewer signs of such conservative bias in their predictions. A more fine-grained analysis indicates that detection effectiveness can also depend on the specific semantic category of the fake information, unveiling category-level weaknesses that can be exploited to further bypass detection.

These findings open several interesting directions for future research. From the detection side, improving LLM-based detection could involve targeted fine-tuning or prompt engineering strategies. From the attack perspective, future work could explore category-aware misinformation generation or adversarial prompting to further evade automated detectors. Finally, this work highlights the potential of using knowledge graphs as a structured foundation for generating deceptive content, offering a systematic approach to crafting realistic misinformation. It also underscores the dual role of LLMs, both as powerful generators of human-like text and as emerging tools for fact verification. Together, these insights pave the way for future efforts at the intersection of knowledge-based generation and trustworthy AI.

Acknowledgments. This work has been supported by the MUR PRIN-2022-PNRR ASSISTANTS (P2022WEAH7) project, under the program EU RESTART funded by the European Commission.

References

1. Abdin, M., et al.: Phi-4 technical report. arXiv preprint arXiv:2412.08905 (2024)
2. Achiam, J., et al.: Gpt-4 technical report. arXiv preprint arXiv:2303.08774 (2023)
3. Almazrouei, E., et al.: The falcon series of open language models. arXiv preprint arXiv:2311.16867 (2023)
4. Axelsson, A., Skantze, G.: Using large language models for zero-shot natural language generation from knowledge graphs. arXiv preprint arXiv:2307.07312 (2023)

5. Bollacker, K.D., Evans, C., Paritosh, P.K., Sturge, T., Taylor, J.: Freebase: a collaboratively created graph database for structuring human knowledge. In: SIGMOD Conference (2008). https://api.semanticscholar.org/CorpusID:207167677
6. Brau, F., Rossolini, G., Biondi, A., Buttazzo, G.: On the minimal adversarial perturbation for deep neural networks with provable estimation error. IEEE Trans. Pattern Anal. Mach. Intell. **45**(4), 5038–5052 (2022)
7. Chen, C., Shu, K.: Combating misinformation in the age of LLMS: opportunities and challenges. AI Mag. **45**(3), 354–368 (2024)
8. Di Mauro, A., Xu, Z., Rim, W.B., Sztyler, T., Lawrence, C.: Generating and evaluating plausible explanations for knowledge graph completion. In: Proceedings of the 62nd Annual Meeting of the Association for Computational Linguistics (Volume 1: Long Papers), pp. 12106–12118 (2024)
9. Huang, Y., Shu, K., Yu, P.S., Sun, L.: From creation to clarification: ChatGPT's journey through the fake news quagmire. In: Companion Proceedings of the ACM Web Conference 2024, pp. 513–516 (2024)
10. Huang, Y., Sun, L.: FakeGPT: fake news generation, explanation and detection of large language models. arXiv preprint arXiv:2310.05046 (2023)
11. Kau, A., He, X., Nambissan, A., Astudillo, A., Yin, H., Aryani, A.: Combining knowledge graphs and large language models. arXiv preprint arXiv:2407.06564 (2024)
12. Koka, S., Vuong, A., Kataria, A.: Evaluating the efficacy of large language models in detecting fake news: a comparative analysis. arXiv preprint arXiv:2406.06584 (2024)
13. Luo, L., Li, Y.F., Haffari, G., Pan, S.: Reasoning on graphs: faithful and interpretable large language model reasoning. arXiv preprint arXiv:2310.01061 (2023)
14. Papageorgiou, E., Chronis, C., Varlamis, I., Himeur, Y.: A survey on the use of large language models (LLMs) in fake news. Future Internet **16**(8), 298 (2024)
15. Sallami, D., Chang, Y.C., Aïmeur, E.: From deception to detection: the dual roles of large language models in fake news. arXiv preprint arXiv:2409.17416 (2024)
16. Schneider, P., Klettner, M., Simperl, E., Matthes, F.: A comparative analysis of conversational large language models in knowledge-based text generation. arXiv preprint arXiv:2402.01495 (2024)
17. Shu, K., Wang, S., Lee, D., Liu, H.: Mining disinformation and fake news: Concepts, methods, and recent advancements. In: Disinformation, Misinformation, and Fake News in Social Media: Emerging Research Challenges and Opportunities, pp. 1–19 (2020)
18. Touvron, H., et al.: Llama: open and efficient foundation language models. arXiv preprint arXiv:2302.13971 (2023)
19. Vrandečić, D., Krötzsch, M.: Wikidata: a free collaborative knowledgebase. Commun. ACM **57**(10), 78–85 (2014)
20. Wang, C., et al.: Survey on factuality in large language models: knowledge, retrieval and domain-specificity. arXiv preprint arXiv:2310.07521 (2023)
21. Wang, L.Z., et al.: Megafake: a theory-driven dataset of fake news generated by large language models. arXiv preprint arXiv:2408.11871 (2024)
22. Wang, L., Li, Y., Aslan, O., Vinyals, O.: Wikigraphs: a wikipedia text-knowledge graph paired dataset. arXiv preprint arXiv:2107.09556 (2021)
23. Wang, T., Liao, X., Chow, K.P., Lin, X., Wang, Y.: Deepfake detection: a comprehensive survey from the reliability perspective. ACM Comput. Surv. **57**(3), 1–35 (2024)
24. Yang, A., et al.: Qwen2. 5 technical report. arXiv preprint arXiv:2412.15115 (2024)

Correction to: Quantum-Safe Hybrid Cryptographic Framework for Multimedia Application

Amna Shifa

Correction to:
Chapter 13 in: B. Coppens et al. (Eds.): ***Availability, Reliability and Security*, LNCS 15997,**
https://doi.org/10.1007/978-3-032-00639-4_13

The original version of this chapter was inadvertently published without the Acknowledgments section. It has been included in this corrected version.

The updated version of this chapter can be found at
https://doi.org/10.1007/978-3-032-00639-4_13

B. Coppens et al. (Eds.): ARES 2025 Workshops, LNCS 15997, p. C1, 2026.
https://doi.org/10.1007/978-3-032-00639-4_20

Author Index

B. Coppens et al. (Eds.): ARES 2025 Workshops, LNCS 15997, pp. 351–352, 2025.
https://doi.org/10.1007/978-3-032-00639-4

The manufacturer's authorised representative in the EU is Springer
Nature Customer Service Centre GmbH, Europaplatz 3, 69115 Heidelberg,
Germany. If you have any concerns regarding our products, please
contact ProductSafety@springernature.com

Printed and bound by CPI Group (UK) Ltd, Croydon, CR0 4YY
28/04/2026
02098521-0010